P9-CQX-453

Adobe® Illustrator® CS6

CLASSROOM IN A BOOK®

The official training workbook from Adobe Systems

Adobe® Illustrator® CS6 Classroom in a Book®

© 2012 Adobe Systems Incorporated and its licensors. All rights reserved.

If this guide is distributed with software that includes an end user agreement, this guide, as well as the software described in it, is furnished under license and may be used or copied only in accordance with the terms of such license. Except as permitted by any such license, no part of this guide may be reproduced, stored in a retrieval system, or transmitted, in any form or by any means, electronic, mechanical, recording, or otherwise, without the prior written permission of Adobe Systems Incorporated. Please note that the content in this guide is protected under copyright law even if it is not distributed with software that includes an end user license agreement.

The content of this guide is furnished for informational use only, is subject to change without notice, and should not be construed as a commitment by Adobe Systems Incorporated. Adobe Systems Incorporated assumes no responsibility or liability for any errors or inaccuracies that may appear in the informational content contained in this guide.

Please remember that existing artwork or images that you may want to include in your project may be protected under copyright law. The unauthorized incorporation of such material into your new work could be a violation of the rights of the copyright owner. Please be sure to obtain any permission required from the copyright owner.

Any references to company names in sample files are for demonstration purposes only and are not intended to refer to any actual organization.

Adobe, the Adobe logo, Acrobat, Classroom in a Book, Flash, Flex, Illustrator, InDesign, Photoshop, PostScript, and PostScript 3 are either registered trademarks or trademarks of Adobe Systems Incorporated in the United States and/or other countries.

Apple, Mac OS, and Macintosh are trademarks of Apple, registered in the U.S. and other countries. Microsoft, Windows, and Windows XP are either registered trademarks or trademarks of Microsoft Corporation in the U.S. and/or other countries. Wacom and Intuos are trademarks of Wacom Company Ltd. All rights reserved. All other trademarks are the property of their respective owners.

Adobe Systems Incorporated, 345 Park Avenue, San Jose, California 95110-2704, USA

Notice to U.S. Government End Users. The Software and Documentation are "Commercial Items," as that term is defined at 48 C.F.R. §2.101, consisting of "Commercial Computer Software" and "Commercial Computer Software Documentation," as such terms are used in 48 C.F.R. §12.212 or 48 C.F.R. §227.7202, as applicable. Consistent with 48 C.F.R. §12.212 or 48 C.F.R. §§227.7202-1 through 227.7202-4, as applicable, the Commercial Computer Software and Commercial Computer Software Documentation are being licensed to U.S. Government end users (a) only as Commercial Items and (b) with only those rights as are granted to all other end users pursuant to the terms and conditions herein. Unpublished-rights reserved under the copyright laws of the United States. Adobe Systems Incorporated, 345 Park Avenue, San Jose, CA 95110-2704, USA. For U.S. Government End Users, Adobe agrees to comply with all applicable equal opportunity laws including, if appropriate, the provisions of Executive Order 11246, as amended, Section 402 of the Vietnam Era Veterans Readjustment Assistance Act of 1974 (38 USC 4212), and Section 503 of the Rehabilitation Act of 1973, as amended, and the regulations at 41 CFR Parts 60-1 through 60-60, 60-250, and 60-741. The affirmative action clause and regulations contained in the preceding sentence shall be incorporated by reference.

Adobe Press books are published by Peachpit, a division of Pearson Education located in Berkeley, California. For the latest on Adobe Press books, go to www.adobepress.com. To report errors, please send a note to errata@peachpit.com. For information on getting permission for reprints and excerpts, contact permissions@peachpit.com.

Printed and bound in the United States of America

ISBN-13:   978-0-321-82248-2
ISBN-10:   0-321-82248-X

9 8 7 6 5 4 3 2

WHAT'S ON THE DISC

Here is an overview of the contents of the Classroom in a Book disc

The *Adobe Illustrator CS6 Classroom in a Book* disc includes the lesson files that you'll need to complete the exercises in this book, as well as other content to help you learn more about Adobe Illustrator CS6 and use it with greater efficiency and ease. The diagram below represents the contents of the disc, which should help you locate the files you need.

Lesson files

Each lesson has its own folder inside the Lessons folder. You will need to copy these lesson folders to your hard drive before you can begin each lesson.

Name
▶ 🗀 Lesson01
▶ 🗀 Lesson02
▶ 🗀 Lesson03
▶ 🗀 Lesson04
▶ 🗀 Lesson05
▶ 🗀 Lesson06
▶ 🗀 Lesson07
▶ 🗀 Lesson08
▶ 🗀 Lesson09
▶ 🗀 Lesson10
▶ 🗀 Lesson11
▶ 🗀 Lesson12

Online resources

Links to Adobe Community Help, product Help and Support pages, Adobe certification programs, Adobe TV, and other useful online resources can be found inside a handy HTML file. Just open it in your Web browser and click on the links, including a special link to this book's product page where you can access updates and bonus material.

Adobe Press

ADOBE PRESS

Find information about other Adobe Press titles, covering the full spectrum of Adobe products, in the Online Resources file.

CONTENTS

1   GETTING TO KNOW THE WORK AREA

4 TRANSFORMING OBJECTS

13 APPLYING APPEARANCE ATTRIBUTES AND GRAPHIC STYLES

14 WORKING WITH SYMBOLS

GETTING STARTED

Adobe® Illustrator® CS6 is the industry-standard illustration application for print, multimedia, and online graphics. Whether you are a designer or a technical illustrator producing artwork for print publishing, an artist producing multimedia graphics, or a creator of web pages or online content, Adobe Illustrator offers you the tools you need to get professional-quality results.

About Classroom in a Book

Adobe Illustrator CS6 Classroom in a Book® is part of the official training series for Adobe graphics and publishing software developed with the support of Adobe product experts.

The lessons are designed so that you can learn at your own pace. If you're new to Adobe Illustrator, you'll learn the fundamentals you need to master to put the application to work. If you are an experienced user, you'll find that *Classroom in a Book* teaches many advanced features, including tips and techniques for using the latest version of Adobe Illustrator.

Although each lesson provides step-by-step instructions for creating a specific project, there's room for exploration and experimentation. You can follow the book from start to finish, or do only the lessons that correspond to your interests and needs. Each lesson concludes with a review section summarizing what you've covered.

Prerequisites

Before beginning to use *Adobe Illustrator CS6 Classroom in a Book*, you should have working knowledge of your computer and its operating system. Make sure that you know how to use the mouse and standard menus and commands, and also how to open, save, and close files. If you need to review these techniques, see the printed or online documentation for your Windows or Mac OS.

● **Note:** When instructions differ by platform, Windows commands appear first, and then the Mac OS commands, with the platform noted in parentheses. For example, "press the Alt (Windows) or Option (Mac OS) key and click away from the artwork." In some instances, common commands may be abbreviated with the Windows commands first, followed by a slash and the Mac OS commands, without any parenthetical reference. For example, "press Alt/ Option" or "press Ctrl/Command+click."

Installing the program

Before you begin using *Adobe Illustrator CS6 Classroom in a Book*, make sure that your system is set up correctly and that you've installed the required software and hardware.

The Adobe Illustrator CS6 software is not included on the Classroom in a Book CD; you must purchase the software separately. For complete instructions on installing the software, see the Adobe Illustrator Read Me file on the application DVD or on the web at www.adobe.com/support.

Fonts used in this book

The Classroom in a Book lesson files use the fonts that come with Adobe Illustrator CS6 and install with the product for your convenience. These fonts are installed in the following locations:

* Windows: [startup drive]\Windows\Fonts\
* Mac OS X: [startup drive]/Library/Fonts/

For more information about fonts and installation, see the Adobe Illustrator CS6 Read Me file on the application DVD or on the web at www.adobe.com/support.

Copying the Classroom in a Book files

The Classroom in a Book CD includes folders containing all the electronic files for the lessons. Each lesson has its own folder. You must install these folders on your hard disk to use the files for the lessons. To save room on your hard disk, you can install the folder for each lesson as you need it.

To install the Classroom in a Book files

1 Insert the Classroom in a Book CD into your CD-ROM drive.

2 Do one of the following:

* Copy the entire Lessons folder onto your hard disk.
* Copy only the specific lesson folder that you need onto your hard disk.

Restoring default preferences

The preferences file controls how command settings appear on your screen when you open the Adobe Illustrator program. Each time you quit Adobe Illustrator, the position of the panels and certain command settings are recorded in different preference files. If you want to restore the tools and settings to their original default settings, you can delete the current Adobe Illustrator CS6 preferences file. Adobe Illustrator creates a new preferences file, if one doesn't already exist, the next time you start the program and save a file.

You must restore the default preferences for Illustrator before you begin each lesson. This ensures that the tools and panels function as described in this book. When you have finished the book, you can restore your saved settings.

To save current Illustrator preferences

1 Exit Adobe Illustrator CS6.

2 Locate the AIPrefs (Windows) or Adobe Illustrator Prefs (Mac OS) file, as follows.

- (Windows XP SP3) The AIPrefs file is located in the folder [startup drive]\ Documents and Settings\[username]\Application Data\Adobe\Adobe Illustrator CS6 Settings\en_US*\x86 or x64.

- (Windows Vista or Windows 7) The AIPrefs file is located in the folder [startup drive]\Users\[username]\AppData\Roaming\Adobe\Adobe Illustrator CS6 Settings\en_US*\x86 or x64.

- (Mac OS 10.6 and 10.7**) The Adobe Illustrator Prefs file is located in the folder [startup drive]/Users/[username]/Library/Preferences/Adobe Illustrator CS6 Settings/en_US*.

*Folder name may be different depending on the language version you have installed.

**On Mac OS 10.7 (Lion) the Library folder is hidden by default.

● **Note:** If you cannot locate the preferences file, try using your operating system's Find command, and search for AIPrefs (Windows) or Adobe Illustrator Prefs (Mac OS).

If you can't find the file, you either haven't started Adobe Illustrator CS6 yet or you have moved the preferences file. The preferences file is created after you quit the program the first time and is updated thereafter.

3 Copy the file and save it to another folder on your hard disk.

4 Start Adobe Illustrator CS6.

▶ **Tip:** To quickly locate and delete the Adobe Illustrator preferences file each time you begin a new lesson, create a shortcut (Windows) or an alias (Mac OS) to the Adobe Illustrator CS6 Settings folder.

● **Note:** In Windows XP, the Application Data folder is hidden by default. The same is true for the AppData folder in Windows Vista and Window 7. To make either one visible, open Folder Options in Control Panel and click the View tab. In the Advanced Settings pane, find Hidden Files and folders and select Show Hidden Files and Folders or Show hidden files, folders, or drives.

To delete current Illustrator preferences

1 Exit Adobe Illustrator CS6.

2 Locate the AIPrefs (Windows) or Adobe Illustrator Prefs (Mac OS) file, as follows.

- (Windows XP SP3) The AIPrefs file is located in the folder [startup drive]\ Documents and Settings\[username]\Application Data\Adobe\Adobe Illustrator CS6 Settings\en_US*\x86 or x64.

- (Windows Vista or Windows 7) The AIPrefs file is located in the folder [startup drive]\Users\[username]\AppData\Roaming\Adobe\Adobe Illustrator CS6 Settings\en_US*\x86 or x64.

- (Mac OS 10.6 and 10.7**) The Adobe Illustrator Prefs file is located in the folder [startup drive]/Users/[username]/Library/Preferences/Adobe Illustrator CS6 Settings/en_US*.

*Folder name may be different depending on the language version you have installed.

**On Mac OS 10.7 (Lion) the Library folder is hidden by default.

● **Note:** If you cannot locate the preferences file, try using your operating system's Find command, and search for AIPrefs (Windows) or Adobe Illustrator Prefs (Mac OS).

3 Delete the preferences file.

4 Start Adobe Illustrator CS6.

To restore saved preferences after completing the lessons

1 Exit Adobe Illustrator CS6.

2 Delete the current preferences file. Find the original preferences file that you saved and move it to the Adobe Illustrator CS6 Settings folder.

● **Note:** You can move the original preferences file rather than renaming it.

Additional resources

Adobe Illustrator CS6 Classroom in a Book is not meant to replace documentation that comes with the program or to be a comprehensive reference for every feature. Only the commands and options used in the lessons are explained in this book. For comprehensive information about program features and tutorials, please refer to these resources:

Adobe Community Help: Community Help brings together active Adobe product users, Adobe product team members, authors, and experts to give you the most useful, relevant, and up-to-date information about Adobe products.

● **Note:** In Windows XP, the Application Data folder is hidden by default. The same is true for the AppData folder in Windows Vista and Window 7. To make either one visible, open Folder Options in Control Panel and click the View tab. In the Advanced Settings pane, find Hidden Files and folders and select Show Hidden Files and Folders or Show hidden files, folders, or drives.

To access Community Help: To invoke Help, press F1 or choose Help > Illustrator Help.

Adobe content is updated based on community feedback and contributions. You can add comments to both content or forums—including links to web content, publish your own content using Community Publishing, or contribute Cookbook Recipes. Find out how to contribute at www.adobe.com/community/publishing/download.html

See community.adobe.com/help/profile/faq.html for answers to frequently asked questions about Community Help.

Adobe Illustrator Help and Support: www.adobe.com/support/illustrator is where you can find and browse Help and Support content on adobe.com.

Adobe Forums: forums.adobe.com lets you tap into peer-to-peer discussions, questions and answers on Adobe products.

Adobe TV: tv.adobe.com is an online video resource for expert instruction and inspiration about Adobe products, including a How To channel to get you started with your product.

Adobe Design Center: www.adobe.com/designcenter offers thoughtful articles on design and design issues, a gallery showcasing the work of top-notch designers, tutorials, and more.

Adobe Developer Connection: www.adobe.com/devnet is your source for technical articles, code samples, and how-to videos that cover Adobe developer products and technologies.

Resources for educators: www.adobe.com/education offers a treasure trove of information for instructors who teach classes on Adobe software. Find solutions for education at all levels, including free curricula that use an integrated approach to teaching Adobe software and can be used to prepare for the Adobe Certified Associate exams.

Also check out these useful links:

Adobe Marketplace & Exchange: www.adobe.com/cfusion/exchange is a central resource for finding tools, services, extensions, code samples and more to supplement and extend your Adobe products.

Adobe Illustrator CS6 product home page: www.adobe.com/products/illustrator

Adobe Labs: http://labs.adobe.com gives you access to early builds of cutting-edge technology, as well as forums where you can interact with both the Adobe development teams building that technology and other like-minded members of the community.

Adobe certification

The Adobe training and certification programs are designed to help Adobe customers improve and promote their product-proficiency skills. There are four levels of certification:

- Adobe Certified Associate (ACA)
- Adobe Certified Expert (ACE)
- Adobe Certified Instructor (ACI)
- Adobe Authorized Training Center (AATC)

The Adobe Certified Associate (ACA) credential certifies that individuals have the entry-level skills to plan, design, build, and maintain effective communications using different forms of digital media.

The Adobe Certified Expert program is a way for expert users to upgrade their credentials. You can use Adobe certification as a catalyst for getting a raise, finding a job, or promoting your expertise.

If you are an ACE-level instructor, the Adobe Certified Instructor program takes your skills to the next level and gives you access to a wide range of Adobe resources.

Adobe Authorized Training Centers offer instructor-led courses and training on Adobe products, employing only Adobe Certified Instructors. A directory of AATCs is available at http://partners.adobe.com.

For information on the Adobe Certified programs, visit www.adobe.com/support/certification/main.html.

Checking for updates

Adobe periodically provides updates to software. You can easily obtain these updates through Adobe Updater, as long as you have an active Internet connection.

1   In Illustrator, choose Help > Updates. The Adobe Updater automatically checks for updates available for your Adobe software.

2   In the Adobe Application Manager dialog box, select the updates you want to install, and then click Download And Install Updates to install them.

● **Note:** Please note that when applying the updates for Illustrator, the Adobe Application Manager dialog box will ask you to close Illustrator if the application is running in the background. Close Illustrator, continue the update, and then launch Illustrator again when the updates are completed.

▶ **Tip:** The Adobe Application Manager dialog box shows all of the Adobe updates for installed applications, independent of the Adobe application from which it is invoked (Illustrator in this case). You can choose to update other Adobe applications too (if their corresponding update is available) from the dialog box.

3   When you are finished investigating updates, close the window and return to Illustrator.

WHAT'S NEW IN ADOBE ILLUSTRATOR CS6

Adobe Illustrator CS6 is packed with new and innovative features to help you produce artwork more efficiently for print, web, and digital video publication. In this section, you'll learn about many of these new features—how they function and how you can use them in your work.

Efficient, flexible interface

Over 40 new enhancements to the Illustrator user interface (UI) make working with your favorite tools smoother, more efficient, and more intuitive.

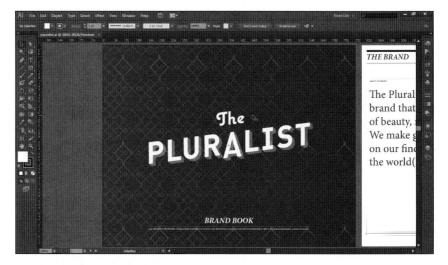

The tools, panels, and controls are still where you expect them, but daily tasks take fewer steps and your interactions are faster and more direct—from inline editing of layer names to navigating the font menu. Panel updates include expandable color-sampling areas and hex-value editing in the Color panel. You can edit names of layers, styles, and swatches directly in the panel, and the Character panel shows glyphs previously requiring multiple clicks to access.

Adjustable user interface brightness

Use adjustable UI brightness to set your working preference for every day or for a particular project. Match the look of your video tools or Adobe Photoshop CS6, or simply use it to put the visual focus on your artwork.

Image Trace

A completely new tracing engine in Illustrator CS6 makes the conversion of raster images to editable vector artwork easy and clean. Get sharper lines, with better shape fitting and more accurate color selection than with the Live Trace feature, introduced in CS2. Image Trace provides many of the same benefits but with far better results, produced more quickly, using intuitive, easy controls. No more struggling with complex options.

Pattern creation

Easily create and edit seamlessly tiled vector patterns. Freely experiment with various types of layout or precisely control tiling and overlaps with automatically seamless repeats.

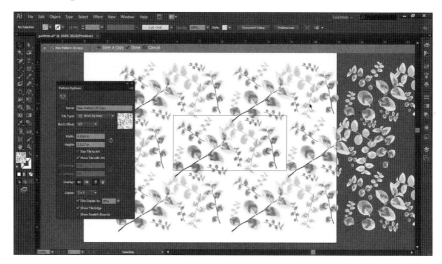

Mercury Performance System

The underlying power of the new Illustrator CS6 is apparent in many different ways. Native 64-bit support on Mac OS and Windows provides access to all the available RAM on your system. Overall performance optimization is apparent when you open, save, and export large files. Previews are faster, and interaction in general is more responsive.

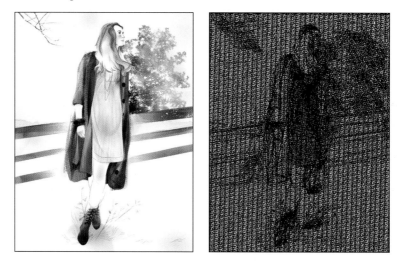

Gradients on strokes

Design creatively with gradients on strokes that can be applied along the length, across the width, or within a stroke. Transform a simple path into a visually complex and compelling shape. With complete control over gradient placement and opacity, you can use strokes rather than fills to create sophisticated artwork.

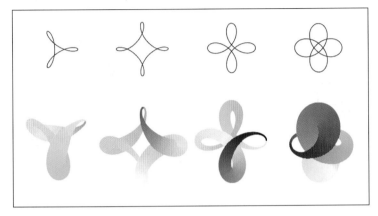

Other enhancements

- **Transform panel**—Quickly access the critical Scale Strokes & Effects option right in the Transform panel. Scale Strokes & Effects is now also available in the updated Transform Effect panel.

- **Transparency panel**—Create opacity masks and work with them more easily, thanks to new Make Mask and Release buttons. All of the Illustrator masking functionality is now exposed in the Transparency panel.

- **Control panel**—Find what you need right when you need it, using a more efficient Control panel with increased consistency across options—no matter what the context, including placement of anchor point controls, clipping masks, envelope distortions, and more.

- **Improved Gaussian Blur**—The Gaussian Blur effect has been specifically optimized for speed, improving the performance of drop shadows and glows, and live preview while applying or editing the effect has also been added.

Although this list touches on just a few of the new and enhanced features of Illustrator CS6, it exemplifies Adobe's commitment to providing the best tools possible for your publishing needs. We hope you enjoy working with Illustrator CS6 as much as we do.

—The *Adobe Illustrator CS6 Classroom in a Book* Team

A QUICK TOUR OF
ADOBE ILLUSTRATOR CS6

Lesson overview

In this interactive demonstration of Adobe Illustrator CS6, you'll get an overview of the application, while using a few of the exciting new features.

 This lesson takes approximately an hour to complete. You'll need to first copy the Lesson00 folder onto your hard disk.

In this demonstration of Adobe Illustrator CS6, you will be introduced to new and exciting application features, like gradients on a stroke and pattern creation, as well as some key fundamentals for working in the application.

Getting started

For the first lesson of this book, you will be taken through a quick tour of the tools and features in Adobe Illustrator CS6, giving you a sense of the possibilities. Along the way, you will build a sign for a chocolate company.

● **Note:** If you have not already done so, copy the Lesson00 folder from the Lessons folder on the *Adobe Illustrator CS6 Classroom in a Book* CD onto your hard disk. See "Copying the Classroom in a Book files" on page 2.

1 To ensure that the tools and panels function exactly as described in this lesson, delete or deactivate (by renaming) the Adobe Illustrator CS6 preferences file. See "Restoring default preferences" on page 3.

2 Start Adobe Illustrator CS6.

3 Choose File > Open, and open the L00end.ai file in the Lesson00 folder in the Lessons folder on your hard disk. This is the final artwork file. You can leave it open for reference or choose File > Close to close it. For this lesson, you will start with a blank document.

4 Choose Window > Workspace > Reset Essentials.

● **Note:** If you don't see "Reset Essentials" in the Workspace menu, choose Window > Workspace > Essentials before choosing Window > Workspace > Reset Essentials.

Working with artboards

An Illustrator document can contain up to 100 artboards (artboards are similar to pages in a program like Adobe InDesign®). Next, you will create a document with two artboards.

● **Note:** Read more about creating new documents in Lesson 3, "Creating and Editing Shapes." Read more about editing artboards in Lesson 4, "Transforming Objects."

1 Choose File > New.

2 In the New Document dialog box, name the file **signage** and leave Print selected for the Profile. Change the Number Of Artboards to **2** and the Units to Inches. Click OK. A new blank document appears.

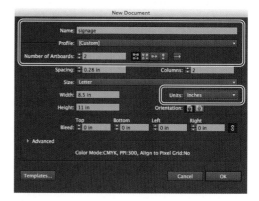

3 Choose File > Save As. In the Save As dialog box, leave the name as signage.ai and navigate to the Lesson00 folder. Leave the Save As Type option set to Adobe Illustrator (*.AI) (Windows) or the Format option set to Adobe Illustrator (ai) (Mac OS), and click Save. In the Illustrator Options dialog box, leave the Illustrator options at their default settings and then click OK.

4 Choose View > Rulers > Show Rulers to show rulers in the Document window.

5 Select the Artboard tool (⊞) in the Tools panel. Click the center of the white artboard with the 01 - Artboard 1 label in the upper-left corner to select it. In the Control panel, above the artboards, click the Landscape button (▣).

6 Position the pointer over the selected artboard, and drag it to the left until there is a gray gap between the two artboards. Illustrator allows you to have artboards of differing sizes and orientations.

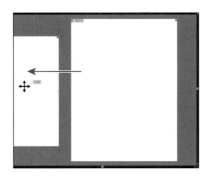

7 Select the Selection tool (▶) to stop editing the artboards. Click the artboard on the right (the vertical artboard) to make it the active artboard. Choose View > Fit Artboard In Window.

Drawing shapes and lines

Drawing shapes is the cornerstone of Illustrator, and you will create many of them throughout these lessons. Next, you will create several shapes.

● **Note:** Read more about creating and editing shapes in Lesson 3, "Creating and Editing Shapes."

1 Select the Line Segment tool (╱) in the Tools panel, and position the pointer on the top of the artboard, close to the left edge (see the circle in the figure). Press and hold the Shift key, click and drag straight down to the bottom edge of the artboard. Release the mouse button and then the Shift key.

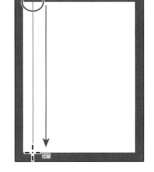

2 In the Control panel above the Document window, type **30 pt** in the Stroke weight field and press Enter or Return.

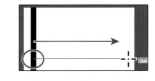

3 With the Line Segment tool (╱) still selected, position the pointer over the center of the line you just created, about a third of the way down from the top. Press and hold the Shift key, and drag to the right, almost to the right edge of the artboard. Release the mouse button and then the Shift key.

● **Note:** Depending on the resolution of your screen, the Transform options (the Y value) may not appear in the Control panel. If they do not appear, you can click the word "Transform" to see the Transform panel or you can choose Window > Transform.

4 In the Control panel, change the Stroke weight to **50 pt**. Type **3.65 in** into the field to the right of the Y value to position the line vertically. Press Enter or Return.

5 Select the Rectangle tool (▦) in the Tools panel. Position the pointer below the horizontal line you just created (circled in the figure). Click and drag to create a rectangle that has a Width of 5.8 in and a Height of 3 in as shown in the gray measurement label that appears next to the pointer. The new rectangle will have a stroke weight of 50 pt, which you will change.

● **Note:** Depending on the resolution of your screen, the Transform options may not appear in the Control panel. If they do not appear, you can click the word "Transform" to see the Transform panel or you can choose Window > Transform.

6 Change the W (width) in the Control panel to **5.8 in**, if it isn't already and press Enter or Return. Press the letter D to apply the default fill and stroke to the rectangle.

7 Select the Selection tool (▶) in the Tools panel, and drag the rectangle so that it is positioned as you see in the figure. It doesn't have to be exact.

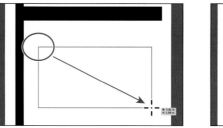 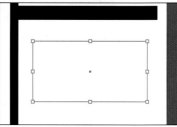

▶ **Tip:** The spiral shapes were created with the Spiral tool (◉) in the Line Segment tool (╱) group in the Tools panel.

8 Choose File > Open, and open the extras.ai file in the Lesson00 folder in the Lessons folder on your hard disk.

9 With the Selection tool, click on the spirals to select them all. Choose Edit > Copy. Leave the extras.ai file open, click the signage.ai file tab at the top of the Document window, and then choose Edit > Paste.

10 With the Selection tool, drag the spirals into position, as you see in the figure, and then choose Select > Deselect.

The spiral paths are grouped together, which means that if you select one, you select them all.

Applying color

Applying colors to artwork is a common Illustrator task. Experimenting and applying color is easy using the Color panel, Swatches panel, Color Guide panel, and Edit Colors/Recolor Artwork dialog box.

▶ **Tip:** When you position the pointer over a swatch, a tool tip appears showing the swatch name.

1 With the Selection tool (▶) selected, click to select the rectangle you drew. Click the Fill color in the Control panel to reveal the Swatches panel. Select the Black swatch. Press the Escape key to hide the panel.

2 Click the Stroke box, toward the bottom of the Tools panel.

3 Click the Swatches panel icon (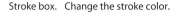) on the right side of the workspace to expand the Swatches panel. Position the pointer over the brown colors. Click the brown color with the tool tip that shows "C=40 M=65 Y=90 K=35."

● **Note:** The stroke color of the rectangle will be hard to see on the selected rectangle because it is small, and that's okay.

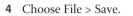

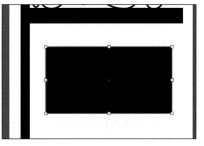

Stroke box.   Change the stroke color.   The result.

4 Choose File > Save.

Working with the Shape Builder tool

The Shape Builder tool is an interactive tool for creating complex shapes by merging and erasing simpler shapes. Next, you will change the rectangle you created, using the Shape Builder tool.

● **Note:** Read more about working with the Shape Builder tool in Lesson 3, "Creating and Editing Shapes."

1 Select the Ellipse tool (●) from the Rectangle group in the Tools panel by clicking and holding down on the Rectangle tool (■).

2 Position the pointer over the upper-left corner of the black rectangle (circled in the figure). The green word "anchor" appears. Click and drag down and to the right

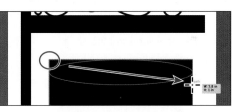

edge of the rectangle, until you see a height of approximately 1 in in the gray measurement label. Release the mouse button.

3 Select the Selection tool (▶) in the Tools panel. Position the pointer over the blue center point of the ellipse, and drag straight up. Stop dragging when the pointer snaps to the top edge of the rectangle (and the pointer turns white). Release the mouse button.

4 Select the Ellipse tool (●) in the Tools panel, and click anywhere on the artboard. In the Ellipse dialog box, change the Width to **1 in** and the Height to **1 in**. Click OK.

Note: The values you see in the gray measurement label will most likely be different and that's okay.

5 Select the Selection tool (▶) in the Tools panel. Drag the center of the new circle onto the lower-left point of the rectangle. It will snap.

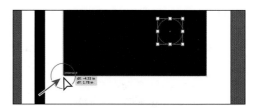

6 Press the Alt (Windows) or Option (Mac OS) key, and drag the circle from its center point to the lower-right point of the rectangle. Release the mouse button when the word

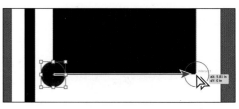

"intersect" appears, and then release the modifier key to create a copy of the circle.

7 Press the Shift key, and click to select the other small circle, the ellipse, and the rectangle to select all four shapes. As you move the pointer around the artwork, the edges of each object will highlight.

8 Select the Shape Builder tool (🔷) in the Tools panel. Position the pointer just above the ellipse at the top of the selected shapes (see the X in the figure), and drag down into the rectangle. This combines those two shapes into one.

9 Position the pointer where the red X is, in the second part of the figure. Holding down the Alt (Windows) or Options (Mac OS) key, drag into the portion of the circle that overlaps the corner of the rectangle so that the circle is cut out of the rectangle in the lower-left corner. Release the mouse button and then the key. Do the same for the circle in the lower-right corner. This removes the highlighted shapes.

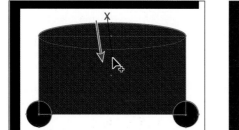

Working with the Width tool

The Width tool allows you to create a variable width stroke and to save the width as a profile that can be applied to other objects.

1 Select the Zoom tool (🔍) in the Tools panel, and click several times, slowly, on the right end of the horizontal path, just below the spirals, to zoom in to it.

2 Select the Width tool (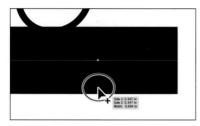) in the Tools panel. Position the pointer as shown in the first part of the figure. When the pointer shows a plus sign (+) next to it, drag up toward the center of the line. When the gray measurement label shows a Width of approximately .4 in, release the mouse button. It's okay if your measurements don't exactly match the measurements included here.

● **Note:** Read more about the Width tool in Lesson 3, "Creating and Editing Shapes."

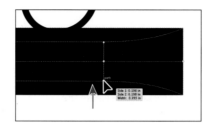

3 Position the pointer a little to the right of where you just dragged the stroke. Click and drag down, away from the center of the line. When the gray measurement label shows a Width of approximately .6 in, release the mouse button.

4 Position the pointer on the right end of the black line (see the circled pointer in the figure below). When the cursor shows a tilde (~) next to it and a green line appears on the end of the line, click and drag up to the center of the line. When the measurement label shows a Width of 0, release the mouse button.

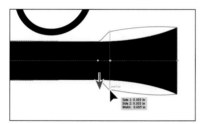 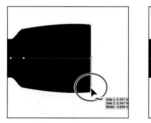 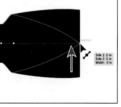

5 Choose View > Fit Artboard In Window.

6 Select the Selection tool (▶), and click on the swirls to select them. Press the Down Arrow key on your keyboard several times to move the swirls down so that they are touching the path you just edited.

7 Choose Object > Arrange > Send To Back, and then choose Select > Deselect.

Creating and editing gradients

Gradients are color blends of two or more colors that you can apply to the fill or stroke of artwork. Next, you will apply a gradient to the stroke of a path.

1 With the Selection tool (▶), click to select the path with the arrowhead that you just edited.

● **Note:** Read more about working with gradients in Lesson 10, "Blending Colors and Shapes."

2 Click the Gradient panel icon () on the right side of the workspace.

3 Click the Stroke box (circled in the figure) so that you can apply the gradient to the stroke of the line. Click the Gradient menu button (▼) to the left of the word "Type," and choose White, Black from the menu. Click the Apply Gradient Across Stroke button (▣).

● **Note:** In the color panel that appears, you may only see a K (black) slider and that's okay.

4 Double-click the white color stop on the left side of the gradient slider in the Gradient panel (circled in the figure below). Click the Color button (▣), if it's not already selected, and drag the K (black) slider to the right until **80** shows in the % field to the right of the slider. Press the Escape key to close the colors panel.

5 Position the pointer over the black color stop on the right end of the gradient slider, and drag it to the left, to approximately the position shown in the figure.

6 With the Selection tool, Shift-click the swirls and choose Object > Arrange > Send To Back. Choose Select > Deselect, and then choose File > Save.

Change the color stop.

Drag the color stop.

The result.

Placing Adobe Photoshop images in Illustrator

▶ **Tip:** Read more about Layer Comps and placing Photoshop images in Lesson 15, "Combining Illustrator CS6 Graphics with Other Adobe Applications."

In Illustrator, you can place Photoshop® files and choose Layer Comps before you place images on the artboard. Next, you will place an image of wood.

1 Choose File > Place. In the Place dialog box, navigate to the Lesson00 folder in the Lessons folder and select the wood.psd file. Make sure that the Link option in the dialog box is selected, and click Place.

Illustrator recognizes when a file has been saved with Layer Comps and opens the Photoshop Import Options dialog box. The file in this example has been saved with two different Layer Comps.

2 In the Photoshop Import Options dialog box, select Show Preview. Choose without text from the Layer Comp menu, and then click OK at the bottom of the dialog box. The image of the wood is placed on the artboard.

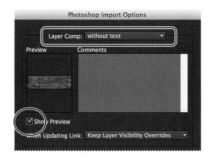 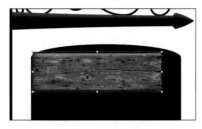

Using Image Trace

You can use Image Trace to convert photographs (raster images) into vector artwork. Next, you will trace the Photoshop file.

● **Note:** Read more about Image Trace in Lesson 3, "Creating and Editing Shapes."

1 With the image still selected, click the Image Trace button in the Control panel. The image is converted to vector paths, but it is not yet editable.

2 Click the Image Trace Panel button (▦) in the Control panel, above the artwork. Click the Auto-Color button (▦) at the top of the Image Trace panel that appears.

3 In the Image Trace panel, drag the Colors slider to the left until **4** shows in the field to the right. Close the Image Trace panel.

The Image Trace panel has many options for changing how the image is traced.

4 Click the Expand button in the Control panel to make the object editable. The wood image is now a series of vector shapes that are grouped together.

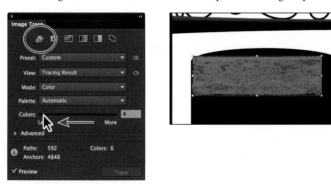

5 Choose Select > Deselect and then File > Save.

Working with the Color Guide panel

● **Note:** Read more about the Color Guide panel and recoloring artwork in Lesson 6, "Color and Painting."

The Color Guide panel can be used as a tool for color inspiration while you create your artwork. Next, you will create and save a series of colors.

1   Click the Swatches panel icon () to show the panel. Position the pointer over the brown swatches. Click the brown swatch that shows a tool tip with "C=40 M=65 Y=90 K=35."

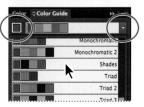

● **Note:** At this point, the colors you see at the top of the Color Guide panel may not match the figure and that's okay.

2   Click the Color Guide panel icon () on the right side of the workspace. Click the Set Base Color To The Current Color icon (■) (circled on the left in the figure). Choose Shades from the Harmony Rules menu.

3   Click the Save Color Group To Swatch Panel button (🖼) at the bottom of the Color Guide panel. This saves the colors at the top of the Color Guide panel as a color group in the Swatches panel.

4   Click the Swatches panel icon () to show the panel, and scroll down to see the new brown colors at the bottom of the panel in a group (folder).

Creating and applying a pattern

● **Note:** Read more about patterns in Lesson 6, "Color and Painting."

In addition to colors, the Swatches panel can also contain pattern swatches. Illustrator provides sample swatches of each type in the default Swatches panel and lets you create your own patterns. In this section, you will focus on creating, applying, and editing a pattern made of the wood.

1   With the Selection tool (▶), select the traced wood on the artboard. Choose Object > Pattern > Make. Click OK in the dialog box that appears.

You can make a pattern from selected artwork or start with nothing. The pattern is added as a saved swatch in the Swatches panel.

2   In the Pattern Options panel, change the Name of the pattern to **wood grain**. Choose Brick By Row from the Tile Type menu. Select Size Tile To Art. Change the H Spacing and V Spacing to **-0.2 in**.

3 With the Selection tool (▶) selected, choose Select > All On Active Artboard. This selects the wood group. The rest of the wood shapes that you see as part of the repeating pattern are there to help you visualize what the pattern will look like.

4 Press the Shift key, and drag the lower, right bounding point of the selected wood group on the artboard to the right and down until the gray measurement label shows a Width of approximately 6 in. Release the mouse button and then the Shift key.

5 Click Done in the upper-left corner of the Document window to finish editing the pattern.

6 Click to select the wood group on the artboard, and press the Backspace or Delete key to delete it.

7 With the Selection tool, click to select the black sign shape. Click the Fill color in the Control panel, and choose the wood grain pattern swatch in the panel. Press the Escape key to hide the Swatches panel.

Next, you will edit the pattern swatch.

8 Click the Swatches panel icon (▦) on the right side of the workspace to reveal it (if it isn't showing). In the Swatches panel, double-click the swatch named wood grain to edit the pattern.

9 With the Selection tool selected, choose Select > All On Active Artboard.

10 Choose Edit > Edit Colors > Adjust Color Balance. In the Adjust Colors dialog box, change the Cyan value to **80** and the Magenta value to **80**. Click OK.

11 Click Done in the upper-left corner of the Document window to finish editing the pattern. The wood pattern now has a purple cast to it.

● **Note:** You're wood pattern may not be positioned within the sign shape exactly the same as in the figures and that's okay.

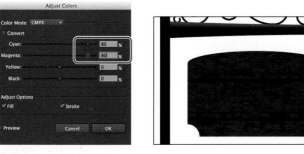

12 Choose Window > Workspace > Reset Essentials to reset the panels.

Working with type

● **Note:** Read more about working with type in Lesson 7, "Working with Type."

Next, you will add some text to the sign and apply formatting.

1 Select the Zoom tool (🔍) in the Tools panel, and click three times, slowly, in the blank area below the sign shape with the wood grain fill, to zoom in.

2 Select the Type tool (**T**) in the Tools panel, and click once in the blank area of the artboard below. You will reposition the text later in the lesson. Type **Fine Handmade Chocolates**. With the cursor in the text, choose Select > All to select the text.

▶ **Tip:** If you don't see the Character options in the Control panel, click the word "Character" to see the Character panel.

3 In the Control panel, select the font name in the Font field (to the right of the word "Character"). Type **adobe cas** to filter the font list to Adobe Caslon Pro (you may not need to type the entire phrase). Type **26 pt** in the Font Size field, and press the Enter or Return key.

4 With the text still selected, change the Stroke color in the Control panel to None (▱), if necessary, and the Fill color to gray (C=0 M=0 Y=0 K=40).

5 Select the Selection tool (▸), and drag the text area up on top of the sign shape. See the figure for placement help.

6 Click the extras.ai tab at the top of the Document window.

● **Note:** Read more about creating outlines in the section "Creating text outlines" in Lesson 7, "Working with Type."

7 With the Selection tool, click to select the text shapes "Coco's." Choose Edit > Copy, and then choose File > Close. The text shapes "Coco's" were converted to outlines (shapes) using the Type > Create Outlines command.

8 With the signage.ai file showing again, choose View > Fit Artboard In Window.

9 Choose Edit > Paste. With the Selection tool, drag the pasted text shapes onto the sign rectangle, above the other text. See the figure for placement help.

10 Choose File > Save.

Working with drawing modes

● **Note:** Read more about drawing modes in Lesson 3, "Creating and Editing Shapes."

Drawing modes allow you to draw inside of or behind existing shapes or to draw in the default Normal mode, which typically layers shapes on top of each other. Next, you will paint inside of a rectangle, using a drawing mode.

1 Select the Rectangle tool (■) from the Ellipse tool (⬭) group in the Tools panel. Position the pointer under the purple sign shape and click. In the Rectangle dialog box, change the Width to **4.8 in** and the Height to **.75 in**. Click OK.

2 Press the letter D to apply the default stroke and fill.

3 Select the Selection tool (▶), and drag the new rectangle from its top edge to the bottom of the sign shape. A green alignment guide will appear when it snaps.

4 Click the Drawing Modes button (▣) at the bottom of the Tools panel, and choose Draw Inside.

● **Note:** If the Tools panel you see is displayed as a double column, you can simply click the Draw Inside button (▣) at the bottom of the Tools panel.

Create a rectangle.   Drag the rectangle into position.   Enter Draw Inside mode.

Notice that the rectangle now has dotted lines around the corners, indicating that content that you paste or draw will be inside the rectangle shape.

5 Choose Select > Deselect and then File > Save.

Working with brushes

Brushes let you stylize the appearance of paths. You can apply brush strokes to existing paths, or you can use the Paintbrush tool to draw a path and apply a brush stroke simultaneously.

● **Note:** Read more about working with brushes in Lesson 11, "Working with Brushes."

1 Click the Brushes panel icon (🖌) on the right side of the workspace to expand the Brushes panel. Scroll down in the panel, and click the Mop brush.

2 Change the Fill color in the Control panel to None (☐) and the Stroke color to the brown color with the tool tip "C=40 M=65 Y=90 K=35."

3 Select the Paintbrush tool (🖌) in the Tools panel. Position the pointer over the left end of the rectangle you just created. Click and drag from left to right, past the right edge of the rectangle. Repeat this several times to partially fill the rectangle with the brown-colored strokes. The idea is to create a wood grain.

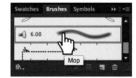

4 Double-click the Mop brush in the Brushes panel to edit it. In the Bristle Brush Options dialog box that appears, change the Size to **4 mm**, the Paint Opacity to **50%**, and the Stiffness to **20%**. Click OK.

5 In the dialog box that appears, click Leave Strokes so as not to change the strokes you already painted on the artboard.

6 Click the Stroke color in the Control panel, and select a light brown color.

7 With the Paintbrush tool selected, paint more strokes in the rectangle so that it looks more like wood grain. Select other brown stroke colors in the Control panel and try adding some new strokes to enhance the wood grain.

Note: If the Tools panel you see is displayed as a double column, you can click the Draw Normal button (icon) at the bottom of the Tools panel.

8 Click the Drawing Modes button (icon) at the bottom of the Tools panel, and choose Draw Normal.

9 Select the Selection tool (icon) in the Tools panel. Click to select the "Fine Handmade Chocolates" text object. Choose Edit > Copy, and then choose Edit > Paste In Place.

10 Drag the copied text object down on top of the rectangle that contains the painting. Center it vertically as best you can.

11 Select the Type tool (**T**) in the Tools panel, and click the copied text object to insert the cursor. Choose Select > All to select the text, and type **Hours Mon–Sat 10am–6pm**. Do not type the period.

12 Select the Selection tool, and, with the text object selected, in the Control panel change the Font Style to Bold and the Fill color to Black.

13 Choose Select > Deselect, and then choose File > Save.

Using the Appearance panel and effects

Note: Read more about working with the Appearance panel in Lesson 13, "Applying Appearance Attributes and Graphic Styles."

The Appearance panel allows you to control an object's attributes, such as stroke, fill, and effects.

1 With the Selection tool (icon), click to select the purple sign shape.

2 Click the Appearance panel icon (icon) on the right side of the workspace.

3 Click the Stroke color box in the Appearance panel (to the right of the word "Stroke"), and then click it again to open the Swatches panel. Choose Black from the Swatches panel. Change the Stroke weight to the right of the color to **10 pt**. Click the underlined word "Stroke," and, in the Stroke panel that appears, click Align Stroke To Inside (icon). Press the Escape key to hide the panel that appears.

4   Click the Add New Stroke button (■) at the bottom of the Appearance panel to add a new stroke to the shape. Click the Stroke color at the top of the list in the Appearance panel, and select White. Press the Escape key to hide the Swatches panel. Change the Stroke weight to **5 pt**.

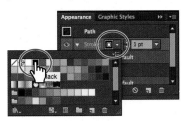

Change the stroke color.

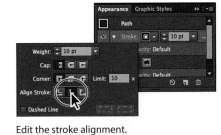

Edit the stroke alignment.

Add a new stroke.

5   Choose Effect > Path > Offset Path. In the Offset Path dialog box, change the Offset to **-0.1 in**. Click OK.

6   Click the word "Fill" in the Appearance panel to apply the next effect to the fill of the path. You may need to scroll down in the panel.

7   Click the Add New Effect button (fx.) at the bottom of the Appearance panel, and choose Stylize > Inner Glow. In the Inner Glow dialog box, choose Darken from the Mode menu. Click the white color preview square next to the Blending Mode menu to specify a color for the glow in the Color Picker dialog box. Change the K value to **100%**, and make sure that the C, M, and Y values are **0%**. Click OK in the Color Picker. Change the Blur to **1 in**, and click OK.

8   With the Selection tool, click the text "Fine Handmade Chocolates."

9   Choose Effect > Stylize > Drop Shadow. In the Drop Shadow dialog box, change the Opacity to **75%** (if necessary), the X Offset and Y Offset to **.02 in**, and the Blur to **.03 in**. Click OK.

10 With the Selection tool, click the text that begins with "Hours..."

11 Choose Effect > Drop Shadow. In the Drop Shadow dialog box, choose Normal from the Mode menu. Change the X Offset and Y Offset to **.01 in**, and the Blur to **0**. Click the black color preview square next to the word "Color." In the Color Picker that appears, change the C, M, Y, and K values all to **0%**, to make white and then click OK. Click OK in the Drop Shadow dialog box.

Working with strokes

Aside from changing the color and weight of strokes, you can also format them in many other ways. That's what you'll do next to create chains to hang the sign.

1 Select the Zoom tool (🔍) in the Tools panel, and click twice, slowly, in the blank area above the purple sign shape, to zoom in.

2 Select the Ellipse tool (⬭) in the Rectangle tool (▪) group. Position the pointer just off the upper-left corner of the purple sign, in the blank area, and click. In the Ellipse dialog box, change the Width to **.35 in** and the Height to **.45 in**. Click OK.

3 In the Control panel, change the Fill color to None, the Stroke color to Black, and the Stroke weight to **5 pt**.

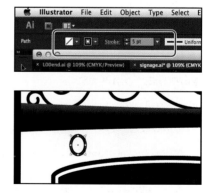

● **Note:** If the spacing is not exactly like you see in the figure, that's okay.

4 Select the Selection tool (▶), and drag the ellipse by its edge into the position you see in the figure.

5 Select the Line Segment tool (╱) in the Tools panel. Position the pointer above the ellipse, on the horizontal path. When the word "intersect" appears and a green line runs through the center of the ellipse, press the Shift key and click and drag down. Drag until the gray measurement label shows a distance of **1.3 in**. Release the mouse button and then the Shift key.

6 Make sure that the Stroke weight in the Control panel is **5 pt**. With the line selected, click the underlined word "Stroke" in the Control panel to reveal the Stroke panel.

Click the Round Cap button (). Select Dashed Line, and select the Aligns Dashes To Corners And Path Ends... button (■■■), if it's not selected. Type **75 pt** into the first Dash field, and press the Enter or Return key to close the Stroke panel.

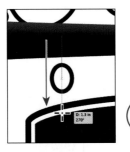

Position the pointer.	Drag to create a line.	Change the Stroke options.

7 Select the Selection tool (▶) in the Tools panel. Shift-click the edge of the ellipse to select both objects. In the Control panel, click the Horizontal Align Center button (▲) and the Vertical Align Center button (♦). Choose Object > Group.

8 With the chain group selected, choose Object > Arrange > Send To Back.

9 With the Selection tool, begin dragging the chain group to the right, by the edge of one of the objects. As you drag, press Alt+Shift (Windows) or Option+Shift (Mac OS). Drag the group toward the right edge of the sign shape. See the figure for placement help. Release the mouse button and then the modifier keys.

● **Note:** The Align options may not appear in the Control panel. If you don't see the Align options, click the word Align in the Control panel to open the Align panel. The number of options displayed in the Control panel depends on your screen resolution.

10 Press the Shift key, and click the edge of one of the objects in the original chain group. Choose Object > Group, and leave the group selected.

Aligning content

Next, you'll align the content for the sign horizontally.

1 Choose View > Fit Artboard In Window.

2 With the Selection tool (▶), position the pointer just to the left of the chains group. Click and drag across the chains, the purple sign, the "Coco's" text shapes, the "Fine Handmade Chocolates" text, the painted sign, and the text beneath it, to select them all.

● **Note:** Read more about aligning content in Lesson 2, "Selecting and Aligning."

3 Click the Horizontal Align Center button (▲) in the Control panel to center align all of the objects to each other horizontally.

Working with perspective

You will now create some chocolate pieces in perspective.

● **Note:** Read more about perspective in Lesson 9, "Working with Perspective Drawing."

1 Click the First button (⏮) in the lower-left corner of the Document window to navigate to the first artboard and to fit it into the Document window.

2 Select the Perspective Grid tool (▦) in the Tools panel to show the grid.

3 Choose View > Perspective Grid > Two Point Perspective > [2P-Normal View]. This centers the grid on the first artboard.

● **Note:** Pressing the number 1 may not appear to do anything, but when working with the Perspective Grid, the numbers 1, 2, 3, 4 are shortcuts for switching grid planes.

4 Select the Rectangle tool (▭) from the Ellipse tool (⬭) group in the Tools panel. Position the pointer over the Origin point at the bottom of the grid (circled in the figure). Press the number 1 on the keyboard to ensure that you draw on the left grid plane. Click and drag up and to the left to create a rectangle that is three gridlines wide and two gridlines high.

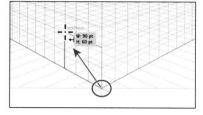

5 In the Control panel, change the Fill color to the medium brown swatch with the tool tip that displays "C=40 M=70 Y=100 K=50," and the Stroke weight to **0**.

6 Click the Right Grid(3) in the Plane Switching Widget in the upper-left corner of the Document window to select the right grid.

7 With the Rectangle tool selected, position the pointer over the origin point again. Click and drag up and to the right to create a rectangle that is three gridlines wide and two gridlines high.

8 In the Control panel, change the Fill color to the darker brown swatch with the tool tip "C=50 M=70 Y=80 K=70." Press the Escape key to hide the Swatches panel.

9 Click the Horizontal Grid(2) in the Plane Switching Widget (see the figure at right). Choose Select > Deselect, if available.

10 Position the pointer over the upper-left point of the first rectangle you drew (circled in the figure). Click and drag across, snapping the pointer to the upper-right point of the second rectangle you drew.

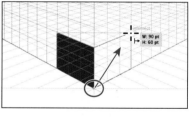

11 In the Control panel, change the Fill color to the lighter brown swatch with the tool tip "C=40 M=65 Y=90 K=35." Press the Escape key to hide the Swatches panel.

12 Choose Select > All On Active Artboard. Choose Object > Group.

13 Choose View > Perspective Grid > Hide Grid, and leave the group selected.

Working with symbols

A symbol is a reusable art object stored in the Symbols panel. You will now create a symbol from artwork.

● **Note:** Read more about working with symbols in Lesson 14, "Working with Symbols."

1 Click the Symbols panel icon (⬚) on the right side of the workspace.

2 Select the Selection tool (▶). With the group still selected on the first artboard, click the New Symbol button (⬚) at the bottom of the Symbols panel.

3 In the Symbol Options dialog box, name the symbol **chocolate**, and choose Graphic from the Type menu. Click OK. The group of objects now appears as a saved symbol in the Symbols panel.

4 Press the Delete or Backspace key to delete the original group on the first artboard. Click the Next button (▶) in the lower-left corner of the Document window to navigate to the second artboard.

5 From the Symbols panel, drag the chocolate symbol onto the center of the sign, above the "Coco's" text.

● **Note:** Your chocolate symbols may be in different locations than those in the figure. That's okay. Use the figure as a guide.

6 Hold down the Shift+Alt (Windows) or Shift+Option (Mac OS) keys and, with the Selection tool (▶), drag a bounding point toward the center of the chocolate to make it smaller, while maintaining its proportions. Release the mouse button and then the keys when it roughly matches the size in the figure.

7 Drag out one more chocolate symbol from the Symbols panel. Resize the chocolate piece, making it smaller than the first. Position it as in the figure, and leave it selected.

Drag the symbol onto the artboard.

Resize the symbol.

The result.

8 Choose Select > Same > Symbol Instance. Choose Object > Group.

9 Click the Graphic Styles panel icon (⬚). Click the Drop Shadow graphic style to apply the appearance formatting.

10 Choose File > Save and then File > Close.

1 GETTING TO KNOW THE WORK AREA

Lesson overview

In this lesson, you'll explore the workspace and learn how to do the following:

- Open an Adobe Illustrator CS6 file.
- Adjust the user interface brightness.
- Work with the Tools panel.
- Work with panels.
- Reset and save your workspace.
- Use viewing options to enlarge and reduce artwork.
- Navigate multiple artboards and documents.
- Understand rulers.
- Explore document groups.
- Use Illustrator Help.

 This lesson takes approximately 45 minutes to complete. If needed, remove the previous lesson folder from your hard disk and copy the Lesson01 folder onto it.

Created with pur[e]

Here at Uncle Henry's Farm we have
about 1200 acres, growing a large variety
of fruits and vegetables, including
peaches, nectarines, apples, apricots,
raspberries, strawberries, blackberries,
and boysenberries.

Our first fruit trees in Seattle were
planted in 1951. Our first commercial
cherry harvest was in 1954 with the work
of picking and processing performed by
family members of all ages. Our first
apple line included four Brier apple
corers, with the washing, sorting, and can
filling all done by hand.

Our nectarine operation has grown into a
thriving business. We have many
pickers on hand throughout the

Pumpkin Festival!

October 24th - 26th, 2010

It's that time of year again! Come join us from
October 24th – 26th as we celebrate our
favorite time of year.

At the farm we'll have thousands of pumpkins
to choose from, hayrides, cider, games for the
kids, and more! The farm comes to life when the
pumpkin festival is back.

U-Pick Calendar

Fruit	Best Time
Peaches	July – August
Apples	September –
Nectarines	July – August
Strawberries	June – Augus
Rasberries	May – July

To make the best use of the extensive
drawing, painting, and editing capabilities of
Adobe Illustrator CS6, it's important to learn how to
navigate the workspace. The workspace consists of the
Application bar, the menus, Tools panel, Control panel,
Document window, and the default set of panels.

Getting started

You'll be working in multiple art files during this lesson, but before you begin, restore the default preferences for Adobe Illustrator CS6. Then, open the finished art file for this lesson to see an illustration.

1   To ensure that the tools and panels function exactly as described in this lesson, delete or deactivate (by renaming) the Adobe Illustrator CS6 preferences file. See "Restoring default preferences" on page 3.

Note: If you have not already done so, copy the Lesson01 folder from the Lessons folder on the *Adobe Illustrator CS6 Classroom in a Book* CD onto your hard disk. See "Copying the Classroom in a Book files" on page 2.

2   Double-click the Adobe Illustrator CS6 icon to start Adobe Illustrator.

3   Choose Window > Workspace > Reset Essentials to ensure that the workspace is set to the default settings.

Note: If you don't see "Reset Essentials" in the Workspace menu, choose Window > Workspace > Essentials before choosing Window > Workspace > Reset Essentials.

Note: Due to the differences in Color Settings from one system to another, a Missing Profile dialog box may appear as you open various exercise files. Click OK if you see this dialog box.

4   Choose File > Open to open the L1start_1.ai file. In the Lesson01 folder in the Lessons folder on your hard disk, select the L1start_1.ai file and click Open.

5   Choose View > Fit Artboard In Window.

Choosing to fit the artboard in the window fits the active artboard into the Document window so that you can see the entire artboard.

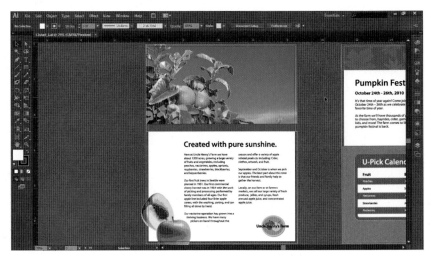

The artwork file contains the front and back of a brochure.

When the file is open and Illustrator is fully launched, the Application bar, menus, Tools panel, Control panel, and panel groups appear on the screen. Docked on the right side of the screen, you will see the default panels that appear as icons. Illustrator also consolidates many of your most frequently accessed options in the Control panel below the menu bar. This lets you work with fewer visible panels and gives you a larger area in which to work.

You will use the L1start_1.ai file to practice navigating, zooming, and investigating an Illustrator document and the workspace.

6 Choose File > Save As. In the Save As dialog box, name the file **brochure.ai** and save it in the Lesson01 folder. Leave the Save As Type option set to Adobe Illustrator (*.AI) (Windows), or leave the Format option set to Adobe Illustrator (ai) (Mac OS). Click Save. If a warning dialog box appears referencing spot colors and transparency, click Continue. In the Illustrator Options dialog box, leave the options at their default settings and click OK.

Note: The Illustrator Options dialog box contains options that can control how the file is saved, allow you to save to a previous version of Illustrator, and more.

Why use Adobe Illustrator?

Vector graphics (sometimes called vector shapes or vector objects) are made up of lines and curves defined by mathematical objects called vectors, which describe an image according to its geometric characteristics. You'll learn more about lines and curves in Lesson 5, "Drawing with the Pen and Pencil Tools."

You can freely move or modify vector graphics without losing detail or clarity, because they are resolution-independent—they maintain crisp edges when resized, printed to a PostScript printer, saved in a PDF file, or imported into a vector-based graphics application. As a result, vector graphics are the best choice for artwork, such as logos, that will be used at various sizes and in various output media.

The vector objects you create using the drawing and shape tools in Adobe Illustrator and the Adobe Creative Suite® are examples of vector graphics.

—From Illustrator Help

Understanding the workspace

● **Note:** The figures in this lesson are taken using the Windows operating system and may look slightly different from what you see, especially if you are using the Mac OS.

You create and manipulate your documents and files using various elements such as panels, bars, and windows. Any arrangement of these elements is called a workspace. When you first start Illustrator, you see the default workspace, which you can customize for the tasks you perform. You can create and save multiple workspaces—one for editing and another for viewing, for example—and switch between them as you work. Below, the areas of the default workspace are described:

A. Application bar
B. Control panel

C. Panels

D. Tools panel

E. Document window

F. Status bar

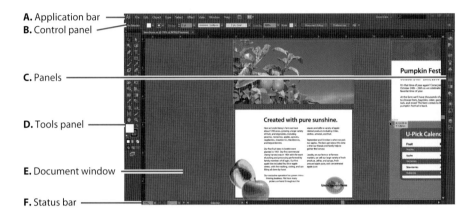

A. The **Application bar** across the top contains a workspace switcher, a menu bar (Windows only, depending on screen resolution), and application controls.

● **Note:** For the Mac OS, the menu items appear above the Application bar.

B. The **Control panel** displays options for the currently selected object.

C. **Panels** help you monitor and modify your work. Certain panels are displayed by default, but you can add any panel by choosing it from the Window menu. Many panels have menus with panel-specific options. Panels can be grouped, stacked, docked, or free-floating.

D. The **Tools panel** contains tools for creating and editing images, artwork, page elements, and more. Related tools are grouped together.

E. The **Document window** displays the file you're working on.

F. The **Status bar** appears at the lower-left edge of the Document window. It displays information and navigation controls.

Adjusting the user interface brightness

Similar to Adobe After Effects® or Adobe Photoshop CS6, Illustrator supports a brightness adjustment for the application user interface. This is a program preference setting that allows you to choose a brightness setting from four preset levels or to specify a custom value.

In this section, you will change the setting to see its effect, and then you will change it back to the program default.

1 Choose Edit > Preferences > User Interface (Windows) or Illustrator > Preferences > User Interface (Mac OS).

2 Choose Light from the Brightness menu of the User Interface options.

You can adjust the brightness of the user interface using set options in the Brightness menu.

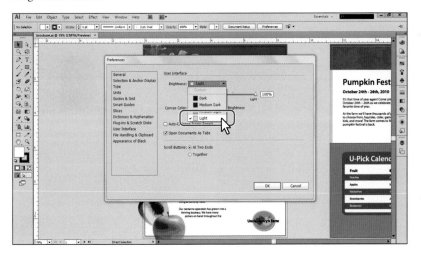

3 Drag the Brightness slider to the left until you see a value of 50%.

You can drag the Brightness slider beneath the Brightness menu to the left or to the right to adjust the overall brightness using a custom value.

4 Choose Medium Dark from the Brightness menu.

5 Select White for the Canvas Color option beneath the Brightness slider.

The canvas is the area outside of the artboards in your document.

6 Click Cancel so as not to save the preference settings.

Working with the Tools panel

The Tools panel contains selection tools, drawing and painting tools, editing tools, viewing tools, the Fill and Stroke boxes, Drawing modes, and screen modes. As you work through the lessons, you'll learn about the specific function of each tool.

● **Note:** The Tools panel shown here and throughout the lesson has two columns. You may see a single-column Tools panel, depending on your screen resolution and workspace.

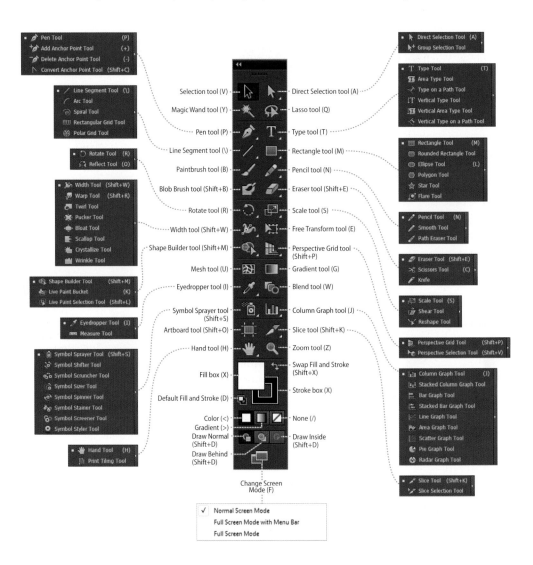

1 Position the pointer over the Selection tool (▶) in the Tools panel. Notice that the name and keyboard shortcut are displayed.

▶ **Tip:** You can turn the tool tips on or off by choosing Edit > Preferences > General (Windows) or Illustrator > Preferences > General (Mac OS) and deselecting Show Tool Tips.

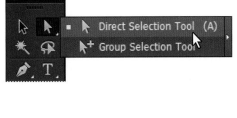

▶ **Tip:** Because the default keyboard shortcuts work only when you do not have a text insertion point, you can also add other keyboard shortcuts to select tools, even when you are editing text. To do this, choose Edit > Keyboard Shortcuts. For more information, see "Keyboard Shortcuts" in Illustrator Help.

2 Position the pointer over the Direct Selection tool (▷) and click and hold down the mouse button. You'll see additional selection tools. Drag to the right. Release the mouse button over the additional tool to select it.

Any tool in the Tools panel that displays a small triangle contains additional tools that can be selected in this way.

▶ **Tip:** You can also select hidden tools by pressing the Alt key (Windows) or the Option key (Mac OS) and clicking the tool in the Tools panel. Each click selects the next hidden tool in the hidden tool sequence.

3 Click and hold down the mouse button on the Rectangle tool (■). Drag the pointer over the arrow at the end of the hidden tools panel, and release the mouse button. This separates the tools from the Tools panel so that you can access them at all times.

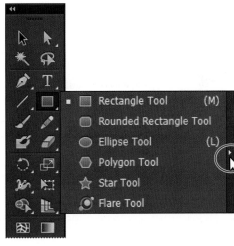

▶ **Tip:** You can also collapse the floating tool panels or dock them to the workspace or each other.

4 Click the Close button (X) in the upper-right corner (Windows) or upper-left corner (Mac OS) on the floating tool panel's title bar to close it. The tools return to the Tools panel.

Next, you'll learn how to resize and float the Tools panel.

5 Click the double arrow in the upper-left corner of the Tools panel to collapse the two columns into one column, which conserves screen space. Click the double arrow again to expand to two columns.

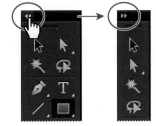

6 Click the dark gray title bar at the top of the Tools panel or the dashed line beneath the title bar, and drag the panel into the workspace. The Tools panel is now floating in the workspace.

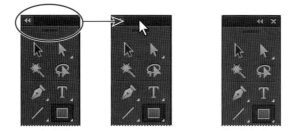

Drag the Tools panel so that it floats in the workspace.

▶ **Tip:** You can also double-click the title bar at the top of the Tools panel to switch between two columns and one column. Just be careful not to double-click the X or the double arrow.

7 With the Tools panel floating in the workspace, click the double arrow in the title bar to display the Tools panel in a single column. Click again to display the Tools panel in two columns.

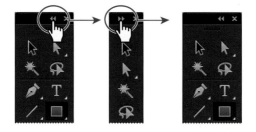

8 To dock the Tools panel again, drag its title bar or the dashed line below it to the left side of the application window (Windows) or screen (Mac OS). When the pointer reaches the left edge, a translucent blue border, called the drop zone, appears. Release the mouse button to fit the Tools panel neatly into the side of the workspace.

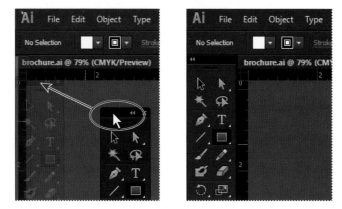

Click and drag to dock the Tools panel at the edge of the workspace.

Exploring the Control panel

The Control panel is context-sensitive, meaning that it offers quick access to options, commands, and other panels relevant to the currently selected object(s). You can click text that is underlined to display a related panel. For example, click the underlined word Stroke to display the Stroke panel. By default, the Control panel is docked at the top of the application window (Windows) or screen (Mac OS); however, you can dock it at the bottom, float it, or hide it altogether.

1   Select the Selection tool (▶) in the Tools panel, and click the middle of the reddish bar close to the center of the page.

Notice that information for that object appears in the Control panel, including the word "Path," color options, Stroke, and more.

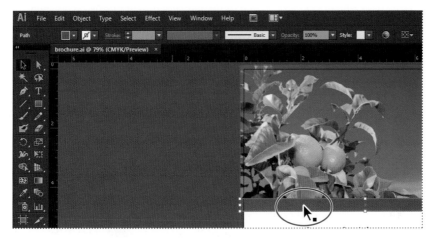

2   With any tool, drag the gripper bar (the dashed line along the left edge) of the Control panel into the workspace.

Once the Control panel is free-floating, you can drag the dark gray gripper bar that appears on the left edge of the Control panel to move it to the top or bottom of the workspace.

Tip: You can also dock the Control panel by choosing Dock To Top or Dock To Bottom from the Control panel menu on the right side of the Control panel (▼≣).

3 Drag the Control panel by the dark gray gripper bar on the left end to the bottom of the application window (Windows) or screen (Mac OS). When the pointer reaches the bottom of the Application window (Windows) or screen (Mac OS), a blue line appears, indicating the drop zone in which it will be docked when you release the mouse button.

Tip: To move the Control panel back to the top of the workspace, you can also choose Window > Workspace > Reset Essentials. This resets the Essentials workspace. You'll learn more about resetting workspaces later in the lesson.

4 Drag the Control panel to the top of the Document window by the gripper bar on the left end of the panel. When the pointer reaches the bottom of the Application bar, a blue line appears indicating the drop zone. When you release the mouse button, the panel is docked.

5 Choose Select > Deselect so that the path is no longer selected.

Working with panels

Panels, which are located in the Window menu, give you quick access to many tools that make modifying artwork easier. By default, some panels are docked and appear as icons on the right side of the workspace. Next, you'll experiment with hiding, closing, and opening panels.

1 First, choose Reset Essentials from the workspace switcher in the upper-right corner of the Application bar to reset the panels to their original location.

Tip: You can also choose Window > Workspace > Reset Essentials to reset the panels.

2 Click the Swatches panel icon (▦) on the right side of the workspace to expand the panel, or choose Window > Swatches. Notice that the Swatches panel appears with two other panels—the Brushes panel and Symbols panel. They are all part of the same panel group. Click the Symbols panel tab to view the Symbols panel.

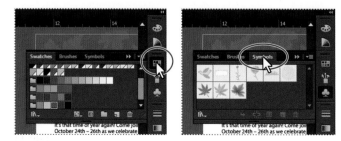

3 Now click the Color panel icon (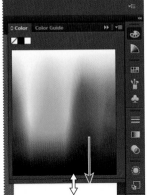). Notice that a new panel group appears, and the panel group that contained the Swatches panel collapses.

4 Click and drag the gripper bar at the bottom of the Color panel down to resize the panel, showing more of the color spectrum.

5 Click the Color panel icon (🎨) to collapse the panel group.

▶ **Tip:** To find a hidden panel, choose the panel name from the Window menu. A check mark to the left of the panel name indicates that the panel is already open and in front of other panels in its panel group. If you choose a panel name that is already selected in the Window menu, the panel and its group collapses.

▶ **Tip:** To collapse a panel back to an icon, you can click its tab, its icon, or the double arrow in the panel title bar.

6 Click the double arrow at the top of the dock to expand the panels. Click the double arrow again to collapse the panels. Use this method to show more than one panel group at a time. Your panels may look different when expanded, and that's okay.

Click to expand. Click to collapse. The dock collapsed.

▶ **Tip:** To expand or collapse the panel dock, you can also double-click the panel dock title bar at the top.

7 To increase the width of all the panels in the dock, drag the left edge of the docked panels to the left until text appears. To decrease the width, click and drag the left edge of the docked panels to the right until the text disappears.

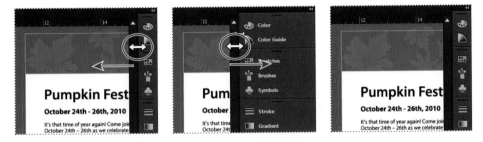

8 Choose Window > Workspace > Reset Essentials to reset the workspace.

9 Drag the Swatches panel icon (▦) to remove the panel from the dock and make it a free-floating panel. Notice that the panel stays collapsed as an icon when it is free-floating. Click the double arrow in the Swatches panel title bar to expand the panel so you can see its contents.

You can also move panels from one panel group to another. In this way you can create custom panel groups that contain the panels you use most often.

▶ **Tip:** To close a panel, drag the panel away from the dock and click the X in the panel title bar. You can also right-click or Ctrl-click a docked panel tab and choose Close from the menu.

10 Drag the Swatches panel by the panel tab, the panel title bar, or the area behind the panel tab onto the Brushes and Symbols panel icons. Release the mouse button when you see a blue outline around the Brushes panel group.

Next, you'll organize the panels to create more room in your workspace.

11 Choose Reset Essentials from the workspace switcher in the Application bar, to make sure that the panels are reset to their default state.

12 Click the double arrow at the top of the dock to expand the panels. Click the Color Guide panel tab to make sure it's selected. Double-click the panel tab to reduce the size of the panel. Double-click the tab again to minimize the panel. This can also be done when a panel is free-floating (not docked).

● **Note:** Many panels only require that you double-click the panel tab twice to return to the full-size view of the panel. If you double-click one more time, the panel fully expands.

▶ **Tip:** To reduce and expand the panel size, instead of double-clicking the panel tab, you can click the small arrow icon to the left of the panel name in the panel tab, if present.

13 Click the Appearance panel tab to expand that panel. Depending on your screen resolution, it may already be expanded.

Next, you will resize a panel group, which can make it easier to see more important panels.

14 Click the Symbols panel tab. Drag the dividing line between the Symbols panel group and the Stroke panel group up to resize the group.

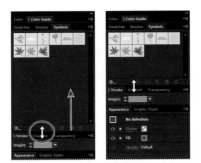

● **Note:** You may not be able to drag the divider very far, depending on your screen size, screen resolution, and number of panels expanded.

15 Choose Reset Essentials from the workspace switcher in the Application bar.

Next, you'll arrange panel groups. Panel groups can be docked, undocked, and arranged in either collapsed or expanded modes.

16 Choose Window > Align to open the Align panel group. Drag the title bar of the Align panel group to the docked panels on the right side of the workspace. Position the pointer below the group that the Symbols panel icon (▦) is in so that a single blue line appears. Release the mouse button to create a new group in the dock.

● **Note:** If you drag a group into the dock and drop it into an existing group, the two groups merge. Reset the workspace and open the panel group to try again.

Next, you will drag a panel from one group to another in the docked panels.

Tip: You can also reorder entire panel groups in the dock by dragging the double gray line at the top of each panel group up or down.

17 Drag the Transform panel icon (▦) up so that the pointer is just below the Color panel icon (▦). A blue line appears between the Color panel icon and the Color Guide panel icon, outlining the Color panel group in blue. Release the mouse button.

Arranging the panels in groups can help you work faster.

Resetting and saving your workspace

You can reset your panels and Tools panel to their default position, which you've been doing throughout this lesson. You can also save the position of panels so that you can easily access them at any time by creating a workspace. Next, you will create a workspace to access a group of commonly used panels.

1 Choose Reset Essentials from the workspace switcher in the Application bar.

Tip: Docking panels next to each other on the right side of the workspace is a great way to conserve space. A docked panel can also be collapsed and resized to conserve even more space.

2 Choose Window > Pathfinder. Click and drag the Pathfinder panel tab to the right side of the workspace. When the pointer approaches the left edge of the docked panels, a blue line appears. Release the mouse button to dock the panel. Click the Close button (X) in the upper-right corner (Windows) or upper-left corner (Mac OS) to close the remaining panel group, which contains the Align and Transform panels.

3 Choose Window > Workspace > New Workspace. Change the Name to **Navigation** in the New Workspace dialog box, and click OK. The workspace named Navigation is now saved with Illustrator until you remove it.

4 Choose Window > Workspace > Essentials, and then choose Window > Workspace > Reset Essentials. Notice that the panels return to their default positions. Choose Window > Workspace > Navigation. Toggle between the two workspaces using the Window > Workspace command, and return to the Essentials workspace before starting the next exercise.

Note: To delete saved workspaces, choose Window > Workspace > Manage Workspaces. Select the workspace name, and click the Delete Workspace button.

▶ **Tip:** To change a saved workspace, reset the panels as you'd like them to appear and then choose Window > Workspace > New Workspace. In the New Workspace dialog box, name the workspace with the original name. A message appears in the dialog box warning that you will overwrite an existing workspace with the same name if you click OK. Click OK.

Using panel menus

Most panels have a panel menu in the upper-right corner. Clicking the panel menu button (▾≡) gives you access to additional options for the selected panel, including changing the panel display in some cases.

Next, you will change the display of the Symbols panel using its panel menu.

1   Click the Symbols panel icon (▨) on the right side of the workspace. You can also choose Window > Symbols to display this panel.

2   Click the panel menu button (▾≡) in the upper-right corner of the Symbols panel.

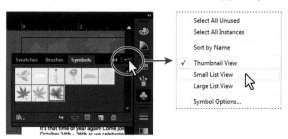

3   Choose Small List View from the panel menu.

This displays the symbol names, together with thumbnails. Because the options in the panel menu apply only to the active panel, only the Symbols panel view is affected.

4   Click the Symbols panel menu and choose Thumbnail View, to return the symbols to their original view. Click the Symbols panel tab to hide the panel again.

In addition to the panel menus, context-sensitive menus display commands relevant to the active tool, selection, or panel.

5   Position the pointer over the Document window or a panel. Then, right-click (Windows) or Ctrl-click (Mac OS) to show a context menu with specific options.

The context-sensitive menu shown here is displayed when you right-click (Windows) or Ctrl-click (Mac OS) the artboard with nothing selected.

Note: If you position the pointer over a panel, like the Swatches panel, and right-click (Windows) or Ctrl-click (Mac OS), you can close a panel or a panel group in the context menu that appears.

Changing the view of artwork

When working in files, it's likely that you'll need to change the magnification level and navigate between artboards. The magnification level, which can range from 3.13% to 6400%, is displayed in the title bar (or document tab) next to the file name and in the lower-left corner of the Document window. Using any of the viewing tools and commands affects only the display of the artwork, not the actual size of the artwork.

Using the view commands

To enlarge or reduce the view of artwork using the View menu, do one of the following:

- Choose View > Zoom In to enlarge the display of the brochure.ai artwork.

▶ **Tip:** Zoom in using the keyboard shortcut Ctrl++ (Windows) or Command++ (Mac OS).

- Choose View > Zoom Out to reduce the view of the brochure.ai artwork.

▶ **Tip:** Zoom out using the keyboard shortcut Ctrl+– (Windows) or Command+–(Mac OS) .

Each time you choose a Zoom option, the view of the artwork is resized to the closest preset zoom level. The preset zoom levels appear in a menu in the lower-left corner of the Document window, identified by a down arrow next to a percentage.

You can also use the View menu to fit the artwork for the active artboard to your screen, to fit all artboards into the view area, or to view artwork at actual size.

▶ **Tip:** You can also double-click the Hand tool in the Tools panel to fit the active artboard in the Document window.

1 Choose View > Fit Artboard In Window. A reduced view of the active artboard is displayed in the window.

● **Note:** Because the canvas (the area outside the artboards) extends to 227", you can easily lose sight of your illustration. By choosing View > Fit Artboard In Window, or using the keyboard shortcuts Ctrl+0 (Windows) or Command+0 (Mac OS), artwork is centered in the viewing area.

2 To display artwork at actual size, choose View > Actual Size.

The artwork is displayed at 100%. The actual size of your artwork determines how much of it can be viewed on-screen at 100%.

▶ **Tip:** You can also double-click the Zoom tool in the Tools panel to display artwork at 100%.

3 Choose View > Fit All In Window.

You will see all artboards in the document displayed in the Document window. You can learn more about navigating artboards in the section "Navigating multiple artboards," later in this lesson.

4 Choose View > Fit Artboard In Window before continuing to the next section.

Using the Zoom tool

In addition to the View menu options, you can use the Zoom tool (🔍) to magnify and reduce the view of artwork to predefined magnification levels.

1   Select the Zoom tool (🔍) in the Tools panel, and then move the pointer into the Document window.

Notice that a plus sign (+) appears at the center of the Zoom tool pointer.

2   Position the Zoom tool over the title text "Created with..." in the center of the artboard, and click once. The artwork is displayed at a higher magnification.

3   Click two more times on the "Created with..." text. The view is increased again, and you'll notice that the area you clicked is magnified.

Next, you'll reduce the view of the artwork.

4   With the Zoom tool still selected, position the pointer over the text "Created with..." and hold down the Alt (Windows) or Option (Mac OS) key. A minus sign (−) appears at the center of the Zoom tool pointer. Continue holding the key down for the next step.

5   With the Alt or Option key pressed, click the artwork twice to reduce the view of the artwork.

> ● **Note:** The percent of the magnification is determined by the size of the marquee you draw with the Zoom tool—the smaller the marquee, the higher the level of magnification.

For a more controlled zoom, you can drag a marquee around a specific area of your artwork. This magnifies only the selected area.

6   Choose View > Fit Artboard In Window.

7   With the Zoom tool still selected, click and drag a marquee around the Uncle Henry's Farm logo in the lower-right corner of the artboard. When you see the marquee around the area you are dragging, release the mouse button. The marqueed area is now enlarged to fit the size of the Document window.

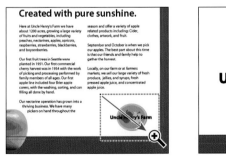
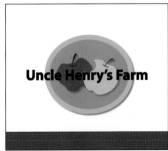

8   Double-click the Hand tool (✋) in the Tools panel to fit the artboard in the Document window.

The Zoom tool is used frequently during the editing process to enlarge and reduce the view of artwork. Because of this, Illustrator allows you to select it using the keyboard at any time without first deselecting any other tool you may be using.

9   Before selecting the Zoom tool using the keyboard, select any other tool in the Tools panel and move the pointer into the Document window.

● **Note:** In certain versions of Mac OS, the keyboard shortcuts for the Zoom tool (steps 10 and 11) open Spotlight or Finder. If you decide to use these shortcuts in Illustrator, you may want to turn off or change those keyboard shortcuts in the Mac OS System Preferences.

10 Now hold down Control+spacebar (Windows) or Command+spacebar (Mac OS) to use the Zoom tool. Click or drag to zoom in on any area of the artwork, and then release the keys.

11 To zoom out using the keyboard, hold down Control+Alt+spacebar (Windows) or Command+Option+spacebar (Mac OS). Click the desired area to reduce the view of the artwork, and then release the keys.

12 Double-click the Hand tool in the Tools panel to fit the artboard in the Document window.

Scrolling through a document

You can use the Hand tool to pan to different areas of a document. Using the Hand tool allows you to push the document around much like you would a piece of paper on your desk.

1   Select the Hand tool (🖐) in the Tools panel.

2   Drag down in the Document window. As you drag, the artwork moves with the hand.

As with the Zoom tool (🔍), you can select the Hand tool with a keyboard shortcut without first deselecting the active tool.

3   Click any other tool except the Type tool (T) in the Tools panel, and move the pointer into the Document window.

4   Hold down the spacebar to select the Hand tool from the keyboard, and then drag to bring the artwork back into the center of your view.

5   Double-click the Hand tool to fit the active artboard in the Document window.

● **Note:** The spacebar shortcut for the Hand tool does not work when the Type tool is active and your cursor is in text.

Viewing artwork

When you open a file, it is automatically displayed in Preview mode, which shows how the artwork will print. When you're working with large or complex illustrations, you may want to view only the outlines, or wireframes, of objects in your artwork so that the screen doesn't have to redraw the artwork each time you make a change. This is called Outline mode. Outline mode can be helpful when selecting objects, as you will see in Lesson 3, "Creating and Editing Shapes."

1 Choose View > Logo Zoom (at the bottom of the View menu) to zoom in to a preset area of the image. This custom view was saved with the document.

▶ **Tip:** To save time when working with large or complex documents, you can create your own custom views within a document so that you can quickly jump to specific areas and zoom levels. Set up the view that you want to save, and then choose View > New View. Name the view, and click OK; it is saved with the document.

2 Choose View > Outline.

Only the outlines of the objects are displayed. Use this view to find objects that might not be visible in Preview mode.

3 Choose View > Preview to see all the attributes of the artwork.

If you prefer keyboard shortcuts, use Control+Y (Windows) or Command+Y (Mac OS) to toggle between Preview and Outline modes.

4 Choose View > Overprint Preview to view any lines or shapes that are set to overprint.

This view is helpful for those in the print industry who need to see how inks interact when set to overprint. You may not actually see much of a change in the logo when you change to this mode.

● **Note:** When switching between viewing modes, visual changes may not be readily apparent. Zooming in and out (View > Zoom In and View > Zoom Out) may help you see the differences more easily.

5 Choose View > Pixel Preview to see how the artwork will look when it is rasterized and viewed on-screen in a web browser. Choose View > Pixel Preview to deselect pixel preview.

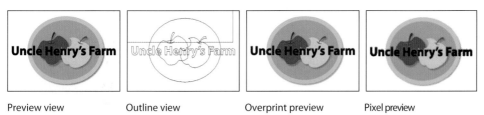

Preview view   Outline view   Overprint preview   Pixel preview

6 Choose View > Fit Artboard In Window to view the entire active artboard.

Navigating multiple artboards

Illustrator allows for multiple artboards within a single file. This is a great way to create a multi-page document so that you can have collateral pieces like a brochure, a postcard, and a business card in the same document. You can easily share content between pieces, create multi-page PDFs, and print multiple pages by creating multiple artboards.

Multiple artboards can be added when you initially create an Illustrator document by choosing File > New. You can also add or remove artboards after the document is created using the Artboard tool in the Tools panel.

Next, you will learn how to efficiently navigate a document with multiple artboards.

1   Select the Selection tool (▶) in the Tools panel.

2   Choose View > Fit All In Window. Notice that there are two artboards in the document.

The artboards in a document can be arranged in any order, orientation, or artboard size–they can even overlap. Suppose that you want to create a four-page brochure. You can create different artboards for every page of the brochure, all with the same size and orientation. They can be arranged horizontally or vertically or in whatever way you like.

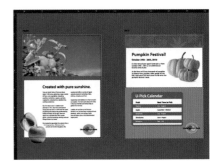

The brochure.ai document has two artboards, which are the front and back of a color brochure.

3   Press Ctrl+– (Windows) or Command+– (Mac OS) until you can see the logo in the upper-left corner of the canvas, which is outside the artboards.

4   Choose View > Fit Artboard In Window.

This command fits the currently active artboard in the window. The active artboard is identified in the Artboard Navigation menu in the lower-left corner of the Document window.

Note: Learn how to work more with artboards in Lesson 4, "Transforming Objects."

5   Choose 2 from the Artboard Navigation menu. The back of the brochure appears in the Document window.

6   Choose View > Zoom Out. Notice that zooming occurs on the currently active artboard.

Notice the arrows to the right and left of the Artboard Navigation menu. You can use these to navigate to the first (), previous (), next (), and last () artboards.

7   Click the Previous navigation button to view the previous artboard (artboard #1) in the Document window.

⬤ **Note:** Since there are only two artboards in this document, you could have also clicked the First button () in this step.

8   Choose View > Fit Artboard In Window to make sure that the first artboard (artboard #1) is fit in the Document window.

Another method for navigating multiple artboards is to use the Artboards panel. Next, you will open the Artboards panel and navigate the document.

9   Choose Reset Essentials from the workspace switcher in the Application bar to reset the Essentials workspace.

10 Choose Window > Artboards to expand the Artboards panel on the right side of the workspace.

The Artboards panel lists all artboards in the document. This panel allows you to navigate between artboards, rename artboards, add or delete artboards, edit artboard settings, and more.

Next, you will focus on navigating the document using this panel.

11 Double-click the number 2 in the Artboards panel. This fits Artboard 2 in the Document window.

⬤ **Note:** Double-clicking the artboard name in the Artboards panel allows you to change the name of the artboard. Clicking the artboard icon () to the right of the artboard name in the panel allows you to edit artboard options.

12 Choose View > Zoom In to zoom in on the second artboard.

13 Double-click the 1 to the left of Artboard 1 in the Artboards panel to show the first artboard in the Document window.

Notice that when you double-click to navigate to an artboard, that artboard is fit in the Document window.

14 Click the Artboards panel icon () in the dock to collapse the Artboards panel.

Artboard overview

Note: You can have up to 100 artboards per document, depending on the size of the artboards. You can specify the number of artboards for a document when you create it, and you can add and remove artboards at any time while working in a document. You can create artboards of different sizes, resize them with the Artboard tool, and position them on the screen—they can even overlap each other.

Artboards represent the regions that can contain printable artwork (similar to pages in a program like Adobe InDesign). You can use artboards to crop areas for printing or placement purposes. Multiple artboards are useful for creating a variety of things such as multiple page PDFs, printed pages with different sizes or different elements, independent elements for websites, video storyboards, or individual items for animation in Adobe Flash® or Adobe After Effects.

A. Printable area
B. Nonprintable area
C. Edge of the page
D. Artboard
E. Bleed area
F. Canvas

A B C D E F

A. Printable area is bounded by the innermost dotted lines and represents the portion of the page on which the selected printer can print. Many printers cannot print to the edge of the paper. Don't get confused by what is considered nonprintable.

B. Nonprintable area is between the two sets of dotted lines representing any nonprintable margin of the page. This example shows the nonprintable area of an 8.5" x 11" page for a standard laser printer. The printable and nonprintable area is determined by the printer selected in the Print Options dialog box.

C. Edge of the page is indicated by the outermost set of dotted lines.

D. Artboard is bounded by solid lines and represents the entire region that can contain printable artwork.

E. Bleed area is the amount of artwork that falls outside of the printing bounding box, or outside the crop area and trim marks. You can include bleed in your artwork as a margin of error—to ensure that the ink is still printed to the edge of the page after the page is trimmed.

F. Canvas is the area outside the artboard that extends to the edge of the 227" square window. Objects placed on the canvas are visible on-screen, but they do not print.

—From Illustrator Help

Using the Navigator panel

The Navigator panel is another way to navigate a document with a single artboard or multiple artboards. This is useful when you need to see all artboards in the document in one window and edit content in any of those artboards in a zoomed in view.

1 Choose Window > Navigator to open the Navigator panel. It is free-floating in the workspace.

2 In the Navigator panel, drag the slider to the left to approximately 50% to decrease the level of magnification. As you drag the slider, the red box in the Navigator panel, called the proxy view area, becomes larger, indicating the area of the document that is being shown. Depending on the zoom percentage, you may or may not see the proxy view area yet, but you will.

Note: Dragging the slider in the Navigator panel tends to jump the magnification to set values. To zoom more precisely, type in a value in the lower-left corner of the Navigator panel.

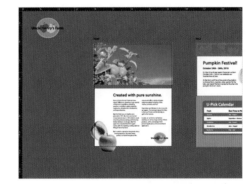

3 Click the larger mountain icon () in the lower-right corner of the Navigator panel several times to zoom in to the brochure until the percentage in the Navigator panel shows approximately 150%.

4 Position the pointer inside the proxy view area (the red box) of the Navigator panel. The pointer becomes a hand ( ).

5 Drag the hand in the proxy view area of the Navigator panel to pan to different parts of the artwork. Drag the proxy view area over the logo in the lower-right corner of the brochure cover.

Note: The percentage and proxy view area in your Navigator panel may appear differently. That's okay.

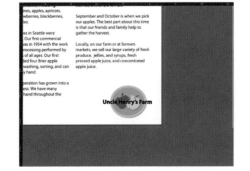

6 In the Navigator panel, move the pointer outside of the proxy view area and click. This moves the box and displays a different area of the artwork in the Document window.

> ▶ **Tip:** Choosing Panel Options from the Navigator panel menu allows you to customize the Navigator panel. For example, you can change the color of the view box.

7 Choose View > Fit Artboard In Window.

● **Note:** The percentage and proxy view area in your Navigator panel may appear differently. That's okay.

8 Deselect View Artboard Contents Only in the Navigator panel menu (▼≣) so that you see any artwork that is on the canvas as well. Notice the logo on the canvas.

> ● **Note:** You may need to adjust the slider in the Navigator panel to see the logo in the proxy view area.

9 Close the Navigator panel group by clicking the Close button (X) in the upper-right corner (Windows) or upper-left corner (Mac OS).

Understanding rulers

Rulers can help you accurately place and measure objects in your document and are displayed in each document by default. Horizontal and vertical rulers appear at the top and left sides of each Document window. The place where 0 appears on each ruler is called the ruler origin.

Next, you will explore the rulers by turning them on and off and noticing where the ruler origin is located on each artboard.

1 Choose View > Rulers > Hide Rulers to hide the rulers.

2 Choose View > Rulers > Show Rulers to show them again.

Notice that the 0 for the horizontal ruler is aligned with the left edge of the first artboard, and the 0 for the vertical ruler (on the left side of the Document window) is aligned with the top edge of the artboard.

3 Navigate to the second artboard by choosing 2 from the Artboard Navigation menu.

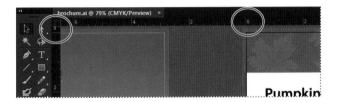

Notice that the rulers start at 0 in the upper-left corner in this second artboard as well. Each artboard has its own ruler system, with the zeros for horizontal and vertical rulers starting in the upper-left corner of each artboard. You will learn about changing the zero point and other ruler options in Lesson 4, "Transforming Objects."

4   Navigate back to the first artboard by choosing 1 from the Artboard Navigation menu.

Arranging multiple documents

When you open more than one Illustrator file, the Document windows are tabbed. You can arrange the open documents in other ways, such as side by side, so that you can easily compare or drag items from one document to another. You can also use the Arrange Documents window to quickly display your open documents in a variety of configurations.

Next, you will open several documents.

1   Choose File > Open and, in the Lesson01 folder, Shift-click to select the L1start_2.ai and L1start_3.ai files that are located in the Lessons folder on your hard disk. Click Open to open both files at once.

You should now have three Illustrator files open: brochure.ai, L1start_2.ai, and L1start_3.ai. Each file has its own tab at the top of the Document window. These documents are considered a group of Document windows. You can create document groups to loosely associate files while they are open.

2   Click the brochure.ai document tab to show the brochure.ai Document window.

3   Click and drag the brochure.ai document tab to the right so that it is between the L1start_2.ai and L1start_3.ai document tabs.

● **Note:** Your tabs may be in a slightly different order. That's okay. Be careful to drag directly to the right. Otherwise, you could undock the Document window and create a new group. If that happens, choose Window > Arrange > Consolidate All Windows.

Dragging the document tabs allows you to change the order of the documents. This can be very useful if you use the document shortcuts to navigate to the next or previous document.

▶ **Tip:** You can cycle between open documents by pressing Ctrl+F6 (next document), Ctrl+Shift+F6 (previous document) (Windows) or Command+~ (next document), Command+Shift+~ (previous document) (Mac OS).

4 Drag the document tabs in the following order, from left to right: brochure.ai, L1start_2.ai, L1start_3.ai.

These three documents are versions of marketing pieces. To see all of them at one time, you can arrange the Document windows by cascading the windows or tiling them. Cascading allows you to cascade (stack) different document groups and is discussed further in the next section. Tiling shows multiple Document windows at one time, in various arrangements.

Next, you will tile the open documents so that you can see them all at one time.

5 On the Mac OS (Windows users can skip to the next step), choose Window > Application Frame. Then, click the green button in the upper-left corner of the Application window so that the it fits as well as possible.

Mac OS users can use the Application frame to group all the workspace elements in a single, integrated window, similar to working in Windows. If you move or resize the Application frame, the elements respond to each other so that they don't overlap.

6 Choose Window > Arrange > Tile.

This shows all three Document windows arranged in a pattern.

Note: Your documents may be tiled in a different order. That's okay.

7 Click in each of the Document windows to activate the documents. Choose View > Fit Artboard In Window for each of the documents. Also, make sure that artboard #1 is showing for each document in the Document window.

With documents tiled, you can drag the dividing lines between each of the Document windows to reveal more or less of a particular document. You can also drag objects between documents to copy them from one document to another.

8 Click in the L1start_3.ai Document window. With the Selection tool, drag the wagon wheel image (behind the pumpkins on the artboard) to the L1start_2.ai Document window and release the mouse button. This copies the image from L1start_3.ai to L1start_2.ai.

● **Note:** After dragging the content in step 8, notice that the document tab for L1start_2.ai now has an asterisk to the right of the file name. This indicates that the file needs to be saved.

● **Note:** When you drag content between tiled documents, a plus sign (+) appears next to the pointer, as shown in the figure below. Depending on your operating system, the pointer may look different.

To change the arrangement of the tiled windows, it's possible to drag document tabs to new positions. However, it's easier to use the Arrange Documents window to quickly arrange open documents in a variety of configurations.

9 Click the Arrange Documents button (▣▾) in the Application bar to display the Arrange Documents window. Click the Tile All Vertically button (▥) to tile the documents vertically.

● **Note:** On the Mac OS, the menu bar is above the Application bar. Also, depending on the resolution of your screen, the Windows menus may appear in the Application bar.

10 Click the Arrange Documents button (▣▾) in the Application bar to display the Arrange Documents window again. Click the 2-Up vertical button (▥) in the Arrange Documents window.

Notice that two of the documents appear as tabs in one of the tiled areas.

11 Click to select the L1start_2.ai tab if it is not already selected. Then, click the Close button (X) on the L1start_2.ai document tab to close the document. If a dialog box appears asking you to save the document, click No (Windows) or Don't Save (Mac OS).

Tip: You can also choose Window > Arrange > Consolidate All Windows to return the two documents to tabs in the same group.

12 Click the Arrange Documents button (▦▾) in the Application bar, and click the Consolidate All button (▦) in the Arrange Documents window. This returns the two documents to tabs in the same group. Keep the brochure.ai and L1start_3.ai documents open.

Exploring document groups

By default, open documents in Illustrator are arranged as tabs in a single group of windows. You can create multiple groups of files for easier navigation and temporarily associate files together. This can be helpful if you are working on a large project that requires you to create and edit multiple pieces. Grouping documents lets you float the groups so that they are separate from the application window (Windows) or screen (Mac OS).

Next, you will create and work with two groups of files.

1 Click to select the L1start_3.ai file tab, if not already selected.

2 Choose Window > Arrange > Float All In Windows. This creates separate groups for all open documents. By default, the groups are cascaded with one on top of the other.

Document windows floating in separate groups

3 Click the title bar for brochure.ai, and notice that L1start_3.ai is not visible. L1start_3.ai is now behind brochure.ai.

4 Choose File > Open and, in the Lesson01 folder, select the L1start_2.ai file, which is located in the Lessons folder on your hard disk. Click Open. Notice that the newly opened document is added as a document tab to the group that contains brochure.ai.

● **Note:** When you open a document or create a new document, that document is added to the currently selected group.

5 Choose Window > Arrange > Cascade to reveal both groups.

6 Click the Minimize button in the upper-right corner (Windows) or the upper-left corner (Mac OS) of the L1start_3.ai group.

● **Note:** If you cannot select the L1start_3.ai group, choose Window > L1start_3.ai at the bottom of the Window menu.

7 Choose Window > L1start_3.ai to show the document again.

8 Click the Close box (Windows) or Close button (Mac OS) to close the L1start_3.ai group. If a dialog box appears asking you to save the document, click No (Windows) or Don't Save (Mac OS).

9 Drag the document tab for L1start_2.ai down until the document appears to float freely. This is another way to create a floating group of documents.

10 Close the L1start_2.ai file, and leave brochure.ai open. If a dialog box appears asking you to save the document, click No (Windows) or Don't Save (Mac OS).

11 On Windows (Mac OS users can skip to the next step), choose Window > Arrange > Consolidate All Windows.

12 On the Mac OS, choose Window > Application Frame to deselect the Application frame.

13 Choose View > Fit Artboard In Window to fit the first artboard of brochure.ai in the Document window.

14 Choose File > Close to close the document without saving.

Finding resources for using Illustrator

For complete and up-to-date information about using Illustrator panels, tools, and other application features, visit the Adobe website. By choosing Help > Illustrator Help, you'll be connected to the Adobe Community Help website, where you can search Illustrator Help and support documents, as well as other websites relevant to Illustrator users. Community Help brings together active Adobe product users, Adobe product team members, authors, and experts to give you the most useful, relevant, and up-to-date information about Adobe products.

If you choose Help > Illustrator Help, you can also download a PDF of the Illustrator Help content by clicking the download button.

For additional resources, such as tips and techniques and the latest product information, check out the Illustrator Help page at:

helpx.adobe.com/illustrator.html.

Review questions

1 Describe two ways to change the view of a document.

2 How do you select tools in Illustrator?

3 Describe three ways to navigate between artboards in Illustrator.

4 How do you save panel locations and visibility preferences?

5 Describe how arranging Document windows can be helpful.

Review answers

1 You can choose commands from the View menu to zoom in or out of a document or to fit it to your screen; you can also use the Zoom tool in the Tools panel and click or drag over a document to enlarge or reduce the view. In addition, you can use keyboard shortcuts to magnify or reduce the display of artwork. You can also use the Navigator panel to scroll artwork or change its magnification without using the Document window.

2 To select a tool, you can either click the tool in the Tools panel or press the keyboard shortcut for that tool. For example, you can press V to select the Selection tool from the keyboard. Selected tools remain active until you click a different tool.

3 You can choose the artboard number from the Artboard Navigation menu at the lower-left of the Document window, you can use the Artboard Navigation arrows in the lower-left of the Document window to go to the first, previous, next, and last artboards, you can use the Artboards panel to navigate to an artboard, or you can use the Navigator panel to drag the proxy view area to navigate between artboards.

4 Choose Window > Workspace > New Workspace to create custom work areas and make it easier to find the controls that you need.

5 Arranging Document windows allows you to tile windows or cascade document groups. This can be useful if you are working on multiple Illustrator files and you need to compare or share content between them.

2 SELECTING AND ALIGNING

Lesson overview

In this lesson, you'll learn how to do the following:

- Differentiate between the various selection tools and employ different selection techniques.

- Recognize Smart Guides.

- Save selections for future use.

- Use tools and commands to align shapes and points to each other and the artboard.

- Group and ungroup items.

- Work in Isolation mode.

- Arrange content.

- Select behind content.

- Copy items with the Selection tool.

- Hide and lock items for organizational purposes.

 This lesson takes approximately an hour to complete. If needed, remove the previous lesson folder from your hard disk and copy the Lesson02 folder onto it.

Selecting content in Adobe Illustrator is one of the more important things you'll do. In this lesson, you learn how to locate and select objects using the selection tools; protect other objects by grouping, hiding, and locking them; align objects to each other and the artboard; and much more.

Getting started

When changing colors or size and adding effects or attributes, you must first select the object to which you are applying the changes. In this lesson, you will learn the fundamentals of using the selection tools. More advanced selection techniques using layers are discussed in Lesson 8, "Working with Layers."

1 To ensure that the tools and panels function exactly as described in this lesson, delete or deactivate (by renaming) the Adobe Illustrator CS6 preferences file. See "Restoring default preferences" on page 3.

2 Start Adobe Illustrator CS6.

⬤ **Note:** If you have not already done so, copy the Lesson02 folder from the Lessons folder on the *Adobe Illustrator CS6 Classroom in a Book* CD onto your hard disk. See "Copying the Classroom in a Book files" on page 2.

⬤ **Note:** In Mac OS, when opening lesson files, you may need to click the round, green button in the upper-left corner of the Document window to maximize the window's size.

3 Choose File > Open, and open the L2start_1.ai file in the Lesson02 folder, located in the Lessons folder on your hard disk. Choose View > Fit Artboard In Window.

4 Choose Window > Workspace > Essentials, make sure it's selected, and then choose Window > Workspace > Reset Essentials to reset the workspace.

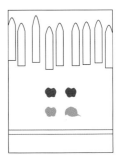

Selecting objects

Whether you are starting artwork from scratch or editing existing artwork in Illustrator, you will need to become familiar with selecting objects. There are many methods and tools for selecting objects, and in this section, you will explore the main selection tools, including the Selection and Direct Selection tools.

Using the Selection tool

The Selection tool in the Tools panel lets you select entire objects.

1 Select the Selection tool (▶) in the Tools panel, if it's not already selected. Position the pointer over different shapes without clicking. The icon that appears as you pass over objects (▶.) indicates that there is an object that can be selected under the pointer. When you hover over an object, it is also outlined in blue.

2 Select the Zoom tool (🔍) in the Tools panel, and drag a marquee around the four colored shapes (the apples and hat) in the center of the page, to zoom in.

3 Select the Selection tool, and then position the pointer over the edge of the red apple on the left. A word such as "path" or "anchor" may appear, because Smart Guides are turned on by default. Smart Guides are snap-to guides that help you

align, edit, and transform objects or artboards. Smart Guides are discussed in more detail in Lesson 3, "Creating and Editing Shapes."

4 Click the left red apple on its edge or anywhere in its center to select it. A bounding box with eight handles appears.

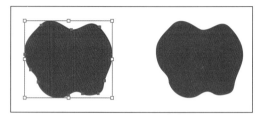

The bounding box is used when making changes to objects, such as resizing or rotating them. The bounding box also indicates that an item is selected and ready to be modified. The color of the bounding box indicates which layer the object is on. Layers are discussed more in Lesson 8, "Working with Layers."

5 Using the Selection tool, click the red apple on the right. Notice that the left red apple is now deselected and only the right apple is selected.

6 Hold down the Shift key, and click the left red apple to add it to the selection. Both red apples are now selected.

Note: To select an item without a fill, you must click the stroke (border).

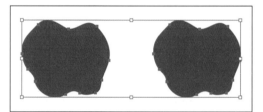

7 Reposition the apples anywhere in the document by clicking the center of either selected apple and dragging in one motion. Because both apples are selected, they move together.

As you drag, you may notice the green lines that appear. These are called alignment guides and are visible because Smart Guides are turned on (View > Smart Guides). As you drag, the objects are aligned to other objects on the artboard. Also notice the gray box, or measurement label, that shows the object's distance from its original position. Measurement labels also appear because Smart Guides are turned on.

8 Deselect the apples by clicking the artboard where there are no objects or by choosing Select > Deselect.

9 Revert to the last saved version of the document by choosing File > Revert. In the Revert dialog box, click Revert.

▶ **Tip:** To select all objects, choose Select > All. To select all objects in a single artboard, choose Select > All On Active Artboard. To learn more about artboards, see Lesson 3, "Creating and Editing Shapes."

Using the Direct Selection tool

The Direct Selection tool selects points or path segments within an object so that it can be reshaped. Next, you will select anchor points and path segments using the Direct Selection tool.

1   Choose View > Fit Artboard In Window.

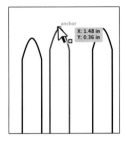

2   Select the Direct Selection tool (⟍) in the Tools panel. Without clicking, position the pointer over the top edge of one of the fence pickets you see above the red apples.

Note: The measurements you see in the gray measurement label may be different than what you see in the figure, and that's okay.

When the Direct Selection tool is over an anchor point of a path or object, a label, such as the word "anchor" or "path," appears. This label is showing because Smart Guides are selected. Also notice the small dot that appears in the center of the box to the right of the cursor. When you position the Direct Selection tool over an anchor point, a dot appears in the small box next to the cursor, indicating that the cursor is positioned over an anchor point.

3   Click the top point of the same picket. Note that only the point you selected is solid, indicating that it is selected, while the other points in the picket are hollow and not selected.

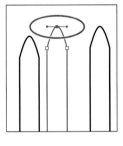

Also notice the blue direction lines extending from the selected anchor point. At the end of the direction lines are direction points. The angle and length of the direction lines determine the shape and size of the curved segments. Moving the direction points reshapes the curves.

4   With the Direct Selection tool still selected, drag the individual point down to edit the shape of the object. Try clicking another point, and notice that the previous point is deselected.

Note: The gray measurement label that appears as you drag the anchor point has the values dX and dY. dX indicates the distance the pointer has moved along the x axis (horizontal), and dY indicates the distance the pointer has moved along the y axis (vertical).

▶ **Tip:** Using the Shift key, you can select multiple points to move them together.

5   Revert to the last saved version of the file by choosing File > Revert. In the Revert dialog box, click Revert.

Selection and anchor point preferences

You can change selection preferences and how anchor points appear in the Illustrator Preferences dialog box.

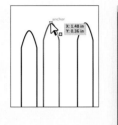

Choose Edit > Preferences > Selection & Anchor Display (Windows) or Illustrator > Preferences > Selection & Anchor Display (Mac OS). You can change the size of anchor points (called anchors in the dialog box) or the display of the direction lines (called handles in the dialog box).

As you move the pointer over anchor points in your artwork, they are highlighted. You can also turn off the highlighting of anchor points as the pointer hovers over them. Highlighting anchor points makes it easier to determine which point you are about to select. You will learn more about anchor points and anchor point handles in Lesson 5, "Drawing with the Pen and Pencil Tools."

Creating selections with a marquee

Some selections may be easier to make by creating a marquee around the objects that you want to select.

1   Choose View > Fit Artboard In Window.

2   Select the Selection tool (▶) in the Tools panel. Instead of Shift-clicking to select multiple objects, position the pointer above and to the left of the upper-left red apple, and then drag downward and to the right to create a marquee that overlaps just the tops of the apples.

▶ **Tip:** When dragging with the Selection tool, you only need to encompass a small part of an object to include it in the selection.

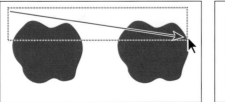

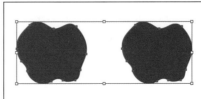

3 Choose Select > Deselect, or click where there are no objects.

Now, you will use the Direct Selection tool (↖) to select multiple points in objects.

4 Select the Direct Selection tool. Click outside the top of one of the fence pickets above the red apples, and drag across to select the tops of two pickets in the top row. Only the top points become selected.

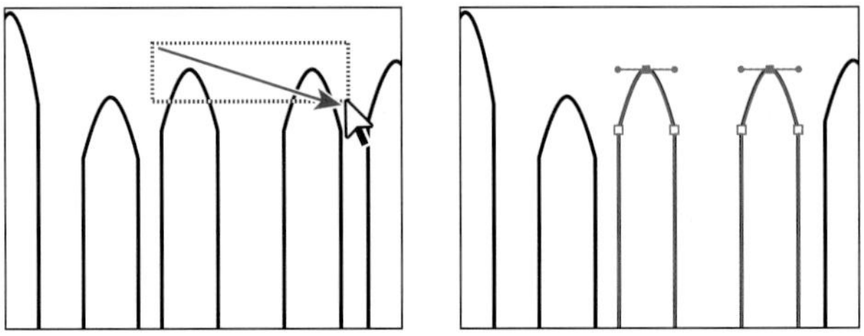

5 Click one of the selected anchor points, and drag to see how the anchor points reposition together. Use this method when selecting points so that you don't have to click exactly on the anchor point that you want to select.

Note: Selecting points using this method might take some practice. You'll need to drag across only the points you want selected; otherwise, more will be selected. You can always click away from the objects to deselect them and then try again.

6 Choose Select > Deselect.

7 With the Direct Selection tool, try dragging across the tops of the red apples. Notice how multiple points in each apple are selected.

8 Choose Select > Deselect.

Creating selections with the Magic Wand tool

You can use the Magic Wand tool to select all objects in a document that have the same or similar color or pattern fill attributes.

Tip: You can customize the Magic Wand tool to select objects based on options, like stroke weight, stroke color, and more, by double-clicking the Magic Wand tool in the Tools panel. You can also change the tolerances used to identify similar objects.

1 Select the Magic Wand tool (✨) in the Tools panel. Click the orange apple, and notice that the orange hat is selected as well. No bounding box (a box surrounding the two shapes) appears, because the Magic Wand tool is still selected.

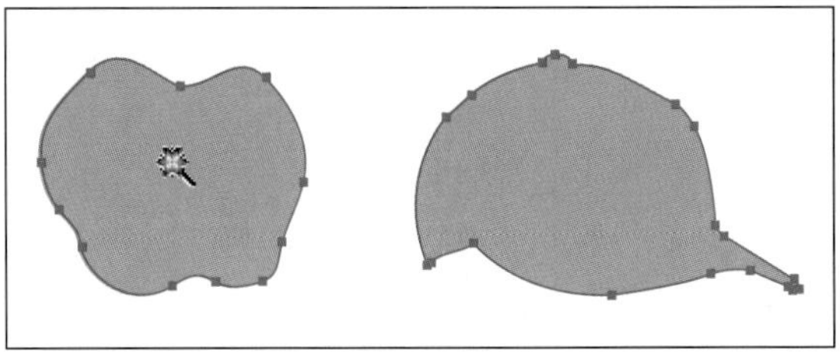

When selecting with the Magic Wand tool, objects with the same fill color are selected as well.

2 Click one of the red apples with the Magic Wand tool. Notice that both red apples are selected and that the orange apple and hat are deselected.

3 Holding down the Shift key, click the orange hat with the Magic Wand tool, and then release the key. This adds the orange hat and orange apple to the selection, because they have the same fill color (orange). With the Magic Wand tool still selected, hold down the Alt (Windows) or Option (Mac OS) key, click the orange hat to deselect the orange objects, and then release the key.

4 Choose Select > Deselect, or click where there are no objects.

Selecting similar objects

You can also select objects based on fill color, stroke color, stroke weight, and more using the Select Similar Objects button or the Select > Same command. The fill is a color applied to the interior area of an object, the stroke is its outline (border), and the stroke weight is the size of the stroke.

Next, you will select several objects with the same stroke applied.

1 Revert to the last saved version of the file by choosing File > Revert. In the Revert dialog box, click Revert. Choose View > Fit Artboard In Window.

2 With the Selection tool (▶), click to select one of the white fence picket objects at the top of the artboard.

3 Click the arrow to the right of the Select Similar Objects button (▣▾) in the Control panel to show a menu. Choose Fill Color to select all objects on any artboard with the same fill color (white) as the selected object.

Notice that all of the pickets at the top are selected, in addition to the white rectangle at the bottom of the artboard.

4 Choose Select > Deselect.

5 Select one of the white picket shapes at the top of the artboard again, and then choose Select > Same > Stroke Weight.

All of the fence picket shapes have a 1 pt stroke, so all strokes that are 1 pt are now selected.

6 With the previous selection still active, choose Select > Save Selection. Name the selection **Fence** in the Save Selection dialog box, and click OK so that you'll be able to choose this selection at a later time.

7 Choose Select > Deselect.

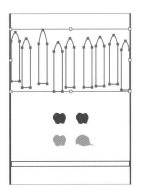

> **Tip:** It is helpful to name selections according to use or function. In step 6, if you name the selection 1 pt stroke, for instance, the name may be misleading if you later change the stroke weight of the object.

Aligning objects

Multiple objects can be aligned or distributed relative to each other, the artboard, or a key object. In this section, you will explore the options for aligning objects and aligning points, as well learn what a key object is.

Aligning objects to each other

● **Note:** The Align options may not appear in the Control panel. If you don't see the Align options, click the word Align in the Control panel to open the Align panel. The number of options displayed in the Control panel depends on your screen resolution.

1 Choose Select > Fence to reselect the fence pickets.

2 Choose Align to Selection from the Align To button () in the Control panel, if it's not already selected. This ensures that the selected objects are aligned to each other.

3 Click the Vertical Align Bottom button (■▮) in the Control panel.

Notice that the bottom edges of all the fence picket objects move to align with the lowest picket.

● **Note:** These are the same options you will see by opening the Align panel (Window > Align).

4 Choose Edit > Undo Align to return the objects to their original positions. Leave the objects selected for the next section.

Aligning to a key object

A key object is an object that you want other objects to align to. You specify a key object by selecting all the objects you want to align, including the key object, and then clicking the key object again. When selected, the key object has a thick blue outline, and the Align To Key Object icon (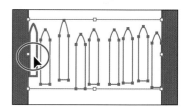) appears in the Control panel and the Align panel.

1 With the fence picket objects still selected, click the left-most picket with the Selection tool (▶).

The thick blue outline indicates that it is the key object which other objects will align to.

▶ **Tip:** In the Align panel, you can also choose Align To Key Object from the Align To option. The object that is in front becomes the key object.

2 In the Align options, which you can view in the Control panel or by clicking with word Align, click the Vertical Align Bottom button (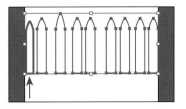). Notice that all of the pickets move to align to the bottom edge of the key object.

> **Note:** To stop aligning and distributing relative to an object, click again on the object to remove the blue outline, or choose Cancel Key Object from the Align panel menu.

3 Choose Select > Deselect.

Aligning points

Next, you'll align two points to each other using the Align panel.

1 With the Direct Selection tool (▶) selected, click the topmost point of the picket that is taller than the rest. Shift-click to select the topmost point of any other picket. In the figure, the picket to the right of the tallest picket is selected.

You select the points in a specific order because the last selected anchor point is the key anchor. Other points align to this point.

2 Click the Vertical Align Top button (⊤⊤) in the Control panel. The first point selected aligns to the second point selected.

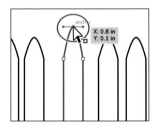
Select the first point.

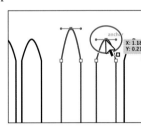
Select the second point.

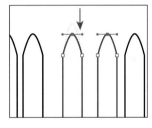
Align the points.

> **Note:** If you don't see the Align options, click the word Align in the Control panel to show the Align panel.

3 Choose Select > Deselect.

Distributing objects

Distributing objects using the Align panel enables you to select multiple objects and to distribute the spacing between those objects equally. Next, you will make the spacing between the fence pickets even, using a distribution method.

1 Select the Selection tool (►) in the Tools panel. Choose Select > Fence to reselect all of the fence pickets.

Note: Using the Horizontal or Vertical Distribute Center buttons distributes the spacing equally between the *centers* of the objects. If the selected objects are not the same size, unexpected results may occur.

2 Click the Horizontal Distribute Center button (🔳) in the Control panel.

This moves all of the fence objects so that the spacing between the *center* of each of them is equal.

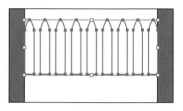

3 Choose Select > Deselect.

4 With the Selection tool (►) selected, hold down the Shift key and drag the right-most fence picket slightly to the right, to keep the picket aligned with the other pickets. Release the mouse button and then the key.

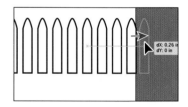

5 Choose Select > Fence to select all of the fence pickets again, and then click the Horizontal Distribute Center button (🔳) again. Notice that, with the right-most picket repositioned, the objects move to redistribute the spacing between the centers of the objects.

Note: When distributing objects horizontally, make sure that the left-most and right-most objects are where you want them, and then distribute the objects between them. For vertical distribution, position the topmost and bottommost objects, and then distribute the objects between them.

6 Choose Select > Deselect.

Aligning to the artboard

You can also align content to the artboard rather than to a selection or a key object. Aligning to the artboard aligns each selected object separately to the artboard. Next, you'll align the leaves shape in the next artboard to the center of the artboard.

Note: The Align options may not appear in the Control panel but are indicated by the word Align. The number of options displayed in the Control panel depends on your screen resolution.

1 Click the Next artboard button (▶) in the lower-left corner of the Document window to navigate to the next artboard in the document, which contains the tree.

2 With the Selection tool selected, click to select the green leaves shape.

3 Click the Align To Selection button (🔲), and choose Align To Artboard in the menu that appears.

4 Click the Horizontal Align Center (⬛) button to align the selection to the horizontal center of the artboard.

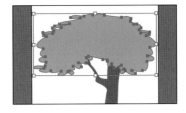

Note: When you want to align all objects to the center of the artboard for a poster, for example, grouping the objects is an important step. Grouping moves the objects together as one object relative to the artboard. If this isn't done, centering everything horizontally moves all the objects to the center, independent of each other.

5 With the Selection tool, click to select the brown tree trunk shape.

6 Click the Horizontal Align Center (⬛) button, and then click the Vertical Align Bottom (⬛) button to align the bottom of the tree trunk to the bottom of the artboard.

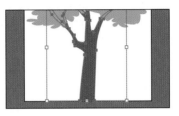

Leave the tree trunk selected for the next step.

Working with groups

You can combine objects in a group so that the objects are treated as a single unit. This way, you can move or transform a number of objects without affecting their individual attributes or relative positions.

Grouping items

Next, you will select multiple objects and create a group from them.

1 With the Selection tool (⬛), press the Shift key and click the green leaves to select them along with the tree trunk you had selected previously.

2 Choose Object > Group, and then choose Select > Deselect.

3 With the Selection tool, click the brown tree trunk. Because the trunk is grouped with the leaves, both are now selected.

Notice that the word "Group" appears on the left side of the Control panel.

▶ **Tip:** To select the objects in a group separately, select the group, and then choose Object > Ungroup. This ungroups them permanently.

4 Choose Select > Deselect.

Working in Isolation mode

Isolation mode isolates groups or sublayers so that you can easily select and edit specific objects or parts of objects without having to ungroup the objects. When you use Isolation mode, you don't need to pay attention to what layer an object is on, nor do you need to manually lock or hide the objects you don't want affected by your edits. All objects outside of the isolated group are locked so that they aren't affected by the edits you make. An isolated object appears in full color, while the rest of the artwork appears dimmed, letting you know which objects you can edit.

Tip: To enter Isolation mode, you can also select a group with the Selection tool and then click the Isolate Selected Object button (▣) in the Control panel.

1 With the Selection tool (▶), click either the green leaves or the brown tree trunk to select the group you created.

2 Double-click the tree trunk to enter Isolation mode.

3 Choose View > Fit All In Window, and notice that the rest of the content in the document appears dimmed (you can't select it).

At the top of the Document window, a gray arrow appears with the words Layer 1 and <Group>. This indicates that you have isolated a group of objects that is on layer 1. You will learn more about layers in Lesson 8, "Working with Layers."

4 Hold down the Shift key, and drag the brown tree trunk slightly to the right. The Shift key constrains its movement to the horizontal.

When you enter Isolation mode, groups are temporarily ungrouped. This enables you to edit objects in the group without having to ungroup.

Tip: To exit Isolation mode, you can also click the gray arrow in the upper-left corner of the Document window until the document is no longer in Isolation mode. Or click the Exit Isolation Mode button (▣) in the Control panel.

5 Double-click outside of the objects within the group to exit Isolation mode.

6 Click to select the green leaves shape.

Notice that it is once again grouped with the tree trunk, and you can now select other objects.

7 Choose Select > Deselect, and then choose View > Fit Artboard In Window.

Adding to a group

Groups can also be nested—they can be grouped within other objects or grouped to form larger groups. In this section, you will explore how to add objects to an existing group.

1 Click the Previous Artboard button (◀) in the lower-left corner of the Document window to navigate to the previous artboard in the document, which contains the fence objects.

2 With the Selection tool (▶), drag a marquee across the pickets at the top of the artboard to select them all.

3 Choose Object > Group.

4 With Align To Artboard chosen from the Align To Selection button (▦▾) menu, click the Horizontal Align Center (▤) button to align the group to the horizontal center of the artboard. Choose Select > Deselect.

5 With the Selection tool, holding down the Shift key, drag the white rectangle at the bottom of the artboard on top of the group of pickets. You needn't pay attention to the alignment.

6 With the Selection tool, Shift-click a picket object to select the grouped objects as well.

7 Choose Object > Group.

You have created a nested group—a group within a group. Nesting is a common technique used when designing artwork. It's a great way to keep associated content together.

8 Choose Select > Deselect.

9 With the Selection tool, click one of the grouped objects. All objects in the group become selected.

10 Click a blank area on the artboard to deselect the objects.

11 Hold down on the Direct Selection tool (▷) in the Tools panel, and drag to the right to access the Group Selection tool (▷⁺). The Group Selection tool adds the object's parent group(s) to the current selection.

12 Click the left-most fence picket once to select the object. Click again to select the object's parent group (the group of pickets). The Group Selection tool adds each group to the selection in the order in which it was grouped.

▶ **Tip:** If you were to click a third time, the white rectangle would also become selected.

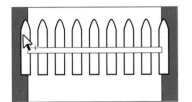

Click once to select a picket.

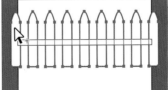

Click twice to select the parent group.

13 Choose Select > Deselect.

14 With the Selection tool, click any of the grouped objects to select the group. Choose Object > Ungroup to ungroup the objects. Choose Select > Deselect.

● **Note:** To ungroup all of the selected objects, even the fence pickets, choose Object > Ungroup twice.

15 Click to select the fence pickets. Notice that they are still grouped.

16 Choose Select > Deselect.

Exploring object arrangement

As you create objects, Illustrator stacks them in order on the artboards, beginning with the first object created. The order in which objects are stacked (called stack order) determines how they display when they overlap. You can change the stacking order of objects in your artwork at any time using either the Layers panel or Object > Arrange commands.

Arranging objects

Next, you will work with the Arrange commands to change how objects are stacked.

1   With the Selection tool (▶) selected, position the pointer over a red apple and click to select it.

2   Choose View > Fit All In Window to see both artboards in the document.

3   Drag the selected red apple on top of the leaves in the tree. Release the mouse, and notice that the red apple goes behind the tree, but it is still selected.

    It is behind the tree because it was probably created before the tree, which means it is lower in the stack of shapes.

4   With the apple still selected, choose Object > Arrange > Bring to Front. This brings the apple to the front of the stack, making it the topmost object.

About arranging objects

As you create more complex artwork, you may need to send content behind or bring it in front of other content, by doing any of the following:

*   To move an object to the top or bottom position in its group or layer, select the object you want to move and choose Object > Arrange > Bring To Front or Object > Arrange > Send To Back.

*   To move an object by one object to the front or one object to the back of a stack, select the object you want to move and choose Object > Arrange > Bring Forward or Object > Arrange > Send Backward.

—From Illustrator Help

Selecting objects behind

When you stack objects on top of each other, sometimes it becomes difficult to select objects that are underneath. Next, you will learn how to select an object through a stack of objects.

1   With the Selection tool (▶), select the other red apple on the left artboard, drag it onto the green leaves shape on the right artboard, and then release the mouse.

Notice that the apple seems to disappear again. The apple went behind the leaves of the tree, but is still selected. This time you will deselect the apple and then select it again by selecting through objects.

2   Click the red apple again. Notice that you have selected the object on top, which is the tree group, instead.

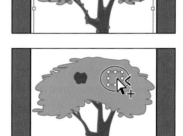

3   With the pointer still positioned over the location of the apple, behind the tree, hold down the Ctrl (Windows) or Command (Mac OS) key and click. Notice the angled bracket displayed with the pointer (▶<). Click once more to select through the leaves of the tree to the apple.

Note: To select the hidden apple, make sure that you click where the apple and the tree overlap. Otherwise, nothing will happen.

4   Choose Object > Arrange > Bring To Front to bring the apple on top of the tree.

5   Choose Select > Deselect.

Note: You may also see a plus symbol (+) next to the pointer when selecting behind. That's okay.

▶ **Tip:** You can add more apples to the tree for practice, if you like.

Hiding objects

When working on complex artwork, selections may become more difficult to control. In this section, you'll combine some of the techniques you've already learned with additional features that make selecting objects easier.

1   With the Selection tool (▶), drag a marquee across the fence pickets and the white rectangle on top to select them. Drag them to the bottom of the right artboard with the tree on it.

2   Choose Object > Arrange > Bring to Front. On the artboard with the tree, click a blank area to make that artboard the active artboard.

3   Choose View > Fit Artboard In Window.

4 Click somewhere to deselect the objects, and then click to select the white rectangle on top of the group of pickets. Choose Object > Arrange > Send Backward one or more times until the white rectangle is behind the picket group. Choose Select > Deselect.

5 Using the Selection tool (▶), select the picket group and choose Object > Hide > Selection or press Ctrl+3 (Windows) or Command+3 (Mac OS). The picket group is hidden so that you can more easily select other objects.

6 Click to select the white rectangle and, holding down the Alt (Windows) or Option (Mac OS) key, drag the rectangle down to create a copy. Release the mouse button and then the modifier key.

7 Choose Object > Show All to show the picket group again.

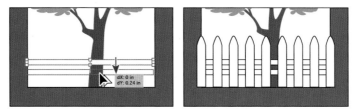

8 Choose Select > Same > Fill Color to select all three parts of the fence, including the picket group. Choose Object > Group.

9 With Align To Artboard chosen from the Align To Selection button (▦▾) menu, click the Horizontal Align Center (≡) button to align the group to the horizontal center of the artboard. Choose Select > Deselect.

10 Choose File > Save to save the file, and then choose File > Close.

Applying selection techniques

As stated earlier, selecting objects is an important part of working with Illustrator. In this part of the lesson, you will use most of the techniques discussed previously in this lesson to get more practice and to learn a few new ones.

1 Choose File > Open, and open the L2start_2.ai file in the Lesson02 folder, located in the Lessons folder on your hard disk.

2 Choose View > Fit All In Window.

Artboard #2 (the artboard on the right) shows the final artwork. Artboard #1 (the artboard on the left) shows the artwork in progress that you need to finish.

3 Choose View > Fit Artboard In Window to fit artboard #1 in the Document window.

4 Choose View > Smart Guides to temporarily deselect the Smart Guides.

5 With the Selection tool (➤), drag the steering wheel shape in the upper-right corner into place. Drag the black rounded rectangle in the upper-left corner of the artboard on the front of the bus, as shown in the figure.

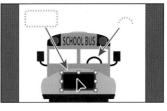

6 With the Selection tool, select the headlight shapes (the circles) in the lower-right corner of the artboard by dragging a marquee across them. Choose Object > Group.

7 Drag the center of the headlight group to slide it to its new location to the right of the newly aligned rounded rectangle.

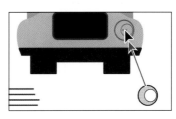

Note: You drag from the center to avoid grabbing a bounding box handle and accidently resizing the shapes.

8 Double-click the center of the headlight group to enter Isolation mode. Click to select the white shape and drag it so that it's visually centered on the other shapes. Choose Select > Deselect. Press the Escape key to exit Isolation mode.

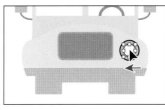

Tip: You could align the shapes using the Align options in the Control panel.

9 With the Selection tool, press the Alt+Shift (Windows) or Option+Shift (Mac OS) keys and drag the headlight group to the left to duplicate it. Release the mouse button, and then the modifier keys.

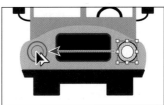

10 Shift-click the rounded rectangle and the headlight group to the right to select all three objects.

11 In the Control panel, choose Align To Selection from the Align To Selection button (⬛▾) menu, and then click the Horizontal Distribute Center (❙❙❙) button. Choose Object > Group.

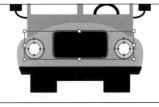

Note: If you don't see the Align panel options in the Control panel, either click the word Align in the Control panel or choose Window > Align.

12 Shift-click the orange shape behind the selected group. Click the orange shape again to make it the key object. Click the Horizontal Align Center (≜) button and then the Vertical Align Center (╪) button to align the rounded rectangle group to the orange shape.

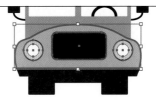

▶ **Tip:** Locking objects is a great way to keep from selecting or editing content and can be used in conjunction with hiding objects.

13 With the Selection tool, Shift-click the orange shape to deselect it. With the group of objects that contains the headlights selected, choose Object > Lock > Selection to keep them in position. You cannot select the shapes until you choose Object > Unlock All. Leave them locked.

14 Select the Zoom tool (🔍) in the Tools panel, and click three times, slowly, on the dome at the top of the bus, above the text, "SCHOOL BUS."

15 Select the Direct Selection tool (◹), select the top anchor point in the dome, and then begin dragging up to make the dome taller. As you drag, press the Shift key to constrain the movement. Release the mouse button and then the key.

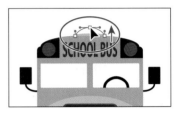

16 Double-click the Hand tool (✋) to fit the artboard in the Document window.

17 Select the Zoom tool (🔍), and click three times on the four lines in the lower-left corner to zoom in.

18 With the Selection tool (▸), drag a marquee across the four lines to select them.

19 In the Control panel, click the Horizontal Align Left (▤) button.

20 Choose View > Smart Guides to turn them back on.

21 With the Direct Selection tool (◹), click the right end of the top, shorter line to select the anchor point (the word "anchor" appears). Click and drag that point to the right until the anchor point aligns with the other lines.

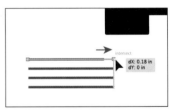

22 With the Selection tool, drag a marquee around the lines to select them. Choose Object > Group to group them.

23 Double-click the Hand tool (✋) to fit the artboard in the Document window.

● **Note:** You may want to turn the Smart Guides off (View > Smart Guides) so that you can more easily drag the group of lines onto the bus. You can then align the group of lines with the other content, if you want.

24 With the Selection tool, drag the line group to position it on the rounded rectangle between the headlights.

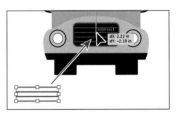

Notice that you need to drag one of the lines, not between the lines, to move the group. You could also align the lines group to the black rounded rectangle using the Align options in the Control panel.

25 Choose Select > Deselect.

26 Choose File > Save and then File > Close.

Review questions

1 How can you select an object that has no fill?

2 Name two ways you can select an item in a group without choosing Object > Ungroup.

3 Of the two Selection tools (Selection and Direct Selection), which allows you to edit the individual anchor points of an object?

4 What should you do after creating a selection that you are going to use repeatedly?

5 If you are unable to select an object, because the object you want to select is underneath another, name two ways to select the blocked object.

6 To align objects to the artboard, what do you need to first select in the Align panel or Control panel before you choose an alignment option?

Review answers

1 You can select items that have no fill by clicking the stroke or dragging a marquee across the object.

2 Using the Group Selection tool, you can click once to select an individual item within a group. Click again to add the next grouped items to the selection. Read Lesson 8, "Working with Layers," to see how you can use layers to make complex selections. You can also double-click the group to enter Isolation mode, edit the shapes as needed, and then exit Isolation mode by pressing the Escape key or by double-clicking outside of the group.

3 Using the Direct Selection tool, you can select one or more individual anchor points and make changes to the shape of an object.

4 For any selection that you anticipate using again, choose Select > Save Selection. Name the selection so that you can reselect it at any time from the Select menu.

5 If your access to an object is blocked, you can choose Object > Hide > Selection to hide the blocking object. The object is not deleted, just hidden in the same position until you choose Object > Show All. You can also use the Selection tool to select behind content by pressing the Ctrl (Windows) or Command (Mac OS) key and then clicking on the overlapping objects until the object you want to select is selected.

6 To align objects to an artboard, first select the Align To Artboard option.

3 CREATING AND EDITING SHAPES

Lesson overview

In this lesson, you'll learn how to do the following:

- Create a document with multiple artboards.
- Use tools and commands to create basic shapes.
- Work with drawing modes.
- Use rulers and Smart Guides as drawing aids.
- Scale and duplicate objects.
- Join and outline objects.
- Edit strokes with the Width tool.
- Work with the Shape Builder tool.
- Work with Pathfinder commands to create shapes.
- Use Image Trace to create shapes.

This lesson takes approximately an hour and a half to complete. If needed, remove the previous lesson folder from your hard disk and copy the Lesson03 folder onto it.

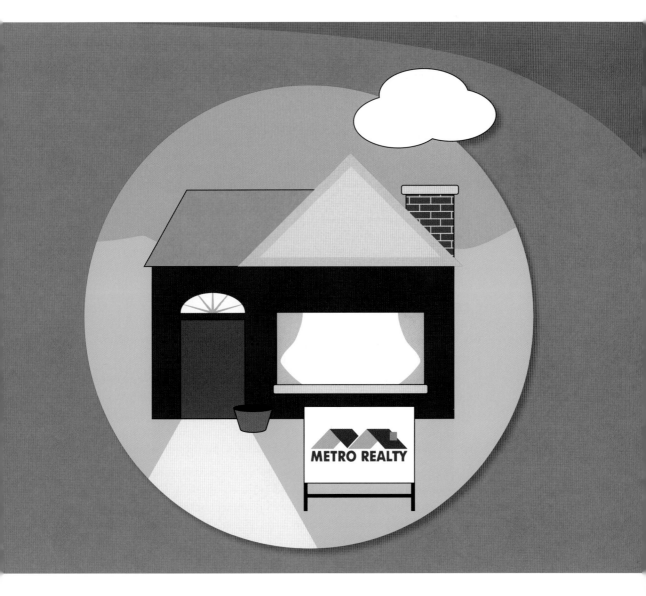

You can create documents with multiple artboards and many kinds of objects by starting with a basic shape and then editing it to create new shapes. In this lesson, you'll create a new document, and then create and edit some basic shapes for an illustration.

Getting started

In this lesson, you'll create an illustration for a brochure.

1 To ensure that the tools and panels function as described in this lesson, delete or deactivate (by renaming) the Adobe Illustrator CS6 preferences file. See "Restoring default preferences" on page 3.

2 Start Adobe Illustrator CS6.

● **Note:** If you have not already done so, copy the Lesson03 folder from the Lessons folder on the *Adobe Illustrator CS6 Classroom in a Book* CD onto your hard disk. See "Copying the Classroom in a Book files" on page 2.

● **Note:** In Mac OS, when opening lesson files, you may need to click the round, green button in the upper-left corner of the Document window to maximize the window's size.

3 Choose File > Open. Locate the file named L3end.ai, which is in the Lesson03 folder in the Lessons folder that you copied onto your hard disk. These are the finished illustrations that you will create throughout this lesson. Choose View > Fit All In Window and leave the file open for reference, or choose File > Close.

Creating a new document

You will now create a document that will have two artboards, each with an illustration that you will later combine.

1 Choose File > New to open a new, untitled document. In the New Document dialog box, change the Name to **homesale**, choose Print from the New Document Profile menu (if it isn't already selected), and change the Units to Inches. When you change the units, the New Document Profile automatically changes to [Custom]. Keep the dialog box open for the next step.

Using document profiles, you can set up a document for different kinds of output, such as print, web, video, and more. For example, if you are designing a web page mockup, you can use a web document profile, which automatically displays the page size and units in pixels, changes the color mode to RGB, and changes the raster effects to Screen (72 ppi).

● **Note:** The spacing value is the distance between each artboard.

2 Change the Number Of Artboards option to **2** to create two artboards. Click the Arrange By Row button (⬚), and make sure that the Left To Right Layout arrow (⬚) is showing. In the Spacing field, type **1**. Click the word "Width," and type **8** in the Width field. Type **8** in the Height field. You don't need to type the **in** for inches, since the units are set to inches (it's assumed). Click OK.

3 Choose File > Save As. In the Save As dialog box, ensure that the name of the file is **homesale** (Windows) or **homesale.ai** (Mac OS), and choose the Lesson03 folder. Leave the Save As Type option set to Adobe Illustrator (*.AI) (Windows) or the Format option set to Adobe Illustrator (ai) (Mac OS), and click Save. In the Illustrator Options dialog box, leave the Illustrator options at their default settings, and click OK.

Set up multiple artboards

Illustrator allows you to create multiple artboards. Setting up the artboards requires an understanding of the initial artboard settings in the New Document dialog box. After specifying the number of artboards for your document, you can set the order you'd like them laid out on screen. They are defined as follows:

- **Grid By Row:** Arranges multiple artboards in the specified number of rows. Choose the number of rows from the Rows menu. The default value creates the most square appearance possible with the specified number of artboards.

- **Grid By Column:** Arranges multiple artboards in the specified number of columns. Choose the number of columns from the Columns menu. The default value creates the most square appearance possible with the specified number of artboards.

- **Arrange By Row:** Arranges artboards in one straight row.

- **Arrange By Column:** Arranges artboards in one straight column.

- **Change To Right-To-Left Layout:** Arranges multiple artboards in the specified row or column format, but displays them from right to left.

—From Illustrator Help

4 Click the Document Setup button in the Control panel.

This button opens the Document Setup dialog box, where you can change the artboard size, units, bleeds, and more, after a document is created.

● **Note:** If the Document Setup button does not appear in the Control panel, it may mean that content in the document is selected. You can also choose File > Document Setup.

5 In the Bleed section of the Document Setup dialog box, change the value in the Top field to **.125** in, either by clicking the up arrow to the left of the field once or by typing the value, and all four fields change. Click OK.

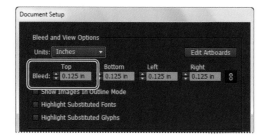

Notice the red line that appears around both artboards. The red line indicates the bleed area. Typical bleeds for printing are about 1/8 of an inch.

What is a bleed?

Bleed is the amount of artwork that falls outside of the printing bounding box, or outside the artboard. You can include bleed in your artwork as a margin of error—to ensure that the ink is still printed to the edge of the page after the page is trimmed or that an image can be stripped into a keyline in a document.

—From Illustrator Help

Working with basic shapes

In the first part of this lesson, you'll create a house using basic shapes, like rectangles, ellipses, rounded rectangles, and polygons. You'll begin this exercise by setting up the workspace.

Tip: You can change the units for the current document by right-clicking (Windows) or Ctrl-clicking (Mac OS) the horizontal or vertical ruler and choosing a new unit from the context menu.

1 Choose Window > Workspace > Essentials (if it's not already selected), and then choose Window > Workspace > Reset Essentials.

2 Choose View > Rulers > Show Rulers, or press Ctrl+R (Windows) or Command+R (Mac OS), to display rulers along the top and left side of the Document window, if they are not already showing.

The ruler units are inches because you specified Units as inches in the New Document dialog box. You can change the ruler units for all documents or for the current document only. The ruler unit applies to measuring objects, moving and transforming objects, setting grid and guide spacing, and creating shapes. It does not affect the units used in the Character, Paragraph, and Stroke panels. The units used in these panels are specified in the Units category in the program preferences (Edit > Preferences [Windows] or Illustrator > Preferences [Mac OS]).

Understanding drawing modes

Before starting to draw shapes in Illustrator, notice the three drawing modes found at the bottom of the Tools panel: Draw Normal, Draw Behind, and Draw Inside.

Each drawing mode allows you to draw shapes in a different way.

Draw Normal — — Draw Inside
Draw Behind

Note: If the Tools panel you see is a single column, select a drawing mode by clicking the Drawing Modes button (⬛) at the bottom of the Tools panel and choosing a drawing mode from the menu that appears.

- **Draw Normal mode:** You start every document by drawing shapes in Normal mode, which stacks shapes on top of each other.

- **Draw Behind mode:** This mode allows you to draw objects behind other objects without choosing layers or paying attention to the stacking order.

- **Draw Inside mode:** This mode lets you draw objects or place images inside other objects, including live text, automatically creating a clipping mask of the selected object.

Note: To learn more about clipping masks, see Lesson 15, "Combining Illustrator CS6 Graphics with Other Adobe Applications."

As you create shapes in the following sections, you will be using the different drawing modes and learning how they affect your shapes.

Creating rectangles

First, you'll create a series of rectangles.

1 Choose View > Fit Artboard In Window. Make sure that 1 is showing in the Artboard Navigation area in the lower-left corner of the Document window, which indicates that the first artboard is showing.

2 Choose Window > Transform to open the Transform panel.

   The Transform panel is useful for editing properties, such as the width and height of an existing shape.

3 Select the Rectangle tool (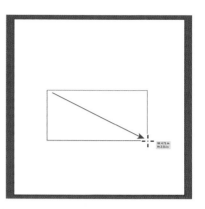) in the Tools panel, and start dragging from just to the left of the center on the artboard, down and to the right. See the figure for placement on the artboard. As you drag, notice the tool tip that appears as a gray box next to the cursor, indicating the width and height of the shape as you draw. This is called the measurement label and is a part of the Smart Guides, which will be discussed further in this lesson. Drag down and to the right until the rectangle is approximately 4.7 in wide and has a height of 2.3 in.

When you release the mouse button, the rectangle is selected, and its center point appears. The center point lets you drag to align the object with other elements in your artwork. Also, by default, shapes are filled with a white color and have a black stroke (border). A shape with a fill can be selected and moved by first positioning the pointer anywhere inside the shape.

▶ **Tip:** Holding down the Alt (Windows) or Option (Mac OS) key as you drag with the Rectangle, Rounded Rectangle, or Ellipse tools draws a shape from its center point rather than from its upper-left corner. Holding down the Shift key as you draw with the Rectangle, Rounded Rectangle, or Ellipse tools selected draws a shape in perfect proportion (a square, rounded corner square, or circle).

4 In the Transform panel, if necessary, change the size of the selected object by typing **4.7** for the width (W:) and **2.3** for the height (H:). Typing the **in** for inches isn't necessary and will be added automatically.

5 Close the Transform panel group by clicking the Close button (X) in the upper-right corner of the group title bar (Windows) or in the upper-left corner (Mac OS).

6 With the new rectangle still selected, click the Fill color (⬜▾) in the Control panel and change the fill color to a dark brown. When you position the pointer over the swatches in the panel that appears, a tooltip showing "C=50 M=70 Y=80 K=70" appears over the correct swatch. Press the Escape key to hide the Swatches panel.

● **Note:** You will learn more about working with color in Lesson 6, "Color and Painting."

Next, you will create another rectangle using a different method.

7 With the Rectangle tool still selected, position the pointer over the rectangle on the artboard and click. The Rectangle dialog box appears.

8 In the Rectangle dialog box, change the Width to **1 in**, press the Tab key, and type **1.6** in the Height field. Click OK.

9 With the new rectangle still selected, click the Fill color (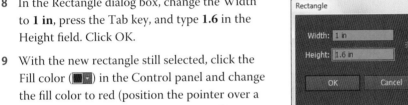) in the Control panel and change the fill color to red (position the pointer over a red swatch until the tooltip displays as "C=15 M=100 Y=90 K=10"). Press the Escape key to hide the Swatches panel.

Note: When entering values, if the correct unit appears (such as in for inches), you don't need to type the **in**. If the correct unit does NOT appear, type the **in** and the units will be converted.

10 Select the Selection tool (⬧), and drag the new rectangle for the door so that the bottom edge snaps to the bottom edge of the brown rectangle and is closer to the left edge of the brown rectangle.

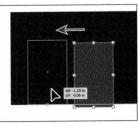

The snapping of the two shapes is caused by the Smart Guides being turned on. Also, the values you see in the measurement label may not be the same as you see in the figure, and that's okay.

Another way to make a shape is to make a copy of that shape. Next, you'll copy the door shape and create shapes for a window and the chimney.

1 With the Selection tool selected, position the pointer over the red filled rectangle. Press the Alt (Windows) or Option (Mac OS) key, and drag directly to the right. When a green line appears indicating that you are snapping to the horizontal center of the brown rectangle and the vertical center of the red rectangle, release the mouse button and then the Alt or Option key. The measurements you see may be different than the figure and that's okay.

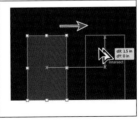

2 With the new rectangle still selected, click the Fill color in the Control panel and change the color to white to fill the new shape.

3 Drag the lower-right bounding point of the white rectangle to the right to change the width of the shape to approximately 2.3 in with a height of 1.1 in, as seen in the measurement label.

> **Tip:** You can always zoom in closer to the artwork for more precision or enter the values in the Transform panel after you draw the shape.

4 With the Selection tool, press the Alt (Windows) or Option (Mac OS) key, and drag the white rectangle from its center straight up so that the bottom edge snaps to the top edge of the brown rectangle.

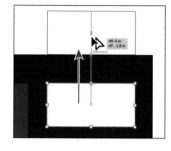

5 Drag the left, middle bounding point of the rectangle to the right until a width of approximately .75 in shows in the measurement label.

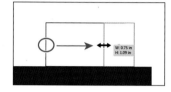

6 Drag the new rectangle to the right until the right edge snaps to the right edge of the brown rectangle.

7 Choose Select > Deselect and then File > Save.

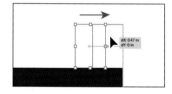

Working with the document grid

The grid allows you to work more precisely by creating a grid behind your artwork in the Document window that objects can snap to, and it does not print. To turn the grid on and use its features, do the following:

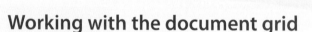

- To use the grid, choose View > Show Grid.

- To hide the grid, choose View > Hide Grid.

- To snap objects to the gridlines, choose View > Snap To Grid, select the object you want to move, and drag it to the desired location. When the object's boundaries come within 2 pixels of a gridline, it snaps to the point.

- To specify the spacing between gridlines, grid style (lines or dots), grid color, or whether grids appear in the front or back of artwork, choose Edit > Preferences > Guides & Grid (Windows) or Illustrator > Preferences > Guides & Grid (Mac OS).

Note: When Snap To Grid is turned on, you cannot use Smart Guides (even if the menu command is selected).

—From Illustrator Help

Creating rounded rectangles

Next, you'll create a rounded rectangle for another part of the illustration.

1 Select the Zoom tool (🔍) in the Tools panel, and click twice on the last white rectangle you created, which will become the chimney of the house.

2 Click and hold down the mouse button on the Rectangle tool (▣), and select the Rounded Rectangle tool (▢) in the Tools panel.

3 Position the pointer on the left edge of the small white rectangle, below the top edge, until you see the word "path." Click and drag down and to the right to the right edge of the white rectangle. Do not release the mouse button yet.

4 Press the Down Arrow key several times to decrease the corner radius (make the corners less rounded). If you've gone too far, you can press the Up Arrow key several times until you achieve the desired roundness. The corner radius of your shape does not have to match the figure exactly. Release the mouse button when the height is approximately .14 in.

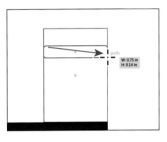

▶ **Tip:** You can also press and hold the Down Arrow or Up Arrow key to change the corner radius faster.

Next, you'll use Smart Guides to help you align the shape you created to the existing shapes.

5 Select the Selection tool (▸) in the Tools panel. Click anywhere inside the rounded rectangle, and drag it up so that it's centered horizontally with the larger white rectangle and so that its bottom snaps to the top of the larger white rectangle, as shown in the figure. When the word "intersect" and the green line(s) appear, release the mouse button.

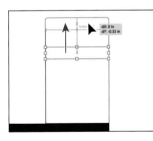

▶ **Tip:** The color of the Smart Guides can be changed from green to another color by choosing Edit > Preferences > Smart Guides (Windows) or Illustrator > Preferences > Smart Guides (Mac OS).

● **Note:** The gray tool tip that appears as you drag the shape indicates the x and y distance that the pointer has moved.

6 With the rounded rectangle selected, click and drag the right, middle bounding point to the right. As you drag, press the Alt (Windows) or Option (Mac OS) key. This allows you to resize from the center of the shape. Drag until the width is approximately .9 in, and release the mouse button and then the modifier key.

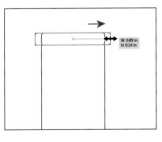

7 With the rounded rectangle still selected, click the Fill color in the Control panel and change the color to a light gray (the tool tip will show "C=0 M=0 Y=0 K=20") to fill the new shape.

8 Choose Select > Deselect.

9 Choose View > Fit Artboard In Window.

10 Select the Rounded Rectangle tool () in the Tools panel. Position the pointer on the larger white window rectangle, and click.

11 In the Rounded Rectangle dialog box, change the Width to **2.4 in** and click OK.

Creating a rounded rectangle this way allows you to enter a width, height, and corner radius. By clicking the artboard with the Rounded Rectangle tool selected, the measurements of the last created rounded rectangle appear by default in the dialog box.

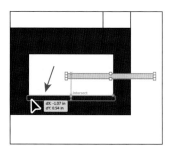

▶ **Tip:** Drawing with the Smart Guides turned on can be very helpful, especially when precision is necessary. If you don't find them useful, you could turn the Smart Guides off by choosing View > Smart Guides.

12 With the Selection tool (▶), drag the rounded rectangle from its center down under the window shape until it's centered horizontally and its top edge snaps to the bottom edge of the window. The green alignment guides will help to snap it into place.

13 Choose File > Save.

Creating ellipses

You can control the shape of polygons, stars, and ellipses by pressing certain modifying keys as you draw. You'll draw an ellipse next, to represent the top of the door.

1 Select the Zoom tool (🔍) in the Tools panel, and click twice on the red rectangle.

2 Click and hold down the mouse button on the Rounded Rectangle tool (), and select the Ellipse tool (⬤). Position the pointer over the upper-left corner of the red rectangle. Notice that the word "anchor" appears. Begin dragging down and to the right, snapping to the right edge of the red rectangle when the word "path" appears. Without releasing the mouse button, drag up or down slightly until

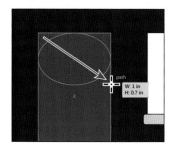

the measurement label shows a height of approximately 0.7 in, and then release the mouse button.

3 Choose View > Hide Bounding Box.

The bounding box, as you saw in previous lessons, allows you to transform the shape. If you turn the bounding box off, you can drag the shape by an edge or an anchor point without transforming it.

4 Select the Selection tool. Click and drag the ellipse up by the right, middle point. Release the mouse button when the center of the ellipse snaps to the top of the red rectangle.

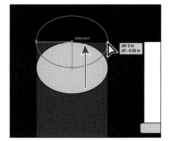

5 Choose View > Show Bounding Box.

6 Choose Window > Transform to open the Transform panel. Click the red rectangle to select it, and note the width in the Transform panel. Click the ellipse again, and see if the widths are the same in the Transform panel. If not, correct the ellipse by typing the same width value as the red rectangle and pressing Enter or Return. Close the Transform panel group.

Note: If you corrected the width in the Transform panel, the ellipse may no longer be aligned with the rectangles. With the Selection tool, drag the ellipse horizontally to align it again.

7 Choose Select > Deselect and then File > Save.

Creating polygons

Now, you'll create two triangles for the roof of the house, using the Polygon tool. Polygons are drawn from the center by default, which is different than the other tools you've worked with so far.

1 Choose View > Fit Artboard In Window.

2 Click and hold down the mouse button on the Ellipse tool ( ), and select the Polygon tool ( ). Position the pointer just above the brown rectangle. Drag to begin drawing a polygon, but don't release the mouse button. Press the Down Arrow key three times to reduce the number of sides on the polygon to three (a triangle). Hold down the Shift

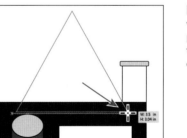

Tip: While drawing with the Polygon tool, press the Up Arrow key to increase the number of sides.

key to straighten the triangle. Without releasing the Shift key, drag down and to the right until the Smart Guides measurement label displays a width of approximately 3.5 in. Release the mouse and then the modifier key.

3 Select the Selection tool (▸) in the Tools panel, and drag the triangle from its center until the bottom of the triangle snaps to the top and right of the larger brown rectangle. The word "intersect" appears when it is snapped. Drag the triangle a little further to the right to hang it over the brown rectangle. See the figure for placement help.

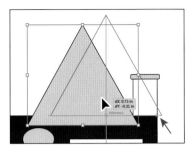

4 With the Selection tool, drag the top, middle bounding point down until the measurement label shows a height of approximately 1.7 in. You may need to zoom out or scroll in the Document window to see the top of the triangle.

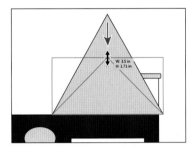

Working with Draw Behind mode

Next, you'll create another triangle behind the one you just drew, using the Draw Behind mode.

● **Note:** If the Tools panel you see is displayed as a single column, you can click the Drawing Modes button (▣) at the bottom of the Tools panel and choose Draw Behind from the menu that appears.

1 Click the Draw Behind button (▣) at the bottom of the Tools panel.

As long as this drawing mode is selected, every shape you create, using the different methods you've learned, will be created behind the other shapes on the page.

2 Select the Polygon tool (⬡) in the Tools panel. Position the pointer just to the left of the triangle you created. Click to open the Polygon dialog box. Click OK, and notice that the new triangle is behind the existing triangle on the artboard.

The values in the Polygon dialog box match the radius and number of sides of the last drawn polygon (before you modified it).

● **Note:** If your larger triangle extends a bit off the top of the artboard don't worry. You will cut off the top of it later in the lesson.

3 Select the Selection tool, and drag the new triangle so that the bottom edge snaps to the top of the brown rectangle, as shown in the figure (the blue outline). With the triangle selected and in place, you can move it to the left, if needed, by pressing the Left Arrow key so that it hangs off the left edge of the brown rectangle a little.

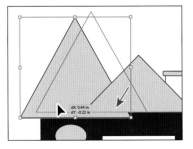

4 With the new triangle still selected, click the Fill color in the Control panel, and change the fill color to a darker gray than the smaller triangle. We chose a swatch with the tool tip values C=0 M=0 Y=0 K=50.

5 Click the Draw Normal button (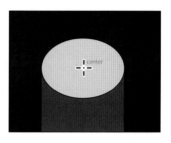) at the bottom of the Tools panel.

Creating stars

Next, you'll create a star for the window above the door, using the Star tool.

1 Select the Zoom tool (Q) in the Tools panel, and click twice on the ellipse at the top of the red door rectangle.

2 Click and hold down the mouse button on the Polygon tool (⬡), and select the Star tool (★) in the Tools panel. Position the pointer in the center of the gray ellipse shape. Notice that the word "center" appears.

▶ **Tip:** The next step uses several keyboard commands for working with stars, so *take it slowly* and reference the figure as you draw. Only release the mouse button when indicated.

3 Click and drag slowly to the right to create a star shape. Without releasing the mouse button, press the Up Arrow key five times to increase the number of points on the star to ten. Drag the mouse until you see a width of approximately .28 in and stop dragging, but don't release the mouse button yet.

Hold down the Control (Windows) or Command (Mac OS) key, and continue dragging to the right. This keeps the inner radius constant. Drag until you see a width of approximately 1.3 in and stop dragging, *without releasing the mouse button*. Release the Control or Command key, but not the mouse. Hold down the Shift key, and drag until the star has a width of about 1.3 in. Release the mouse button and then the Shift key.

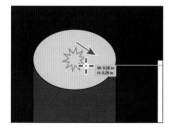
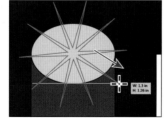
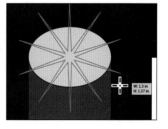

Change the number of points.   Resize the star.   Constrain the star.

4 Change the Stroke weight, to the right of the word "Stroke" in the Control panel, to **0**. Later in the lesson, you will use the ellipse and the star shape to create the window above the door.

5 Choose Select > Deselect and then File > Save.

Tips for drawing polygons, spirals, and stars

You can control the shapes of polygons, spirals, and stars by pressing certain keys as you draw the shapes. Choose any of the following options to control the shape:

- To add or subtract sides on a polygon, points on a star, or number of segments on a spiral, hold down the Up Arrow or Down Arrow key while creating the shape. This only works if the mouse button is held down. When the mouse button is released, the tool remains set to the last specified value.

- To rotate the shape, move the mouse in an arc.

- To keep a side or point at the top, hold down the Shift key.

- To keep the inner radius constant, start creating a shape and then hold down Ctrl (Windows) or Command (Mac OS).

—From Illustrator Help

Changing stroke width and alignment

Every shape, by default, is created with a 1 point stroke. You can easily change the stroke weight of an object to make it thinner or thicker. Strokes are also aligned to the center of a path edge, by default, but you can easily change the alignment as well, using the Stroke panel.

1   Choose View > Fit Artboard In Window.

2   With the Selection tool (↖), click to select the smaller light gray triangle that makes up part of the roof.

3   Select the Zoom tool (🔍) in the Tools panel, and click that triangle once to zoom in.

Note: You can also open the Stroke panel by choosing Window > Stroke.

4   Click the word "Stroke" in the Control panel to open the Stroke panel. In the Stroke panel, change the Stroke weight to **10 pt**. Notice that the stroke of the triangle is centered on the edge of the shape, by default.

5   Click the Align Stroke To Inside button (⬛) in the Stroke panel. This aligns the stroke to the inside edge of the triangle.

You set the stroke to the inside of the triangle so that the bottom edge still visually aligns with the bottom of the other triangle.

6 With the triangle still selected, click the Stroke color in the Control panel (to the left of the word Stroke), and change the stroke color to a darker gray than the fill of that same triangle.

7 Choose File > Save.

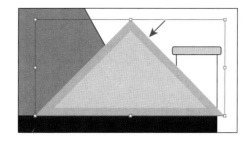

About aligning strokes

If an object is a closed path (such as a square), you can select an option in the Stroke panel to align the stroke along the path to the center (default), inside, or outside:

Working with line segments

Next, you'll work with straight lines and line segments, known as open paths, to create a flower pot. Shapes can be created in many ways in Illustrator, and the simpler way is usually better.

1 Select the Zoom tool (🔍) in the Tools panel, and click four times below the red door to zoom in on the empty artboard space below it.

2 Choose Reset Essentials from the workspace switcher in the Application bar.

You've been working in the default Preview mode, which lets you see how objects are painted with fill and stroke colors. If paint attributes seem distracting, you can work in Outline mode, which you'll do next.

3 Choose View > Outline to switch from Preview to Outline mode.

● **Note:** Outline mode removes all paint attributes, such as colored fills and strokes, to speed up selecting and redrawing artwork. You can't select or drag shapes by clicking in the middle of a shape, because the fill temporarily disappears.

4 Select the Ellipse tool (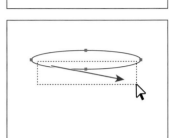) in the Tools panel. Below the house shapes, draw an ellipse that has a width of 0.6 in and a height of 0.1 in, as shown in the measurement label that appears.

● **Note:** When you drag to select, make sure that you do not drag across the points on the left and right ends of the ellipse.

5 Select the Direct Selection tool (⬚) in the Tools panel. Drag across the lower part of the ellipse to select the bottom half.

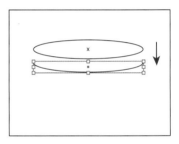

6 Choose Edit > Copy and then Edit > Paste In Front to create a new path that is directly on top of the original.

This copies and pastes only the bottom half of the ellipse as a single path, because that is what you selected with the Direct Selection tool.

7 Select the Selection tool (▶), and press the Down Arrow key about five times to move the new line down.

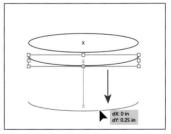

8 Click and drag the line straight down until you see, in the measurement label, a dY of approximately .25 in.

Make sure that you position the pointer directly on the line to select and drag it.

● **Note:** Depending on the resolution of your screen, the Transform options may appear in the Control panel. If they do appear, you can change the W value.

9 Click the word "Transform" in the Control panel to show the Transform panel. Change the Width of the selected line to **.4 in**.

You could also open the Transform panel by choosing Window > Transform.

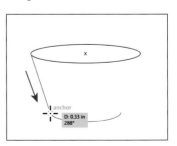

10 Select the Line Segment tool (╱) in the Tools panel. Draw a line by clicking on the left anchor point of the ellipse and dragging to the left anchor point of the new path. The anchor points are highlighted when the line snaps to them. Repeat this on the right side of the ellipse.

11 Choose Select > Deselect.

12 Choose File > Save.

Next, you will take the three line segments that make up part of the flower pot and join them together as one path.

Joining paths

When more than one open path is selected, you can join them together to create a closed path (like a circle). You can also join the end points of two separate paths.

Next, you will join the three paths to create a single closed path.

1 Select the Selection tool (🡤) in the Tools panel. Drag a selection marquee across each of the three paths that you just created, to select them all (not the top ellipse).

2 Choose Object > Path > Join.

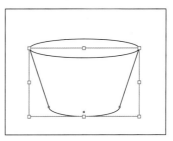

The three paths are converted to a single path. Illustrator identifies the anchor points on the ends of each path and joins the closest points together.

▶ **Tip:** After the paths are selected, you can also join paths by pressing Ctrl+J (Windows) or Command+J (Mac OS).

3 With the path still selected, choose Object > Path > Join once more. Choose Select > Deselect to see the joined path.

This creates a closed path, connecting the two endpoints of the path. If you select a single open path and choose Object > Path > Join, Illustrator creates a path segment between the endpoints of the open path, creating a closed path.

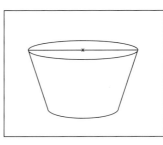

● **Note:** If you only want to fill the shape with a color, it is not necessary to join the path to make a closed path. An open path can have a color fill. It is, however, necessary to do this if you want a stroke to appear around the entire fill area.

4 Choose View > Preview.

5 With the Selection tool, drag a marquee across the two flower pot shapes to select them both. Change the Stroke weight in the Control panel to **1 pt**. Change the Stroke color to black. Change the Fill color to black.

6 Choose Select > Deselect. Click to select the bottom flower pot shape, and choose Object > Arrange > Send To Back.

7 In the Control panel, change the Fill color to a brown (C=35 M=60 Y=80 K=25).

> ● **Note:** To select a path without a fill, click the stroke or drag across the path.

8 Hold down the Shift key, and click the ellipse with the Selection tool to select both flower pot shapes. Choose Object > Group.

Open path vs. closed path

As you draw, you create a line called a path. A path is made up of one or more straight or curved segments. The beginning and end of each segment are marked by anchor points, which work like pins holding a wire in place. A path can be closed (for example, a circle), or open, with distinct endpoints (for example, a wavy line).

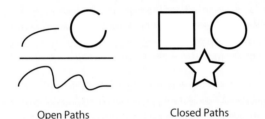

Open Paths   Closed Paths

Both open and closed paths can have fills applied to them.

—From Illustrator Help

Using the Width tool

Not only can you adjust the stroke weight and the alignment of the stroke, but you can also alter regular stroke widths either by using the Width tool (🖉) or by applying width profiles to the stroke. This allows you to create variations along the stroke of a path. Next, you will use the Width tool to create some curtains.

1 Choose View > Fit Artboard In Window. Select the Zoom tool (🔍) in the Tools panel, and then click the white window rectangle three times to zoom in.

2 With the Selection tool, press the Shift key and click the white rectangle, the gray rounded rectangle beneath it, and the brown rectangle, to select them all. Choose Object > Lock > Selection to temporarily lock them.

3 Select the Line Segment tool (╱) in the Tools panel, and position the pointer at the top of the white rectangle, away from the left edge. Hold down the Shift key, and drag straight down, snapping the end of the line to the bottom of the white rectangle. Release the mouse button and then the modifier key.

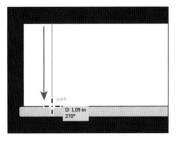

4 Make sure that in the Control panel the Stroke color of the line is black, and that the Stroke weight is **1 pt**.

5 Select the Width tool (✎) in the Tools panel. Position the pointer over the middle of the line, and notice the pointer has a plus symbol next to it (▶₊). Drag to the right, away from the line. Notice that as you drag, you are stretching the stroke to the left and right equally. Release the mouse when the measurement label shows Side 1 and Side 2 at approximately .25 in.

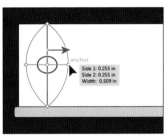

The new point on the stroke of the original line is called the width point. The lines extending from the width point are the handles. Width points created at a corner or at a direct-selected anchor point stick to the anchor point during basic editing of the path.

6 The width point on the stroke (circled in the figure) should still be selected. You can tell it's selected, because it's not hollow like the points at the ends of the handles. Press Delete to remove it.

Because you only created one width point on the stroke, removing that one removed the width completely.

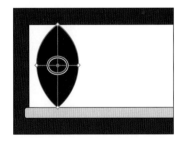

Note: If you need to reselect the point, make sure that the Width tool is selected, position the pointer over the point, and then click it.

7 Position the pointer over the top anchor point of the line, and notice the pointer has a curve next to it (▶﹏). Press the Alt (Windows) or Option (Mac OS) key, and drag to the right until you see that Side 1 is approximately 0.25 in. Release the mouse button and then the modifier key.

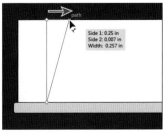

Note: When you edit with the Width tool, you are only editing the stroke of the object.

The modifier key allows you to drag one side of the stroke rather than both sides, as you did previously.

8 Position the pointer over the bottom anchor point of the line. Press the Alt (Windows) or Option (Mac OS) key, and drag to the right until you see that Side 1 is approximately 0.3 in. Release the mouse button and then the modifier key.

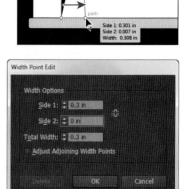

▶ **Tip:** You can use the Width Point Edit dialog box to ensure that width points are the same.

9 With the Width tool still selected, position the pointer over the top width point or handle of the line and double-click to open the Width Point Edit dialog box. Change the Side 1 width to **.3 in**. Make sure that Side 2 is set to **0**, and click OK.

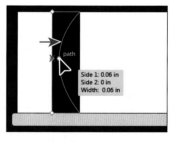

The Width Point Edit dialog box allows you to adjust the sides together or separately, using more precision. Clicking the Adjust Widths Proportionately button (⊞) would link Side 1 with Side 2 so that they adjust together, in proportion. Also, if you select the Adjust Adjoining Width Points option, changes to the selected width point affect neighboring width points as well.

10 Position the pointer over the bottom width point or handle of the line and double-click to open the Width Point Edit dialog box. Change the Side 1 width to **.3** in. Make sure that Side 2 is set to **0**, and click OK.

11 Position the pointer over the middle of the line (indicated by the X in the figure). Click and drag to the right until you see a Side 1 width of approximately .06 in.

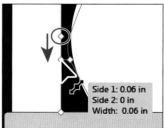

● **Note:** You don't have to position the pointer over the center of the line and drag to create another width point. You can also drag from anywhere in the stroke area.

12 Position the pointer over the new width point you just created (circled in the figure) and, pressing the Alt (Windows) or Option (Mac OS) key, drag the new width point down to create a copy. Release the mouse button and then the key.

13 Click the new width point to select it.

Next, you will select another width point and move them both. You may want to zoom in to the line.

14 With the Width tool, press the Shift key and click the width point above the selected width point to select both. Release the Shift key. Drag the point you just selected down just a bit. Notice that the two width points move together proportionately.

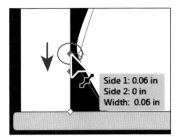

▶ **Tip:** You can drag one width point on top of another width point to create a discontinuous width point. If you double-click a discontinuous width point, the Width Point Edit dialog box allows you to edit both width points.

15 Position the pointer between the top width point and the second width point from the top. See the figure for help. Click and drag to the right until you see a Side 1 width of approximately .2 in.

16 Choose File > Save.

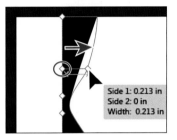

Saving width profiles

After defining the stroke width, you can save the variable width profile from the Stroke panel or the Control panel.

Width profiles can be applied to selected paths by choosing them from the Width Profile drop-down list in the Control panel or Stroke panel. When a stroke with no variable width is selected, the list displays the Uniform option. You can also select the Uniform option to remove a variable width profile from an object. To restore the default width profile set, click the Reset Profiles button at the bottom of the Profile drop-down list.

If you apply a variable width profile to a stroke, it is indicated with an asterisk (*) in the Appearance panel.

—From Illustrator Help

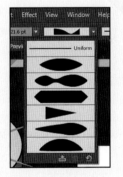

Outlining strokes

Paths, such as a line, can show a stroke color but not a fill color, by default. If you create a line in Illustrator and you want to apply both a stroke and a fill, you can outline the stroke, which converts the line into a closed shape (or compound path).

Next, you will outline the stroke of the curtain you just created.

1   With the line still selected, choose None from the Fill color in the Control panel, if it is not already selected.

◍ **Note:** If the line initially has a color fill, a more complex group is created when you choose Outline Stroke.

2   Choose Object > Path > Outline Stroke. This creates a filled shape that is a closed path.

3   With the new shape selected, click the Fill color in the Control panel and change the color to a light orange that shows "C=0 M=35 Y=85 K=0" in the tool tip. Click the Stroke color, and make sure that the color is None (▨).

4   Select the Selection tool (▶) and begin dragging the left edge of the curtain shape to the left. As you drag, press the Shift key. When it snaps to the left edge of the white window rectangle, release the mouse button and then the key.

5   Drag the right, middle bounding point of the curtain shape to the right to make the curtain a bit wider.

6   Press the Alt (Windows) or Option (Mac OS) key, and drag the curtain shape to the right until its right edge aligns to the right edge of the white rectangle.

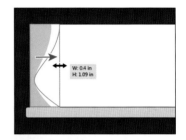

◍ **Note:** Depending on the resolution of your screen, the word "Transform" may not appear in the Control panel. Click the underlined X, Y, W, or H links to open the Transform panel if you see them instead.

7   In the Control panel, click the word "Transform" to open the Transform panel (Window > Transform). Making sure that the center point of the Reference Point Indicator (▦) is selected (to flip the curtain shape around its center), choose Flip Horizontal from the Transform panel menu (▾▤).

8   Choose Object > Unlock All, and then choose Select > Deselect.

9   With the Selection tool, click to select the white window rectangle. Click the word "Stroke" in the Control panel to open the Stroke panel. Click the Align Stroke To Outside button (▮).

10 Click to select the gray rounded rectangle beneath the white window rectangle and curtain shapes. Choose Object > Arrange > Bring To Front.

11 Choose Select > Deselect and then File > Save.

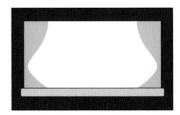

Combining and editing shapes

In Illustrator, you can combine vector objects to create shapes in a variety of ways. The resulting paths or shapes differ depending on the method you use to combine the paths. The first method you will learn for combining shapes involves working with the Shape Builder tool. This tool allows you to visually and intuitively merge, delete, fill, and edit overlapping shapes and paths directly in the artwork.

Working with the Shape Builder tool

Using the Shape Builder tool, you'll change the appearance of the red door and create the window above it. Then, you'll make a cloud.

1 Choose View > Fit Artboard In Window.

2 Select the Selection tool (↖) in the Tools panel, and click to select the star shape. Choose Object > Hide > Selection to temporarily hide it.

3 Select the Zoom tool (🔍) in the Tools panel, and click three times on the top of the red door to zoom in.

4 Choose View > Outline.

5 Select the Rectangle tool (■) in the Tools panel. Position the pointer off the left edge of the top of the door. When the green alignment guide appears, click and drag down and to the right to create a rectangle with an approximate width of 1.2 in and a height of .1 in.

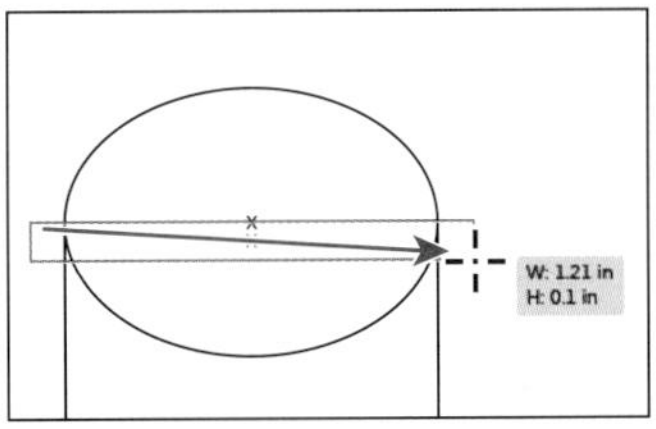

6 Choose View > Preview.

7 With the Selection tool, Shift-click the gray ellipse and the red rectangle to select all three shapes. With the shapes selected, select the Shape Builder tool ( ) in the Tools panel.

Using the Shape Builder tool, you will now combine, delete, and paint these shapes.

8 Position the pointer over the bottom of the ellipse, indicated by the red x in the figure. Drag the pointer down into the red rectangle. See the figure at right. Release the mouse button to combine the shapes.

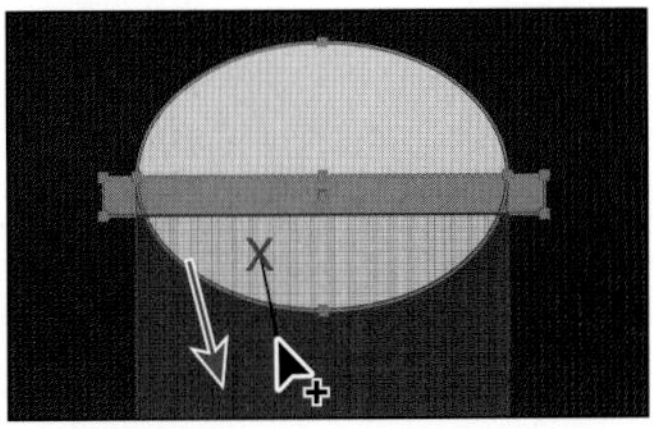

In order to edit shapes with the Shape Builder tool, they need to be selected. When you select the Shape Builder tool, the overlapping shapes are divided into separate objects temporarily. As you drag from one part to another, a red outline appears, showing you what the final shape outline will look like when it merges the shapes together.

▶ **Tip:** Zooming in can help you see what shapes you are going to combine.

9 With the shapes still selected, hold down the Alt (Windows) or Option (Mac OS) key and click the left end of the rectangle to delete it.

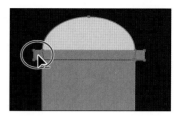

Notice that, with the modifier key held down, the pointer shows a minus sign (▶_).

Next, you will delete a series of shapes using the Shape Builder tool.

10 With the Shape Builder tool still selected, position the pointer off the left edge of the small rectangle below the ellipse, indicated by the red x in the figure. Hold down the Alt (Windows) or Option (Mac OS) key, and drag to the right to delete all of the shapes. Release the mouse button and then the modifier key.

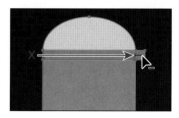

Notice that all of the shapes that will be deleted are highlighted as you drag.

11 With the shapes still selected, change the Fill color in the Control panel to red, with the tool tip showing "C=15 M=100 Y=90 K=10." This won't change anything on the artboard. Position the pointer over the larger rectangle that is the door, and click to apply the red color fill.

You can apply fills to any of the selected shapes by selecting the fill color first and then clicking the shape.

12 Choose Select > Deselect, and then choose View > Fit Artboard In Window.

13 Choose Object > Show All to show the star shape.

Lastly, with the Shape Builder, you will build a simple cloud.

1 Select the Ellipse tool (⬤) in the Tools panel, and draw an ellipse that has an approximate width of 1.4 in and an approximate height of .8 in above the chimney on the house.

2 Select the Selection tool and, pressing the Alt (Windows) or Option (Mac OS) key, drag the ellipse twice to create two copies.

3 With the Selection tool, position the shapes like you see in the figure and select them all.

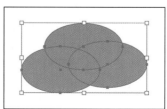

4 Select the Shape Builder tool (⬥) in the Tools panel.

5 Press the Shift key and, starting off the upper-left edge of the shapes, drag a marquee across them all. Release the mouse button and then the key.

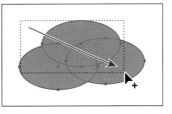

▶ **Tip:** Pressing Shift+Alt (Windows) or Shift+Option (Mac OS) and dragging a marquee across selected shapes with the Shape Builder tool selected allows you to delete a series of shapes within the marquee.

6 Select the Selection tool and, with the shape selected, change the Fill color in the Control panel to white and the Stroke color to black.

7 Choose Select > Deselect and then File > Save.

Shape Builder tool options

You can set up and customize various options such as gap detection, coloring source, and highlighting to get the required merging capability and better visual feedback.

Double-click the Shape Builder Tool icon in the Tools panel to set these options in the Shape Builder Tool Options dialog box.

—From Illustrator Help

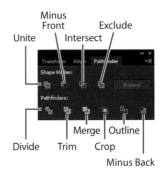

▶ **Tip:** To learn more about the Shape Builder tool options, choose Help > Illustrator Help, and search for "Shape Builder tool options."

Working with Pathfinder effects

Pathfinder effects in the Pathfinder panel let you combine shapes in many different ways to create paths or compound paths, by default. When a Pathfinder effect is applied (such as Merge), the original objects selected are permanently transformed. If the effect results in more than one shape, they are grouped automatically.

Next, you will finish the roof of the house by removing a portion of one of the gray triangles.

1 Choose View > Fit Artboard In Window. Press and hold the spacebar to access the Hand tool. Drag the artboard down a bit so that you can see the gray area above the artboard.

2 Choose Window > Pathfinder to open the Pathfinder panel group.

3 Select the Rectangle tool (■) in the Tools panel. Position the pointer above the artboard on the left edge. Click and draw a rectangle that covers the top part of the larger triangle. See the figure for guidance.

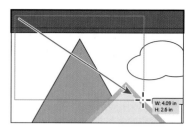

4 With the Selection tool (▸), hold down the Shift key and click the larger triangle to select it as well.

5 With the shapes selected, in the Pathfinder panel, click the Minus Front button (▣).

With the new shape selected, notice the word "Path" on the left side of the Control panel.

6 Choose Object > Arrange > Send To Back.

7 Choose Select > Deselect, and then choose File > Save.

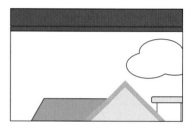

Working with shape modes

Shape modes create paths like Pathfinder effects, but they can also be used to create compound shapes. When several shapes are selected, clicking a shape mode while pressing the Alt (Windows) or Option (Mac OS) key creates a compound shape rather than a path. The original underlying objects of compound shapes are preserved. As a result, you can still select each object within a compound shape.

Next, you will use shape modes to finish the window above the door.

1 Choose View > Fit Artboard In Window.

2 Select the Zoom tool (🔍), and click several times on the star above the red rectangle.

● **Note:** If the star is not showing, you can choose Object > Show All to show the star shape.

3 With the Selection tool, click to select the star, hold down the Shift key, and then click the gray ellipse behind it to select both shapes. Release the Shift key, and then click the ellipse once more to make it the key object.

4 Click the Horizontal Align Center button (≛) in the Control panel.

● **Note:** The Align options may not appear in the Control panel. If you don't see the Align options, click the word "Align" in the Control panel to open the Align panel. The number of options displayed in the Control panel depends on your screen resolution.

5 With the objects selected, hold down the Alt (Windows) or Option (Mac OS) key and click the Minus Front button (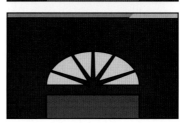) in the Pathfinder panel.

This creates a compound shape that traces the outline of the overlapping area of both objects. You will still be able to edit the star and the ellipse shape separately.

6 Choose Select > Deselect to see the final shape.

The star was removed from the ellipse shape, and the stroke is around the final window shape.

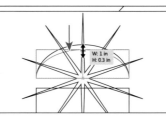

7 With the Selection tool, double-click the window shape above the door to enter Isolation mode.

▶ **Tip:** To edit the original shapes in a compound shape like this one, you can also select them individually with the Direct Selection tool (▸).

8 Choose View > Outline so that you can see the two shapes (the ellipse and the star). Click the edge of the ellipse to select it, if it isn't already selected. In the Control panel, change the Fill color to white.

9 Drag the top, middle bounding point of the ellipse bounding box down to make it shorter. Drag until the measurement tool tip shows a height of approximately 0.3 in. Leave the ellipse selected.

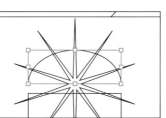

Note: It is easier to resize a shape precisely if you zoom in. You can also change the width and height of the selected shape in the Transform panel.

10 Choose View > Preview.

11 Choose Edit > Copy to copy the ellipse shape. Choose Select > Deselect.

12 Press the Escape key to exit Isolation mode.

13 With the Selection tool, click to select the window shape again. Choose Edit > Paste In Back. In the Control panel, change the Fill color of the ellipse copy to a darker gray (C=0 M=0 Y=0 K=40) and make sure that the Stroke color is None.

14 Choose Select > Deselect. Click to select the window shape again (the compound shape on top). Click the Stroke panel icon (▤) on the right side of the workspace to expand the Stroke panel. Change the Stroke weight to **0** by clicking the down arrow to the left of the field or typing in the value and pressing Enter or Return. Click the Stroke panel tab to collapse the panel. Leave the window compound shape selected.

Tip: You typically expand an object when you want to modify the appearance attributes and other properties of specific elements within it.

You will now expand the window shape. Expanding a compound shape maintains the shape of the compound object, but you can no longer select or edit the original objects.

15 Click the Expand button in the Pathfinder panel. Close the Pathfinder panel group. Choose Select > Deselect.

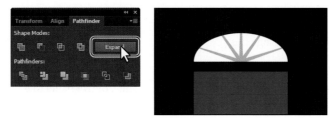

16 Choose View > Fit Artboard In Window, and then File > Save.

Using Draw Inside mode

Next, you will learn how to draw a shape inside of another using the Draw Inside drawing mode.

1 Select the Ellipse tool (⬤) in the Tools panel. Position the pointer over the upper-left corner of the artboard, and click. In the Ellipse dialog box, enter **7 in** for the Width and **7** for the Height. Click OK.

Note: The Align options may not appear in the Control panel. If you don't see the Align options, click the word "Align" in the Control panel to open the Align panel.

2 With the ellipse selected, choose Align To Artboard from the Align To (▦) menu in the Control panel. Click the Horizontal Align Center button (🎲) and the Vertical Align Center button (▮).

3 Change the Fill color to blue (C=70 M=15 Y=0 K=0) in the Control panel.

4 Click the Draw Inside button, located near the bottom of the Tools panel.

This button is active when a single object is selected (path, compound path, or text), and it allows you to draw within the selected object only. Every shape you create will now be drawn inside of the selected shape (the circle). Also,

notice that the blue circle has a dotted open rectangle around it, indicating that, if you draw, paste, or place content, it will be inside of the circle.

Note: If the Tools panel is a single column, to access the drawing modes, click and hold down the Drawing Modes button (▣) at the bottom of the Tools panel and choose Draw Inside from the menu that appears.

5 Choose Select > Deselect.

6 Choose View > Outline to see the rest of the shape outlines.

7 Select the Rectangle tool (■), and draw
a rectangle that starts halfway down the
roof, vertically, and just off the left edge of
the large circle you are drawing inside of.
Make it large enough to cover the bottom
part of the circle. This will become grass.

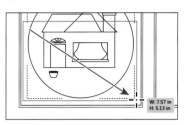

8 Choose View > Preview to see that the
rectangle is inside of the circle.

9 With the rectangle selected, change the Fill color in the Control panel to a green
(C=50 M=0 Y=100 K=0).

Notice that the circle still has the dotted open rectangle around it, indicating
that Draw Inside mode is still active.

Note: The blue circle is masking part of the green rectangle and is referred to as a clipping mask. You can learn more about clipping masks in Lesson 15, "Combining Illustrator CS6 Graphics with Other Adobe Applications."

10 Select the Polygon tool (⬡) in the Tools panel. Position the pointer in the lower
half of the circle, and click. In the Polygon dialog box, change the Radius
to **2.6 in** and the Sides to **3**. Click OK.

Note: If you draw a shape outside of the circle shape, it will seem to disappear. That is because
the circle is masking all shapes drawn inside of it, so only shapes positioned inside of the circle
bounds will appear.

11 In the Control panel, change the
Fill color of the shape to a light gray
(C=0 M=0 Y=0 K=10).

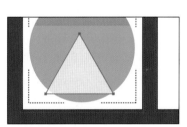

When you are finished drawing content
inside of a shape, you can click the Draw
Normal button so that any new content
you create will be drawn normally. Right
now, if you were to attempt to select the triangle or the rectangle, you would
select the circle instead. If you move the circle, the shapes inside go with it. If
you resize or reshape the circle, the shapes inside also resize or reshape.

12 Choose Select > Deselect. Click the Draw Normal button (▣) at the bottom of
the Tools panel.

Editing content drawn inside

Next, you will edit the shapes inside of the circle.

1 Select the Selection tool (▶), and click to
select the gray triangle. Notice that it selects
the blue circle instead. Double-click the gray
triangle to enter Isolation mode. Click once
more on the gray triangle to select it.

▶ **Tip:** You can separate the shapes by selecting the blue circle with the Selection tool and choosing Object > Clipping Mask > Release. This would make three shapes, stacked on top of each other.

With the gray triangle selected, notice that the Edit Contents button (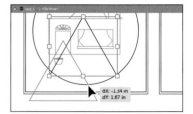) on the left end of the Control panel is selected. Also notice the gray bar along the top of the Document window, indicating that this content is a clip group.

2 Choose View > Outline to see the rest of the shapes. With the Selection tool still selected, drag the triangle from its edge down and to the left until it looks approximately like the figure. This will be a sidewalk that starts at the front door. The dX and dY you see in the measurement label will most likely be different than what you see in the figure, and that's okay.

3 Choose View > Preview to see the fill of the shapes again. Choose View > Fit Artboard In Window.

4 Press the Escape key to exit Isolation mode.

5 Choose Select > Deselect.

● **Note:** Your sidewalk (gray triangle) may not look exactly the same as in the figure and that's okay.

6 With the Selection tool, click to select the green grass shape. Choose Object > Arrange > Send To Back.

7 Choose File > Save.

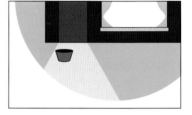

Another way to work with the Draw Inside mode is to paste or place content into a path, compound path, or text.

8 Choose File > Open, and open the pieces.ai file in the Lesson03 folder, located in the Lessons folder on your hard disk.

9 Navigate to the first artboard, with the red brick shapes on it. Select the Selection tool, and click to select the brick group. Choose Edit > Copy. Leave the pieces.ai file open.

10 Click the homesale.ai tab to return to that document.

11 With the Selection tool, click to select the larger chimney rectangle. Click the Draw Inside button, located near the bottom of the Tools panel.

12 Choose Edit > Paste.

The brick group will be pasted into the chimney rectangle and will be selected.

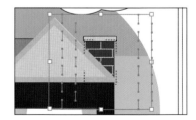

13 Press the Shift+Alt (Windows) or Shift+Option (Mac OS) keys and, with the Selection tool, click and drag the upper, middle bounding down to make the brick pattern smaller. When the pattern fits better, release the mouse button and then the keys.

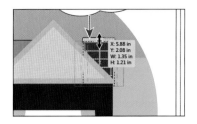

14 Click the Draw Normal button () at the bottom of the Tools panel, and choose Select > Deselect. Choose File > Save.

Using the Eraser tool

The Eraser tool lets you erase any area of your artwork, regardless of the structure. You can use the Eraser tool on paths, compound paths, paths inside Live Paint groups, and clipping paths.

1 Choose View > Fit Artboard In Window.

2 With the Selection tool (▶), double-click the green rectangle behind the house. This enters Isolation mode and lets you edit the shapes in the circle. Click once more on the green rectangle to select it.

By selecting the green rectangle, you'll erase only that shape and nothing else. If you leave all objects deselected, you can erase any object that the tool touches across all layers.

3 Select the Eraser tool (✐) in the Tools panel. With the pointer on the artboard, press and hold the Right Bracket key (]) for a second or two to make the size of the eraser diameter larger. If you make it too large, you can press the Left Bracket key ([) to make it smaller.

4 Position the pointer in the upper-left corner of the green rectangle—beyond the left edge of the circle. Click and drag from left to right, along the top edge of the rectangle, moving the pointer up and down to create hills. When you release the mouse button, the path remains closed (the erased ends are joined).

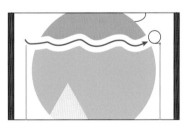

▶ **Tip:** To create a marquee around an area and erase everything inside the area, Alt-drag (Windows) or Option-drag (Mac OS). To constrain the marquee to a square, Alt-Shift-drag (Windows) or Option-Shift-drag (Mac OS).

▶ **Tip:** If you press the Shift key and drag across content, you will constrain the Eraser tool to a vertical, horizontal, or diagonal line.

5 Press the Escape key to exit Isolation mode. Choose Select > Deselect and then File > Save.

Using Image Trace to create shapes

In this part of the lesson, you will learn how to work with the Image Trace command. Image Trace traces existing artwork, like a raster picture from Adobe Photoshop. You can then convert the drawing to vector paths or a Live Paint object. This can be useful for turning a drawing into vector art, tracing raster logos, and much more.

1 Click the Next button (▶) in the status bar in the lower-left corner of the Document window to navigate to the second artboard.

2 Click the pieces.ai tab to show the artwork in the Document window. Click the Next button (▶) in the status bar to navigate to the second artboard. Choose Select > All On Active Artboard to select the realty sign frame. Choose Edit > Copy and then File > Close to close the pieces.ai file without saving.

3 Back in the homesale.ai file, on the second artboard, choose Edit > Paste. With the content selected, choose Object > Hide > Selection to hide the sign frame.

4 Choose File > Place. Select the logo.png file in the Lesson03 folder, located in the Lessons folder on your hard disk, and click Place.

With the placed image selected, the Control panel options change. You will see "Linked File" on the left side of the Control panel, and you can see the name "logo.png" and the resolution (PPI: 72), as well as other information.

5 Click the Image Trace button in the Control panel. The tracing results you see may differ slightly from the figure, and that's okay.

This converts the image into an image tracing object using the default tracing options. That means that you can't edit the vector content yet, but you can change the tracing settings or even the original placed image and then see the updates immediately.

● **Note:** You can also choose Object > Image Trace > Make with raster content selected.

6 Press Ctrl++ (Windows) or Command++ (Mac OS) a few times to zoom in.

7 Select the Selection tool in the Tools panel.

8 Choose 6 Colors from the Preset menu on the left end of the Control panel.

Illustrator comes with preset tracing options that you can apply to your image tracing object. You can then make changes to the tracing settings, if need be, using the default preset as a starting point.

9 Choose Outlines With Source Image from the View menu in the Control panel, and take a look at the image. Choose Tracing Result from that same menu.

An image tracing object is made up of the original source image and the tracing result (which is the vector artwork). By default, only the tracing result is visible. However, you can change the display of both the original image and the tracing result to best suit your needs.

10 Click the Image Trace Panel button (▦) in the Control panel to open the panel. In the panel, click the Auto-Color button (▦) at the top of the panel. The tracing results you see may differ from the figure, and that's okay.

The buttons along the top of the panel are saved settings for converting the image to grayscale, black and white, and more.

Tip: The Image Trace panel can be opened at any time by choosing Window > Image Trace or by choosing the Tracing workspace (Window > Workspace > Tracing).

11 Press and hold the eye icon (◉) to the right of the View menu in the Image Trace panel to see the source image on the artboard. Release the mouse button.

12 In the Image Trace panel, drag the Colors slider to the left until you see **3** in the field to the right of the slider.

● **Note:** Below the buttons at the top of the Image Trace panel, you will see the options Preset and View. These are the same as those in the Control panel. The Mode option allows you to change the color mode of resulting artwork (color, grayscale, or black and white). The Palette option is useful for limiting the color palette or assigning colors from a color group.

Tip: To the right of the Preset menu in the Image Trace panel, you can click the panel options and choose to save your settings as a preset, delete a preset, or rename a preset.

13 Toggle the arrow to the left of the Advanced option, and change the Advanced options as follows:

- Paths: **88%**
- Corners: **90%**
- Noise: **20 px**
- Method: Click the Overlapping button (▦).
- Select the Snap Curves To Lines option.

▶ **Tip:** For information
on Image Trace and the
options in the Image
Trace panel, see "Tracing
artwork" in Illustrator
Help.

14 With the logo image tracing object still
selected, click the Expand button in the
Control panel. Notice that the logo is
no longer an image tracing object but is
composed of shapes and paths that are
grouped together.

15 Close the Image Trace panel.

Cleaning up traced artwork

After tracing, you may need to clean up the resulting vector content.

1 Select the Selection tool, and double-click the logo group to enter Isolation mode.
Click the blue shape on the left, above the "M," and choose Object > Path > Simplify.

● **Note:** You will learn a
lot more about working
with paths and shapes in
Lesson 5, "Drawing with
the Pen and Pencil Tools."

2 In the Simplify dialog box, select
Straight Lines and make sure that the
Angle Threshold is **30** degrees. Select
Preview, if not already selected, to see
the effect. Click OK.

You can apply the Simplify command
to other parts of the logo as well.
By aligning points and using other
methods, you can turn the raster logo
into a viable vector logo.

3 Press the Escape key to exit Isolation mode, and choose View > Fit Artboard
In Window.

4 Choose Object > Show All to show the realty sign frame. With the Selection
tool, click to select the logo and, pressing the Shift key, drag the top, middle
bounding point down until the sign fits into the sign frame.

5 With the Selection tool, move the logo into the
sign frame and visually center it. See the figure
for placement help.

6 Choose Select > All On Active Artboard, and
then choose Object > Group. With the group
selected, choose Edit > Copy.

7 Click the Previous button (◀) in the status bar to
show the first artboard in the Document window, and choose Edit > Paste.

8 Using the Selection tool, drag the sign and resize it, making
it smaller, positioning it like you see in the figure. Drag the
flower pot into position next to the right side of the door.

9 Choose File > Save and then File > Close.

Review questions

1 What are the basic tools for creating shapes?

2 How do you select a shape with no fill?

3 How do you draw a square?

4 How do you change the number of sides on a polygon as you draw?

5 Name two ways you can combine several shapes into one.

6 How can you convert a raster image to editable vector shapes?

Review answers

1 There are six basic shape tools: Rectangle, Rounded Rectangle, Ellipse, Polygon, Star, and Flare. To tear off a group of tools from the Tools panel, position the pointer over the tool that appears in the Tools panel and hold down the mouse button until the group of tools appears. Without releasing the mouse button, drag to the triangle on the right side of the group and then release the mouse button to tear off the group.

2 Items that have no fill can be selected by clicking the stroke.

3 To draw a square, select the Rectangle tool in the Tools panel. Hold down the Shift key and drag to draw the square, or click the artboard to enter equal dimensions for the width and height in the Rectangle dialog box.

4 To change the number of sides on a polygon as you draw, select the Polygon tool in the Tools panel. Start dragging to draw the shape, and hold down the Down Arrow key to reduce the number of sides and the Up Arrow key to increase the number of sides.

5 Using the Shape Builder tool, you can visually and intuitively merge, delete, fill, and edit overlapping shapes and paths directly in the artwork. You can also use the Pathfinder effects to create new shapes out of overlapping objects. You can apply Pathfinder effects by using the Effects menu or the Pathfinder panel.

6 If you want to base a new drawing on an existing piece of artwork, you can trace it. To convert the tracing to paths, click Expand in the Control panel or choose Object > Image Trace > Expand. Use this method if you want to work with the components of the traced artwork as individual objects. The resulting paths are grouped.

4 TRANSFORMING OBJECTS

Lesson overview

In this lesson, you'll learn how to do the following:

- Add, edit, rename, and reorder artboards in an existing document.
- Navigate artboards.
- Select individual objects, objects in a group, and parts of an object.
- Move, scale, and rotate objects using a variety of methods.
- Work with Smart Guides.
- Reflect, shear, and distort objects.
- Adjust the perspective of an object.
- Apply multiple transformations.
- Apply a distortion effect.
- Repeat transformations quickly and easily.
- Copy to multiple artboards.

 This lesson takes approximately an hour to complete. If needed, remove the previous lesson folder from your hard disk and copy the Lesson04 folder onto it.

You can modify objects in many ways as you create artwork, by quickly and precisely controlling their size, shape, and orientation. In this lesson, you'll explore creating and editing artboards, the various Transform commands, and specialized tools, while creating several pieces of artwork.

Getting started

In this lesson, you'll create content and use it to create a flyer, a save the date card, an envelope, and a hang tag. Before you begin, you'll restore the default preferences for Adobe Illustrator, and then open a file containing a composite of the finished artwork to see what you'll create.

1   To ensure that the tools and panels function exactly as described in this lesson, delete or deactivate (by renaming) the Adobe Illustrator CS6 preferences file. See "Restoring default preferences" on page 3.

2   Start Adobe Illustrator CS6.

●   **Note:** If you have not already done so, copy the Lesson04 folder from the Lessons folder on the *Adobe Illustrator CS6 Classroom in a Book* CD onto your hard disk. See "Copying the Classroom in a Book files" on page 2.

3   Choose File > Open, and open the L4end_1.ai file in the Lesson04 folder, located in the Lessons folder on your hard disk.

This file contains the three pieces of finished artwork: a flyer, a save the date card (front and back), and an envelope. This lesson contains a fictitious business name, address, and website address, made up for the purposes of the project.

4   Choose View > Fit All In Window, and leave the artwork on-screen as you work. If you don't want to leave the file open, choose File > Close (without saving).

To begin working, you'll open an existing art file set up for the flyer artwork.

●   **Note:** In Mac OS, you may need to click the round, green button in the upper-left corner of the Document window to maximize the window's size.

5   Choose File > Open to open the L4start_1.ai file in the Lesson04 folder, located in the Lessons folder on your hard disk. This file has been saved with the rulers showing.

6   Choose File > Save As. In the Save As dialog box, name the file **recycle.ai**, and navigate to the Lesson04 folder. Leave the Save As Type option set to Adobe Illustrator (*.AI) (Windows) or the Format option set to Adobe Illustrator (ai) (Mac OS), and then click Save. In the Illustrator Options dialog box, leave the Illustrator options at their default settings and then click OK.

●   **Note:** If you don't see "Reset Essentials" in the Workspace menu, choose Window > Workspace > Essentials before choosing Window > Workspace > Reset Essentials.

7   Choose Window > Workspace > Reset Essentials.

Working with artboards

Artboards represent the regions that can contain printable artwork, similar to pages in Adobe InDesign. You can use multiple artboards for creating a variety of things, such as multiple-page PDF files, printed pages with different sizes or different elements, independent elements for websites, video storyboards, or individual items for animation.

Adding artboards to the document

You can add and remove artboards at any time while working in a document. You can create artboards in different sizes, resize them with the Artboard tool or Artboards panel, and position them anywhere in the Document window. All artboards are numbered and can have a unique name assigned to them.

Next, you will add more artboards to create the save the date card (front and back) and envelope.

1   Choose View > Fit Artboard In Window. This is the first artboard.

2   Press the spacebar to temporarily access the Hand tool (✋). Drag the artboard to the left until you see the canvas off the right side of the artboard.

3   Select the Artboard tool (⊞) in the Tools panel. Position the Artboard tool cursor to the right of the existing artboard and in line with the top edge of the existing artboard until a green alignment guide appears. Drag down and to the right to create an artboard that is 9 in (width) by 4 in (height). The measurement label indicates when the artboard is the correct size.

▶ **Tip:** If you zoom in on an artboard, the measurement label has smaller increments.

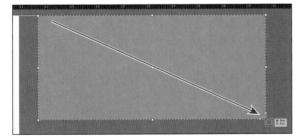

4   Click the New Artboard button (▣) in the Control panel. This allows you to create a duplicate of the last selected artboard.

5   Position the pointer below the lower-left corner of the new artboard. When a vertical green alignment guide appears, click to create a new artboard. This is artboard #3.

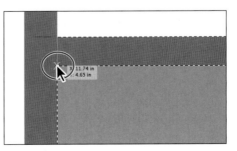

6   Select the Selection tool (▶) in the Tools panel.

7 Click the Artboards panel icon (▦) on the right side of the workspace to expand the Artboards panel.

Notice that Artboard 3 is highlighted in the panel. The active artboard is always highlighted in this panel.

The Artboards panel allows you to see how many artboards the document currently contains. It also allows you to reorder, rename, add, and delete artboards and to choose many other options related to artboards.

Next, you will create a copy of an artboard using this panel.

8 Click the New Artboard button (▦) at the bottom of the panel to create a copy of Artboard 3, called Artboard 4.

Notice that a copy is placed to the right of Artboard 2 in the Document window (the first artboard you created).

▶ **Tip:** With the Artboard tool (⊞), you can also copy an artboard by holding down the Alt (Windows) or Option (Mac OS) key and dragging it until the copied artboard clears the original. When creating new artboards, you can place them anywhere; you can even overlap them.

9 Click the Artboards panel icon (▦) to collapse the panel.

10 Choose View > Fit All In Window.

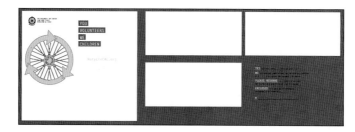

Editing artboards

You can edit or delete artboards at any time by using the Artboard tool, menu commands, or the Artboards panel. Next, you will reposition and change the sizes of several of the artboards using multiple methods.

1 Select the Artboard tool (⊞) in the Tools panel, and click Artboard 4, on the right, to select it.

Next, you will resize an artboard by entering values in the Control panel.

2 Select the upper-left point in the reference point locator (▦) in the Control panel.

This allows you to resize an artboard from the upper-left corner of the artboard. By default, artboards are resized from their center.

3 With the artboard named "04 – Artboard 4" selected, notice the bounding points around the artboard and the dashed box. In the Control panel, change the width to **9.5 in** and press Enter or Return. Make sure that the height is **4 in**.

● **Note:** If you don't see the Width and Height fields in the Control panel, click the Artboard Options button (▤) in the Control panel and enter the values in the dialog box that appears.

You will see the Constrain Width and Height Proportions button (▨) in the Control panel, between the Width and Height fields. This button, if selected, allows both fields to change in proportion to each other.

Another way to resize an artboard is to drag the active artboard handles using the Artboard tool, which is what you'll do next.

4 With Artboard 4 (04 – Artboard 4) still selected, choose View > Fit Artboard In Window.

5 With the Artboard tool selected, drag the bottom-center bounding point of the artboard down until the height is approximately 4.15 in, as shown in the measurement label.

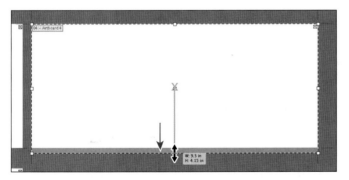

▶ **Tip:** To delete an artboard, select the artboard with the Artboard tool and either press Delete, click the Delete Artboard button (▥) in the Control panel, or click the Delete icon (☒) in the upper-right corner of an artboard. You can delete all but one artboard.

6 With Artboard 4 (04 – Artboard 4) still selected, click the Show Center Mark button (▣) in the Control panel to show a center mark for the active artboard only. The center mark can be used for many purposes, including working with video content.

7 Select the Selection tool (▶), and choose View > Fit All In Window.

Notice the black outline around the artboard, which indicates that Artboard 4 is the currently active artboard.

● **Note:** Clicking the Artboard Options button (▤) in the Control panel, with the Artboard tool selected also allows you to display the center mark for an artboard.

8   Click the Artboards panel icon (▦) to expand the Artboards panel (Window >
    Artboards). Click the name "Artboard 1" in the Artboards panel to make it the
    active artboard.

    This is the original artboard. Notice that a dark border appears around
    Artboard 1 in the Document window. This indicates that it is active. There can
    be only one active artboard at a time. Commands such as View > Fit Artboard
    In Window apply to the active artboard.

    Next, you will edit the active artboard size by choosing a preset value.

9   Click the Artboard Options button (▣) to the right
    of the name "Artboard 1" in the Artboards panel.
    This opens the Artboard Options dialog box.

    ▶ **Tip:** You also may have noticed that this button appears to the
    right of each artboard. It allows access to the artboard options for
    each artboard but also indicates the orientation of the artboard.

10 Locate the reference point locator (▦) to the left of
    the X and Y values, and make sure that the upper-left point is still selected. This
    ensures that the artboard will be resized from the upper-left corner.

11 Choose Letter from the Preset
    menu in the Artboard Options
    dialog box. Click OK.

    The Preset menu lets you change
    a selected artboard to a set size.
    Notice that the sizes in the Preset
    menu include typical print, video,
    tablet (Apple iPad, for instance),
    and web sizes. You can also fit the artboard to the artwork bounds or the selected
    art, which is a great way to fit an artboard to a logo, for instance.

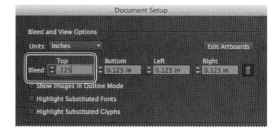

12 Click the Document Setup button in the Control panel.

    ▶ **Tip:** You can also access the Document Setup dialog box by choosing File > Document Setup.

▶ **Tip:** To learn more
about the Document
Setup dialog box,
search for "document
setup" in Illustrator Help
(Help > Illustrator Help).

13 In the Document Setup
    dialog box, change the
    Top Bleed option to **.125**
    by clicking the up arrow to
    the left of the field. Notice
    that all the values change
    together, because Make
    All Settings The Same (▣)
    is selected. Click OK.

The Document Setup dialog box contains many useful options for the current document, including units, type options, transparency settings, and more.

● **Note:** All changes made in the Document Setup dialog box apply to all artboards in the document.

14 Select the Artboard tool (⊞) in the Tools panel.

15 Click the upper-right artboard (04 – Artboard 4), and drag it below the original letter-sized artboard (01 – Artboard 1). Align the left edges of the artboards.

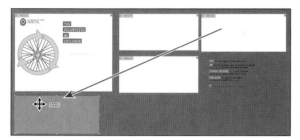

● **Note:** When you drag an artboard with content on it, the art moves with the artboard by default. If you want to move an artboard, but not the art on it, select the Artboard tool, and then click to deselect Move/Copy Artwork With Artboard (▣).

You can drag artboards at any time and even overlap them, if necessary.

16 Select the Selection tool (▶) in the Tools panel.

17 Choose Window > Workspace > Reset Essentials.

18 Choose File > Save.

Renaming artboards

By default, artboards are assigned a number and a name. When you navigate the artboards in a document, it can be helpful to name them.

Next, you are going to rename the artboards so that the names are more useful.

1 Click the Artboards panel icon (▦) to expand the Artboards panel.

2 Double-click the name "Artboard 1" in the Artboards panel. Change the name to **Flyer** and press Enter or Return.

▶ **Tip:** You can also change the name of an artboard by clicking the Artboard Options button (▤) in the Artboards panel and changing the name in the Artboard Options dialog box. Another way is to double-click the Artboard tool in the Tools panel to change the name for the currently active artboard in the Artboard Options dialog box. You can make an artboard the currently active artboard by clicking the artboard with the Selection tool.

You will now rename the rest of the artboards.

3 Double-click the name "Artboard 2" in the panel, and change the name to **Card-front**.

4 Do the same for the remaining two artboards, changing "Artboard 3" to **Card-back** and "Artboard 4" to **Envelope**.

5 Choose File > Save, and keep the Artboards panel expanded for the next steps.

Reordering artboards

When you navigate your document, the order in which the artboards appear can be important, especially if you are navigating the document using the Next artboard and Previous artboard buttons. By default, artboards are ordered according to the order in which they are created, but you can change that order. Next, you will reorder the artboards so that the two sides of the card are in the correct order.

1 With the Artboards panel still open, click the name "Envelope" in the panel. This makes the Envelope artboard the active artboard.

2 Choose View > Fit All In Window.

3 Position the pointer over the Envelope artboard listed in the Artboards panel. Click and drag up until a line appears between the Flyer and Card-front artboards. Release the mouse button.

▶ **Tip:** You can also reorder the artboards by selecting an artboard in the Artboards panel and clicking the Move Up or Move Down button at the bottom of the panel.

This moves the artboard up in order so that it becomes the second artboard. Notice that it does nothing to the artboards in the Document window.

4 Double-click to the right or left of the name "Flyer" in the Artboards panel to fit that artboard in the Document window.

5 Click the Next Artboard button (▶) in the lower-left corner of the Document window to navigate to the next artboard (Envelope). This fits the Envelope artboard in the Document window.

If you had not changed the order, the next artboard would have been the Card-front.

Now that the artboards are set up, you will concentrate on transforming artwork to create the content for the artboards.

Transforming content

Transforming content allows you to move, rotate, reflect, scale, and shear objects. Objects can be transformed using the Transform panel, selection tools, specialized tools, Transform commands, guides, Smart Guides, and more. In this part of the lesson, you will transform content using a variety of methods.

Working with rulers and guides

Rulers help you accurately place and measure objects. The point where 0 appears on each ruler (horizontal and vertical) is called the ruler origin. The ruler origin can be reset depending on which artboard is active. There are also two types of rulers available: global rulers and artboard rulers. Artboard rulers, which are the default, set the ruler origin to the upper-left corner of the active artboard. Global rulers set the ruler origin at the upper-left corner of the first artboard.

Guides are non-printing lines that help you align objects. You can create horizontal and vertical ruler guides by dragging them from the rulers. Next, you will create a guide and then reset the origin and create a new guide.

1   In the Artboards panel, double-click to the right or left of the Card-front artboard name to navigate to that artboard.

2   Shift-drag from the left vertical ruler toward the right to create a vertical guide at 1/2 inch on the horizontal ruler. The Shift key snaps the guide to the ruler units as you drag. Release the mouse button, and then the Shift key. The guide will be selected.

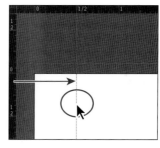

Tip: To change the units for a document, choose File > Document Setup or, with nothing selected, click the Document Setup button in the Control panel. You can also right-click (Windows) or Ctrl-click (Mac OS) either ruler to change the units.

If you don't see the rulers, you can choose View > Rulers > Show Rulers. Also, you will see finer increments in the rulers the more you zoom in to the artboard.

Note: Notice that the rulers show 0 at the upper-left corner of the artboard. If they don't show 0, choose View > Rulers > (and make sure that you see) Change To Global Rulers. If you see Change To Artboard Rulers, choose it.

3   With the guide selected, change the X value in the Control panel to **.25 in** and press Enter or Return.

Note: If you don't see the X value, you can click the word "Transform" or open the Transform panel (Window > Transform).

Guides are similar to drawn objects in that they can be selected like a drawn line, and they can be deleted by pressing the Backspace or Delete key.

4 Position the pointer in the upper-left corner of the Document window, where the rulers intersect (▦), and drag the pointer to the upper-right corner of the artboard, not the red bleed guides. The word "intersect" will appear.

As you drag, a cross hair in the window and in the rulers indicates the changing ruler origin. This sets the ruler origin (0,0) to the upper-right corner of the artboard.

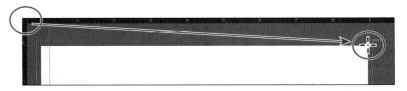

5 Shift-drag from the left vertical ruler toward the right to 1/4 inch inside the right edge of the artboard to create a new guide. Release the mouse button and then the key.

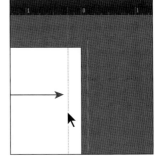

Look at the X value in the Control panel and, after releasing the mouse button, you should see -0.25 in. The X axis runs horizontal, and the Y axis runs vertical. Measurements to the right (horizontal) and below (vertical) the ruler origin are positive. Measurements to the left (horizontal) and above (vertical) the ruler origin are negative.

6 Position the pointer in the upper-left corner of the Document window, where the rulers intersect, and double-click to reset the ruler origin.

7 Choose View > Guides > Lock Guides to prevent them from being accidentally moved. Choose View > Fit All In Window.

The guides are no longer selected and are aqua in color, by default.

▶ **Tip:** To change guide settings, choose Edit > Preferences > Guides & Grid (Windows) or Illustrator > Preferences > Guides & Grid (Mac OS).

8 Choose File > Save.

Scaling objects

Objects are scaled by enlarging or reducing them horizontally (along the X axis) and vertically (along the Y axis) relative to a fixed reference point that you designate. If you don't designate an origin, objects are scaled from their center point. So far in the lessons, you scaled most content with the selection tools. In this lesson, you'll use several other methods to scale the objects.

First, you'll set the preference to scale strokes and effects. Then, you'll scale a logo by using the Scale command and aligning the logo to the guides provided.

1 Choose Edit > Preferences > General (Windows) or Illustrator > Preferences > General (Mac OS), and select Scale Strokes & Effects. This scales the stroke width of any object scaled in this lesson. Click OK.

Tip: You can also select Scale Strokes & Effects in the Transform panel.

2 Click to select the large yellow/green wheel logo on the Flyer artboard. Alt-drag (Windows) or Option-drag (Mac OS) the object to the upper-right artboard. Release the mouse button and then the key, when in position.

3 Select the Zoom tool (🔍) in the Tools panel, and click twice, slowly, on the new wheel logo to zoom in.

4 Choose View > Hide Edges. This hides the inside edges of the shapes, not the bounding box.

5 Double-click the Scale tool (⬚) in the Tools panel.

6 In the Scale dialog box, select the Preview option. Change Uniform to **50%**. Deselect and then select Preview to see the change in size. Click OK.

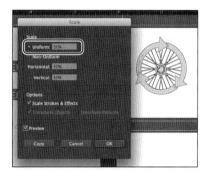

Tip: The Scale dialog box can also be accessed by choosing Object > Transform > Scale.

7 With the Selection tool (▶) selected, position the pointer over the left anchor point of the bottom, left arrow in the wheel. When you see the word "anchor" appear, drag the wheel to the left until the anchor snaps to the guide. The pointer will turn white when it is snapped.

Note: When snapping to a point, the snapping alignment depends on the position of the pointer, not the edges of the dragged object. Also, you can snap points to guides because the View > Snap To Point command is selected by default.

Note: You may need to turn off the Smart Guides in order to snap the content to the guide (View > Smart Guides). If you do turn them off, turn them back on after you have completed the step.

8 Choose View > Fit All In Window, and then choose View > Show Edges.

9 Choose View > Outline.

10 With the Selection tool, drag a marquee across the text that starts with, "YOU DONATE YOUR," and ends with, "KEEP MAKING ART," on the first artboard (Flyer) to select it all. Choose Edit > Copy.

11 Choose 3 Card-front from the Artboard Navigation menu in the lower-left corner of the Document window to return to the card artboard.

12 Choose Edit > Paste In Place.

This command pastes the grouped content in the same relative position on the card artboard as it was on the Flyer artboard.

Note: Depending on the resolution of your screen, the Transform options may not appear in the Control panel. If they do not appear, you can click the word "Transform" to see the Transform panel, or you can also choose Window > Transform.

13 In the Control panel, click the middle-left reference point of the reference point locator (⊞) to set the reference point. Click to select the Constrain Width And Height Proportions icon (⊞), located between the W and H fields. Type **75%** in the Width (W) field, and then press Enter or Return to decrease the size of the grouped text.

14 Choose View > Preview, and then choose File > Save.

You will position the text, along with other content, later in the lesson.

Reflecting objects

When you reflect an object, Illustrator creates a reflection of the object across an invisible vertical or horizontal axis. Copying objects while reflecting allows you to create a mirror image of the object, based on an invisible axis. In a similar way to scaling and rotating, when you reflect an object, you either designate the reference point or use the object's center point by default. Next, you'll move content onto an artboard and use the Reflect tool to flip it 90° across the vertical axis and copy it.

1 Choose View > Fit All In Window. Press Ctrl+– (Windows) or Command+– (Mac OS) twice to zoom out to see the bicycle off the left edge of the Flyer artboard.

2 With the Selection tool (⬉), click to select the bicycle. Choose Edit > Cut.

3 Choose 4 Card-back from the Artboard Navigation menu in the lower-left corner of the Document window to return to the card artboard.

4 Choose Edit > Paste to paste the bicycle in the center of the Document window.

5 With the Selection tool (⬉), drag the bicycle down into the lower-right corner of the artboard. Try to approximately align the right side of the bicycle with the right guide, using the figure as a guide. It doesn't have to be exact.

6 With the bicycle still selected, choose Edit > Copy and Edit > Paste In Front to put a copy directly on top.

7 Select the Reflect tool (⬕), which is nested within the Rotate tool (⟳) in the Tools panel. Click the left edge of the front bicycle tire (the word "anchor" or "path" may appear).

This will set the point of the axis on the left edge of the bicycle rather than the center, which is the default.

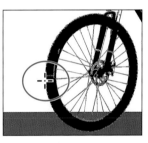

▶ **Tip:** You can reflect and copy in one step. With the Reflect tool (⬕) selected, Alt-click (Windows) or Option-click (Mac OS) to set a point to reflect around and open the Reflect dialog box, in one step. Select Vertical, and then click Copy.

8 With the bicycle copy still selected, position the pointer off the left edge and drag clockwise. As you are dragging, hold down the Shift key. When the measurement label shows −90°, release the mouse and then the modifier key.

The Shift key constrains the rotation to 45° as it is reflected. Leave the new bicycle where it is for now. You'll move it a bit later.

Rotating objects

Objects are rotated by turning them around a designated reference point. You can rotate objects by displaying their bounding boxes and moving the pointer to an outside corner. You can also rotate objects using the Transform panel to set a reference point and a rotation angle.

You'll rotate the wheels using the Rotate tool.

1   Choose 1 Flyer from the Artboard Navigation menu in the lower-left corner of the Document window. Select the Zoom tool (🔍), and drag a marquee across the small, black wheel logo in the upper-left corner of the Flyer artboard.

2   With the Selection tool (▶), select the small black wheel. Choose Object > Transform > Rotate.

By default, the wheel logo will rotate around its center.

▶ **Tip:** To access the Rotate dialog box, you can also double-click the Rotate tool (◯) in the Tools panel. The Transform panel (Window > Transform) also has a rotate option.

3   In the Rotate dialog box, make sure that Preview is selected. Change the angle to **20**, and then click OK to rotate the wheel around the center.

● **Note:** If you select an object and then select the Rotate tool, you can Alt-click (Windows) or Option-click (Mac OS) anywhere on the object (or artboard) to set a reference point and open the Rotate dialog box.

4   Choose View > Fit All In Window. Select the Selection tool (▶) and, with the small wheel logo selected, press the Shift key and click the text to the right of logo that begins, "THE CHILDREN'S ART CENTER," to select both. Choose Edit > Cut.

5   Choose 2 Envelope from the Artboard Navigation menu.

6   Choose Edit > Paste In Place. Click the word "Transform" in the Control panel to open the Transform panel. With the middle, left point chosen in the reference point locator (▦), change the X value to **1.7 in** and the Y value to **0.6 in**. Press Enter or Return to hide the panel again.

Next, you'll rotate content manually, using the Rotate tool.

7   Choose View > Fit All In Window.

8   With the Selection tool, click to select the large yellow/green wheel logo on the Flyer artboard. Choose View > Hide Edges.

9   Select the Rotate tool (⟳) which is nested within the Reflect tool (⟲) in the Tools panel. Click in the approximate center of the wheel part of the logo to set the reference point (✛) (just above where the reference point is by default). Position the pointer to the right of the wheel logo, and drag up. Notice that the movement is constrained to a circle rotating around the reference point. When the measurement label shows approximately 20°, release the mouse button.

Next, you will rotate the wheel logo on the 3 Card-front artboard in the same way.

10 Choose 3 Card-front from the Artboard Navigation menu in the lower-left corner of the Document window. Select the Selection tool, and click to select the yellow/green wheel logo.

11 Select the Rotate tool (⟳), and click in the approximate center of the wheel part of the logo to set the reference point (✛) (just above where the reference point is by default). Position the pointer to the right of the wheel logo, and drag up. When the measurement label shows approximately 20°, release the mouse button.

12 Choose View > Show Edges, and then choose File > Save.

Distorting objects

You can distort the original shapes of objects in different ways, using various tools. Now, you'll distort a logo shape, first using the Pucker & Bloat effect, and then applying the Twist effect to twirl the shape.

1   Click the First button (◀) in the status bar to navigate to the first artboard.

2   Click the Layers panel icon to open the panel, and then click the visibility column to the left of the Flyer Background layer name to show that content.

3   Select the Selection tool (▶), and click to select the white triangle in the lower-right corner of the Flyer artboard.

4   Choose Effect > Distort & Transform > Pucker & Bloat.

5 In the Pucker & Bloat dialog box, select Preview and drag the slider to the left to change the value to roughly **–60%**, which distorts the triangle. Click OK.

6 Choose Effect > Distort & Transform > Twist. Change the Angle to **20**, select Preview if not already selected, and then click OK.

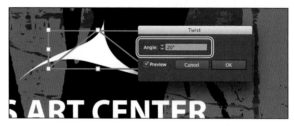

Twist distortion is applied as an effect, which maintains the original shape and lets you remove or edit the effect at any time, in the Appearance panel. Learn more about using effects in Lesson 12, "Applying Effects."

7 Choose Select > Deselect and then File > Save.

Shearing objects

Shearing an object slants, or skews, the sides of the object along the axis you specify, keeping opposite sides parallel and making the object asymmetrical.

Next, you'll copy a bicycle object and apply shear to it.

1 Click the Artboards panel tab. Double-click the 4 to the left of the Card-back artboard name. Click the Artboards panel tab to collapse the panel group.

2 Select the Selection tool (▶). Click to select the bicycle shape on the left. Choose Object > Hide > Selection. Click to select the remaining bicycle shape.

3 Choose Edit > Copy, and then choose Edit > Paste In Front to paste a copy directly on top of the original.

4 Select the Shear tool (↗), nested within the Scale tool (⬜) in the Tools panel. Position the pointer at the bottom of the bicycle shape, between the wheels, and click to set the reference point.

5   Drag from the approximate center of the bicycle to the left, and stop when the sheared copy looks like what you see in the figure. Release the mouse button.

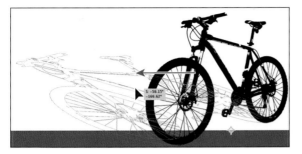

6   Change the opacity in the Control panel to **20%.**

7   Choose Object > Arrange > Send Backward to put the copy behind the original bicycle shape.

▶ **Tip:** In the Transform panel, you can also shear, rotate, and change the scale as well as the position on the X and Y axes.

8   Choose Object > Show All to show and select the reflected bicycle copy you hid earlier. Choose Edit > Cut to cut the bicycle from the artboard.

9   Choose 2 Envelope from the Artboard Navigation menu in the lower-left corner of the Document window. Choose Edit > Paste.

10 Choose Select > Deselect and then File > Save.

Positioning objects precisely

You can use the Smart Guides and the Transform panel to move objects to exact coordinates on the X and Y axes and to control the position of objects in relation to the edge of the artboard.

You'll add content to the backgrounds of both sides of the cards and then position it precisely.

1   Choose View > Fit All In Window to see all of the artboards.

2   Press Ctrl+– (Windows) or Command+– (Mac OS) once to zoom out. You should see the two images off the left edge of the Flyer artboard.

3 With the Selection tool (▶), click to select the top, darker image.

4 Click the Artboards panel icon (▦), if the panel isn't showing. Click once on the 3 Card-front artboard name in the list to make it the active artboard.

The ruler origin is now in the upper-left corner of that artboard.

5 Click the upper-left point of the reference point locator (▦) in the Control panel. Then, change the X value to **0** and the Y value to **0**.

6 Choose Object > Arrange > Send to Back, and then Select > Deselect.

The image should now be precisely positioned on the artboard, since it was the same size as the artboard to begin with.

7 Choose View > Fit Artboard In Window to fit the 3 Card-front artboard in the Document window.

8 With the Selection tool, hold down the Shift key and, in the text on the right, click/drag to the left from the word, "YOU," until the right edge of the "h" in "MAY 19th" is aligned with the right guide. Release the mouse button and then the Shift key.

9   In the Artboards panel, click once on the 4 Card-back artboard name in the list
    to make it the active artboard. Click the Artboards panel tab to collapse
    the panel group.

10 Choose View > Fit All In Window to see all of the artboards.

11 Press Ctrl+– (Windows) or Command+– (Mac OS) once to zoom out. You
    should see the second, lighter image off the left edge of the Flyer artboard.

12 With the Selection tool, click to select the image off the left side of the
    Flyer artboard.

13 With the upper-left point of the reference
    point locator (▦) selected in the Control panel,
    change the X value to **0** and the Y value to **0**.

14 Choose Object > Arrange > Send to Back.

15 Choose View > Fit Artboard In Window to fit
    the 4 Card-back artboard in the Document window.

16 Press Ctrl+– (Windows) or Command+– (Mac OS) twice to zoom out. You
    should see the text group off the right edge of the artboard.

17 With the Selection tool, click to select the text
    group. With the upper-left point of the reference
    point locator (▦) in the Control panel selected,
    change the X value to **0** and the Y value to **0**.

18 Choose View > Fit Artboard In Window.

19 Using the Selection tool, position the pointer
    over the upper-left word, "YES," and drag
    the text group down and to the right. When
    the measurement label shows dX: 0.25 in and
    dY: 0.5 in, release the mouse button.

● **Note:** The dX
or dY appears as a
negative value in the
measurement label
if you drag content
up or to the left on
an artboard.

The dY in the measurement label indicates the distance moved along the Y axis
(vertically), and the dX indicates the distance moved along the X axis (horizontally).

20 With the text group still selected, choose Object > Arrange > Bring To Front, to
    bring the text on top of the other content on the artboard.

21 Click away from the artwork to deselect it, and then choose File > Save.

Changing perspective

Next, you'll use the Free Transform tool to change the perspective of content. The Free Transform tool is a multipurpose tool that, besides letting you change the perspective of an object, combines the functions of scaling, shearing, reflecting, and rotating.

1 Choose 2 Envelope from the Artboard Navigation menu in the lower-left corner of the Document window.

2 Click to select the bicycle on the artboard with the Selection tool (↖). Select the Free Transform tool (◼) in the Tools panel.

3 Position the pointer over the upper-middle point of the bounding box around the bicycle. *Extra attention is required in the rest of this step, so follow directions closely.* Slowly drag the point down and to the right. *While dragging,* press the Control (Windows) or Command (Mac OS)

key to transform the object. When the measurement label shows a width of approximately 4.75 in and a height of approximately 1.5 in, release the mouse button and then the modifier key.

Pressing the Ctrl (Windows) or Command (Mac OS) key as you drag distorts an object from the anchor point or bounding box handle that you're dragging.

● **Note:** Take your time on this step. The process is specific, and you can always choose to undo if you make a mistake.

4 Position the pointer over the upper-left corner of the bounding box, and begin dragging down. *While dragging,* press the Shift+Control+Alt (Windows) or Shift+Option+Command (Mac OS) keys to transform the object. When the measurement label shows a width of approximately

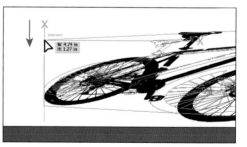

4.75 in and a height of approximately 1.25 in, release the mouse button and then the modifier keys. If the values you see don't match exactly, that's okay.

5 With the Selection tool, drag the bicycle to the left until the left edge is close to the edge of the artboard. Change the Opacity to **20%** in the Control panel. See the figure for placement help.

6 Choose Select > Deselect, and then File > Save.

Applying multiple transformations

Next, you will learn about the Transform Each command and how to apply a series of transformations multiple times.

1 With the 2 Envelope artboard showing in the Document window, select the Zoom tool (🔍), and drag a marquee across the upper-left corner of the artboard. Make sure you can still see the corner of the artboard and the wheel.

2 With the Selection tool (▶), double-click the small wheel logo. Click to select the wheel shape (not the "RE-CYCLE IT" text), and then choose Edit > Copy.

3 Press the Escape key to exit Isolation mode, and then choose Edit > Paste In Front.

4 Choose Object > Transform > Transform Each. In the Transform Each dialog box, select Preview. Ensure that center point of the reference point locator (▦) is selected in the dialog box. Change the Move Horizontal to **−0.45 in**. Change the Rotate Angle to **20**. Leave the other settings as they are, and then click **Copy**.

> **Tip:** You can also apply transformations to selected content as an effect (Effect > Distort & Transform > Transform). Transforming as an effect has the advantage of letting you change or remove the transformation in the Appearance panel at any time. You will learn more about the Appearance panel in Lesson 13, "Applying Appearance Attributes and Graphic Styles."

The options in the Transform Each dialog box let you apply multiple types of transformations in a random manner, if you want. It also allows you to transform multiple selected objects on the artboard, independently of each other.

5 With the new wheel selected, change the Fill color to a darker gray (C=0 M=0 Y=0 K=60) in the Control panel and choose Object > Arrange > Send To Back.

6 Choose Object > Transform > Transform Again to create one more wheel.

7 With the new wheel selected, change the Fill color to a lighter gray (C=0 M=0 Y=0 K=30) in the Control panel and choose Object > Arrange > Send To Back.

8 Press Ctrl+D (Windows) or Command+D (Mac OS) to transform the last selected wheel, creating a total of four wheel shapes.

9 Change the Fill color of the last wheel to a lighter gray (C=0 M=0 Y=0 K=10) in the Control panel, and choose Object > Arrange > Send To Back.

10 Choose File > Save and File > Close.

Using the Free Distort effect

Now, you'll explore a slightly different way of distorting objects. Free Distort is an effect that lets you distort a selection by moving any of its four corner points.

1 Choose File > Open, and open the L4start_2.ai file in the Lesson04 folder, located in the Lessons folder on your hard disk.

2 Choose File > Save As. In the Save As dialog box, change the name to **hangtags.ai**, and navigate to the Lesson04 folder. Leave the Save As Type option set to Adobe Illustrator (*.AI) (Windows) or the Format option set to Adobe Illustrator (ai) (Mac OS), and then click Save. In the Illustrator Options dialog box, leave the Illustrator options at their default settings, and then click OK.

3 Choose View > Fit Artboard In Window to fit Artboard 1 in the window.

▶ **Tip:** In this case, the text was selected with the Selection tool, and the Type > Create Outlines command was applied to convert the text to shapes. It is not necessary to apply the Create Outlines command to text prior to applying the Free Distort command.

4 With the Selection tool (▶), double-click the text, "RE-CYCLE IT" to enter Isolation mode. Click to select the text shapes.

5 Choose Effect > Distort & Transform > Free Distort.

6 In the Free Distort dialog box, drag one or more of the handles to distort the selection. In the figure, we dragged the upper-right point up and the bottom-right point in toward the center. Click OK.

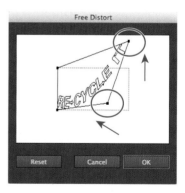

7 Double-click outside the artwork to exit Isolation mode and to deselect it.

Now, you'll create multiple copies of the business card content.

▶ **Tip:** To print the cards on a single page, choose File > Print and select Ignore Artboards to fit all the artboards on a single page.

8 Choose Select > All On Active Artboard.

9 Choose Edit > Cut.

10 Choose View > Fit All In Window, and then choose Edit > Paste On All Artboards.

11 Choose Select > Deselect. Then, choose View > Guides > Hide Guides to hide the red bleed guides.

12 Choose File > Save and then File > Close.

Review questions

1 Name two ways to change the size of an existing active artboard.

2 How can you rename an artboard?

3 What is the ruler origin?

4 Explain several ways you can resize an object.

5 What transformations can you make using the Transform panel?

6 What does the square icon (▦) indicate, and how does it affect transformations?

Review answers

1 Double-click the Artboard tool (⌗), and edit the dimensions of the active artboard in the Artboard Options dialog box. Select the Artboard tool, position the pointer over an edge or corner of the artboard, and drag to resize. Select the Artboard tool, click in an artboard in the Document window and change the dimensions in the Control panel.

2 To rename an artboard, you can select the Artboard tool and click to select an artboard. Then, change the name in the Name field in the Control panel. You can also double-click the name of the artboard in the Artboards panel to rename it or click the Options button in the Artboards panel to enter the name in the Artboard Options dialog box.

3 The ruler origin is the point where 0 (zero) appears on each ruler. By default, the ruler origin is set to be 0 (zero) in the top-left corner of the active artboard.

4 You can resize an object in several ways: By selecting it and dragging handles on its bounding box, by using the Scale tool or the Transform panel, or by choosing Object > Transform > Scale to specify exact dimensions. You can also scale by choosing Effect > Distort & Transform > Transform.

5 You use the Transform panel for making the following transformations: Moving or precisely placing objects in your artwork (by specifying the X and Y coordinates and the reference point), scaling, rotating, shearing, and flipping.

6 The square icon, called the reference point locator, indicates the bounding box of the selected objects. Select a reference point in the square to indicate the reference point from which the objects (as a group) move, scale, rotate, shear, or reflect.

5 DRAWING WITH THE PEN AND PENCIL TOOLS

Lesson overview

In this lesson, you'll learn how to do the following:

- Draw curved lines.

- Draw straight lines.

- Use template layers.

- End path segments and split lines.

- Select and adjust curve segments.

- Create dashed lines and add arrowheads.

- Draw and edit with the Pencil tool.

 This lesson takes approximately an hour and a half to complete. If needed, remove the previous lesson folder from your hard disk and copy the Lesson05 folder onto it.

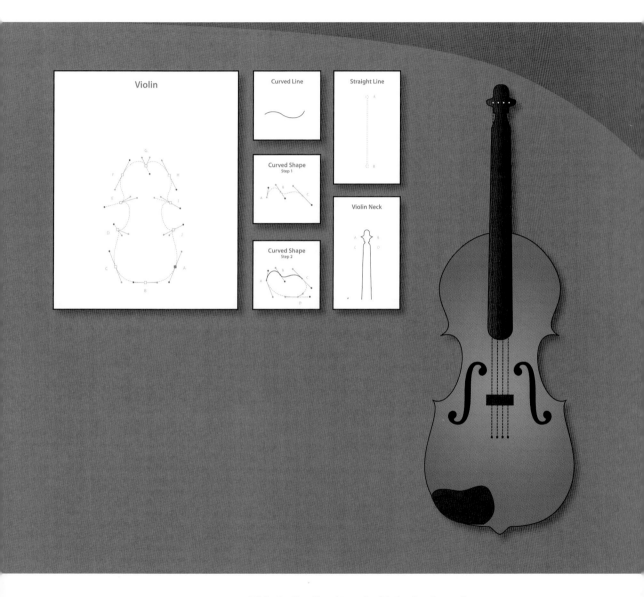

While the Pencil tool is preferable for drawing and editing freeform lines, the Pen tool is excellent for drawing precisely, including straight lines, Bezier curves, and complex shapes. You'll practice using the Pen tool on a blank artboard and then use it to create an illustration of a violin.

Getting started

In the first part of this lesson, you learn how to manipulate the Pen tool on a blank artboard.

1 To ensure that the tools and panels function exactly as described in this lesson, delete or deactivate (by renaming) the Adobe Illustrator CS6 preferences file. See "Restoring default preferences" on page 3.

2 Start Adobe Illustrator CS6.

   ● **Note:** If you have not already done so, copy the Lesson05 folder from the Lessons folder on the *Adobe Illustrator CS6 Classroom in a Book* CD onto your hard disk. See "Copying the Classroom in a Book files" on page 2.

● **Note:** In Mac OS, when opening lesson files, you may need to click the round, green button in the upper-left corner of the Document window to maximize the window's size.

3 Open the L5start_1.ai file in the Lesson05 folder, located in the Lessons folder on your hard disk.

   The top artboard shows the path that you will create. Use the bottom artboard for this exercise.

4 Choose File > Save As. In the Save As dialog box, navigate to the Lesson05 folder and open it. Rename the file to **path1.ai**. Choose Adobe Illustrator (*.AI) from the Save As Type menu (Windows), or choose Adobe Illustrator (ai) from the Format menu (Mac OS). Click Save and, in the Illustrator Options dialog box, leave the default settings, and then click OK.

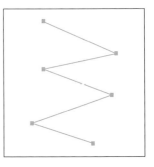

Starting with the Pen tool

1 Press Alt+Ctrl+0 (zero) (Windows) or Option+Command+0 (zero) (Mac OS) to fit both artboards in the window. Then, hold down the Shift key and press the Tab key once to close all the panels except for the Tools panel. You don't need the panels for the first part of this lesson.

2 Choose View > Smart Guides to deselect the Smart Guides.

3 In the Control panel, click the Fill color and choose the None swatch (☐). Then, click the Stroke color and make sure that the black swatch is selected.

4 Make sure the Stroke weight is 1 pt in the Control panel.

When you draw with the Pen tool, it is best to have no fill on the path you create. You can add a fill later, if necessary.

● **Note:** If you see a cross hair instead of the Pen icon, the Caps Lock key is active. Caps Lock turns tool icons into cross hairs for increased precision.

5 Select the Pen tool (✐) in the Tools panel. Notice the asterisk next to the Pen icon (✎.), indicating that you are starting a path. Click toward the top of the bottom artboard to set the first point, and then move the pointer to the right of the original anchor point. The asterisk disappears.

6 Click down and to the right of the original point to create the next anchor point in the path.

● **Note:** The first segment you draw is not visible until you click a second anchor point. If direction handles appear, you have accidentally dragged with the Pen tool; choose Edit > Undo Pen, and then click again.

7 Click a third anchor point beneath the initial anchor point to create a zigzag pattern. Create a zigzag that has six anchor points, which means you will click the artboard a total of six times.

One of the many benefits of using the Pen tool is that you can create custom paths and continue to edit the anchor points that make up the path. Notice that only the last anchor point is selected (not hollow), like the rest of the anchor points.

Next, you'll see how the Selection tools work with the Pen tool.

8 Select the Selection tool (▶) in the Tools panel, and position the pointer directly over the zigzag path. When the pointer shows a solid black box (▶.) next to it, click to select the path and all of the anchor points. Notice that all of the anchor points become solid, signifying that all anchor points are selected. Drag the path to a new location anywhere on the artboard. All the anchor points travel together, maintaining the zigzag path.

9 Deselect the zigzag path in one of the following ways:

• With the Selection tool, click an empty area of the artboard.

• Choose Select > Deselect.

• If the Pen tool were still selected, you could Ctrl-click (Windows) or Command-click (Mac OS) in a blank area of the artboard to deselect the path. This temporarily selects the Selection tool. When you release the Ctrl or Command key, the Pen tool is again selected.

10 In the Tools panel, select the Direct Selection tool (▷) and position the pointer over any anchor point. The pointer shows a small box with a dot in the center (▷.), indicating that, if you click, you will select an anchor point. Click that same point in the zigzag, or drag a marquee selection around an anchor point.

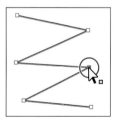

The selected anchor point turns solid, and the deselected anchor points are hollow.

11 With the anchor point selected, drag to reposition it. The anchor point moves, but the others remain stationary. Use this technique to edit a path.

12 Choose Select > Deselect.

Note: If the entire zigzag path disappears, choose Edit > Undo Cut and try again.

13 With the Direct Selection tool, click any line segment that is between two anchor points, and then choose Edit > Cut. This cuts only the selected segment from the zigzag.

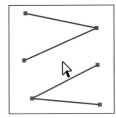

When you position the pointer over a line segment *that is not already selected*, a black square appears next to the Direct Selection tool pointer ( ). The solid square indicates that you are selecting a line segment.

14 Select the Pen tool, and position the pointer over one of the end anchor points that was connected to the line segment that was cut. Notice that the Pen tool shows a forward slash (/), indicating a continuation of an existing path. Click the point. Notice that it becomes solid. Only active points appear solid.

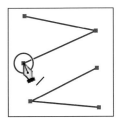

15 Position the pointer over the other anchor point that was connected to the cut line segment. The pointer now shows a merge symbol next to it ( ), indicating that you are connecting to another path. Click the point to reconnect the paths.

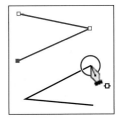

16 Choose File > Save and then File > Close.

Creating straight lines

In Lesson 4, "Transforming Objects," you learned that using the Shift key and Smart Guides in combination with shape tools constrains the shape of objects. The Shift key and Smart Guides also constrain the Pen tool to create paths of 45°.

Next, you will learn how to draw straight lines and constrain angles.

1 Open the L5start_2.ai file in the Lesson05 folder, located in the Lessons folder on your hard disk. The top artboard shows the path that you will create. Use the bottom artboard for this exercise.

2 Choose File > Save As. In the Save As dialog box, navigate to the Lesson05 folder and open it. Name the file **path2.ai**. Choose Adobe Illustrator (*.AI) from the Save As Type menu (Windows), or choose Adobe Illustrator (ai) from the Format menu (Mac OS). Click Save and, in the Illustrator Options dialog box, leave the default settings and then click OK.

3 Choose View > Smart Guides to select the Smart Guides, and then choose View> Fit All In Window.

4 With the Pen tool () selected, and without dragging, click once on the left side of the bottom artboard (toward the top) to set the first point.

5 Move the pointer to the right of the original anchor point 1.5 inches, as indicated by the measurement label. It doesn't have to be exact. A green construction guide appears when the pointer is vertically aligned with the previous anchor point. Click to set another anchor point.

▶ **Tip:** If Smart Guides are deselected, the measurement label and construction guides won't appear. If you don't use Smart Guides, you can press the Shift key and click to create straight lines.

As you've learned in previous lessons, the measurement label and construction guide are part of the Smart Guides. When working with the Pen tool, you will learn that you can achieve finer measurements in the measurement label when you zoom in.

6 Click to set three more points, following the same shape as shown in the top half of the artboard.

● **Note:** The points you set don't have to be in exactly the same position as the path at the top of the artboard. Also, the measurement you see in your measurement label may not match what you see in the figure, and that's okay.

7 Press the Shift key, and move the pointer to the right and down, until it is aligned with the bottom two points and the green alignment guide appears. Click to set an anchor point, and then release the modifier key.

Pressing the Shift key creates angled lines constrained to 45˚. The Smart Guides will show a green construction guide when the pointer is aligned with the existing points, which can be very useful when you are drawing paths with straight lines.

8 Position the pointer below the last point, and click to set the last anchor point for the shape.

9 Choose File > Save, and then choose File > Close.

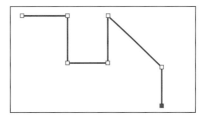

Creating curved paths

In this part of the lesson, you'll learn how to draw smooth, curved lines with the Pen tool. In vector drawing applications, such as Illustrator, you draw a curve, called a Bezier curve, with control points. By setting anchor points and dragging direction handles, you can define the shape of the curve. Although drawing curves this way can take some time to learn, it gives you the greatest control and flexibility in creating paths.

1 Open the L5start_3.ai file in the Lesson05 folder. Choose View > Fit All In Window.

● **Note:** See Lesson 8, "Working with Layers," for information about creating layers.

This file contains a template layer that you can trace to practice using the Pen tool (✐). You will draw in the bottom artboard for this exercise.

2 Choose File > Save As. In the Save As dialog box, navigate to the Lesson05 folder. Change the name to **path3.ai**. Choose Adobe Illustrator (*.AI) from the Save As Type menu (Windows), or choose Adobe Illustrator (ai) from the Format menu (Mac OS). Click Save and, in the Illustrator Options dialog box, leave the default settings and then click OK.

3 In the Control panel, click the Fill color (▢) and choose the None swatch (☑). Then, click the Stroke color (▣) and make sure that the black swatch is selected.

4 Make sure the Stroke weight is 1 pt in the Control panel.

5 With the Pen tool (✐), click on the left side of the bottom artboard to create the initial anchor point. Click another location, and drag away from the point to create a curved path.

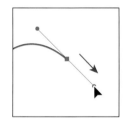

Continue clicking and dragging at different locations on the page. The goal for this exercise is not to create anything specific but to get accustomed to the feel of the Bezier curve.

Notice that as you drag, direction handles appear. Direction handles consist of direction lines that end in round direction points. The angle and length of the direction handles determine the shape and size of the curve. Direction handles do not print and are not visible when the anchor is inactive.

6 Choose Select > Deselect.

7 Select the Direct Selection tool (▸) in the Tools panel, and click the line between two points (called a line segment) to display the direction handles. Click and drag the end of a direction handle as you see in the figure. Moving the direction handles reshapes the curve.

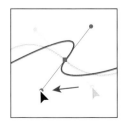

8 Leave the file open for the next section.

Components of a path

As you draw, you create a line called a path. A path is made up of one or more straight or curved segments. The beginning and end of each segment are marked by anchor points, which work like pins holding a wire in place. A path can be closed (for example, a circle) or open, with distinct endpoints (for example, a wavy line). You change the shape of a path by dragging its anchor points, the direction points at the end of direction lines that appear at anchor points, or the path segment itself.

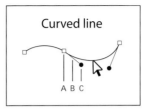

Curved line

A. Anchor point
B. Direction line
C. Direction point

Paths can have two kinds of anchor points: corner points and smooth points. At a corner point, a path abruptly changes direction. At a smooth point, path segments are connected as a continuous curve.

You can draw a path using any combination of corner and smooth points. If you draw the wrong kind of point, you can always change it.

—From Illustrator Help

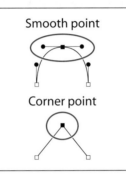

Smooth point

Corner point

Building a curve

In this part of the lesson, you will learn how to control the direction handles to control curves. You will use the top artboard to trace shapes.

1   Press Z to switch to the Zoom tool (🔍), and drag a marquee around the curve in the top artboard, labeled A.

2   Choose View > Smart Guides to deselect them.

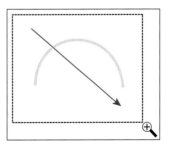

● **Note:** The artboard
may scroll as you drag.
If you lose visibility
of the curve, choose
View > Zoom Out until
you see the curve and
anchor point. Pressing
the spacebar allows you
to use the Hand tool to
reposition the artwork.

3 Select the Pen tool (✐) in the Tools panel. Click
at the base of the left side of the arch, and drag
up to create a direction line going the same
direction as the arch. Remember to always
follow the direction of the curve. Release the
mouse button when the direction line is above
the gray arch.

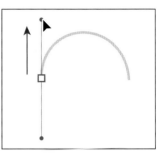

▶ **Tip:** If you make a mistake while drawing with the
Pen tool, choose Edit > Undo Pen to undo the points you
have set.

4 Click the lower-right base of the gray arch path,
and drag down. Release the mouse button when
the path you are creating looks like the arch.

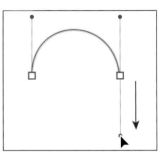

● **Note:** Pulling the direction handle longer makes a steeper
slope; when the direction handle is shorter, the slope is flatter.

5 If the path you created is not aligned exactly
with the template, use the Direct Selection
tool (▷) to select the anchor points one at a
time. Then, adjust the direction handles until your path follows the template
more accurately.

6 Select the Selection tool (▶), and click the artboard in an area with no objects,
or choose Select > Deselect. Deselecting the first path allows you to create a new
path. If you click somewhere on the artboard with the Pen tool while path A is
still selected, the path connects to the next point you draw.

▶ **Tip:** To deselect objects, you can also press the Ctrl (Windows) or Command (Mac OS) key to
temporarily switch to the Selection or Direct Selection tool, whichever was last used. Then, click the
artboard where there are no objects.

7 Choose File > Save.

8 Zoom out to see path B.

9 Select the Pen tool, and drag up from the left
base of path B in the direction of the arch. Click
and drag down on the next square point to
the right, adjusting the arch with the direction
handle before you release the mouse button.
This creates the same type of arch shape you
created for path A.

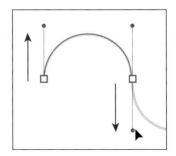

● **Note:** Don't worry if the path you draw is not exact. You
can correct the line with the Direct Selection tool when the
path is complete.

10 Continue along the path, alternating between dragging up and down. Put anchor points only where there are square boxes. If you make a mistake as you draw, you can undo your work by choosing Edit > Undo Pen.

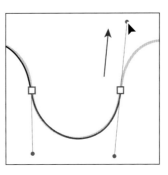

11 When the path is complete, select the Direct Selection tool and click to select an anchor point. When the anchor is selected, the direction handles appear and you can readjust the curve of the path.

12 Practice repeating these paths in the work area.

13 Choose File > Save and then File > Close.

Converting smooth points to corner points

When creating curves, the direction handles help to determine the shape and size of the curved segments. If you've created a smooth point by dragging out direction handles, as you did in the previous section, you can convert that point to a corner point. In the next part of the lesson, you will practice converting smooth points to corner points.

1 Open the L5start_4.ai file in the Lesson05 folder. Choose View > Fit All In Window.

On the top artboard, you can see the paths that you will create, labeled A and B. You will use the top artboard as a template for the exercise, creating your paths directly on top of those. Use the bottom artboard for additional practice on your own.

2 Choose File > Save As. In the Save As dialog box, navigate to the Lesson05 folder. Change the name to **path4.ai**. Choose Adobe Illustrator (*.AI) from the Save As Type menu (Windows), or choose Adobe Illustrator (ai) from the Format menu (Mac OS). In the Illustrator Options dialog box, leave the default settings and then click OK.

3 In the top artboard, use the Zoom tool (🔍) and drag a marquee around path A.

4 In the Control panel, click the Fill color and choose the None swatch (▱). Then, click the Stroke color and make sure that the black swatch is selected.

5 Make sure the Stroke weight is 1 pt in the Control panel.

● **Note:** If you're paths don't match the gray template path exactly in these sections, that's okay! The purpose is to get used to how the Pen tool works.

Note: Pressing
the Shift key when
dragging constrains the
tool to multiples of 45°.

6 Select the Pen tool (✐) and, pressing the Shift key, click the first anchor point and drag up. Release the mouse button and then the Shift key when the direction line is slightly above the arch. Click the next anchor point to the right, and, pressing the Shift key, drag down. When the curve looks correct, release the mouse button and then the Shift key. Leave the path selected.

Next, you will split the direction lines to convert a smooth point to a corner point.

▶ **Tip:** After you draw
a path, you can also
select single or multiple
anchor points and click
the Convert Selected
Anchor Points To Corner
button (⬛) or Convert
Selected Anchor Points
To Smooth button (⬛)
in the Control panel.

7 Press the Alt (Windows) or Option (Mac OS) key, and position the pointer over either the last anchor point created or the bottom direction point. When you see the caret (^) symbol appear next to the Pen tool pointer, click and drag a direction line up. Release the mouse button and then the modifier key. If you do not see the caret (^), you will create an additional loop.

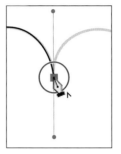
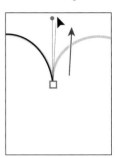

Note: If you don't click exactly
on the anchor point or the direction
point at the end of the direction line, a
warning dialog box appears. Click OK,
and try again.

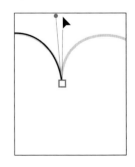

Adobe Illustrator

Please use the convert anchor point tool on an anchor point of a path.

☐ Don't Show Again   OK

You can practice adjusting the direction handles with the Direct Selection tool when the path is completed.

8 Position the Pen tool pointer over the next black square point on the template path, and drag down. Release the mouse button when the path looks similar to the template path.

9 Press the Alt (Windows) or Option (Mac OS) key and, after the caret (^) appears, position the pointer over the last anchor point or direction point and drag up. Release the mouse button and then the modifier key.

10 For the fourth anchor point, click the next square on the template path and drag down until the path looks correct. Do not release the mouse button.

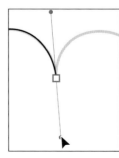
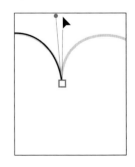

11 Press the Alt (Windows) or Option (Mac OS) key, and drag the direction handle up for the next curve. Release the mouse button and then the modifier key.

12 Continue this process using the Alt (Windows) or Option (Mac OS) key to create corner points until the path is completed. Use the Direct Selection tool (▸) to fine-tune the path, and then deselect the path.

Next, you will switch from a curve to a straight line.

1 Choose View > Fit Artboard In Window. You can also press Ctrl+0 (zero) (Windows) or Command+0 (zero) (Mac OS). Use the Zoom tool to drag a marquee around path B to enlarge its view.

2 With the Pen tool (✐), click the first anchor point on the left side of the gray template path and drag up. Release the mouse button when the path looks right. Then, drag down from the second anchor point and release the mouse button when the arch matches the template.

> This method of creating an arch should be familiar to you by now.

You will now continue the path as a straight line.

Pressing the Shift key and clicking does not produce a straight line, because the last point you created is a smooth anchor point. The figure shows what the path would look like if you clicked with the Pen tool on the last point.

3 Click the last point created to delete the leading direction line from the path, as shown in the figure.

4 Press the Shift key, and click the next point in the template path to the right to set the next point, creating a straight segment.

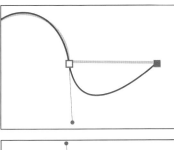

5 For the next arch, position the pointer over the last point created (notice that the carat appears [✎]) and then drag down from that point. This creates a new direction line.

6 Click the next point, and drag up to complete the arch. Click the last anchor point you just created, to remove the direction line.

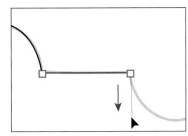

7 Shift-click the next point to create the second straight segment.

8 Click and drag up from the last point created, and then click and drag down on the last point to create the final arch. Practice repeating these paths in the lower artboard. Use the Direct Selection tool to adjust your path, if necessary.

9 Choose File > Save and then File > Close.

Creating the violin illustration

In this next part of the lesson, you'll create an illustration of a violin. You'll use the new skills you learned in the previous exercises, and you'll also learn some additional Pen tool techniques.

Note: The S shaped scrolls in the final artwork were added as an extra touch and will not be covered in this lesson.

1 Choose File > Open, and open the L5end_5.ai file in the Lesson05 folder, located in the Lessons folder.

2 Choose View > Fit All In Window to see the finished artwork. (Use the Hand tool [🖐] to move the artwork to where you want it.) If you don't want to leave the artwork open, choose File > Close.

3 Choose File > Open, and open the L5start_5.ai file in the Lesson05 folder.

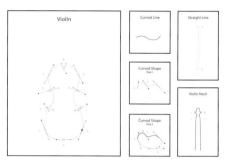

4 Choose File > Save As, name the file **violin.ai**, and select the Lesson05 folder in the Save As dialog box. Choose Adobe Illustrator (*.AI) from the Save As Type menu (Windows), or choose Adobe Illustrator (ai) from the Format menu (Mac OS), and click Save. In the Illustrator Options dialog box, leave the options set at the defaults, and then click OK.

5 In the Control panel, click the Fill color and choose the None swatch (⊘). Then, click the Stroke color and make sure that the black swatch is selected.

6 Make sure the Stroke weight is 1 pt in the Control panel.

Drawing curves

In this part of the lesson, you will review drawing curves by drawing the violin, its neck, the strings, and a curved path.

Selecting a curved path

You'll first examine a single curve and then draw a series of curves together, using the template guidelines to help you.

1 Choose 2 Curved Line from the Artboard Navigation menu in the lower-left corner of the Document window.

2 Choose View > Fit Artboard In Window if the artboard is not fit into the Document window.

3 Select the Direct Selection tool (↖), and click one of the segments of the curved line to view its anchor points and direction handles, which extend from the points. The Direct Selection tool lets you select and edit individual segments in the curved line.

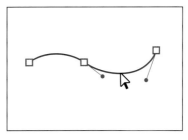

With a curve selected, you can also select the stroke and fill of the curve. When you do this, the next line you draw will have the same attributes. For more information about these attributes, see Lesson 6, "Color and Painting."

Drawing a curved path

Next, you'll draw the first curve of the curved shape.

1 Choose 3 Curved Shape step 1 from the Artboard Navigation menu in the lower-left corner of the Document window.

Instead of clicking with the Pen tool (✐) to start a path, you will drag with it to set the starting point and the direction of the path's curve.

2 Select the Pen tool (✐), and position it over point A on the template. Drag from point A to the red dot above it.

Next, you'll create the second anchor point with direction lines.

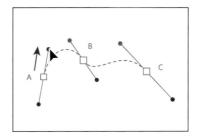

3 Drag with the Pen tool from point B to the next red dot.

The two anchor points are connected with a line segment which has a curve that is controlled by the direction handles you created. Notice that, if you vary the angle of dragging, you change the shape of the curve.

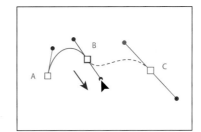

4 To complete the curved line, position the pointer over point C and drag from point C to the last red dot.

5 Control-click (Windows) or Command-click (Mac OS) away from the path to stop drawing that path.

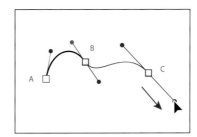

▶ **Tip:** You can also end a path by clicking the Pen tool, pressing P for the Pen tool shortcut, or choosing Select > Deselect.

Drawing a closed path with curves

Next, you'll finish drawing the curved shape by adding to an existing curved path. Even after you stop drawing a path, you can return to the path and edit it.

1 Choose 4 Curved Shape step 2 from the Artboard Navigation menu in the lower-left corner of the Document window.

Note: The dotted template lines are guides only. The shapes you create do not need to follow the lines exactly.

Next, you'll add a corner point to the path. A corner point lets you change the direction of the curve. A smooth point lets you draw a continuous curve.

2 Position the Pen tool ( ) over point A.

The slash (/) next to the Pen tool pointer indicates that the cursor is over an end anchor point of an open path. By clicking that point, you can continue the path rather than starting a new one.

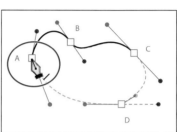

3 Press the Alt (Windows) or Option (Mac OS) key, and notice that the status bar in the lower-left corner of the Document window displays **Pen: Make Corner**. Press the Alt (Windows) or Option (Mac OS) key, and drag the Pen tool from anchor point A to the gray dot. Release the mouse button and then the modifier key.

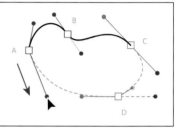

4 With the Pen tool, drag from point D to the red dot to the right, and don't let go of the mouse button. Press the Alt (Windows) or Option (Mac OS) key, and drag the direction line from the red dot to the gold dot. Release the mouse button and then the modifier key.

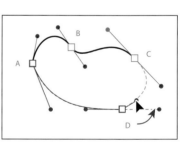

So far, you've drawn open paths, where there are two distinct endpoints. Next, you'll close a path using a smooth point.

5 Position the pointer over anchor point C on the template. A circle appears to the right of the Pen tool ( ) pointer, indicating that you can click to close the path.

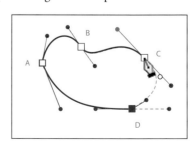

6 Drag from point C to the gray dot, as shown in the figure. As you drag, pay attention to the line segments on either side of point C.

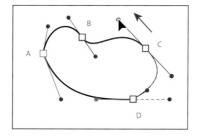

Notice that the direction handles that appear on both sides of a smooth point where you close the path are aligned along the same angle.

7 Control-click (Windows) or Command-click (Mac OS) away from the line, and choose File > Save.

Drawing the violin shape

Next, you'll draw a single, continuous path that consists of smooth points and corner points. This closed shape will become the body of the violin.

1 Choose View > Violin to display the violin in the Document window. You may wish to zoom in further as you work through this section.

2 With the Pen tool (✐) selected, starting at the blue square (point A), drag from point A to the red dot to set the starting anchor point and direction of the first curve.

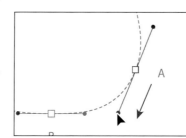

Note: You do not have to start at the blue square (point A) to draw this shape. You can set anchor points for a path with the Pen tool in a clockwise or counter-clockwise direction.

3 With the Pen tool, begin dragging from point B to the red dot on the left. As you drag, hold down the Shift key. Release the mouse button and then the Shift key when the pointer reaches the red dot.

4 Drag from point C to the red dot.

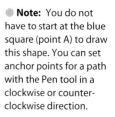

5 Drag from point D to the red dot. Don't release the mouse button yet. When the pointer reaches the red dot, hold down the Alt (Windows) or Option (Mac OS) key and drag from the red dot to the gold dot. Release the mouse button and then the modifier key. This splits the direction lines.

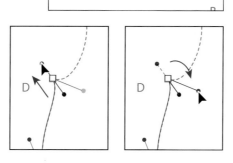

6 With the Pen tool, drag from point E to the red dot, press the Alt (Windows) or Option (Mac OS) key, and then drag the direction handle from the red dot to the gold dot. Release the mouse button and then the modifier key.

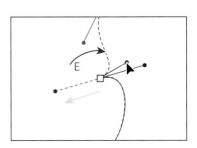

7 Drag from point F to the red dot.

8 With the Pen tool, drag from point G to the red dot. Holding the mouse button down, press the Alt (Windows) or Option (Mac OS) key and drag the direction handle from the red dot to the gold dot. Release the mouse button and then the modifier key.

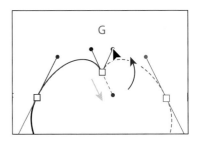

9 Drag from point H to the red dot.

10 Continue drawing the points at I and J by first dragging from the anchor point to the red dot and then pressing the Alt (Windows) or Option (Mac OS) key and dragging the direction handle from the red dot to the gold dot.

Next, you'll complete the drawing of the violin by closing the path.

11 Position the Pen tool over point A. Notice that an open circle appears next to the Pen tool pointer (⟨ꞏ⟩), indicating that the path will close when you click.

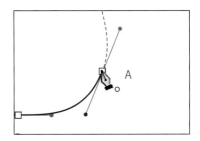

12 Drag down and to the left, to the red dot below point A.

As you drag down, another direction line appears above the point. As you drag, you are reshaping the path.

13 Ctrl-click (Windows) or Command-click (Mac OS) away from the path to deselect it, and then choose File > Save.

▶ **Tip:** Pen tool practice is important and encouraged. To speed up the process of drawing symmetrical objects and to ensure that they are perfectly symmetrical, however, you can also draw half of the object and then reflect and join a copy. To learn more about reflecting objects, see Lesson 4, "Transforming Objects."

Creating the strings

There are many ways to create straight paths, including using the Pen tool. Next, you'll draw a straight line for the strings of the violin using the Pen tool.

1   Choose 5 Strings from the Artboard Navigation menu in the lower-left corner of the Document window.

2   Choose Window > Workspace > Reset Essentials.

> **Note:** If you don't see "Reset Essentials" when choosing Window > Workspace > Reset Essentials, first choose the Window > Workspace > Essentials and then choose Window > Workspace > Reset Essentials. You can also choose the same commands in the workspace switcher in the Application bar.

3   In the Control panel, make sure that None (☑) is chosen for the Fill color and black is the Stroke color. Also make sure that the Stroke weight is 1 pt.

> **Note:** When drawing with the Pen tool, it can be easier to draw paths with no fill. You can also change the fill and other properties of the path later.

4   Choose View > Hide Bounding Box to hide the bounding boxes of selected objects.

5   Select the Pen tool (✐), and place it in the middle of the circle (point A) on the artboard. Notice that the pointer has an asterisk next to it, indicating that your next click begins a new path. Click to create the starting anchor point.

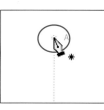

6   Pressing the Shift key, click point B to create the ending anchor point. The Shift key constrains the placement of the anchor point to a multiple of 45°.

After clicking to create point B, a caret (^) appears next to the Pen tool when the pointer is positioned over the new point, indicating that you can create a direction line for a curve by dragging the Pen tool from this anchor point. The caret disappears when you move the Pen tool away from the anchor point.

7   Press the letter V to switch to the Selection tool (▶). The straight line will still be selected. Click in a blank area to deselect this line so that you can draw other lines that aren't connected to this path.

Next, you'll make the straight line thicker by changing its stroke weight.

> **Note:** If you don't see the Stroke weight option in the Control panel, click the line again, even though it may still be selected. This indicates to Illustrator that you are no longer drawing. You can also expand the Stroke panel by clicking its icon on the right side of the workspace.

8   With the Selection tool, click the line you just drew. In the Control panel, change the Stroke weight to **3 pt**. Leave the line segment selected.

Splitting a path

To continue creating the strings, you'll split a path using the Scissors tool and then adjust the segments.

Note: If you click the stroke of a closed shape (a circle, for example) with the Scissors tool, it simply cuts the path so that it becomes open (a path with two end points).

1   With the line selected, in the Tools panel, click and hold down the Eraser tool (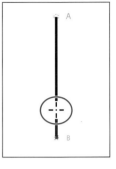) to reveal the Scissors tool ( ). Select the Scissors tool, and click about three-fourths of the way down the line to make a cut. See the figure for placement help.

If you don't click directly on the path, you will see a warning dialog box. You can simply click OK and try again. Cuts made with the Scissors tool must be on a line or a curve rather than on an endpoint. When you click with the Scissors tool, a new anchor point appears and is selected. The Scissors tool has split the line into two lines.

2   Select the Direct Selection tool ( ), and click directly on the top path to select it and show the anchor points. Click to select the bottom anchor point of that selected path. Begin dragging that point up, and as you drag, hold down the Shift key to widen the gap between the two split segments. Release the mouse button and then the key. Leave the top path selected.

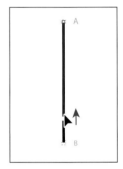

Adding arrowheads

You can add arrowheads to both ends of an open path using the Stroke panel. There are many different arrowhead styles to choose from in Illustrator, as well as arrowhead editing options.

Next, you'll add different arrowheads to the paths.

1   With the top line segment still selected, open the Stroke panel by clicking the Stroke panel icon ( ) on the right side of the workspace.

2   In the Stroke panel, choose Arrow 24 from the menu directly to the right of the word "Arrowheads." This adds an arrowhead to the start (top) of the line.

Note: If necessary, click the double arrows on the left side of the Stroke panel tab or choose Show Options from the panel menu to expand the panel so that you can see all of the content.

3   In the Stroke panel, change the Scale (beneath the start of the line arrowhead menu) to **30%** by clicking the word "Scale," typing the value in the field, and then pressing Enter or Return.

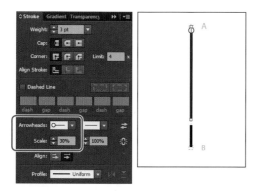

4   With the Selection tool (▸), click to select the lower, shorter path. In the Stroke panel, choose Arrow 22 from the arrowheads menu to the far right of the word "Arrowheads." This adds an arrowhead to the end of the line, as shown in the figure.

▶ **Tip:** Click the Swap Start And End Arrowheads button (⬌) in the Stroke panel to swap the starting and ending arrowheads on selected lines.

5   In the Stroke panel, change the Scale (beneath the end of the line arrowhead menu) to **40%** by typing the value in the field and then press Enter or Return.

Notice that the arrowheads are positioned inside the endpoints of the line, by default. Next, you will extend the arrowheads beyond the ends of the paths.

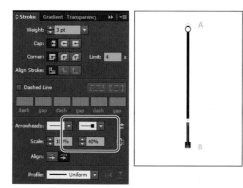

▶ **Tip:** The Link Start And End Arrowhead Scales button (⬡) to the right of the Scale values in the Stroke panel allows you to link the scale values together so that, if one changes, the other changes proportionately.

6   With the Selection tool, Shift-click to select the upper line segment so both lines are selected. Click the Extend Arrow Tip Beyond End of Path button (⬛) beneath the Scale value in the Stroke panel.

Notice that the arrowheads on both lines move slightly beyond the end of the lines. Leave both lines selected for the next steps.

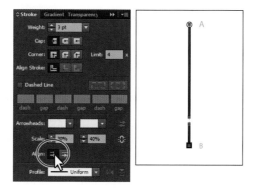

Creating a dashed line

Dashed lines apply to the stroke of an object and can be added to a closed path or an open path. Dashes are created by specifying a sequence of dash lengths and the gaps between them.

Next, you'll apply a dash to both paths.

▶ **Tip:** The Preserve Exact Dash And Gap Lengths button (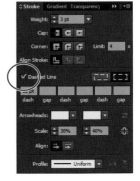) allows you to retain the appearance of the dashes without aligning to the corners or the dash ends.

1 With both paths still selected, make sure that the Butt Cap button ( ) is selected in the Stroke panel to the right of the word "Cap." Select Dashed Line in the middle of the Stroke panel.

   By default, this creates a repeating dash pattern of 12 pt dash, 12 pt gap.

   ▶ **Tip:** To learn about the Cap and Corner options in the Stroke panel, search for "Change the caps or joins of a line" in Illustrator Help.

Next, you will change the size of the dash.

2 In the Stroke panel, select the 12 pt value in the first Dash field on the left, below the Dashed Line check box. Change the value to **3 pt**, and press Enter or Return to set the value.

   This creates a 3 pt dash, 3 pt gap repeating line pattern. Next, you will adjust the gap between each dash, using the Stroke panel.

3 Insert the cursor in the Gap field to the right of the first Dash value. Type **1 pt**, and press Enter or Return to set the value. This creates a 3 pt dash, 1 pt gap line pattern.

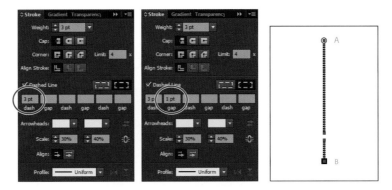

▶ **Tip:** If you want to create a custom dash pattern that has multiple dash and gap sizes, continue adding values in the next dash and gap fields in the Stroke panel. This pattern will be repeated in the line segment.

4 With both lines still selected, choose Object > Group.

5 Choose Select > Deselect and then File > Save.

Editing curves

In this part of the lesson, you'll adjust the curves you've drawn by dragging either the curve's anchor points or direction handles. You can also edit a curve by moving the line. You will hide the template layer to make editing the path easier.

1 Choose 4 Curved Shape step 2 from the Artboard Navigation menu in the lower-left corner of the Document window.

2 Choose Window > Workspace > Reset Essentials. Then, click the Layers panel icon ( ) on the right side of the workspace to expand the Layers panel. Click the Template Layer icon ( ) in the Layers panel to make the template layer invisible.

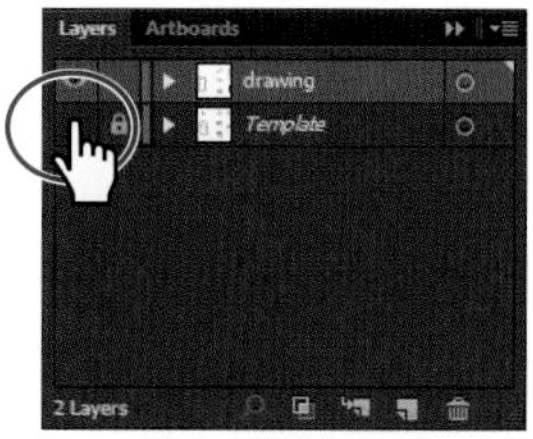

Tip: To learn more about layers, see Lesson 8, "Working with Layers."

3 Select the Direct Selection tool ( ), and click the outline of the curved shape. All of the points will appear.

Clicking with the Direct Selection tool displays the curve's direction handles for the selected line segment and lets you adjust the shape of individual curved segments. Clicking with the Selection tool ( ) selects the entire path.

4 Click the anchor point that is at the top, just to the left of center on the curved shape, to select it. Press the Down Arrow key three times to nudge the point down.

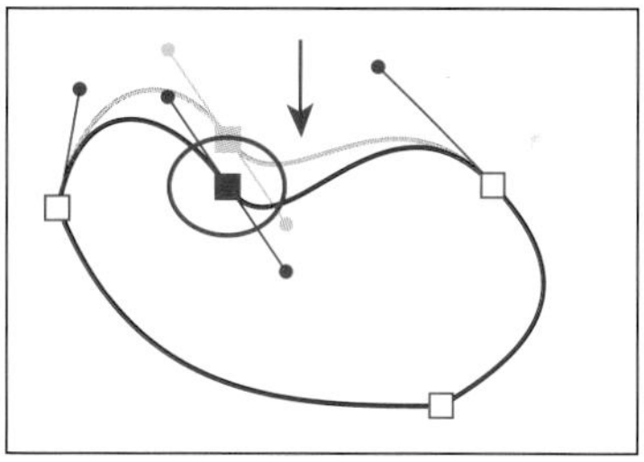

Note: You can also drag the anchor point with the Direct Selection tool.

Tip: Pressing and holding down the Shift key and then pressing an arrow key moves the point five times further than pressing the arrow key without the modifier key.

5 With the Direct Selection tool, drag across the top half of the shape to select the top two anchor points.

Notice that, when both points are selected, the handles disappear.

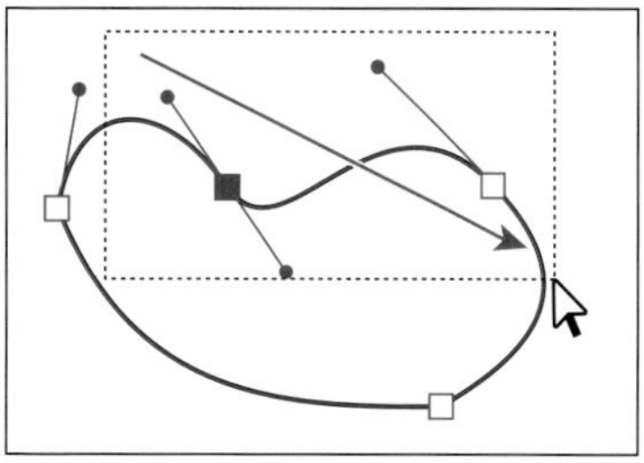

6 In the Control panel, click Show Handles For Multiple Selected Anchor Points ( ), to the right of the word Handles, to see the direction lines for both selected points.

Note: If you don't select both points the first time, try dragging across them again. If you have at least one of the anchor points selected, you can also Shift-click with the Direct Selection tool on the other anchor point to add it to the selection.

7 For the selected point on the right, drag the bottom control handle up and to the left to edit the curve.

As you drag, notice that both direction lines for the point are moving. Also notice that you can control the length of each direction line independently.

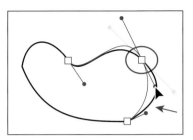

8 For the selected point on the left, drag the bottom control handle up and to the right to reshape the curve.

9 Choose Select > Deselect.

10 Choose File > Save.

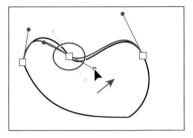

Deleting and adding anchor points

It can be easier to work with paths if you don't add more anchor points than necessary. A path with fewer points is easier to edit, display, and print. You can reduce a path's complexity or change its overall shape by deleting unnecessary points. You can also reshape a path by adding points to it.

Next, you will delete an anchor point and then add points to the path.

1 Choose 1 Violin from the Artboard Navigation menu in the lower-left corner of the Document window.

2 Select the Zoom tool (🔍) in the Tools panel, and click once in the center of the violin shape to zoom in. You need to see the whole violin shape for the next steps.

3 Select the Direct Selection tool (▷) in the Tools panel, and then click the edge of the violin.

4 Position the pointer over the top corner point of the violin. Click to select the anchor point.

5 In the Control panel, click Remove Selected Anchor Points (✏) to delete the anchor point.

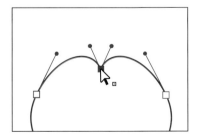

6 With the Direct Selection tool, position the pointer over the top part of the path. Click and begin dragging the path up to reshape the top curve. As you drag, hold down the Shift key. When the path is reshaped, release the mouse button and then the modifier key. Leave the shape selected.

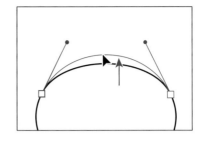

● **Note:** Don't use the Delete, Backspace, or Clear keys or the Edit > Cut or Edit > Clear command to delete anchor points; you will delete the point and the line segments that connect to that point.

▶ **Tip:** You can also delete a point by selecting the Pen tool and clicking an anchor point.

Next, you will add anchor points and reshape the bottom of the violin.

1 Select the Zoom tool (🔍) in the Tools panel, and click twice, slowly, on the bottom part of the violin shape to zoom in.

2 Select the Pen tool (✐) in the Tools panel, and position the pointer over the violin path to the right of the bottom anchor point. A plus sign (+) appears to the right of the Pen tool pointer. Click to add another point to the path.

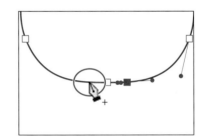

▶ **Tip:** Another way to add anchor points is to select the Add Anchor Point tool (⁺✐) in the Tools panel, position the pointer over a path, and click to add a point.

3 Position the pointer over the path to the left of the bottom anchor point until a plus sign (+) appears to the right of the pointer. Click to add another point, making three points in a row.

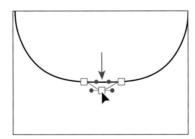

4 With the Direct Selection tool (▷), click to select the bottom-center point. Begin dragging the point down and, as you drag, hold down the Shift key. Drag the point down just a bit. Release the mouse button and then the modifier key.

You may need to zoom in.

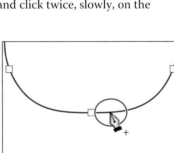

▶ **Tip:** When adding points to a shape that is symmetrical, it can be difficult to make sure that they are the same distance from the bottom-center point. You can select the points and distribute their spacing based on the bottom-center point. To learn more about distributing points, see Lesson 2, "Selecting and Aligning."

5 Choose Select > Deselect and then File > Save.

Converting between smooth points and corner points

Next, you'll finish the violin neck by adjusting a path. You'll be converting a smooth point on the curve to a corner point and a corner point to a smooth point.

1 Choose 6 Violin Neck from the Artboard Navigation menu in the lower-left corner of the Document window.

2 In the Layers panel, click the blank box to the left of the Template layer lock icon (⬛) to turn on the visibility for the template layer again.

3 Select the Zoom tool (🔍) in the Tools panel, and click three times in the middle of the points A, B, C, and D.

Note: When dragging a direction handle with Direct Selection tool, both handles remain parallel to each other but they can each be made longer or shorter independent of each other.

4 With the Direct Selection tool (▶), position the pointer over point A on the left side of the shape. When an open square with a dot in the center (▶₀) appears next to the pointer, click the anchor point to select it.

5 With the point selected, click the Convert Selected Anchor Points To Smooth button (⬛) in the Control panel.

6 With the Direct Selection tool, hold down the Shift key and click and drag the bottom direction handle down to reshape the bottom half of the curve. Release the mouse button and then the key to match the figure.

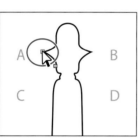 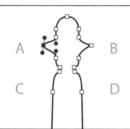 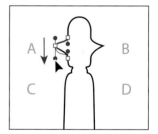

Select the point.   Convert the anchor point.   Drag the direction point down.

7 Perform steps 4–6 on point B on the right side of the shape.

8 With the Direct Selection tool, click the point to the right of the letter C to select it. With the point selected, click the Convert Selected Anchor Points To Corner button (◤) in the Control panel.

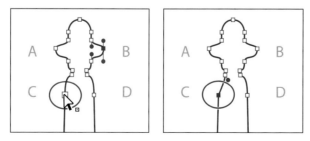

9 Select point D with the Direct Selection tool, and convert it to a corner point as well.

10 With the Direct Selection tool, click to select the top point of the neck shape. In the Control panel, click the Cut Path At Selected Anchor Points button (). Choose Select > Deselect.

11 With the Selection tool (➤), hold down the Shift key and drag the right side of the neck shape a little to the right. Release the mouse button and then the modifier key. This creates a gap between the two open paths.

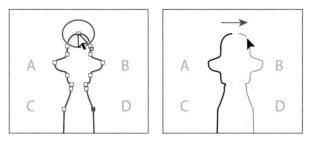

12 With the Direct Selection tool, drag a marquee across the top two points of both paths. Then click the Connect Selected End Points button (▦) in the Control panel to create a straight line connecting the two paths.

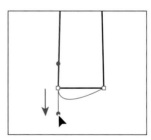

13 Choose View > Fit Artboard In Window.

14 Select the Selection tool in the Tools panel, and then click the path to select it (even though it looks selected). Choose Object > Path > Join to join the open endpoints at the bottom of the neck shape. Leave the shape selected.

15 Select the Convert Anchor Point tool (Ͷ), which is nested in the Pen tool in the Tools panel.

16 Drag the bottom-left anchor point of the neck shape down. As you drag, press the Shift key to constrain the movement. Release the mouse and then the Shift key.

The Convert Anchor Point tool also allows you to convert points from smooth to corner points, corner to smooth points, and much more.

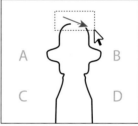

● **Note:** Make sure to press the Shift key *after* you start dragging away from the point.

17 Drag up from the bottom-right corner of the neck shape, pressing the Shift key as you drag, to make a smooth point. This makes the bottom of the shape round. Release the mouse button and then the modifier key.

18 Choose Select > Deselect, and then choose File > Save.

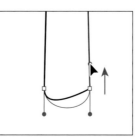

● **Note:** As mentioned earlier in the lesson, if you don't click on the point exactly, a warning dialog box may appear.

Drawing with the Pencil tool

The Pencil tool lets you draw open and closed paths as if you were drawing with a pencil on paper. Anchor points are created by Illustrator and are placed on the path as you draw. However, you can adjust the points when the path is complete. The number of anchor points set down is determined by the length and complexity of the path and by tolerance settings in the Pencil Tool Options dialog box. The Pencil tool is most useful for freeform drawing and for creating more organic shapes.

Next, you will draw a few lines that will be a chin rest on the curved shape you drew earlier.

1　Choose 4 Curved Shape step 2 from the Artboard Navigation menu in the lower-left corner of the Document window.

2　In the Layers panel (⬛), click the Template Layer icon (⬛) to hide the template layer. Click the Layers panel icon or panel tab to collapse the panel.

3　Double-click the Pencil tool (✎) in the Tools panel. In the Pencil Tool Options dialog box, drag the Smoothness slider to the right until the value is **100%**. This reduces the number of points on the paths drawn with the Pencil tool and makes them appear smoother. Click OK.

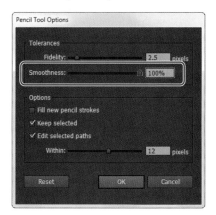

4　With the Pencil tool selected, click the Stroke color in the Control panel and select black in the Swatches panel that appears. Then, click the Fill color in the Control panel and choose None (⬜), if not already selected.

● **Note:** The colors may already be set for the stroke and fill.

5　Position the pointer inside the curved shape, on the left side of the shape. When you see an x to the right of the Pencil tool pointer, drag from the left side toward the right side to create an arc inside the curved shape. See the figure for position and shape.

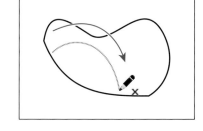

The x that appears to the right of the pointer before you begin drawing indicates that you are about to create a new path. If you don't see the x, it means that you are about to redraw a shape that the pointer is near. If necessary, move the pointer further from the edge of the curved shape.

▶ **Tip:** To create a closed path, such as a circle, select the Pencil tool and press the Alt (Windows) or Option (Mac OS) key and drag. The Pencil tool displays a small circle to indicate that you're creating a closed path. When the path is the size and shape you want, release the mouse button but don't release the Alt or Option key until the path closes. The beginning and ending anchor points are connected with the shortest line possible.

Notice that, as you draw, the path may not look perfectly smooth. When you release the mouse button, the path is smoothed based on the Smoothness value that you set in the Pencil Tool Options dialog box.

6 Position the pointer anywhere over the newly created path. Notice that the x is no longer next to the Pencil tool pointer. This indicates that if you drag to start drawing, you will edit the path from that point rather than draw a new path.

Next, you will set more options for the Pencil tool and then draw another curve to the right of the curved line you just drew.

7 Double-click the Pencil tool (✐) in the Tools panel.

8 In the Pencil Tool Options dialog box, deselect Edit Selected Paths. Change the Fidelity value to **10** pixels. Click OK.

9 With the Pencil tool, click the end of the curved path you just drew and drag to the right to draw another arc shape.

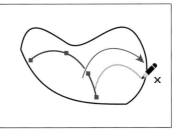

10 Choose Select > Deselect.

▶ **Tip:** The higher the Fidelity value, the greater the distance between anchor points and the fewer the anchor points created. Fewer anchor points can make the path smoother and less complex.

Editing with the Pencil tool

Using the Pencil tool, you can also edit any path and add freeform lines and shapes to any shape. Next, you will edit the curved shape using the Pencil tool.

1 With the Selection tool (▶), select the closed curved path (not the arcs you drew with the Pencil tool).

2 Double-click the Pencil tool. In the Pencil Tool Options dialog box, click Reset. Make sure that the Edit Selected Paths option is selected (this is important for the next steps). Ensure that the Fidelity is **10**, and change the Smoothness to **30%**. Click OK.

3 Position the Pencil tool on the top left of the curved path (not on the point), and notice that the x disappears from the pointer. This indicates that you are about to redraw the selected path.

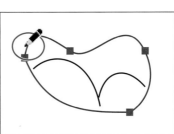

● **Note:** Depending on where you begin to redraw the path and in which direction you drag, you may get unexpected results. Try redrawing if that happens.

Tip: If the shape doesn't look like you want it to, you can choose Edit > Undo Pencil or try dragging with the Pencil tool across the same area again.

4   Drag to the right to edit the curve of the path. When the pointer is back on the path, release the mouse button to see the shape.

5   Choose Select > All On Active Artboard.

Note: Your curved path result may not look exactly as you see in the figure. That's okay. If you want, edit the path again, using the Pencil tool.

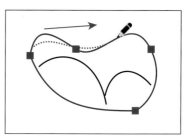

6   Choose Object > Group.

7   With the group selected, double-click the Scale tool (⟐) in the Tools panel. In the Scale dialog box that appears, change the Uniform Scale to **70%** and then click OK.

8   Choose Select > Deselect and then File > Save.

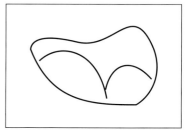

Finishing the violin illustration

To complete the illustration, you'll make some minor modifications and assemble and paint the objects.

Assembling the parts

1   Choose View > Fit All In Window. Choose Reset Essentials from the workspace switcher in the Application bar.

2   Choose View > Show Bounding Box so that you can see the bounding boxes of selected objects as you transform them.

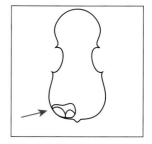

Note: It may be easier to drag the curved shape group by dragging a path in the group rather than trying to drag the shape from its middle, since it has no fill.

3   Select the Selection tool (▸) in the Tools panel, and move the curved shape group you just edited to the bottom left of the violin, as shown in the figure.

4   Shift-click the edge of the violin shape to select both shapes, and then choose Object > Group.

5   Choose Object > Lock > Selection.

6   With the Selection tool, move the violin neck to the top of the violin body. Using the rulers as a guide, position the neck about an inch from the top of the artboard and align it as close to the center of the violin body as you can (you will align it more precisely later).

7   With the violin neck still selected, choose Object > Arrange > Bring to Front.

8   Select the Direct Selection tool (▸) in the Tools panel, and drag a marquee across the bottom of the neck shape. Holding down the Shift key, drag one of

the bottom points of the neck shape down. Release the mouse button and then the key. See the figure for approximate length.

9 Choose Object > Lock > Selection.

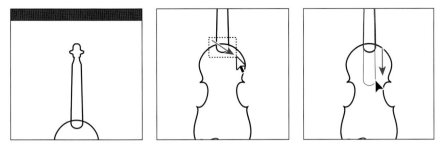

10 With the Selection tool, drag the dashed line group (from the 5 Strings artboard) onto the center of the violin shape. Drag it so that the bottom of the dashed line is above the curved shaped and on the left edge of the violin neck shape. See the figure below for placement.

11 Choose Object > Arrange > Bring To Front.

12 Select the Direct Selection tool in the Tools panel. Click to select the top point of the dashed line group. Begin dragging the top point of the dashed line group up. While dragging, hold down the Shift key, and drag until the point is just below the top of the violin neck. Release the mouse button and then the key.

13 With the Selection tool, click to select the dashed line group. Double-click the Selection tool in the Tools panel to open the Move dialog box.

14 In the Move dialog box, change Horizontal to **0.1 in** and make sure that Vertical is **0**. Click Copy to copy and move the dashed line group to the right.

15 With the copied line group still selected, choose Object > Transform > Transform Again twice, until there are four dotted line groups.

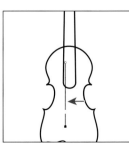
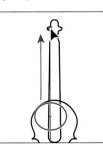
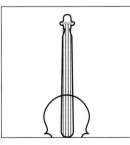

Drag the line group into place.   Drag to reshape the line.   Copy the line group.

16 Choose Select > All On Active Artboard and then Object > Group.

17 In the Control panel, change the Stroke weight to **1 pt**.

18 Select the Zoom tool (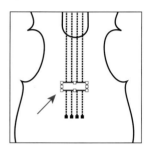) in the Tools panel, and click the bottom portion of the dotted line groups three times.

19 Select the Rectangle tool in the Tools panel. Click anywhere in the artwork. In the Rectangle dialog box, change the Width to **.5 in** and the Height to **.18 in**. Click OK.

20 With the Rectangle on the page and selected, press the letter D to apply the default stroke and fill to it.

●**Note:** You may need to adjust the height of the rectangle so that it fits into the gap between your dashed lines more accurately.

21 With the Selection tool, drag the Rectangle to where you cut the dotted lines. See the figure for positioning.

22 Choose View > Fit Artboard In Window.

23 Choose Object > Unlock All and then Select > All On Active Artboard.

24 In the Control panel, choose Align To Artboard from the Align to menu (▦) and then click the Horizontal Align Center (≣) button.

●**Note:** If you don't see the align options in the Control panel, click the word "Align" or choose Window > Align.

25 Choose Select > Deselect and then File > Save.

Painting the artwork

In the color illustration, the fills are painted with custom-made colors called Violin, Neck, and Gray, which are provided in the Swatches panel. To learn more about painting options in Illustrator, see Lesson 6, "Color and Painting."

●**Note:** To change the color of the curved shape, double-click the shape to enter Isolation mode and change the color. Then, press the Escape key to exit.

1 With the Selection tool (▶), select an object, and then change the Fill color in the Control panel. Apply the swatch named Violin to the violin shape, the swatch named Gray to the rectangle and the curved shape group, and the swatch named Neck to the neck shape.

2 Choose File > Save and then File > Close.

Review questions

1 Describe how to draw straight vertical, horizontal, or diagonal lines using the Pen tool.

2 How do you draw a curved line using the Pen tool?

3 How do you draw a corner point on a curved line?

4 Name two ways to convert a smooth point on a curve to a corner point.

5 Which tool would you use to edit a segment on a curved line?

6 How can you change the way the Pencil tool works?

Review answers

1 To draw a straight line, click twice with the Pen tool. The first click sets the starting anchor point, and the second click sets the ending anchor point of the line. To constrain the straight line vertically, horizontally, or along a 45° diagonal, press the Shift key as you click to create the second anchor point with the Pen tool.

2 To draw a curved line with the Pen tool, click to create the starting anchor point, drag to set the direction of the curve, and then click to end the curve.

3 To draw a corner point on a curved line, press the Alt (Windows) or Option (Mac OS) key and drag the direction handle on the endpoint of the curve to change the direction of the path. Continue dragging to draw the next curved segment on the path.

4 Use the Direct Selection tool to select the anchor point, and then use the Convert Anchor Point tool to drag a direction handle to change the direction. Another method is to choose a point or points with the Direct Selection tool and then click the Convert Selected Anchor Points To Corner button ( ) in the Control panel.

5 To edit a segment on a curved line, select the Direct Selection tool and drag the segment to move it, or drag a direction handle on an anchor point to adjust the length and shape of the segment.

6 Double-click the Pencil tool to open the Pencil Tool Options dialog box, where you can change the smoothness, fidelity, and more.

6 COLOR AND PAINTING

Lesson overview

In this lesson, you'll learn how to do the following:

- Use color modes and color controls.

- Create, edit, and paint with colors using the Control panel and shortcuts.

- Name and save colors, create color groups, and build a color palette.

- Use the Color Guide panel and the Edit Colors/Recolor Artwork features.

- Copy paint and appearance attributes from one object to another.

- Create and paint with patterns.

- Work with Live Paint.

 This lesson takes approximately an hour and a half to complete. If needed, remove the previous lesson folder from your hard disk and copy the Lesson06 folder onto it.

Spice up your illustrations with colors by taking
advantage of color controls in Adobe Illustrator CS6.
In this information-packed lesson, you'll discover how
to create and paint fills and strokes, use the Color
Guide panel for inspiration, work with color groups,
recolor artwork, create patterns, and more.

Getting started

In this lesson, you will learn about the fundamentals of color and create and edit colors using the Color panel, Swatches panel, and more.

1 To ensure that the tools and panels function exactly as described in this lesson, delete or deactivate (by renaming) the Adobe Illustrator CS6 preferences file. See "Restoring default preferences" on page 3.

2 Start Adobe Illustrator CS6.

   ● **Note:** If you have not already done so, copy the Lesson06 folder from the Lessons folder on the *Adobe Illustrator CS6 Classroom in a Book* CD onto your hard disk. See "Copying the Classroom in a Book files" on page 2.

3 Choose File > Open, and open the L6end_1.ai file in the Lesson06 folder, located in the Lessons folder, to view a final version of the label you will paint. Leave it open for reference.

● **Note:** In Mac OS, when opening lesson files, you may need to click the round, green button in the upper-left corner of the Document window to maximize the window's size.

4 Choose File > Open. In the Open dialog box, navigate to the Lesson06 folder in the Lessons folder. Open the L6start_1.ai file. This file has some components already in it. You will create and apply color as necessary to complete the labels.

5 Choose File > Save As. In the Save As dialog box, navigate to the Lesson06 folder and name it **label.ai**. Leave the Save As Type option set to Adobe Illustrator (*.AI) (Windows) or the Format option set to Adobe Illustrator (ai) (Mac OS), and click Save. In the Illustrator Options dialog box, leave the options at their default settings and then click OK.

● **Note:** If you don't see "Reset Essentials" in the menu, choose Window > Workspace > Essentials before choosing Window > Workspace > Reset Essentials.

6 Choose Window > Workspace > Reset Essentials.

Understanding color

When working with color in Illustrator, you first need to understand color modes (also called color models). When you apply color to artwork, keep in mind the final medium in which the artwork will be published (print or web, for instance) so that you can use the correct color mode and color definitions. First, you will learn about color modes, and then you will learn the basic color controls.

Color modes

Before starting a new illustration, you must first decide which color mode the artwork should use, CMYK or RGB.

- **CMYK**—Cyan, magenta, yellow, and black are the colors used in four-color process printing. These four colors are combined and overlapped in a screen pattern to create a multitude of other colors. Select this mode for printing.

- **RGB**—Red, green, and blue light are added together in various ways to create an array of colors. Select this mode if you are using images for on-screen presentations or the Internet.

When creating a new document, you select a color mode by choosing File > New and picking the appropriate document Profile, such as Print, which uses CMYK for the color mode. You can change the color mode by clicking the arrow to the left of Advanced and selecting a Color Mode.

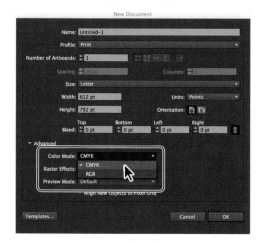

When a color mode is selected, the applicable panels open, displaying colors in either the CMYK or RGB mode. You can change the color mode of a document after a file is created by choosing File > Document Color Mode and then selecting either CMYK or RGB in the menu.

Understanding the color controls

In this lesson, you will learn about the traditional methods of coloring objects in Illustrator. This includes painting objects with colors and patterns using a combination of panels and tools, such as the Control panel, Color panel, Swatches panel, Gradient panel, Stroke panel, Color Guide panel, Color Picker, and the paint buttons in the Tools panel. You'll begin by looking at finished artwork to which color has already been applied.

1 Click the L6end_1.ai document tab at the top of the Document window.

2 Choose 1 from the Artboard Navigation menu in the lower-left corner of the Document window and then choose View > Fit Artboard In Window.

3 Select the Selection tool (▶), and then click the green shape behind the text "Pizza Sauce."

● **Note:** Depending on your screen resolution, your Tools panel may be displayed in a double column rather than in a single column.

Objects in Illustrator can have a fill, a stroke, or both. In the Tools panel, notice that the Fill box appears in the foreground, indicating that it is selected. This is the default setting. The Fill box is green for this object. Behind the Fill box, the Stroke box has a yellow outline.

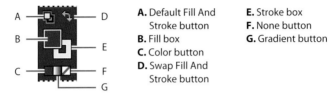

A. Default Fill And Stroke button
B. Fill box
C. Color button
D. Swap Fill And Stroke button
E. Stroke box
F. None button
G. Gradient button

4 Click the Appearance panel icon (⬤) on the right side of the workspace.

The Fill and Stroke attributes of the selected object also appear in the Appearance panel. You can add, edit, or delete appearance attributes, which you can apply to other objects, layers, and groups. You'll use this panel later in later lessons.

A. Object selected
B. Stroke color
C. Fill color

▶ **Tip:** Shift-click the color spectrum bar at the bottom of the Color panel to rotate through different color modes, such as CMYK and RGB.

5 Click the Color panel icon (▦) on the right side of the workspace. Click the double-arrow to the left of the word "Color" in the panel tab to expand the panel, if necessary. The Color panel displays the current color of the fill and stroke. The CMYK sliders in the Color panel show the percentages of cyan, magenta, yellow, and black. The color spectrum bar is at the bottom of the Color panel.

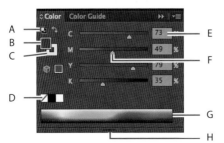

A. Default Fill And Stroke button
B. Fill box
C. Stroke box
D. None box
E. Color value
F. Color slider
G. Color spectrum bar
H. Drag to expand the color spectrum

The color spectrum bar lets you quickly and visually select a fill or stroke color from a spectrum of colors. You can also choose white or black by clicking the appropriate color box.

6   Click the Swatches panel icon (▦) on the right side of the workspace. You can name and save document colors, gradients, and patterns in the Swatches panel, for instant access. When an object has a fill or stroke that contains a color, gradient, pattern, or tint applied in the Swatches panel, the applied swatch is highlighted in the panel.

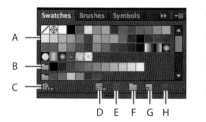

A
B
C
    D E F G H

A. Swatch
B. Color group
C. Swatch Libraries menu
D. Show Swatch Kinds menu
E. Swatch options

F. New Color group
G. New Swatch
H. Delete Swatch

7   Click the Color Guide panel icon (▨) on the right side of the workspace. Click the green swatch in the upper-left corner of the panel to set the base color as the color of the selected object (labeled A in the figure below). Click the Harmony Rules menu, and choose Complementary 2 (labeled D in the figure).

The Color Guide can provide color inspiration while you create your artwork. It helps you pick color tints, analogous colors, and much more. In this panel, you can also access the Edit or Apply Colors feature, which lets you edit and create colors.

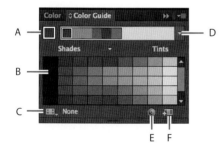

A
B
C
    E F

D

A. Set base color to the current color
B. Color variations
C. Limits the color group to colors in a swatch library

D. Harmony Rules menu and active color group
E. Edit Or Apply Colors button
F. Save color group to Swatch panel

● **Note:** The colors you see in the panel may be different and that's okay.

8   Click the Color panel icon (▣). Using the Selection tool (▸), click various shapes in the L6end_1.ai file to see how their paint attributes are reflected in the panel.

9   Leave the L6end_1.ai file open for reference, or choose File > Close to close it without saving your changes.

10 Click the label.ai document tab at the top of the Document window if you did not close the L6end_1.ai document.

Creating color

In this project, you will be working on artwork in the CMYK color mode, which means that will create your own color from any combination of cyan, magenta, yellow, and black. You can create color in a variety of ways, depending on the artwork. If you want to create a color that is specific to your company, for instance, you can use a swatch library. If you are trying to match color in artwork, you can use the Eyedropper tool to sample color or the Color Picker to enter exact values.

Next, you will create color using different methods and then apply that color to objects.

Building and saving a custom color

First, you will create a color using the Color panel, and then you will save the color as a swatch in the Swatches panel.

● **Note:** If an object is selected when you create a color, the color is applied to the selected object.

1 Choose Select > Deselect to ensure that nothing is selected.

2 Choose 1 from the Artboard Navigation menu in the lower-left corner of the Document window (if not selected), then choose View > Fit Artboard In Window.

▶ **Tip:** The values are each a percentage of 100.

3 If the Color panel is not visible, click the Color panel icon (▦). If the CMYK sliders are not visible, choose the CMYK color model from the Color panel menu (▼☰). Click the Stroke box, and type the following values in the CMYK text fields: C=**19**, M=**88**, Y=**78**, K=**22**.

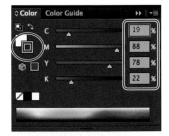

▶ **Tip:** To save a color you made in the Color panel, you can also click the New Swatch button at the bottom of the Swatches panel to open the New Swatch dialog box.

4 Click the Swatches panel icon (▦), and choose New Swatch from the Swatches panel menu (▼☰). In the New Swatch dialog box, name the color **label background** and, leaving the rest of the options as they are, click OK.

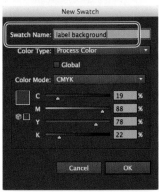

▶ **Tip:** If you want to load swatches from one saved document into another, click the Swatch Libraries Menu button (▥) at the bottom of the Swatches panel and choose Other Library. Then, locate the document with the swatches that you want to import.

Notice that the swatch is highlighted in the Swatches panel (it has a white border around it). New colors added to the Swatches panel are saved with the current document only. Opening a new file displays a default set of swatches.

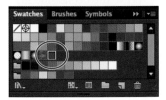

5 With the Selection tool (▶), click anywhere in the white-filled background shape on the artboard to select it. Click the Fill box at the bottom of the Tools panel. Click the Swatches panel icon (▦) if the panel is not showing, and select the label background swatch. Choose Select > Deselect.

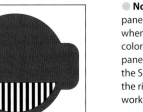

Note: The Swatches panel that appears when you click Fill color in the Control panel is the same as the Swatches panel on the right side of the workspace.

Next, you will create another swatch using a similar method.

6 In the Swatches panel, click the New Swatch (▦) button at the bottom of the panel to create a copy of the selected swatch.

7 In the New Swatch dialog box, change the name to **label background stroke** and change the values to C=**19**, M=**46**, Y=**60**, K=**0**. Click OK.

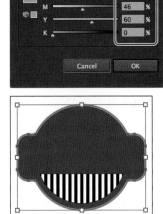

● **Note:** If the shape had still been selected, it would be filled with the new color.

8 With the Selection tool (▶), click the shape again to select it. Click the Stroke color in the Control panel. When the Swatches panel appears, select the label background stroke swatch.

9 Change the Stroke weight in the Control panel to **7 pt**. Leave the Swatches panel showing.

Editing a swatch

After a color is created and saved in the Swatches panel, you can edit that color. Next, you will edit the label background swatch that you just saved.

1 Select the Stroke box in the Tools panel. This expands the Color panel. Click the Swatches panel icon (▦) on the right side of the workspace.

2 With the shape still selected, double-click the label background stroke swatch in the Swatches panel. In the Swatch Options dialog box, change the values to C=**2**, M=**15**, Y=**71**, K=**20**. Select Preview to see the changes to the logo shape. Change the K value to **0**, and then click OK.

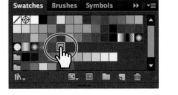

▶ **Tip:** You can position the pointer over a color swatch in the Swatches panel to see a tool tip indicating the name of the swatch.

When you create a swatch and then edit it, the objects that already have that swatch color applied need to be selected to apply the change.

Next, you will change the logo background swatch to a global color. When you edit it, a global color automatically updates throughout the artwork, regardless of whether the objects that use that global color are selected.

3 With the shape still selected, click the Fill box in the Tools panel.

4 Double-click the label background swatch in the Swatches panel to open the Swatch Options dialog box. Select Global, and then click OK.

5 Choose Select > Deselect.

Note: The white triangle in the lower-right corner of a swatch icon (▣) in the Swatches panel indicates a global color.

6 Double-click the label background swatch in the Swatches panel again to open the Swatch Options dialog box. Change the K value (black) to **70**. Select Preview to see the changes. Notice how the shape fill changes, even though the shape is not selected. That's the purpose of a global color. Click Cancel so that the color change is not saved.

7 Choose File > Save.

Using Illustrator swatch libraries

Note: Most, but not all, of the libraries that come with Illustrator are CMYK colors.

Swatch libraries are collections of preset colors, such as PANTONE and TOYO, and thematic libraries, such as Earthtone and Ice Cream. Illustrator has default swatch libraries that appear as separate panels and cannot be edited. When you apply color from a library to artwork, the color in the library becomes a swatch that is saved in the Swatches panel for that document. Libraries are a great starting point for creating colors.

Next, you will create a yellow spot color using a PANTONE+ library for another shape in the label. When this color is defined, it could be a warm, dark, or light yellow. This is why most printers and designers rely on a color matching system, like the PANTONE system, to help maintain color consistency and to give a wider range of colors, in some cases.

Spot versus process colors

You can designate colors as either spot or process color types, which correspond to the two main ink types used in commercial printing.

- A process color is printed using a combination of the four standard process inks: cyan (C), magenta (M), yellow (Y), and black (K) (CMYK).

- A spot color is a special premixed ink that is used instead of, or in addition to, CMYK process inks. A spot color requires its own printing plate on a printing press.

Creating a spot color

In this section, you will see how to load a color library, such as the PANTONE color system, and how to add a PANTONE Matching System (PMS) color to the Swatches panel.

1 In the Swatches panel, click the Swatch Libraries Menu button (▦). Choose Color Books > PANTONE+ Solid Coated.

   The PANTONE+ solid coated library appears in its own panel.

2 Type **100** in the Find field. The PANTONE 100 C swatch is highlighted in the swatches. Click the highlighted swatch to add it to the Swatches panel. Close the PANTONE+ Solid Coated panel. The PANTONE color appears in the Swatches panel.

● **Note:** When you exit Illustrator and then relaunch it, the PANTONE library panel does not reopen. To automatically open the panel whenever Illustrator opens, choose Persistent from the PANTONE+ Solid Coated panel menu.

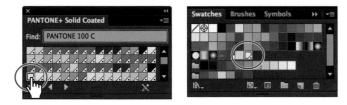

3 Position the pointer on the artboard and, holding down the spacebar, drag to the right so that you can see both the white-filled shape off the left edge and the content on the first artboard.

4 With the Selection tool (▶), click the white-filled shape off the left edge of artboard 1 to select it. From the Fill color in the Control panel, choose the PANTONE 100 C color to fill the shape. Change the Stroke color to None (⬜).

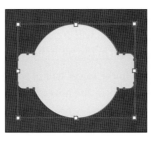

5 With the shape still selected, Shift-click to select the original red label background shape on the first artboard. Release the Shift key.

6   Choose View > Fit Artboard In Window.

Note: To learn more about what key objects are and how to work with them, see Lesson 2, "Selecting and Aligning."

7   With the Selection tool, click the red shape once more to make it the key object.

8   In the Control panel, click the Horizontal Align Center button (≛) and the Vertical Align Center button (╫═) to align the yellow shape to the red label shape.

Note: If you don't see the Align options, click the word "Align" in the Control panel to reveal the Align panel.

9   Choose Select > Deselect.

10 Choose File > Save. Keep the file open.

Why does my PANTONE swatch look different from the other swatches in the Swatches panel?

In the Swatches panel, the color type is identified by the icon that appears next to the name of the color. You can identify spot-color swatches by the spot-color icon (◉) when the panel is in List view or by the dot in the lower corner (◳) when the panel is in Thumbnail view. Process colors do not have a spot-color icon or a dot.

By default, the PANTONE solid coated swatch is defined as a spot color. A spot color is not created from a combination of CMYK inks but is its own solid ink color. A press operator uses a premixed PMS color in the press, offering more consistent color.

A triangle indicates that the color is global. If a global color is edited, all color references used in the illustration are updated. Any color can be global, not only PANTONE colors. To learn more about spot colors, search for "spot colors" in Illustrator Help (Help > Illustrator Help).

Using the Color Picker

The Color Picker lets you select color in a color field and in a spectrum by either defining colors numerically or by clicking a swatch.

Next, you will create a color using the Color Picker and then save the color as a swatch in the Swatches panel.

1   In the lower half of artboard 1, with the Selection tool (▶), click one of the white bars in the lower part of the label shape to select the underlying white shape.

2 Double-click the Fill box in the Tools panel to open the Color Picker.

> **Tip:** You can double-click the Fill box or Stroke box in the Color panel to access the Color Picker.

> **Tip:** If you work in Adobe Photoshop or Adobe InDesign, the Color Picker may be familiar, because those programs also have a Color Picker feature.

3 In the Color Picker dialog box, type these values into the CMYK text fields: C=**0**, M=**11**, Y=**54**, and K=**0**.

Notice that the slider in the color spectrum bar and the circle in the color field move as you enter the CMYK values. The color spectrum shows the hue, and the color field shows saturation (horizontally) and brightness (vertically).

4 Select S (saturation) to change the color spectrum displayed in the Color Picker. The color spectrum bar becomes the saturation of the orange color. Drag the color spectrum slider up until the S value is **60%**, and then click OK.

The white shape is filled with the yellow/orange color you just made in the Color Picker.

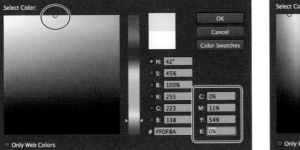
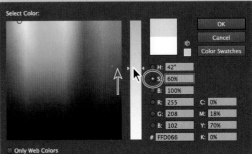

● **Note:** The Color Swatches button in the Color Picker shows you the swatches in the Swatches panel and the default color books (the sets of swatches that come with Illustrator) and lets you select a color from one. You can return to the color models view by clicking the Color Models button and editing the swatch color values, if necessary.

5 Change the Stroke color in the Control panel to None (☑).

Next, you will save the color in the Swatches panel.

6 Ensure that the Fill box is selected (in front) at the bottom of the Tools panel.

This ensures that, when you create a new swatch, it is created using the fill of the selected shape.

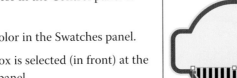

7 Click the Swatches panel icon (▦) to show the panel, if it's not already showing.

8 Click the New Swatch button (▣) at the bottom of the Swatches panel, and name the color **yellow/orange** in the New Swatch dialog box. Select Global, and then click OK to see the color appear as a swatch in the Swatches panel.

9 Choose Select > Deselect and then File > Save.

Creating and saving a tint of a color

A tint is a mixture of color with white to make the color lighter. You can create a tint from a global process color, like CMYK, or from a spot color.

Next, you will create a tint of the yellow/orange swatch.

1 With the Selection tool, click one of the black bars in the lower half of the artboard. Change the fill color in the Control panel to the yellow/orange color you just made.

2 Click the Color panel icon () to expand the Color panel.

3 Make sure that the Fill box is selected in the Color panel, and then drag the tint slider to the left to change the tint value to **20%**.

● **Note:** You may need to choose Show Options from the Color panel menu to see the slider.

4 Click the Swatches panel icon (🏭) on the right side of the workspace. Click the New Swatch button (🗂) at the bottom of the panel to save the tint. Notice the tint swatch in the Swatches panel. Position the pointer over the swatch icon to see its name, yellow/orange 20%.

5 Choose File > Save.

Copying appearance attributes

You can use the Eyedropper tool to copy appearance attributes from one object to another, including character, paragraph, fill, and stroke attributes.

1 Using the Selection tool (▶), select one of the black bars that has not yet been colored and then choose Select > Same > Fill Color to select the remaining black rectangles.

2 Using the Eyedropper tool (✐), click the bar with the yellow/orange 20% fill applied. All the bars that are black pick up the attributes from the painted bar.

3 With the Selection tool, Shift-click to select the original bar.

4 Choose Object > Group.

5 Choose Select > Deselect and then File > Save.

Creating color groups

In Illustrator, you can save colors in color groups, which consist of related color swatches in the Swatches panel. Organizing colors by their use, such as grouping all colors for a logo, is helpful for organization and to be able to edit all of those colors together, if necessary. Only spot, process, and global colors can be in a group.

Next, you will create a color group using the label colors you've created.

1   In the Swatches panel, click a blank area of the panel to deselect the color swatches. Click the label background swatch (red) and, holding down the Shift key, click the yellow/orange swatch to the right to select four color swatches.

▶ **Tip:** To select multiple colors that are not next to each other in the Swatches panel, Ctrl-click (Windows) or Command-click (Mac OS) the swatches you want to select.

2   Click the New Color Group button (▤) at the bottom of the Swatches panel. Change the Name to **label base** in the New Color Group dialog box, and click OK to save the group.

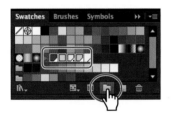 

● **Note:** If objects are selected when you click the New Color Group button, an expanded New Color Group dialog box appears. In this dialog box, you can create a color group from the colors in the artwork and convert the colors to global colors.

3   With the Selection tool (▶), click a blank area of the Swatches panel to deselect the color group you just created.

4   In the Swatches panel, double-click the yellow/orange swatch in the label base color group to open the Swatch Options dialog box. Change the values to C=0, M=**12**, Y=**54**, and K=**0**. Click OK.

5   Click the yellow/orange 20% swatch, and drag it between the PANTONE 100 C swatch and the yellow/orange swatch in the label base color group.

You can also reorder the swatches within the group by dragging them.

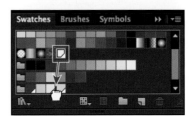

6 Drag the PANTONE 100 C swatch to the right of the yellow/orange swatch.

● **Note:** If you drag the PANTONE 100 C swatch too far to the right, you may pull it out of the group. If that happens, you can always drag it back into the group.

7 Choose File > Save.

Working with the Color Guide panel

The Color Guide panel can provide you with color inspiration as you create your artwork. Use it to pick harmony rules such as color tints, analogous colors, and much more. In this panel, you can also access the Edit Color/Recolor Artwork feature, which allows you to edit and create colors.

Next, you will use the Color Guide panel to select different colors for a second label and then you'll save those colors as a color group in the Swatches panel.

1 Choose 2 from the Artboard Navigation menu in the lower-left corner of the Document window.

2 With the Selection tool (▶), click the red background shape of the label. Make sure that the Fill box is selected in the Tools panel.

● **Note:** The colors you see in the Color Guide panel may be different from what you see in the figure. That's okay.

3 Click the Color Guide panel icon (▣) on the right side of the workspace to open the panel. Click the Set Base Color To The Current Color button (■).

This allows the Color Guide panel to suggest colors based on the color showing in the Set Base Color To The Current Color button.

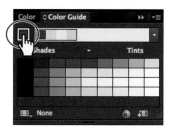

Next, you'll experiment with the colors in the label.

4 Choose Complementary 2 from the Harmony Rules menu to the right of the Set Base Color To The Current Color button in the Color Guide panel.

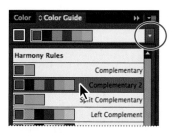

5 Click the Save Color Group To Swatch Panel button (▤) to save the colors in the Complementary 2 harmony rule in the Swatches panel.

6 Click the Swatches panel icon (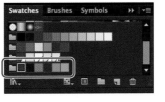). Scroll down to see the new group added.

You can apply these colors to the artwork, and you can edit them.

7 Click the Color Guide icon (■) to open the Color Guide panel.

Next, you'll experiment with the colors.

8 In the color variations in the Color Guide panel, select the fifth color from the left, in the second row. Notice that the logo changes color. Click the Set Base Color To The Current Color button (■) to try a new group of colors using the Complementary 2 harmony rule. Click the Save Color Group To Swatch Panel button (■) to save the colors in the Swatches panel.

● **Note:** If you choose a different color variation than the one suggested, your color will differ from those in the rest of this section.

9 Choose File > Save.

Editing a color group

When you create color groups, either in the Swatches panel or in the Color Guide panel, you can edit them individually or as a group in the Edit Colors dialog box. You can also rename a color group, reorder the colors in the group, add or remove colors, and more. In this section, you will learn how to edit colors of a saved color group using the Edit Color dialog box.

1 Choose Select > Deselect, and then click the Swatches panel icon ().

2 Click the folder icon to the left of the last color group to select the group (you may need to scroll down in the Swatches panel).

Notice that the Swatch Options button (▤) changes to the Edit Color Group button (◉) when the group (folder) is selected. The Swatch Options button at the bottom of the panel lets you edit a single, selected color.

● **Note:** If artwork is selected when you click the Edit Color Group button in the Swatches panel, the color group applies to the selected object(s). The Recolor Artwork dialog box appears, allowing you to edit colors for and apply colors to the selected object(s).

3 Click the Edit Color Group button (◉) at the bottom of the Swatches panel to open the Edit Colors dialog box.

On the right side of the Edit Colors dialog box, under Color Groups, all of the existing color groups in the Swatches panel are listed. On the left side of the dialog box, you can edit the colors of each color group, either individually or as a group.

▶ **Tip:** To edit a color group, you can also double-click the folder icon to the left of the color group in the Swatches panel.

Next, you will edit the colors for the color group.

4 In the Edit Colors dialog box, the group of colors you are about to edit is shown in the upper-left corner. Select the name Color Group 2 above the Color Groups, on the right side of the dialog box, and rename the group **label 2**. This will be the name of a new color group you save later in the lesson.

5 In the color wheel, you'll see markers (circles) that represent each color in the group. Drag the largest red marker on the right side of the color wheel up and to the right edge of the color wheel.

6 Change the Brightness by dragging the Adjust Brightness slider below the color wheel to the right, to brighten all the colors at once. Leave the Edit Colors dialog box open.

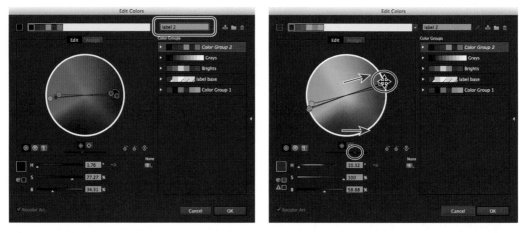

Rename the color group.   Edit the color and brightness.

● **Note:** You can match the H, S, B (hue, saturation, brightness) values below the color wheel in the Edit Colors dialog box to what you see in the figure, if you want to match exactly the color we achieved.

The Recolor Art selection at the bottom of the Edit Colors dialog box is dimmed because no artwork is selected. If artwork is selected when you open this dialog box, the dialog box is called the Recolor Artwork dialog box and any edits you make change the color group and artwork.

● **Note:** The larger marker in the color wheel with the double circle is the base color of the color group.

Next, you will edit the colors in the group independently and then save the colors as a new named group.

7   Click the Unlink Harmony Colors button (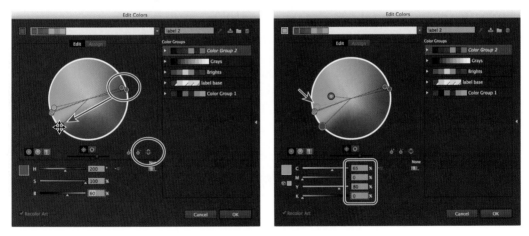) in the Edit Colors dialog box to edit the colors independently. The button will turn into the Link Harmony Colors button ().

The lines between the color markers (circles) and the center of the color wheel become dotted, indicating that the colors can be edited independently.

8   Drag the larger red marker down and to the left, to the edge of the color wheel below the green color markers, to change the red color into a blue.

By moving the color markers away from the center, you increase saturation. By moving the color markers toward the center of the color wheel, you decrease saturation. When a color marker is selected, you can edit the color using the H, S, B sliders below the color wheel.

9   Click the Color Mode button () to the right of the H, S, B values below the color wheel, and choose CMYK from the menu, if the CMYK sliders are not already visible. Click to select one of the green markers in the color wheel, as shown in the figure on the right, below. Change the CMYK values to C=**65**, M=**0**, Y=**80**, and K=**0**. Notice the light green color marker move in the color wheel. Leave the dialog box open.

Edit a single color.   Edit another color.

● **Note:** It's okay if the color markers in your Edit Colors dialog box are different from those shown in the figure above.

10 Click the Color Mode button () and choose HSB from the menu, so that next time you edit colors you will be using the HSB sliders.

11 Click the New Color Group button () in the upper-right corner of the Edit Colors dialog box to save the colors you've edited as a new color group named **label 2**.

▶ **Tip:** To edit a color group and save the changes without creating a new color group, click the Save Changes To Color Group button ().

12 Click OK to close the Edit Colors dialog box. The label 2 color group is automatically saved in the Swatches panel. If a dialog box appears, click Yes to save the changes to the color group in the Swatches panel.

13 Choose File > Save.

Editing color options

You can use the options in the lower portion of the Edit Colors dialog box to edit color, as described in the figure below.

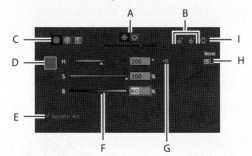

A Show saturation or brightness and hue on color wheel.

B Add and subtract color tools.

C Color display options (smooth color wheel, segmented color wheel, color bars).

D Color of the selected color marker or color bar.

E Selected artwork is recolored when selected (the check box is dimmed when artwork is not selected).

F Color sliders.

G Color Mode button.

H Limit the color group to colors in a swatch library.

I Unlink harmony colors.

Editing colors in artwork

You can also edit the colors in selected artwork, using the Recolor Artwork command. Next, you will edit the colors for the artwork on the second artboard and save the edited colors as a color group.

1 Choose Select > All On Active Artboard.

2 Choose Edit > Edit Colors > Recolor Artwork to open the Recolor Artwork dialog box.

The Recolor Artwork dialog box options allow you to reassign or reduce the colors in your artwork and to create and edit color groups. All the color groups that you create for a document appear in the Color Groups storage area of the Recolor Artwork dialog box and in the Swatches panel. You can select and use these color groups at any time.

Tip: You can also access the Recolor Artwork dialog box by selecting the artwork and then clicking the Recolor Artwork button (🔘) in the Control panel.

3 In the Recolor Artwork dialog box, click the Hide Color Group Storage icon (◀) on the right side of the dialog box.

4 Click the Edit tab to edit the colors in the artwork using the color wheel.

5 Click the Link Harmony Colors icon (⬢) to edit all the colors at the same time. The icon should now look like this ⬢.

6 Click the larger red color circle to select it. At the bottom of the dialog box, change the H value to **336**, the S value to **77**, and the B value to **25**.

Tip: If you want to return to the original logo colors, click the Get Colors From Selected Art button (🔲).

Changing the H (hue) and S (saturation) values is the same as dragging the larger red circle in the color wheel. Changing the B (brightness) value is the same as dragging the Brightness slider.

Hide the color groups.   Edit the larger red color.   The result.

Tip: You can save the edited colors as a color group by clicking the Show Color Group Storage icon (▶) on the right side of the dialog box and then clicking the New Color Group button (🔲).

The edit options in the Recolor Artwork dialog box are the same as the options in the Edit Colors dialog box. Instead of editing color and creating color groups to apply later, you are dynamically editing colors in the selected artwork. Notice the Recolor Art selection in the lower-left corner of the dialog box. When artwork is selected, you are editing the artwork.

7 Click OK in the Recolor Artwork dialog box.

8 Choose Select > Deselect, and then choose File > Save.

Next, you will get a color group from a community of users, using the Kuler panel.

Working with the Kuler panel

The Kuler panel is a portal to themed color groups, such as Ice Cream, created by an online community of designers. You can browse lots of color groups and download them to edit or use. You can also create themed color groups to share with others.

Next, you will download a themed color group for an Italian restaurant and apply color to it.

1 Choose 3 Artboard 3 from the Artboard Navigation menu in the lower-left corner of the Document window.

2 Choose Window > Extensions > Kuler.

● **Note:** You need an Internet connection to access the Kuler themes.

● **Note:** Because the themes are constantly updated and are brought into the Kuler panel via the Internet, your Kuler panel may show different themes from those shown in the figures.

3 In the Kuler panel, click the Highest Rated menu and choose Most Popular. The Kuler panel shows you the newest themes, highest rated themes, and more.

4 To search for themes, type **Italian restaurant** in the Search field at the top of the panel and press Enter or Return. This brings in the themes related to the words "Italian restaurant."

● **Note:** To learn more about the Kuler panel options, search for "Kuler panel" in Illustrator Help (Help > Illustrator Help).

5 Click the Italian Restaurant theme that looks something like this (▉▉▢▢▉▉) in the search results (below the search field). If the Italian Restaurant theme does not appear, select another. Click the Add Selected Theme To Swatches button (▦) to add it to the Swatches panel for the open document.

6 Close the Kuler panel.

7 Click the Swatches panel icon (▦) to open the panel, if it isn't already open.

Notice that the new color group, Italian Restaurant, appears in the panel list of swatches (scroll down, if necessary).

8 Choose File > Save.

Assigning colors to your artwork

The Assign tab of the Recolor Artwork dialog box lets you assign colors from a color group to your artwork. You can assign colors in several ways, including using a new color group chosen from the Harmony Rules menu. Next, you will assign new colors to a third version of the label.

1 Choose Select > All On Active Artboard.

2 Click the Recolor Artwork button () in the Control panel.

3 Click the Show Color Group Storage icon (▶) (the small arrow) on the right side of the dialog box to show the color groups, if they aren't already showing. Make sure that, in the top left of the dialog box, the Assign button is selected.

On the left side of the Recolor Artwork dialog box, notice that the colors of the label are listed in the Current Colors column, in what is called "Hue-Forward" sorting. That means they are arranged, from top to bottom, in the ordering of the color wheel: red, orange, yellow, green, blue, indigo, and violet.

● **Note:** If the colors in the Kuler group you selected earlier were different than what we selected, the colors in this section will also look a little different and that's okay.

4 Under Color Groups in the Recolor Artwork panel, select the Italian Restaurant color group you saved from the Kuler panel.

On the left side of the Recolor Artwork dialog box, notice that the colors of the Italian Restaurant color group are assigned to the colors in the label. The Current Colors column shows what the color was in the label, and the New column shows what the color has become (or been "reassigned to"). Also, notice that the two yellow colors in the original label are now next to each other and are mapped to a single color. This is because there are only five colors in the Italian Restaurant group and six in the label.

● **Note:** If the colors of the label do not change, make sure that Recolor Art is selected at the bottom of the Recolor Artwork dialog box.

5 Click the Hide Color Group Storage icon (◾) to hide the color groups. Drag the dialog box by the title bar at the top so that you can see the artwork.

6 In the New column of the Recolor Artwork dialog box, drag the red color down on top of the green color below it. See the first part of the figure below.

This swaps the green and red colors in the artwork order and changes the color in the artwork on the artboard.

7 Drag the colors back to their original order.

The colors in the New column show what you see in the artwork. If you click one of the colors, notice that the HSB sliders at the bottom of the dialog box let you edit that one color.

8 Double-click the darker brown color at the bottom of the New column.

9 In the Color Picker dialog box, click the Color Swatches button to see the document swatches. Select label background in the Color Swatches list. Click OK to return to the Recolor Artwork dialog box.

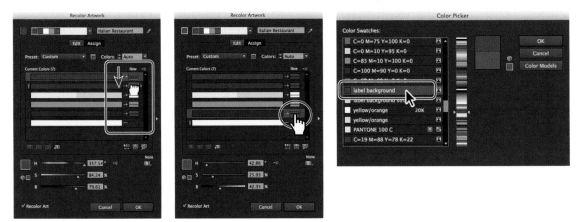

Reorder the New colors.   Double-click the brown color.   Select the label background swatch.

Next, you will make a few more changes to the colors in the label and then save the color edits to the Italian Restaurant color group.

10 Click the arrow between the lighter green color in the Current Color column and the light brown color in the New column.

In the artwork, the color on the label changes. By clicking the arrow between a current color and a new color, you prevent the current color in the row (the light green) from being reassigned to the new color (light brown). It stays light green (in this case).

11 Drag the light green bar up on top of the dark brown bar in the current color list. Notice the color change in the artwork.

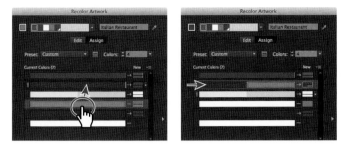

Note: If you want to apply a single color to the selected artwork, you can choose 1 from the Colors menu, above the New column in the Recolor Artwork dialog box. Be sure to finish the steps in this lesson before experimenting with this.

When you drag a color in the current color column onto another row in the same column, you are telling Illustrator to apply the same new color (the green in this case) to both colors. The green color in the New column is split into three sections (![icon]). The darkest color in the row (the dark brown gray) is replaced with the green. The lighter green color is replaced with a proportionally lighter tint of the green.

12 Click the Show Color Group Storage icon (![icon]) to show the color groups on the right side of the dialog box. Click the Save Changes To Color Group button (![icon]) to save the changes to the color group without closing the dialog box. Click OK. The color changes that you made to the color group are saved in the Swatches panel.

Note: Many kinds of color edits can be made to selected artwork in the Recolor Artwork dialog box. To learn more, search for "Working with color groups" in Illustrator Help.

13 Choose Select > Deselect and then File > Save.

Adjusting colors

Next, you will change the original label on artboard 1 to use CMYK colors only. You'll convert the yellow color PANTONE 100 C to CMYK.

1 Choose 1 from the Artboard Navigation menu in the lower-left corner of the Document window.

2 Choose Select > All On Active Artboard.

3 Choose Edit > Edit Colors > Convert To CMYK.

The colors in the selected label, including the yellow PANTONE 100 C, are now CMYK. There are many options in the Edit > Edit Colors menu for converting color, including Recolor With Preset. This command lets you change the color of selected artwork using a chosen number of colors, a color library, and a specific color harmony (such as complementary colors).

Note: Using this method for converting to CMYK does not affect the color swatches in the Swatches panel. It simply converts the selected artwork colors to CMYK.

4 Choose Select > Deselect and then File > Save.

Painting with patterns

In addition to process and spot colors, the Swatches panel can also contain pattern and gradient swatches. Illustrator provides sample swatches of each type in the default Swatches panel and lets you create your own patterns and gradients. In this section, you will focus on creating, applying, and editing patterns. To learn more about working with gradients, see Lesson 10, "Blending Colors and Shapes."

Applying existing patterns

A pattern is artwork saved in the Swatches panel that can be applied to the stroke or fill of an object. You can customize existing patterns and design patterns from scratch with any of the Illustrator tools. All patterns start with a single tile that is tiled (repeated) within a shape, starting at the ruler origin and continuing to the right. Next, you will apply an existing pattern to a shape.

1 Choose Window > Workspace > Reset Essentials.

2 Click the Layers panel icon (●) to expand the Layers panel.

3 In the Layers panel, click to select the visibility column to the left of the layer named pattern.

4 Click the Swatches panel icon (▦). In the Swatches panel, click the Swatch Libraries Menu button (▦▾) at the bottom of the panel and choose Patterns > Decorative > Vonster Patterns to open the pattern library.

5 Using the Selection tool (▶), select the white filled shape toward the top of the artboard. In the Control panel, change the Stroke color to None (▢). Make sure that the Fill box toward the bottom of the Tools panel is selected.

● **Note:** This last step is important. When you apply a pattern swatch, it applies to the stroke or the fill that is selected.

▶ **Tip:** Because some supplied patterns have a clear background, you can create a second fill for the object, using the Appearance panel. For more information, see Lesson 13, "Applying Appearance Attributes and Graphic Styles."

6 Select the Blazer pattern swatch in the Vonster Patterns panel to fill the path with the pattern. Close the Vonster Patterns panel, and notice that the pattern swatch fills the shape and is added to the list in the Swatches panel. Click the Swatches panel icon to collapse the panel.

7 Choose Select > Deselect and then File > Save.

Creating your own pattern

In this section of the lesson, you will create your own custom pattern and add it to the Swatches panel.

1 Select the Rectangle tool (▢) in the Tools panel. Click once in a blank area of the artboard to open the Rectangle dialog box. Change the Width to **34 pt** and the Height to **34 pt**, and then click OK.

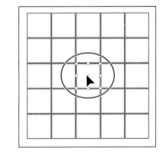

   Notice that the new rectangle has the same pattern fill as the shape in the previous steps. You will use this shape as the basis for your new pattern.

2 With the rectangle selected, press the letter D to set the default stroke (black) and fill (white) on the selected shape. A pattern that you create cannot contain another pattern.

3 With the rectangle selected, choose Object > Pattern > Make. Click OK in the dialog box that appears.

   When you create a pattern, Illustrator enters Pattern Editing mode, which is similar to Isolation mode you've worked with in grouped content. Pattern Editing mode allows you to create and edit patterns interactively, while previewing the changes to the pattern on the artboard. The Pattern Options panel (Window > Pattern Options) also opens, giving you all of the necessary options to create your pattern.

● **Note:** You don't have to have anything selected to start with a blank pattern.

4 Select the Selection tool (▸), and click the center rectangle to select it. Press Ctrl++ (Windows) or Command++ (Mac OS) twice to zoom in.

   Notice the series of lighter colored rectangles around the center rectangle. This is the rectangle shape repeated into a pattern and dimmed to let you focus on the original rectangle.

● **Note:** A pattern can be composed of more than one shape. For instance, to create a flannel pattern for a shirt, you can create three overlapping rectangles or lines, each with varying appearance options.

5 With the shape selected, double-click the Rotate tool (⟳) in the Tools panel. In the Rotate dialog box, change the Angle value to **45**. Click OK.

   Notice the blue rectangle in the center of the pattern. This indicates the tile edge (which is a part of the pattern definition area).

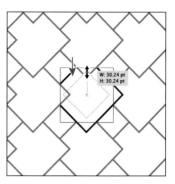

● **Note:** The figure at
right shows the pattern
before resizing.

6 Select the Selection tool and, pressing the
Shift+Alt (Windows) or Shift+Option (Mac
OS) keys, drag the top bounding point of the
selected rectangle down until the width and
height are approximately 30 pt.

Notice that the tile area (the blue box) didn't
change in size and that the rectangles have
more space between them. At this point,
you can edit the existing artwork, add new
artwork, or delete artwork.

7 In the Pattern Options panel, change the Name
to **checker** (the name is what appears in the
Swatches panel as a tool tip). Choose Hex By
Column for the Tile Type.

You have three Tile Type choices: the default
grid pattern, a brick style pattern, or the hex
pattern. The Brick Offset options can be selected
when you choose a brick Tile Type.

8 Click the Pattern Tile Tool button (⊞) in
the upper-left corner of the Pattern Options
panel. Position the pointer over the right,
middle tile size control widget of the blue
tile. Press the Alt (Windows) or Option
(Mac OS) key, and drag the widget to the
right a bit to make it wider.

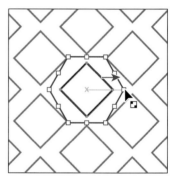

To stop editing the pattern tile, you can
either select any tool in the Tools panel
or click the Pattern Tile Tool button (⊞).

Instead of manually dragging to resize the tile with the Pattern Tile Tool, you
can also enter values in the Width and Height fields in the Pattern Options
panel. You can do this only if Size Tile To Art is not selected.

9 Select Size Tile To Art in the Pattern Options panel.

The Size Tile To Art selection fits the tile area (the blue hex shape) to the
bounds of the artwork, changing the spacing between the repeated objects. You
can manually change the width and the height of the pattern definition area to
include more content or to edit the spacing between.

10 Change the H Spacing to **5** pt, and change the V Spacing to **-5** pt.

▶ **Tip:** The spacing values can be either positive or negative values, to move the tiles apart or to
bring them closer together.

11 For Overlap, click the Bottom In Front button (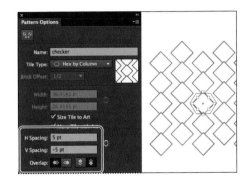), to see the change in the pattern.

The artwork in a pattern may begin to overlap, due to the size of the tile or the spacing values. By default, when objects overlap horizontally, the left object is on top; when objects overlap vertically, the top object is on top.

The Pattern Options panel has a host of other pattern editing options, including the ability to see more or less of the pattern, called Copies. To learn more about the Pattern Options panel, search for "Pattern options" in Illustrator Help.

12 Choose Edit > Undo Pattern Options *twice* to remove the overlap change and the vertical spacing change, but keep the horizontal spacing at 5 pt.

13 Select Show Swatch Bounds at the bottom of the Pattern Options panel to see the dotted area that will be saved in the swatch. Deselect Show Swatch Bounds.

14 With the rectangle still selected, change the Fill color to CMYK Cyan in the Control panel.

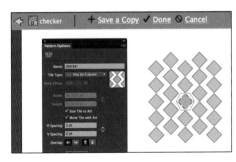

15 Click Done in the bar along the top of the Document window.

16 Choose File > Save.

> **Tip:** If you want to create pattern variations, you can click Save A Copy in the bar along the top of the Document window. This saves the current pattern in the Swatches panel as a copy and allows you to continue creating.

Applying a pattern

You can assign a pattern using a number of different methods. In this lesson, you will use the Swatches panel to apply the pattern. You can also apply the pattern using the Fill color in the Control panel.

1 Choose View > Fit Artboard In Window.

2 With the Selection tool (↖), click the shape filled with the Blazer pattern swatch near the top of the artboard.

3 Select the checker pattern swatch from the Fill color in the Control panel.

4 Choose Select > Deselect and then File > Save.

● **Note:** Your pattern may look different, and that's okay.

Editing a pattern

Next, you will edit the saved pattern and then update all instances in your artwork.

1 In the Swatches panel, double-click the checker pattern swatch to edit it.

▶ **Tip:** You can also select an object filled with a pattern swatch, and with the Fill box selected in the Tools panel, choose Object > Pattern > Edit Pattern.

2 In Pattern Editing mode, with the Selection tool, click to select the center diamond shape in the tile. In the Control panel, change the fill color to the yellow swatch named **label background stroke** (in a color group) and the Stroke weight to **0**.

3 Click Done to exit Pattern Editing mode.

4 Click the shape with the checker pattern fill to select it. Double-click the Scale tool (⬚) in the Tools panel to make the pattern larger without affecting the shape. In the Scale dialog box, change the Uniform Scale to **110%**. Deselect Scale Strokes & Effects, if necessary. Deselect Transform Objects, which selects Transform Patterns, and select Preview to see the change. Click OK.

5 On the artboard, select and delete the original white rectangle that you used to create the pattern.

6 Open the Layers panel, and make all layers visible by selecting the Visibility column to the left of the tomato and top shapes layers. Click the Layers panel icon to collapse the panel group.

7 Choose Select > Deselect and then File > Save.

8 Choose File > Close.

Working with Live Paint

Live Paint lets you paint vector graphics intuitively, by automatically detecting and correcting gaps that otherwise would have affected how fills and strokes were applied. Paths divide the drawing surface into areas, any of which can be colored, regardless of whether the area is bounded by a single path or by segments of multiple paths. Painting objects is like filling in a coloring book or using watercolors to paint a pencil sketch. Live Paint does not edit the underlying shapes.

Creating a Live Paint group

Next, you will open a file and paint objects using the Live Paint Bucket tool.

1 Choose File > Open, and open the L6start_2.ai file in the Lesson06 folder.

● **Note:** The final lesson file L6end_2.ai is in the Lesson06 folder in the Lessons folder if you wish to open it.

2 Choose File > Save As. In the Save As dialog box, name the file **greetingcard.ai** and navigate to the Lesson06 folder. Leave the Save As Type option set to Adobe Illustrator (*.AI) (Windows) or the Format option set to Adobe Illustrator (ai) (Mac OS), and click Save. In the Illustrator Options dialog box, leave the Illustrator options at their default settings and then click OK.

3 Use the Selection tool (▸) to drag a selection across the three white flower shapes on the artboard. The rest of the content is locked.

4 Choose Object > Live Paint > Make.

This creates a Live Paint group that you can now paint using the Live Paint Bucket tool (🪣). Once a Live Paint group is created, each path remains fully editable. When you move or adjust a path's shape, the colors are automatically reapplied to the new regions that are formed by the edited paths.

▶ **Tip:** You can tell it's a Live Paint group because of the special bounding box around all three shapes.

5 Select the Live Paint Bucket tool (🪣) from the Shape Builder tool (🔨) group in the Tools panel. Before painting, click the Fill color in the Control panel and select the yellow/orange swatch in the Swatches panel.

● **Note:** You may need to press the Escape key to hide the Swatches panel.

6 Position the pointer over the center of the Live Paint group. As you move over Live Paint objects, they are highlighted and three color swatches appear above the pointer. The swatches represent the three adjacent swatches in the Swatches panel. The center swatch is the last selected color. Click when the larger, center flower shape is highlighted.

▶ **Tip:** You can also drag across multiple shapes to apply color to them all at once.

7 Move the pointer to the left, to the overlapping shape. Click the Left Arrow key twice to highlight the light yellow color in the three swatches above the pointer. Click to apply the color to the flower.

● **Note:** You can also switch to a color other than the one selected in the group by clicking a color in the Swatches panel.

8 Paint the remaining three flower shapes using the colors you see in the figure at right (yellow, pink, and dark pink). Before clicking to apply a color, press the Left and Right Arrow keys to cycle through the colors in the Swatches panel.

Painting strokes with the Live Paint Bucket tool is just as easy as painting fills. First, you need to enable the option to paint strokes.

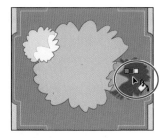

● **Note:** To learn more about the options in the Live Paint Bucket Options dialog box, search for "Paint with the Live Paint Bucket tool" in Illustrator Help.

9 Double-click the Live Paint Bucket tool in the Tools panel. This opens the Live Paint Bucket Options dialog box. Select the Paint Strokes option, and then click OK.

Next, you'll remove the inner black strokes from the shapes and retain the outer black strokes.

10 Position the tip (▶) part of the pointer directly over the stroke, between the center shape and the light yellow filled shape, as shown in the figure. When the Stroke pointer (◣) appears, click the Left Arrow key to select None and then click the stroke to remove the stroke color.

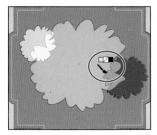

11 Position the pointer directly over the stroke, between the center shape and the light pink filled shape, as shown in the figure. When the Stroke pointer appears, ensure that None appears in the swatches above the pointer and then click the stroke to remove the stroke color.

12 Choose Select > Deselect to see how the strokes are now painted. Then, choose File > Save.

Editing Live Paint regions

When you make a Live Paint group, each path remains editable. When you move or adjust a path, the colors that were previously applied don't just stay where they were, like they do in natural media paintings or image-editing software. Instead, the colors are automatically reapplied to the new regions that are formed by the edited paths. Next, you will edit the paths and add another shape.

1   Select the Selection tool (▶) in the Tools panel, and then hold down the spacebar and drag the artboard to the right to reveal the white flower shape off the left edge of the artboard.

2   Select the flower shape, and choose Edit > Copy.

3   Double-click the Hand tool (✋) to fit the artboard in the Document window.

4   With the Selection tool, double-click the Live Paint group.

    Illustrator enters Isolation mode and allows you to edit each shape independently.

5   Choose Edit > Paste. Drag the pasted flower shape down to the lower left so that it overlaps the center flower, as shown in the figure.

6   Select the Live Paint Bucket tool (🪣) in the Tools panel, and paint the outer half of the pasted flower with dark green and the inner half with light green.

7   Position the pointer directly over the stroke, between the center orange shape and the green-filled shape. When the Stroke pointer appears, click the Left Arrow key to highlight None and then click the stroke to remove the stroke color. Do this for the last remaining stroke inside the green-filled shape as well.

● **Note:** When you move or edit shapes that are part of a Live Paint group, unexpected things can happen. For instance, a stroke may appear where there was none before. Be sure to double-check the shapes to make sure that they look like they should.

8   Select the Selection tool, and drag the green-filled flower shape a little up and to the left, to reposition it. Notice how the color fill changes.

9   Select the Direct Selection tool (▷) in the Tools panel, and position the pointer over the small yellow flower in the upper-left corner. Click one of the anchor points on the edge of the center flower (located in the middle of the small yellow flower), and drag to reposition it.

Notice how the paths are still completely editable and the colors are automatically reapplied to the new regions that are formed by the edited paths.

Next, you will add a white color to the center of the larger flower so that you can add text and make it readable.

10 Press Ctrl++ (Windows) or Command++ (Mac OS) twice to zoom in. Press Escape to exit Isolation mode, and then choose Select > Deselect.

11 Expand the Layers panel by clicking the Layers panel icon (◩) on the right side of the workspace. Click the visibility column for the layer named text (just above the eye icon for the layer named live paint). Collapse the Layers panel group.

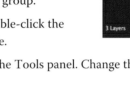

12 Select the Selection tool (▶), and double-click the flower shapes to enter Isolation mode.

13 Select the Line Segment tool (╱) in the Tools panel. Change the Stroke color to white in the Control panel.

14 Click the center of the orange flower and, in the Line Segment Tool Options dialog box, change the Length to **2.55** in and the Angle to **0**. Click OK, and leave the line selected.

● **Note:** If you see the word "Transform," click to reveal the Transform panel and make these changes.

15 Select the Selection tool. In the Control panel, with the center point selected in the reference point locator (▦), change the X value to **4.48** in and the Y value to **1.8** in to position the line and leave a small gap on the right end of the line between the end of the line and the flower shape.

16 Select the Line Segment tool (╱) and draw another line below that by pressing the Shift key and clicking the right edge of the green flower and then dragging to the right, to the point where the line snaps to the left edge of the light pink shape. The Smart Guides (View > Smart Guides) help you snap the line to the shapes.

● **Note:** If the red outline stops at the top line you created, try making the top line shorter on the right side, using the Direct Selection tool.

17 Select the Live Paint Bucket tool in the Tools panel, and position the cursor over the center of the large orange flower, between the lines. *Do not click.*

Note that the bottom line "closes" the bottom of the flower shape, but the top line may not close the top of the path. That means that if you were to click (don't), the color would fill everywhere that the red outline surrounds. The red line in the figure below has been enhanced to see it more easily.

Draw the bottom line.   Hover to see the paint area.

208 LESSON 6 Color and Painting

Working with gap options

Next, you will work with the Gap Options dialog box.

1 Choose Select > All.

2 Choose Object > Live Paint > Gap Options. In the Gap Options dialog box, select Gap Detection, if it is not already selected. Choose Medium Gaps from the Paint Stops At menu.

The Gap Preview Color is set to highlight any gaps it detects in red. Setting the gap detection stops paint from leaking through some of the gaps between objects as you paint. Look at the artwork to see any gaps highlighted in red. The gap between the top line and the right edge of the flower shape should be closed with a red line. If not, you can try choosing Large Gaps from the Paint Stops At menu. Click OK.

Tip: If you click the Close Gaps With Paths button in the Gap Options dialog box, Illustrator will insert actual vector paths to the artwork.

3 Select the Live Paint Bucket tool (⬛), and cross over the space between the two lines you drew. Make sure that white is showing in the swatches above the pointer, and then click to fill the space with white.

4 Choose View > Fit Artboard In Window.

5 Select the Live Paint Selection tool (⬛) in the Tools panel, from the Live Paint Bucket tool group. Click the top yellow/orange shape, and Shift-click the bottom yellow/orange shape, as shown in the figure below. Choose the gradient swatch named background from the Fill color in the Control panel.

Tip: Within a Live Paint group, you can also select content by dragging across artwork with the Live Paint Selection tool.

6 Select the Gradient tool (⬛) in the Tools panel. Make sure that the Fill box is selected towards the bottom of the Tools panel. Drag from the center of the large flower shape (in the white area) down and to the right to create a uniform gradient across both shapes.

7 Select the Selection tool (▸), and press Escape to exit Isolation mode and to see the "Happy Birthday" text on the artboard.

Select the pieces.

Drag with the Gradient tool.

The final result.

8 Choose File > Save then File > Close.

Review questions

1 Describe at least three ways to fill an object with color.

2 How can you save a color?

3 How do you name a color?

4 How can you choose color harmonies for colors?

5 Name two things that the Edit Colors/Recolor Artwork dialog box allows you to do.

6 How do you add pattern swatches to the Swatches panel?

7 Explain what Live Paint allows you to do.

Review answers

1 To fill an object with color, select the object and change the Fill color or Stroke color in the Control panel or select the Fill box in the Tools panel. Then do one of the following:

   • Double-click the Fill or Stroke box in the Tools panel to access the Color Picker.

   • Drag the color sliders, or type values in the text boxes in the Color panel.

   • Click a color swatch in the Swatches panel.

   • Select the Eyedropper tool, and then click a color in the artwork.

   • Choose Window > Swatch Libraries to open another color library, and then click a color swatch in the Color Library panel.

2 You can save a color for painting other objects in your artwork by adding it to the Swatches panel. Select the color, and do one of the following:

   • Drag it from the Fill box, and drop it over the Swatches panel.

   • Click the New Swatch button at the bottom of the Swatches panel.

   • Choose New Swatch from the Swatches panel menu.

   You can also add colors from other color libraries by selecting them in the Color Library panel and choosing Add To Swatches from the panel menu.

3 To name a color, double-click the color swatch in the Swatches panel or select it and choose Swatch Options from the panel menu. Type the name for the color in the Swatch Options dialog box.

4 The Color Guide panel is a tool you can use for inspiration while you create your artwork. The panel suggests color harmonies based on the current color in the Tools panel.

5 You use the Edit Colors/Recolor Artwork dialog box to create and edit color groups, to reassign or reduce the colors in your artwork, and more.

6 Easily create and edit seamlessly tiled vector patterns. Either create content for the pattern or deselect all content and choose Object > Pattern > Make. In Pattern Editing mode you can edit the pattern and preview it.

7 Live Paint lets you paint vector graphics intuitively by automatically detecting and correcting gaps that otherwise would have affected how fills and strokes were applied. Paths divide the drawing surface up into areas, any of which can be colored, regardless of whether the area is bounded by a single path or by segments of multiple paths. Painting objects with Live Paint is like filling in a coloring book or using watercolors to paint a pencil sketch.

7 WORKING WITH TYPE

Lesson overview

In this lesson, you'll learn how to do the following:

- Import text.

- Create columns of type.

- Change text attributes.

- Create and edit paragraph and character styles.

- Copy and apply text attributes by sampling type.

- Wrap type around a graphic.

- Reshape text with a warp.

- Create type on a path and shapes.

- Create text outlines.

 This lesson takes approximately an hour to complete. If needed, remove the previous lesson folder from your hard disk and copy the Lesson07 folder onto it.

Text as a design element plays a major role in your illustrations. Like other objects, type can be painted, scaled, rotated, and so on. In this lesson, discover how to create basic text and interesting text effects.

Getting started

You'll be working in one art file during this lesson, but before you begin, restore the default preferences for Adobe Illustrator CS6. Then, open the finished art file for this lesson to see the illustration.

1 To ensure that the tools and panels function exactly as described in this lesson, delete or deactivate (by renaming) the Adobe Illustrator CS6 preferences file. See "Restoring default preferences" on page 3.

2 Start Adobe Illustrator CS6.

● **Note:** If you have not already done so, copy the Lesson07 folder from the Lessons folder on the *Adobe Illustrator CS6 Classroom in a Book* CD onto your hard disk. See "Copying the Classroom in a Book files" on page 2.

3 Choose File > Open. Locate the file named L7end.ai in the Lesson07 folder in the Lessons folder that you copied onto your hard disk.

In this lesson, you will create the text for this poster. Leave it open for reference, or choose File > Close without saving.

● **Note:** In Mac OS, when opening lesson files, you may need to click the round, green button in the upper-left corner of the Document window to maximize the window's size.

4 Choose File > Open. In the Open dialog box, navigate to the Lesson07 folder in the Lessons folder. Open the L7start.ai file.

This file already has non-text components in it. You will add all of the text elements to complete the poster.

5 Choose File > Save As. In the Save As dialog box, navigate to the Lesson07 folder and name the file **poster.ai**. Leave the Save As Type option set to Adobe Illustrator (*.AI) (Windows) or the Format option set to Adobe Illustrator (ai) (Mac OS), and then click Save. In the Illustrator Options dialog box, leave the Illustrator options at their default settings and then click OK.

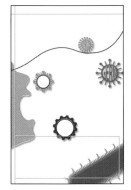

6 Choose View > Smart Guides to deselect the Smart Guides.

7 Choose Window > Workspace > Reset Essentials.

● **Note:** If you don't see "Reset Essentials" in the Workspace menu, choose Window > Workspace > Essentials before choosing Window > Workspace > Reset Essentials.

Working with type

Type features are some of the most powerful tools in Illustrator. You can add a single line of type to your artwork, create columns and rows of text like you do in Adobe InDesign, flow text into a shape or along a path, and work with letterforms as graphic objects.

You can create text in three different ways: as point type, area type, and type on a path. Following is a short description of each type of text:

- **Point type** is a horizontal or vertical line of text that begins where you click and expands as you enter characters. Each line of text is independent—the line expands or shrinks as you edit it but doesn't wrap to the next line. Entering text this way is useful for adding a headline or a few words to your artwork.

- **Area type** uses the boundaries of an object to control the flow of characters, either horizontally or vertically. When the text reaches a boundary, it automatically wraps to fit inside the defined area. Entering text in this way is useful when you want to create one or more paragraphs, such as for a brochure.

- **Type on a path** flows along the edge of an open or closed path. When you enter text horizontally, the characters are parallel to the baseline. When you enter text vertically, the characters are perpendicular to the baseline. In either case, the text flows in the direction in which points were added to the path.

Next, you will create point type and then you will create area type. Later in this lesson, you will also create type on a path.

Creating point type

When typing text directly into a document, you select the Type tool and click where you'd like the text. When the cursor appears, you can begin typing.

Next, you will enter some text at the top of the poster.

1 Select the Zoom tool (🔍) in the Tools panel, and click the upper-left corner of the artboard twice, slowly.

2 Select the Type tool (T), and click where the guides meet in the upper-left corner of the artboard. The cursor appears on the artboard. Type **Help stop the spread of germs that cause colds and other illnesses!**

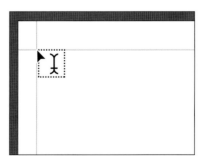

By clicking with the Type tool, you create point type. Point type is a line of text that keeps going until you stop typing or press Return or Enter. It's very useful for headlines.

Note: Point type that is scaled, as in step 3, is printable, but the font size may not be a whole number (such as 12 pt).

3   Select the Selection tool (⬉) in the Tools panel, and notice the bounding box around the text. Drag the bounding point on the right to the right. Notice that the text stretches as you drag any bounding point.

4   Choose Edit > Undo Scale and then View > Fit Artboard In Window.

Creating area type

To create area type, you click with the Type tool where you want the text and drag to create an area type object (also called a text area). When the cursor appears, you can type. You can also convert an existing shape or object to a type object by clicking on or inside the edge of the object with the Type tool.

Next, you will create area type and enter more text.

1   Choose View > Smart Guides to select the Smart Guides.

2   Select the Type tool (**T**), and position the cursor below the text you just created, aligned on the left guide. Drag from the guide down and to the right to create a text area with a width and height of approximately 2 in.

The cursor appears in the new text area.

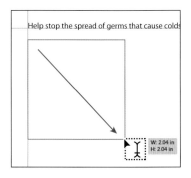

3   Select the Zoom tool (🔍) in the Tools panel, and click twice, slowly, in the center of the new text area.

Note: For now, keep the default settings for type formatting.

4   Select the Type tool (**T**), and type **Cover your mouth and nose when you cough or sneeze**. Do not type the period.

Notice that the text wraps in the text area.

5   Select the Selection tool (⬉), and notice the bounding box around the text. Drag the right center bounding point to the right, noticing how the text wraps within the object. Drag until it approximately aligns with the right edge of the text above it.

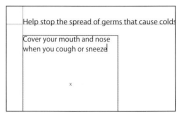

6   Choose Select > Deselect, and then choose File > Save.

Area type versus point type

Illustrator provides visual indications to help you tell the difference between point type and area type. With the Selection tool, click to select text and its bounding box.

Area type has two extra boxes, called ports. Ports are used to thread (flow) text from one type area to another. Working with ports and threading is covered later in this lesson. Point type, when selected, does not have ports; instead, it has a point before the first letter in the first line.

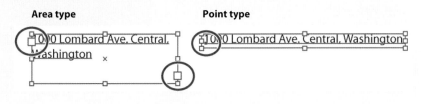

Area type   **Point type**

Importing a plain text file

You can import text into artwork from a file that was created in another application. Illustrator supports the following formats for importing text:

* Microsoft Word (doc)

* Microsoft Word DOCX (docx)

* Microsoft RTF (rtf)

* Plain text (txt)(ASCII) with ANSI, Unicode, Shift JIS, GB2312, Chinese Big 5, Cyrillic, GB18030, Greek, Turkish, Baltic, and Central European encoding.

You can also copy and paste text, but formatting may be lost when text is pasted. One of the advantages of importing text from a file, rather than copying and pasting it, is that imported text retains its character and paragraph formatting. For example, text from an RTF file retains its font and style specifications in Illustrator.

Next, you will place text from a simple text file.

1 Before importing the text, select the Type tool (**T**) and insert the cursor at the end of the text "Cover your mouth and nose when you cough or sneeze." Press Enter or Return, and leave the cursor in the text.

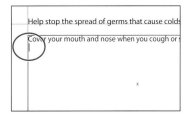

2 Choose File > Place. Navigate to the Lesson07 folder in the Lessons folder, select the L7copy.txt file, and click Place.

● **Note:** Ensure that the cursor is in the text frame before you click. Otherwise, you may create another type area.

3 In the Text Import Options dialog box, you can set options prior to importing text. Leave the default settings, and then click OK.

The text is now placed in the text area. You will learn how to apply attributes to format text later in this lesson. Also, if you see a red plus sign (⊞) in the lower-right corner of the type object, this indicates that the text does not fit within the bounds. You will fix this later in the lesson.

4 Choose File > Save, and leave this file open.

By inserting the cursor in a text area, the text is automatically flowed within the bounds of the area. If you didn't insert the cursor in the text area, and you placed the text, you could click to have Illustrator automatically create a text area that covers most of the page or click and drag to create a new text area in the size and position you want.

Placing Microsoft Word documents

When you place (File > Place) RTF (Rich Text Format) or Word documents (.DOC or .DOCX) in Illustrator, the Microsoft Word Options dialog box appears.

In this dialog box, you can select to keep the generated Table of Contents, footnotes and endnotes, and index text, and even choose to remove the formatting of the text before you place it.

Note: *When you place a Word document and do not select Remove Text Formatting, paragraph styles that were used in Word are brought into Illustrator.*

Working with overflow text and text reflow

Each area type object contains an in port and an out port. The ports enable you to link to other objects and to create a linked copy of the type object. An empty port indicates that all the text is visible and that the object isn't linked. A red plus sign (⊞) in an out port indicates that the object contains additional text, which is called overflow text.

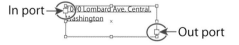

There are two main methods for remedying overflow text:

- Thread the text to another type object.
- Resize the type object or adjust the text.

Threading text

To thread, or continue, text from one object to the next, you have to link the objects. Linked type objects can be of any shape; however, the text must be entered in an object or along a path, not as point type (by simply clicking to create text).

Next, you will thread the overset text to another type object.

1 Use the Selection tool (▶) to select the larger type object.

2 With the Selection tool, click the out port (⊞) of the selected type object. The pointer changes to a loaded text icon (▦) when you move it away.

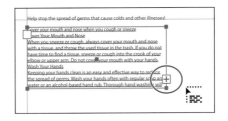

● **Note:** If you double-click, a new type object appears. If this happens, you can either drag the new object where you would like it to be positioned or choose Edit > Undo Link Threaded Text, and the loaded text icon reappears.

3 Choose View > Fit Artboard In Window.

4 Towards the bottom of the artboard, click and drag from the upper-left corner of the aqua guide box, down and to the right corner of the guide box.

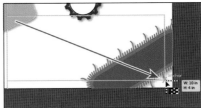

● **Note:** With the loaded text icon, you can simply click the artboard instead of dragging to create a new type object. This creates a much larger type object.

▶ **Tip:** Another way to thread text between objects is to select an area type object, select the object (or objects) you want to link to, and then choose Type > Threaded Text > Create.

5 Choose File > Save.

With the bottom type object still selected, notice the line between the two objects, which is the thread that tells you that the two objects are connected. Notice the out port (▶) of the top type object and the in port (▶) of the bottom type object (both circled in the figure at right). The arrow indicates that an object is linked to another object.

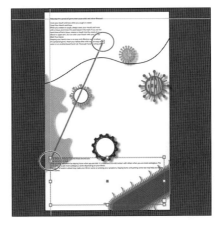

● **Note:** If you delete the second type object (created in the previous step), the text is pulled back into the original object as overflow text. Although not visible, the overflow text is not deleted.

Creating columns of text

You can easily create columns and rows of text by using the Area Type options.

● **Note:** If the cursor is still in the type object, you don't have to select the text area with the Selection tool to access the Area Type options.

1 If the bottom type object is no longer selected, use the Selection tool (▶) to select it.

2 Choose Type > Area Type Options. In the Area Type Options dialog box, select Preview in the lower-left corner. In the Columns section of the dialog box, change Number to **2** and then click OK.

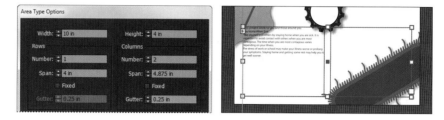

● **Note:** Your text may not look exactly like the figure. That's okay.

3 Choose Select > Deselect.

4 Choose File > Save. Leave this document open.

Area type options

You can use the Area Type Options command to create rows and columns of text. Read about additional options below:

- **Number** specifies the number of rows and columns you want the object to contain.

- **Span** specifies the height of individual rows and the width of individual columns.

- **Fixed** determines what happens to the span of rows and columns if you resize the type area. When this option is selected, resizing the area can change the number of rows and columns, but not their width. Leave this option deselected if you want row and column widths to change when you resize the type area.

- **Gutter** specifies the distance between rows or columns.

- **Inset Spacing** controls the margin between the text and the bounding path. This margin is referred to as the inset spacing.

- **First Baseline** controls the alignment of the first line of text with the top of the object.

- **Text Flow** determines how text flows between rows and columns.

—From Illustrator Help

Formatting type

In this section, you'll discover how to change text attributes, such as size, font, and style. You can quickly change most attributes in the Control panel.

1   Select the Zoom tool (🔍) in the Tools panel, and click twice, slowly, in the center of the top text area that is threaded at the top of the artboard.

2   Select the Type tool (T) in the Tools panel, and insert the cursor anywhere in the text area. Choose Select > All, or press Ctrl+A (Windows) or Command+A (Mac OS) to select all the text in both threaded type objects.

▶ **Tip:** If you double-click text with the Selection or Direct Selection tool, the Type tool becomes selected.

In this next section, you'll learn two different methods for selecting a font. First, you'll change the font of selected text using the Font menu in the Control panel.

3   Click the arrow to the right of the Font menu and scroll to find and select Myriad Pro, if not already selected.

This sets the font for all of the threaded text.

● **Note:** You may see the word "Character" instead of the Font menu listed in the Control panel. Click the word "Character" to reveal the Character panel.

● **Note:** You may need to click the arrow that appears at the bottom of the font list to continue scrolling through the list.

4   Click three times in the first line of the text "Cover your mouth and nose when you cough or sneeze" to select the entire paragraph. Choose Type > Font to see a list of available fonts. Scroll down, and select Minion Pro > Bold. If your font list is long, you may need to scroll quite far to find this font (the list is alphabetized).

● **Note:** Be careful when selecting text. If you attempt to drag across the text to select it, you may wind up creating a new text area.

Tip: Once a font name is selected, you can also press the Up or Down Arrow keys to scroll through the list.

5 Make sure that the text is still selected, and then follow the instructions below. This next method is the most dynamic method for selecting a font.

- Select whatever font is listed in the Font menu in the Control panel, and begin typing the name **Letter Gothic Std**. Illustrator filters through the list and displays the font name in the field.

Tip: You can also click the word "Character" in the Control panel to open the Character panel (Window > Type > Character) and type the name of the font there.

6 Click the arrow in the Font Style menu in the Control panel to see the available styles for Letter Gothic Std, and make sure Bold is selected.

Font styles are specific to each font family. Although you may have the Letter Gothic Std font family on your system, you may not have the bold and italic styles of that family.

Illustrator CS6 Fonts

The following fonts and accompanying documentation are installed and are included in the Documentation folder on the Illustrator CS6 product DVD or in the packaged downloaded file if you download Illustrator CS6 from the Adobe Store. For trial customers, the fonts are not available until after purchase.

Adobe Arabic	Letter Gothic Std
Birch Std	LITHOS PRO
Blackoak Std	MESQUITE STD
Brush Script Std	Adobe Ming Std
Adobe Caslon® Pro	Minion Pro
Chaparral Pro	Myriad Arabic
CHARLEMAGNE STD	Myriad Hebrew
Cooper Black Std	Myriad Pro
Adobe Devanagari	Adobe Myungjo Std
Adobe Fan Heiti Std	Adobe Naskh
Adobe Fangsong Std	Nueva Std
Adobe Garamond® Pro	OCR A Std
Giddyup Std	ORATOR STD
Adobe Gothic Std	Poplar Std
Adobe Hebrew	Prestige Elite Std
Adobe Heiti Std	ROSEWOOD STD
Hobo Std	Adobe Song Std
Adobe Kaiti Std	STENCIL STD
Kozuka Gothic Pro (and Pr6N)	Tekton Pro
Kozuka Mincho Pro (and Pr6N)	TRAJAN PRO

What is OpenType?

If you frequently send files back and forth between platforms, you should be designing your text files using the OpenType format.

OpenType® is a cross-platform font file format developed jointly by Adobe and Microsoft. Adobe has converted the entire Adobe Type Library into this format and now offers thousands of OpenType fonts.

The two main benefits of the OpenType format are its cross-platform compatibility (the same font file works on Macintosh and Windows computers) and its ability to support widely expanded character sets and layout features, which provide richer linguistic support and advanced typographic control.

The OpenType format is an extension of the TrueType SFNT format that also can support Adobe PostScript font data and new typographic features. OpenType fonts containing PostScript data, such as those in the Adobe Type Library, have an .otf suffix in the font file name, while TrueType-based OpenType fonts have a .ttf file name suffix.

OpenType fonts can include an expanded character set and layout features, providing broader linguistic support and more precise typographic control. Feature-rich Adobe OpenType fonts can be distinguished by the word "Pro," which is part of the font name and appears in application font menus. OpenType fonts can be installed and used alongside PostScript Type 1 and TrueType fonts.

—From Adobe.com/type/opentype

Changing the font size

1   With text and Type tool (**T**) still selected, and the cursor in the top threaded text area, choose Select > All.

2   Type **13** in the Font Size field in the Control panel, and press Enter or Return. Notice the text change. Choose 14 pt from the Font Size menu. Leave the text selected.

● **Note:** You may see the word "Character" instead of the Font Size field in the Control panel. Click the word Character to reveal the Character panel.

The Font Size menu has preset sizes. If you want a custom size, select the value that appears in the Font Size field, enter any other value in points, and then press Enter or Return.

▶ **Tip:** You can dynamically change the font size of selected text using keyboard shortcuts. To increase the font size in increments of 2 points, press Ctrl+Shift+> (Windows) or Command+Shift+> (Mac OS). To reduce the font size, press Ctrl+Shift+< (Windows) or Command+Shift+< (Mac OS).

Changing the font color

You can change the font color of the fill and stroke of selected text. In this example, you will change only the fill.

1 With the text still selected, click the Fill color in the Control panel. When the Swatches panel appears, select White. The text fill changes to white.

2 Click the Layers panel icon (■) on the right side of the workspace to expand the panel. Click the visibility column to the left of the background layer. A blue background appears. Click the Layers panel tab to collapse the group.

Tip: Double-click to select a word; triple-click to select an entire paragraph. The end of a paragraph is defined by a hard return (when you press Enter or Return).

3 With the Type tool, click three times to select the second paragraph ("Cover Your Mouth and Nose"). See the figure below for which text to select.

4 Change the Fill color in the Control panel to light yellow (C=0 M=2 Y=60 K=0 will appear in the swatch tool tip).

5 With the text still selected, select the entry in the Font Size field in the Control panel and change the font size by typing **20**. Press Enter or Return.

6 Choose Bold from the Font Style menu in the Control panel to change the font style for the selected text.

7 Choose Select > Deselect.

8 With the Type tool, click three times on the top text on the artboard, which begins with "Help stop the spread..."

9 Change the Fill color in the Control panel to orange (C=0 M=50 Y=100 K=0 will appear in the swatch tool tip).

10 Change the Font Size to **30** and the Font Style to Bold Condensed in the Control panel.

11 Choose Select > Deselect.

12 Chose File > Save.

Changing additional text attributes

You can change many additional text attributes in the Character panel, which you can access by clicking the underlined word "Character" in the Control panel or by choosing Window > Type > Character.

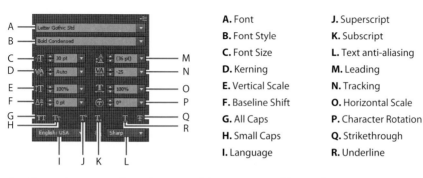

A. Font
B. Font Style
C. Font Size
D. Kerning
E. Vertical Scale
F. Baseline Shift
G. All Caps
H. Small Caps
I. Language

J. Superscript
K. Subscript
L. Text anti-aliasing
M. Leading
N. Tracking
O. Horizontal Scale
P. Character Rotation
Q. Strikethrough
R. Underline

In this section, you will apply some of the many possible attributes to experiment with the different ways you can format text.

1 With the Type tool (T), insert the cursor in the text that begins "Cover your mouth..." With the cursor in the text, triple-click to select the entire paragraph.

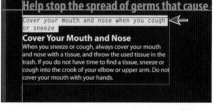

2 With the Zoom tool (🔍), click the selected text once more to zoom in to it.

3 Click the word "Character" in the Control panel to reveal the Character panel (or choose Window > Type > Character). With the text selected, click the Tracking icon (🆚) in the Character panel to select the Tracking field and type **-25**.

Tracking changes the spacing between characters. A positive value pushes the letters apart horizontally; a negative value pulls the letters closer together.

● **Note:** If you choose to open the Character panel (Window > Type > Character), you may need to click the double-arrow next to the word "Character" in the panel tab to reveal more options.

4 Click the Horizontal Scale icon (🆃), and type **50%** in the Horizontal Scale field. Change the Font Size by typing **80** and pressing Enter or Return to close the Character panel.

5 Choose Type > Change Case > UPPERCASE.

6 Choose View > Fit Artboard In Window and then Select > Deselect.

7   Select the Selection tool (▶), and click the text "COVER YOUR" to select the text area. Drag the lower, right bounding point of the text frame to the right and down until you see the text "COVER YOUR MOUTH AND NOSE" on

one line. See the figure for sizing help and how much text to reveal.

8   With the Type tool, select the second line of the first paragraph ("WHEN YOU COUGH OR SNEEZE").

9   Change the Font Size in the Control panel to **48 pt**.

10 Click three times in that same selected text "WHEN YOU COUGH OR SNEEZE" to select the entire paragraph.

11 Click the word "Character" in the Control panel, and change the Leading (▧) to **50 pt**. Press Enter or Return to close the panel.

Leading is the vertical space between lines. Notice the change in the vertical distance between the lines. Adjusting the leading can be useful for fitting text into a text area.

12 Choose Select > Deselect and then File > Save.

Working with glyphs

Glyphs are characters within a certain typeface that may be harder to find, like a bullet point or a registration symbol.

1   Select the Zoom tool (🔍) in the Tools panel, and drag a marquee around the bottom of the text at the bottom of the artboard.

● **Note:** Make sure that you inserted the cursor in the text area and didn't create a new one.

2   Select the Type tool (T) in the Tools panel, and click to place the cursor right after the period in the text "...may help you to get well sooner." Press Enter or Return twice to add two paragraph returns.

3   Type **The Feel Better People**. Don't type the period. Leave the cursor after the last word ("People").

4 Choose Type > Glyphs to open the Glyphs panel.

The Glyphs panel is used to insert type characters, like trademark symbols (™) or bullet points(·). It shows all the characters (glyphs) available for a given font.

Next, you will insert a copyright symbol.

5 In the Glyphs panel, scroll down until you see a copyright symbol (©). Double-click the symbol to insert it at the text insertion point. Close the Glyphs panel.

▶ **Tip:** The Glyphs panel lets you select another font in the bottom of the panel. You can also increase the size of the glyph icons by clicking the larger mountain (⛰) in the lower-right corner or make the icons smaller by clicking the smaller mountain (⛰).

6 With the Type tool, drag to select the copyright symbol (©) you just inserted.

7 Click the word "Character" in the Control panel (or choose Window > Type > Character), and click the Superscript button (T¹) near the bottom of the panel.

8 Click with the Type tool between the word "People" and the copyright symbol to insert the cursor. The Character panel will close.

9 Choose 75 from the Kerning menu in the Character panel.

▶ **Tip:** To remove kerning changes, insert the cursor in the text and choose Auto from the Kerning menu.

Kerning is similar to tracking, but it adds or subtracts space between a pair of characters. It's useful for situations such as this one, when you're working with a glyph.

10 Choose Select > Deselect, and then choose File > Save.

Resizing type objects

In this next section, you'll see how to resize type objects to either make room for additional text or to make sure that threaded frames have the correct text in them.

1 Choose View > Fit Artboard In Window.

2 Select the Zoom tool (🔍) in the Tools panel, and click twice, slowly, in the center of the top text area that is threaded.

3 With the Selection tool (▶), click the text in the top text area that is threaded, to select it. Double-click the out port (▶) in the lower-right corner of the text area.

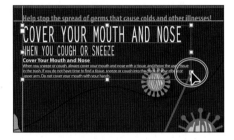

Because the two text areas are threaded, double-clicking the out port of the top text area or the in port of the bottom text area breaks the connection between them. Any text threaded between the two type objects flows back into the first object. The bottom text area is still there, but it has no stroke or fill.

4 Choose View > Smart Guides to turn them off.

5 Using the Selection tool, drag the bottom, middle handle of the bounding box up until the yellow text "Cover Your Mouth and Nose" disappears. The text area changes in size vertically.

6 With the Selection tool, click the out port (⊞) in the lower-right corner of the top type object. The pointer changes to the loaded text icon (▤).

7 Choose View > Fit Artboard In Window.

8 Position the loaded text icon (▤) over the edge of the bottom type object until it changes in appearance to (▶). Click to thread the two objects together.

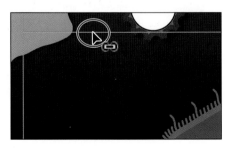

9 Choose Select > Deselect.

When type objects are threaded, you can move them anywhere and still maintain the connection between them. You can even thread between artboards. When type objects are resized, especially those in the beginning of the thread, text can reflow.

10 Choose File > Save.

▶ **Tip:** You can create unique type object shapes by deselecting the type object and choosing the Direct Selection tool (↖). Drag the edge or corner of the type object to adjust the shape of the path. This method is easier to use when View > Hide Bounding Box is selected. Adjusting the type path with the Direct Selection tool is easiest when you're in Outline mode (View > Outline).

● **Note:** If you edit the type object by following the tip, choose Edit > Undo Move before continuing.

Changing paragraph attributes

As with character attributes, you can set paragraph attributes, such as alignment or indenting, before you enter new type or to change the appearance of existing type. If you select several type paths and type containers, you can set attributes for them all at the same time. Most of this type of formatting is done in the Paragraph panel, which you can access by clicking the underlined word "Paragraph" in the Control panel or by choosing Window > Type > Paragraph.

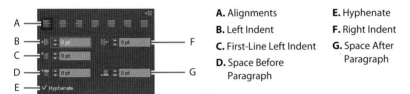

A. Alignments
B. Left Indent
C. First-Line Left Indent
D. Space Before Paragraph
E. Hyphenate
F. Right Indent
G. Space After Paragraph

Now, you'll add more space after all the paragraphs in the main text.

1 Select the Zoom tool (🔍) in the Tools panel, and click twice in the center of the bottom text area (at the bottom of the artboard).

2 Using the Type tool (T), insert the cursor in the second paragraph that begins with "When you sneeze..."

3 Click the word "Paragraph" in the Control panel to open the Paragraph panel.

4 Type **10 pt** in the Space After Paragraph text field (in the bottom-right corner), and press Enter or Return.

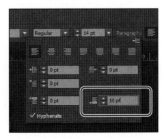

Setting a spacing value after paragraphs, rather than pressing the Return key, is recommended when working with large type objects.

5 Choose Select > Deselect, and then choose File > Save.

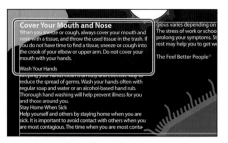

Document setup options

By choosing File > Document Setup, you can access the Document Setup dialog box. In this dialog box, there are many text options, including the Highlight Substituted Fonts and Highlight Substituted Glyphs options, which are in the Bleed And View Options section.

In the Type Options section at the bottom of the dialog box, you can set the document language, change double and single quotes, edit Superscript, Subscript, Small Caps, and more.

Creating and applying text styles

Styles allow you to format text consistently and are helpful when text attributes need to be globally updated. Once a style is created, you only need to edit the saved style. Then, all text formatted with that style is updated.

Illustrator provides two types of styles:

• **Paragraph**—Retains character and paragraph attributes and applies them to an entire paragraph.

• **Character**—Retains the character attributes and applies them to selected text.

Creating and applying a paragraph style

First, you will create a paragraph style for the subheadings.

1 With the Type tool (**T**) selected, insert the cursor in the yellow subhead "Cover Your Mouth and Nose."

   You do not need to select text to create a paragraph style, but you do have to place the text insertion point in the line of text that has the attributes you are going to save.

2 Choose Window > Type > Paragraph Styles, and click the Create New Style button (⬚) at the bottom of the Paragraph Styles panel.

   This creates a new paragraph style in the panel, called Paragraph Style 1. This style captures the character and paragraph formatting from the yellow subhead.

3 Double-click the style name Paragraph Style 1 in the list of styles. Change the name of the style to **Subhead**, and press Enter or Return to edit the name inline.

   By double-clicking the style to edit the name, you are also applying the new style to the yellow subhead (where the cursor is). This means that if you edit the Subhead paragraph style, this first yellow paragraph will update as well.

4 Two paragraphs below the first yellow subhead, click three times on the text "Wash Your Hands" to select it. Select the Subhead style in the Paragraph Styles panel.

   Notice that a plus sign (+) appears to the right of the style name, and the text doesn't look exactly like the "Cover Your Mouth and Nose" text. The plus sign (+) means that the style has an override. An override is any formatting that doesn't match the attributes defined by the style, for example, if you changed the font size for the selected paragraph.

5   Press the Alt (Windows) or Option (Mac OS) key, and select the Subhead style name again in the Paragraph Styles panel to overwrite existing attributes on the selected text. The text attributes of the Subhead style are applied to the selected text.

● **Note:** If you place a Microsoft Word document and choose to keep the formatting, the styles used in the Word document may be brought into the Illustrator document and show up in the Paragraph Styles panel.

6   With the Type tool, click three times in the text "Stay Home When Sick" to select the paragraph. Alt-click (Windows) or Option-click (Mac OS) the Subhead style in the Paragraph Styles panel.

7   Choose Select > Deselect.

Editing a paragraph style

After creating a paragraph style, you can easily edit the style formatting. Then, anywhere the style has been applied, the formatting will be automatically updated.

1   Double-click to the right of the name "Subhead" in the Paragraph Styles panel list to open the Paragraph Style Options dialog box.

▶ **Tip:** You can also choose Paragraph Style Options from the Paragraph Styles panel menu (▼≣).

2   Select the Indents and Spacing category on the left side of the dialog box.

3   Change the Space After to **10 pt**.

Since Preview is selected by default, you can move the dialog box out of the way to see the text change.

4   Click OK. Choose File > Save.

There are many options for working with paragraph styles, most of which are found in the Paragraph Styles panel menu, including duplicating, deleting, and editing paragraph styles.

Sampling text formatting

Using the Eyedropper tool, you can quickly sample type attributes and apply them to text without creating a style.

1   Using the Type tool (**T**), triple-click to select the second main paragraph in the first column, which begins with "Keeping your hands clean..."

2   Select the Eyedropper tool () in the Tools panel, and click in the first paragraph of white text. A letter T appears above the Eyedropper pointer.

    The attributes are immediately applied to your selected text.

3   With the Type tool, click three times in the paragraph after the subhead "Stay Home When Sick" that starts with "Help yourself and others..." to select it. Select the Eyedropper tool after selecting the paragraph, and click the first paragraph of text again. Repeat this for the next paragraph that starts with "The stress of work..."

▶ **Tip:** You could have also created a paragraph style for the white body text.

4   Choose Select > Deselect and then File > Save. Leave the file open.

Creating and applying a character style

Character styles, unlike paragraph styles, can only be applied to selected text and can only contain character formatting. Next, you will create a character style from text styling within the two columns of text.

1   Using the Type tool (**T**), in the first paragraph after the subhead, "Cover Your Mouth and Nose," select the text "Do not cover your mouth with your hands."

2   Choose Italic from the Font Style menu in the Control panel. Click the word "Character," and then click the Underline button (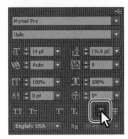) to underline the text as well.

    Note: You may see the word "Character" instead of the Font Style menu in the Control panel. Click the word "Character" to reveal the Character panel.

3   In the Paragraph Styles panel group, click the Character Styles panel tab.

4 In the Character Styles panel, Alt-click (Windows) or Option-click (Mac OS) the Create New Style button (![icon]) at the bottom of the Character Styles panel.

Alt, or Option-clicking the Create New Style button in the Character or Paragraph Styles panel lets you name the style as it is added to the panel.

5 Name the style **emphasis**, and click OK.

The style records the attributes applied to your selected text.

6 With the text still selected, Alt-click (Windows) or Option-click (Mac OS) the style named emphasis in the Character Styles panel to assign the style to that text so that it will update if the style changes.

● **Note:** You must select the entire phrase rather than just placing the cursor in the text.

7 In the next paragraph, after the "Wash Your Hands" subhead, select the text "Wash your hands often" and apply the emphasis style while pressing the Alt (Windows) or Option (Mac OS) key.

8 Choose Select > Deselect.

Editing a character style

After creating a character style, you can easily edit the style formatting, and anywhere the style is applied, the formatting will be automatically updated.

1 Double-click to the right of the emphasis style name in the Character Styles panel (*not* the style name itself). In the Character Style Options dialog box, click the Character Color category on the left side of the dialog box and make sure that the Fill box is selected. Click the light yellow swatch (C=0 M=2 Y=60 K=0) in the Swatches panel that appears. Make sure that Preview is selected, and as you change the style formatting, the text that uses the emphasis style changes automatically. Click OK.

● **Note:** Clicking [Normal Character Style] ensures that any new text you add to the document will not have the style named emphasis applied.

2 Click the style named [Normal Character Style] in the Character Styles panel. Close the Character Styles panel group.

3 Choose Select > Deselect, if necessary, and then File > Save.

Reshaping text with a preset envelope warp

Envelopes are objects that distort or reshape selected objects, such as text. You can use a preset warp shape or a mesh grid as an envelope, or you can create and edit your own envelope using objects on the artboard.

Next, you'll explore the preset warp shapes that Illustrator provides.

1   Select the Type tool (**T**) in the Tools panel. Before typing, in the Control panel, change the Font Family to Myriad Pro (if it is not already selected), the Font Style to Bold, and the font size to **36 pt**.

2   With the Type tool, click on the poster to the right of the orange face, below the green object (you may need to scroll up in the Document window). Exact placement is not important. A cursor appears.

3   Type the word **COLD** (all uppercase). Select the text with the Type tool, and then select the Eyedropper tool (✎). Click the green fill of the object above the text to fill the text with the same green color.

4   Select the Selection tool (▶). With the text area selected, click the Make Envelope button (▦▾) in the Control panel (not the arrow to the right). In the Warp Options dialog box, select Preview. The text appears as an arc.

5   Choose Bulge from the Style menu. Drag the Bend slider to the right to see it bend up further. You can experiment with many combinations. Drag the Horizontal and Vertical Distortion sliders to see the effect on the text. When you are finished experimenting, drag the Distortion sliders to **0%**, make sure that the Bend is **40%**, and then click OK.

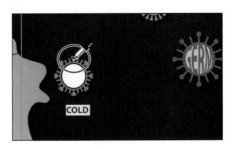

● **Note:** The Make Envelope button (▦▾) does not apply an effect. It just turns the text into an envelope object. The same visual result is achieved by choosing Effect > Warp > Arc Upper. For more information about envelopes, see "Reshape using envelopes" in Illustrator Help.

6   Using the Selection tool, click to select the white placeholder circle on the green object above the text and then press Delete or Backspace to remove it.

7 Drag the envelope object (warped text) into the approximate center of the green object.

If you want to make any changes, you can edit the text and shape that make up the envelope warp object separately. Next, you will edit the text and then the warp shape.

8 Select the Zoom tool (🔍), and click several times on the warped text to zoom in.

9 With the warped text still selected, click the Edit Contents button (▦) in the Control panel. This is how you edit the text in the warped shape.

10 Choose View > Smart Guides to turn them on.

▶ **Tip:** If you double-click with the Selection tool instead of the Type tool, you enter Isolation mode. This is another way to edit the text within the envelope warp object. Press the Escape key to exit Isolation mode.

11 Using the Type tool, position the cursor over the warped text. Notice that the text "COLD" is in blue and is underlined. The Smart Guides show you the original text. Click the text to insert the cursor, and then double-click to select the text.

12 Type **GERM**, and notice that the text warps automatically in the envelope shape. Choose Edit > Undo Typing to return to the original text ("COLD").

Besides editing the text, you can also change the formatting at this point.

13 Select the Selection tool, and make sure that the warped text is still selected. Click the Edit Envelope button (▦) in the Control panel.

Notice the options for the envelope warp object in the Control panel, such as Horizontal, Vertical, and Bend. These are the same options you saw in the Warp Options dialog box when you first created the envelope warp.

Note: Changing the warp style may move the text on the artboard.

14 Change the Bend to **87%** in the Control panel. Make sure that the H (horizontal) Distortion is 0 and the V (vertical) Distortion is 0.

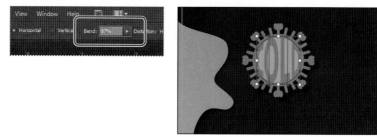

15 Choose View > Smart Guides to turn them off.

16 Select the Direct Selection tool () in the Tools panel. Click to select one of the anchor points to the right of the letter D. Then, drag the selected point to the right a bit to change the warp shape.

17 Choose Edit > Undo Move.

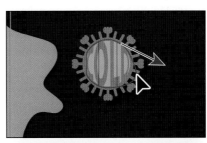

▶ **Tip:** To take the text out of the warped shape, select the text with the Selection tool and choose Object > Envelope Distort > Release. This gives you two objects: the text and an ellipse shape.

18 Select the Selection tool and, holding down the Alt (Windows) or Option (Mac OS) key, drag the right, middle bounding point to the right. The purpose is to remove the gaps between the text and the green shape edge. See the figure for help.

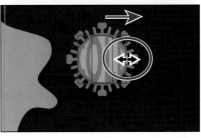

19 Choose Select > Deselect, and then File > Save. Leave the file open.

Reshaping text with an object warp

Another way to reshape text is to create and edit your own warp object, using objects on the artboard.

1 With the Selection tool, click to select the warped text again. Press the Alt (Windows) or Option (Mac OS) key, and drag a copy of the envelope warp object down. Scroll down the artboard, and drop the copy of the envelope warp object on top of the red shape above the two columns of text.

2 Choose Object > Envelope Distort > Release to separate the text area from the envelope. Choose Select > Deselect. Click to select the gray envelope shape and delete it, leaving the text area. Click to select the text area.

3 Select the Eyedropper tool () in the Tools panel, and click the darker red shape surrounding the white circle.

4 With the Selection tool, click to select the white circle and choose Object > Arrange > Bring To Front.

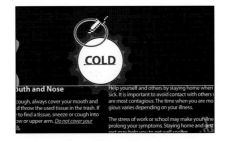

5 Choose Edit > Copy, and then Edit > Paste In Front. There are now two white circles on top of each other, with the top one still selected.

6 Choose Object > Hide > Selection. You will use that white circle later.

7 Choose View > Outline.

8 Press the Shift key, and click the text "COLD" and the edge of the white circle to select both objects. Choose View > Preview, and make sure that both objects are selected.

9 Choose Object > Envelope Distort > Make With Top Object.

This object is now called Envelope Top on the left end of the Control panel. The same editing rules apply to this type of envelope object.

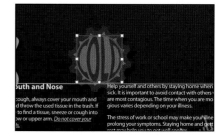

10 Press the Shift key, and select the red object behind the warped text. Choose Object > Group, and then choose File > Save.

Wrapping text around an object

You can create interesting and creative results by wrapping text around an object. Next, you will wrap text around the red object.

1 Choose View > Fit Artboard In Window.

▶ **Tip:** You can also resize the text area to reflow the text by dragging the bottom, middle point up or down.

2 Select the Type tool, and insert the cursor in front of the subhead "Stay Home When Sick." Press Enter or Return once or twice to move the subhead to the top of the next column.

3 Select the red object with the Selection tool and choose Object > Arrange > Bring To Front.

To wrap text around an object, the wrap object must be in the same layer as the text and located directly above the text in the layer hierarchy.

4 With the red object still selected, choose Object > Text Wrap > Make. The text in the two columns wraps around the red shape.

5 With the Selection tool, drag the red shape down a bit to see the effect on the text in the two columns. Choose Edit > Undo Move.

6 Choose Object > Text Wrap > Text Wrap Options. In the Text Wrap Options dialog box, change Offset to **10 pt** and select Preview to see the change. Click OK.

7 Choose Select > Deselect.

8 Choose File > Save. Keep the file open.

Creating text on an open path

Using the Type tools, you can type on paths and shapes to flow text along the edge of an open or closed path.

1 Choose View > Fit Artboard In Window, if necessary. You may wish to zoom in to see the text you type.

2 With the Selection tool (▶), select the wavy path above the orange face shape.

3 With the Type tool (**T**), position the cursor over the left side of the path to see an insertion point with an intersecting wavy path (.ɪ.·). Click when this cursor appears. See the figure for where to click.

The text will start where you click on the path. Also, the stroke attributes of the path change to None and a cursor appears.

4 Type the text **WASH YOUR HANDS**. Note that the new text follows the path.

5 With the Type tool, click three times on the new text to select it.

6 Select the Eyedropper tool (✏) in the Tools panel, and click in the first heading, which begins with "COVER YOUR MOUTH..."

A letter T appears above the Eyedropper pointer (without the Caps Lock key selected).

7 Select the Selection tool (▶) in the Tools panel, and make sure that the text path is selected (not the text). Choose Edit > Copy and then Edit > Paste In Front. Drag the copy straight down, as you see in the figure.

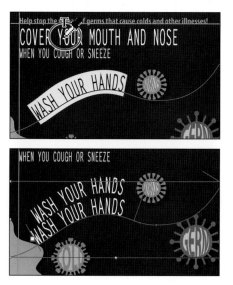

● **Note:** If the text doesn't fit on the path, a small box with a plus sign (+) appears at the end of the path. You can make the font size smaller or the line bigger, among other options.

8 Select the Type tool, and click in the text of the copied path. Click three more times to select the text, and type **STAY HOME WHEN SICK**.

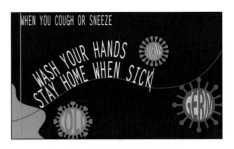

▶ **Tip:** With the path or the text on the path selected, you can choose Type > Type On A Path > Type On A Path Options to set options.

9 Select the Selection tool, and position the pointer over the vertical line on the left edge of the text. When you see this cursor (▶⊦), click and drag to the right. See the figure for how far to drag. Be careful not to drag too far to the right, otherwise, you may see a plus (⊞) in the out port on the right end of the path.

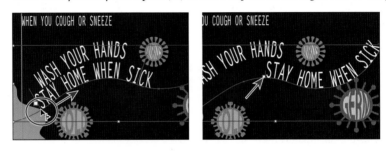

10 With the path still selected, choose Object > Transform > Rotate. In the Rotate dialog box, enter **8** for the Angle and then click OK.

11 Drag the path with the Selection tool to reposition it as you see in the figure.

12 Choose Select > Deselect, and then choose File > Save.

● **Note:** You can apply any character and paragraph formatting you want to the text on the path.

Creating text on closed paths

Now, you will put text on a closed path.

1 Choose Object > Show All.

2 Choose Object > Arrange > Bring To Front.

This will show the white circle that you hid earlier, on top of the red shape.

3 Select the Zoom tool (🔍) in the Tools panel, and click the white circle three times, slowly, to zoom in. With the Selection tool (▶), select the white circle, if it's not already selected.

4 Double-click the Scale tool (⊡) in the Tools panel to open the Scale dialog box. In the Scale dialog box, change Uniform Scale to **155%** and then click OK.

● **Note:** Read more about transforming objects in Lesson 4, "Transforming Objects."

5 Select the Type tool, and position the pointer over the edge of the white circle. The Type cursor (꤮) changes to a Type cursor with a circle (꤮). This indicates that, if you click (*don't click,*) text will be placed inside of the circle, creating a type area.

6 While pressing the Alt (Windows) or Option (Mac OS) key, position the pointer over the left side of the circle (see the figure for location). The insertion point with an intersecting wavy path (꤮) appears. Click, but don't type.

The cursor is now on the path.

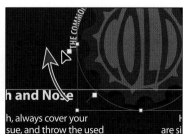

● **Note:** Instead of pressing the Alt (Windows) or Option (Mac OS) key to allow the Type tool to type on a path, you can select the Type On A Path tool (꤮) by holding down the Type tool in the Tools panel.

● **Note:** If you find that after clicking, the cursor jumps to a different part on the circle, choose Edit > Undo Type and position the pointer lower on the circle before you try again.

7 Type **THE COMMON COLD**. The text flows on the circular path. Click three times to select the text.

8 Choose Window > Type > Paragraph Styles. Press the Alt (Windows) or Option (Mac OS) key, and click the style named [Normal Paragraph Style] to make sure that the default formatting is applied to the text. Close the panel group.

9 With the text still selected, in the Control panel, change the font size to **15 pt**, the font to Myriad Pro (if not already selected), the font style to Bold Condensed or something similar, and the Fill color to a light gray (C=1 M=1 Y=13 K=15).

10 To adjust the placement on the path, switch to the Selection tool. Position the pointer over the line on the left end of the text (to the left of the word "THE"). That line is called a bracket. When you see this cursor (꤮), drag up around the circle a bit. See the figure for position.

● **Note:** You may need to zoom in further to see the brackets more easily.

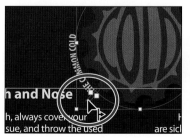

Brackets appear at the beginning of the type, at the end of the path, and at the midpoint between the start and end brackets. All of these brackets can be adjusted to reposition the text in the path.

● Note: To learn about the Type On A Path options, search for "Creating type on a path" in Illustrator Help (Help > Illustrator Help).

11 With the path type object selected with the Selection tool, choose Type > Type On A Path > Type On A Path Options. In the Type On A Path Options dialog box, select Preview and then choose Skew from the Effect menu. Select other options from the Effect menu, and then choose Rainbow. Choose Descender from the Align To Path menu, and change the Spacing to **-12 pt**. Click OK.

12 Choose Select > Deselect.

13 Choose View > Fit Artboard In Window.

14 Choose File > Save, and leave the file open.

Creating text outlines

Converting text to outlines means converting text into vector outlines that you can edit and manipulate as you would any other graphic object. Text outlines are useful for changing the look of large display type, but they are rarely useful for body text or other type at small sizes. The file recipient doesn't need to have your fonts installed in order to open and view the file correctly.

1 Click the Layers panel icon (■) on the right side of the workspace to expand the panel. Click the visibility column to the left of the warped text layer. Click the Layers panel tab to collapse it.

● Note: Always keep your original artwork, because you cannot change outline text back to editable text using this method.

2 With the Selection tool, click the text "AH-CHOO" that appears on the artboard to select it. Choose Type > Create Outlines.

The text is no longer linked to a particular font. Instead, it is now artwork, much like any other vector art in your illustration. The AH-CHOO text was also warped, so the selection doesn't match the yellow text. To have it match, you could choose Object > Expand Appearance.

3 Choose View > Guides > Hide Guides and then choose Select > Deselect.

4 Choose File > Save and then File > Close.

Review questions

1 Name two methods for creating a text area in Adobe Illustrator.

2 What are two benefits of using an OpenType font?

3 What is the difference between a character style and a paragraph style?

4 What are the advantages and disadvantages of converting text to outlines?

Review answers

1 The following methods can be used for creating text areas:

- With the Type tool, click the artboard and start typing when the cursor appears. A text area is created to accommodate the text.

- With the Type tool, drag to create a text area. Type when a cursor appears.

- With the Type tool, click a path or closed shape to convert it to text on a path or in a text area. Alt-clicking (Windows) or Option-clicking (Mac OS) when crossing over the stroke of a closed path creates text around the shape.

2 The two main benefits of OpenType fonts are cross-platform compatibility (they work the same on both Windows and Mac OS) and support of widely expanded character sets and layout features, which provide richer linguistic support and advanced typographic control.

3 A character style can be applied to selected text only. A paragraph style is applied to an entire paragraph. Paragraph styles are best for indents, margins, and line spacing.

4 Converting type to outlines eliminates the need to send the fonts along with the file when sharing with others. You can also fill the type with a gradient and create interesting effects on individual letters. However, when you create outlines from text, you should consider the following:

- Text is no longer editable. The content and font cannot be changed for outlined text. It is best to save a layer with the original text or to use the Outline Object effect.

- Bitmap fonts and outline-protected fonts cannot be converted to outlines.

- Outlining text that is less than 10 points in size is not recommended. When type is converted to outlines, the type loses its hints—instructions built into outline fonts to adjust their shape to display or print optimally at many sizes. When scaling type, adjust its point size before converting it to outlines.

- You must convert all type in a selection to outlines; you cannot convert a single letter within a string of type. To convert a single letter into an outline, create a separate type area containing only that letter.

8 WORKING WITH LAYERS

Lesson overview

In this lesson, you'll learn how to do the following:

- Work with the Layers panel.

- Create, rearrange, and lock layers and sublayers.

- Move objects between layers.

- Locate objects in the Layers panel.

- Copy and paste objects and their layers from one file to another.

- Merge layers into a single layer.

- Apply a drop shadow to a layer.

- Make a layer clipping mask.

- Apply an appearance attribute to objects and layers.

- Isolate content in a layer.

This lesson takes approximately 45 minutes to complete. If needed, remove the previous lesson folder from your hard disk and copy the Lesson08 folder onto it.

Layers let you organize your work into distinct
levels that can be edited and viewed individually
or together. Every Adobe Illustrator document has
at least one layer. Creating multiple layers in your
artwork lets you easily control how artwork is printed,
displayed, selected, and edited.

Getting started

In this lesson, you'll finish the artwork for a television as you explore the various ways to use the Layers panel.

1 To ensure that the tools and panels function exactly as described in this lesson, delete or deactivate (by renaming) the Adobe Illustrator CS6 preferences file. See "Restoring default preferences" on page 3.

2 Start Adobe Illustrator CS6.

   Note: If you have not already done so, copy the Lesson08 folder from the Lessons folder on the *Adobe Illustrator CS6 Classroom in a Book* CD onto your hard disk. See "Copying the Classroom in a Book files" on page 2.

3 Choose File > Open, and open the L8end.ai file in the Lesson08 folder, located in the Lessons folder on your hard disk.

4 Choose View > Fit Artboard In Window.

5 Choose Window > Workspace > Reset Essentials.

Note: If you don't see "Reset Essentials" in the Workspace menu, choose Window > Workspace > Essentials before choosing Window > Workspace > Reset Essentials.

6 Click the Layers panel icon (⬛) on the right side of the workspace, or choose Window > Layers.

Separate layers are used for the objects that make up the artwork, as indicated by the layer names listed in the Layers panel. In the figure below, you can see the Layers panel (Window > Layers) and descriptions of the icons.

Note: The Layers panel in your workspace will *not* look exactly like the figure at right, and that's okay. At this point, you just need to familiarize yourself with the options in the panel.

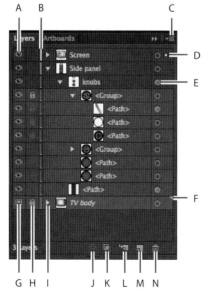

A. Visibility column
B. Layer color
C. Layers panel menu
D. Selection column
E. Target column
F. Current layer indicator
G. Template layer icon
H. Edit column (lock/unlock)
I. Expand/collapse triangle
J. Locate Object
K. Make/Release Clipping Mask
L. Create New Sublayer
M. Create New Layer
N. Delete Selection

7 If you like, you can leave the file open as a visual reference. Otherwise, choose File > Close.

To begin working, you'll open an existing art file that is incomplete.

8 Choose File > Open, and open the L8start.ai file in the Lesson08 folder, located in the Lessons folder on your hard disk.

9 Choose File > Save As, name the file **tv.ai**, and select the Lesson08 folder. Leave the Save As Type option set to Adobe Illustrator (*.AI) (Windows) or the Format option set to Adobe Illustrator (ai) (Mac OS), and then click Save. In the Illustrator Options dialog box, leave the Illustrator options at their default settings and then click OK.

10 Choose View > Fit Artboard In Window.

About layers

When creating complex artwork, it can be a challenge to keep track of all the items in your Document window. Small items get hidden under larger items, and selecting artwork becomes difficult. Layers provide a way to manage all the items that make up your artwork. Think of layers as clear folders that contain artwork. If you reshuffle the folders, you change the stacking order of the items in your artwork. You can move items between folders and create subfolders within folders.

The structure of layers in your document can be as simple or complex as you want it to be. By default, all items are organized in a single, parent layer. However, you can create new layers and move items into them or move elements from one layer to another at any time. The Layers panel provides an easy way to select, hide, lock, and change the appearance attributes of artwork. You can even create template layers, which you can use to trace artwork, and exchange layers with Adobe Photoshop.

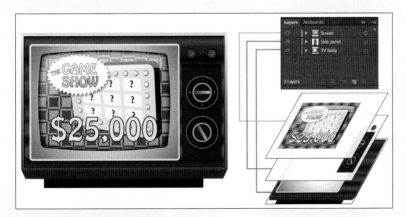

Example of composite art and how layers break out individually.

—From Illustrator Help

Creating layers

By default, every document begins with one layer, called Layer 1. As you create artwork, you can rename and add layers at any time. Placing objects on separate layers lets you more easily select and edit them. For example, by placing type on a separate layer, you can change the type all at once without affecting the rest of the artwork.

Next, you'll change the default layer name and then create two layers using different methods and a sublayer.

1   If the Layers panel isn't visible, click the Layers panel icon (📚) on the right side of the workspace, or choose Window > Layers.

Layer 1 (the default name for the first layer) is highlighted, indicating that it is active.

2   In the Layers panel, double-click the layer name Layer 1 to edit it. Type **Side panel**, and then press Enter or Return.

Instead of keeping all content on one single layer, you'll create several layers and sublayers to better organize the content and to make it easier to select content later.

▶ **Tip:** You can easily delete a layer by selecting the layer or sublayer and clicking the Delete Selection button (🗑) at the bottom of the Layers panel. This deletes the layer or sublayer and all content on it.

3   Click the Create New Layer button (🔲) at the bottom of the Layers panel, or choose New Layer from the Layers panel menu (▼≡).

Layers and sublayers that aren't named are numbered in sequence; for example, the second layer is named Layer 2.

4   Double-click the layer name Layer 2, and change the name to **TV body**.

The new layer is added above the Side panel layer and becomes active. Notice that the new layer has a different layer color (a light red) to the left of the layer name. This will become more important later, as you select content.

Next, you will create a layer and name it in one step, using a modifier key.

5   Alt-click (Windows) or Option-click (Mac OS) the Create New Layer button (🔲) at the bottom of the Layers panel. In the Layer Options dialog box, change the name to **Screen**, and then click OK.

6 Click the layer named Side panel once, and then click the Create New Sublayer button (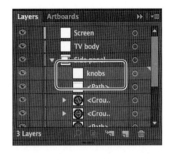) at the bottom of the Layers panel to create a new sublayer in the Side panel layer.

Creating a new sublayer opens the selected layer to show existing sublayers. A sublayer is a layer within another layer. Sublayers are used to organize content within a layer without grouping or ungrouping content.

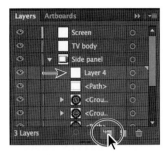

Note: To create a new sublayer and name it in one step, press the Alt (Windows) or Option (Mac OS) key and click the Create New Sublayer button to open the Layer Options dialog box.

7 Double-click the new sublayer name Layer 4, change the name to **knobs**, and then press Enter or Return.

The new sublayer appears directly beneath its main layer, Side panel, and is selected.

Layers and color

By default, Illustrator assigns a unique color to each layer in the Layers panel. The color displays next to the layer name in the panel. The same color displays in the artwork bounding box, path, anchor points, and center point of a selected object.

You can use this color to quickly locate an object's corresponding layer in the Layers panel, and you can change the layer color to suit your needs.

Each layer and sublayer can have a unique color.

—From Illustrator Help

Selecting and moving objects and layers

By rearranging the layers in the Layers panel, you can change the stacking order of objects in your artwork. On an artboard, objects in layers that are higher in the Layers panel list are in front of objects located on layers lower in the list. You can also move objects between layers and sublayers.

First, you'll move the knobs into the knobs sublayer.

Tip: Keeping layers and sublayers closed can make it easier to navigate content in the Layers panel.

1   If the contents of the Side panel layer are not showing in the Layers panel, click the triangle to the left of the Side panel layer name. This reveals the contents of the Side panel layer, which was the original layer.

When a layer or sublayer in the Layers panel contains other items, a triangle appears to the left of the layer or sublayer name. Click the triangle to show or hide the contents. If no triangle appears, the layer contains no additional items.

2   Drag the bottom of the Layers panel down to make the panel taller so that you can see all of the layers.

3   In the artwork, using the Selection tool (▶), click the top smaller knob on the right side of the television.

Notice that the bounding box and points have a blue color that matches the Side panel layer color in the Layers panel. Also notice, in the Layers panel, that the layer name has a small blue box to the far right of the layer name and the object name (<Path>, in this case). This is the selected-art indicator (■) and is meant to show you which layer the selected content is on.

4   Click and drag the <Path> row that has the selected-art indicator showing onto the knobs sublayer. Release the mouse button when you see the knobs sublayer highlighted.

Notice the triangle that appears to the left of the knobs sublayer when you release the mouse button. This indicates that the sublayer has content.

5   Choose Select > Deselect.

6   Click the top <Group> object in the Side panel layer, and then press and hold the Shift key and click the <Group> object directly beneath it in the Layers panel to highlight both objects. See the figure for selection help.

Tip: You can use the Shift key to select multiple sublayers and drag them all at once.

7   Drag either of the highlighted rows onto the knobs sublayer. Release the mouse button when you see the knobs sublayer highlight.

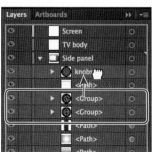

This better organizes the panel and makes it easier to find content later.

8   Click the triangle to the left of the knobs sublayer to show the contents.

Duplicating layer content

You can either use the Layers panel to duplicate layers and other content or use the Edit > Copy or Edit > Cut commands, as you have used in previous lessons.

1   Click the <Path> name in the knobs sublayer. Press the Alt (Windows) or Options (Mac OS) key, and drag the <Path> object up until a line appears just above the current <Path> object. Release the mouse button and then the key.

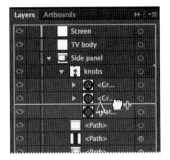

Tip: You can also select the <Path> row in the Layers panel and choose Duplicate <Path> from the Layers panel menu.

Dragging with the modifier key copies the selected content. This is the same as selecting the content on the artboard and choosing Edit > Copy and then Edit > Paste In Front.

2   Drag the left edge of the Layers panel to the left to make it wider so that you can more easily read the layer names.

3   Click the triangle to the left of the knobs sublayer to hide the sublayer contents. Hiding layer and/or sublayer contents makes the Layers panel easier to work with.

4   With the Selection tool (↖) selected, click to select the small knob in the artwork again. Double-click the Selection tool and, in the Move dialog box, change the Horizontal Position to **0.8 in**, make sure that the Vertical Position is **0,** and then click OK.

5   Choose Select > Deselect, and then choose File > Save.

Moving layers

Now, you'll move the screen artwork to the Screen layer, to which you'll later add content from another Illustrator file. You'll also move the artwork for the television body to the TV body layer.

1   In the artwork, using the Selection tool (↖), click the white, rounded corner shape where the screen content will be, to select it.

In the Layers panel, the Side panel layer shows a selected-art indicator (■) to the far right of the layer name.

2 Drag the selected-art indicator (■) from the right of the Side panel layer name straight up to the right of the target icon (◉) on the Screen layer.

This action moves the selected object (<Path>) to the Screen layer. The color of the bounding box and of the anchor points in the artwork changes to the color of the Screen layer, which is green.

3 Choose Select > Deselect.

4 Click the selection column to the right of the bottom <Path> object in the Side panel layer to see which content is selected on the artboard. A blue selected-art indicator (■) will appear in the selection column, as shown.

Clicking the selection column is a way to select the artwork on the artboard.

5 Drag that same <Path> sublayer up onto the TV body layer.

The <Path> object appears on top of most of the other content in the artwork.

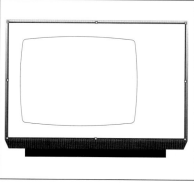

6 Click the bottom <Path> sublayer on the Side panel layer to select it. Shift-click the <Path> sublayer above it to select both sublayers. Drag either selected <Path> sublayer up onto the TV body layer name.

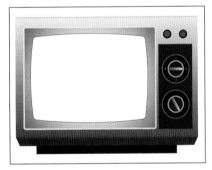

The Side panel content (the knobs) has disappeared. That is because the TV body layer content is higher in the Layers panel and, therefore, higher in the stacking order (on top of the Side panel layer content).

7 Click the triangle to the left of the Side panel layer to hide the layer contents, and then choose Select > Deselect.

8 Click and drag the Side panel layer up between the Screen and TV body layers in the Layers panel. When a line appears between the layers, release the mouse button.

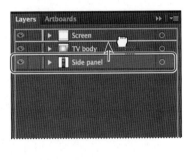

● **Note:** Be careful not to drag the layer into one of the other layers. If the Side panel layer disappears, you can choose Edit > Undo Reorder Layers and try again.

9 Choose File > Save.

Locking layers

As you edit your artwork, you can lock layers to prevent selecting or changing the rest of the artwork. In this section, you will learn how to lock all content on a layer or sublayer. Now, you'll lock all of the layers except the knobs sublayer so that you can easily edit the knobs without affecting objects on other layers.

1 Select the edit column to the right of the eye icon (👁) on the Screen layer to lock the layer.

The lock icon (🔒) indicates that a layer and all its content are locked.

2 Repeat the previous step for the TV body layer.

► **Tip:** Clicking again in the edit column relocks the layer. Pressing the Alt (Windows) or Option (Mac OS) key as you click in the edit column alternately locks and unlocks all other layers.

3 Click the triangle to the left of the Side panel layer to show the layer contents. Select the edit column to the right of the eye icon on the <Path> sublayer below the knobs sublayer.

You can unlock individual layers by deselecting the lock icon (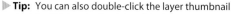).

► **Tip:** You can also double-click the layer thumbnail or double-click just to the right of the layer name to open the Layer Options dialog box. You can then select Lock and click OK.

Now, you'll change the size of the smaller knobs.

4 With the Selection tool (➤) selected, drag a marquee across the two small knobs in the upper-right corner of the television.

By locking all other content, you cannot select it on the artboard. Locking layers can be a great way to more easily select your content.

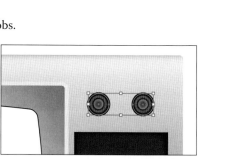

5 Choose Object > Transform > Scale. In the Scale dialog box, change the Uniform Scale to **110**% and then click OK.

6 In the Layers panel, deselect the lock icons (🔒) next to the <Path>, Screen, and TV body layers to unlock them. Click the triangle to the left of the Side panel layer to collapse it.

7 Choose Select > Deselect.

8 Choose File > Save.

Viewing layers

The Layers panel lets you hide layers, sublayers, or individual objects from view. When a layer is hidden, the content on the layer is also locked and cannot be selected or printed. You can also use the Layers panel to display layers or objects individually, in either Preview or Outline mode. Now, you'll change the fill color of part of the television body.

► **Tip:** You can Alt (Windows) or Option (Mac OS) click the layer eye icon to hide or show a layer. Hiding layers prevents them from being changed.

1 In the Layers panel, click the TV body layer to select it and then Alt-click (Windows) or Option-click (Mac OS) the eye icon (👁) to the left of the TV body layer name to hide the other layers.

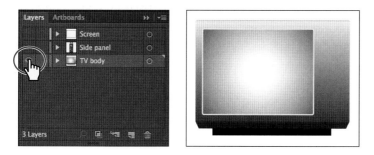

2 Click the triangle to the left of the TV body layer name to show the contents of the layer.

3 Ctrl-click (Windows) or Command-click (Mac OS) the eye icon () to the left of the TV body layer name to view the artwork for that layer in Outline mode.

This action lets you see that there are three shapes. Displaying a layer in Outline mode is also useful for selecting the anchor points or center points on objects.

▶ **Tip:** To view layer artwork in Outline mode, you can also double-click either the layer thumbnail or just to the right of the layer name to open the Layer Options dialog box. You can then deselect Preview and click OK.

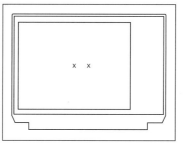

Ctrl-click (Windows) or Command-click (Mac OS) the eye icon to enter Outline mode.

4 Using the Selection tool (▶), on the artboard, click the rectangle just inside the television shape to select it. See the figure for selection help.

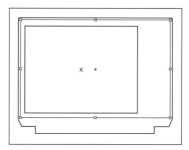

5 With the rectangle selected, click Fill color in the Control panel and then select the Wood Grain swatch in the Swatches panel that appears in the tool tip, to paint the rectangle with a gradient.

6 Ctrl-click (Windows) or Command-click (Mac OS) the eye icon () to the left of the TV body layer name to view the artwork for that layer in Preview mode.

In the Layers panel, notice the selected-art indicator (■) to the right of the bottom <Path> sublayer. Also note that you cannot see the shape on the artboard, since it is on the bottom of the layer stack, behind the other two <Path> objects.

7 Choose Object > Arrange > Bring Forward.

You can now see the selected shape and its gradient fill on the artboard. By choosing an Arrange command, you are moving the content in the layer stack in the Layers panel, much as you did earlier in the lesson by dragging the sublayers in the Layers panel.

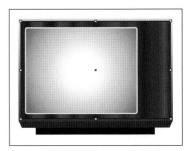

● **Note:** When you first select the Gradient tool, a horizontal line appears in the selected rectangle. This is the default direction of the gradient fill.

8 Select the Gradient tool (▨) in the Tools panel. Make sure that the Fill box is selected at the bottom of the Tools panel. Position the pointer over the bottom, middle of the selected rectangle. Press and hold the Shift key, click the pointer, and drag in a line straight up to the top of the rectangle to change the direction of the gradient. Release the mouse button and then the modifier key.

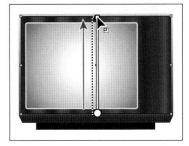

9 Choose Select > Deselect and then File > Save.

10 In the Layers panel, choose Show All Layers from the panel menu (▼≡).

In the Layers panel, you can also Alt-click (Windows) or Option-click (Mac OS) the eye icon () to the left of the TV body layer name to show the other layers.

11 Click the triangle to the left of the TV body layer name to hide the contents of the layer.

12 Choose File > Save.

Pasting layers

To complete the television, you'll copy and paste the remaining pieces of artwork from another file. You can paste a layered file into another file and keep the layers intact.

1   Choose Window > Workspace > Reset Essentials.

2   Choose File > Open, and open the show.ai file, located in the Lesson08 folder in the Lessons folder on your hard disk.

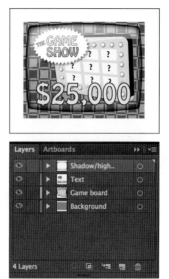

3   To see how the objects in each layer are organized, Alt-click (Windows) or Option-click (Mac OS) the eye icon (👁) for each layer in the Layers panel to show one layer and hide the others. You can also click the triangles (▶) to the left of the layer names to expand and collapse the layers for further inspection. When you're finished, make sure that all the layers are showing and that they are collapsed.

4   Choose Select > All and then Edit > Copy to select and copy the game show content to the clipboard.

5   Choose File > Close to close the show.ai file without saving any changes. If a warning dialog box appears, click No (Windows) or Don't Save (Mac OS).

6   In the tv.ai file, choose Paste Remembers Layers from the Layers panel menu (▾≡). A check mark next to the option indicates that it's selected.

    When Paste Remembers Layers is selected, artwork is pasted into the layer(s) from which it was copied, regardless of which layer is active in the Layers panel. If the option is not selected, all objects are pasted into the active layer and the layers from the original file are not pasted in.

● **Note:** If the target document has a layer of the same name, Illustrator combines the pasted content into a layer of the same name.

7   Choose Edit > Paste to paste the game show content onto the television.

    The Paste Remembers Layers option causes the show.ai layers to be pasted as four separate layers at the top of the Layers panel (Shadow/highlight, Text, Game board, and Background).

8 With the Selection tool, drag the new content on top of the gray, rounded rectangle to center it as best as you can. See the figure for placement help.

Now, you'll move the newly pasted layers into the Screen layer.

9 In the Layers panel, select the Shadow/highlight layer (if not already selected) and Shift-click the Background layer name. Drag any of the four selected layers down on top of the Screen layer. The artwork should not change in appearance.

Drag the selected layers.   The result.

The four pasted layers become sublayers of the Screen layer. Notice that they keep their individual layer colors.

10 Choose Select > Deselect, and then choose File > Save.

Creating a clipping mask

The Layers panel lets you create clipping masks to control whether artwork on a layer (or in a group) is hidden or revealed. A clipping mask is an object or group of objects which masks (with its shape) artwork below it, in the same layer or sublayer, so that only artwork within the shape is visible.

Now, you'll create a clipping mask with the white, rounded rectangle shape at the top of the Screen layer.

1 Drag the bottom of the Layers panel down to reveal all of the layers.

In the Layers panel, a masking object must be above the objects it masks. You can create a clipping mask for an entire layer, a sublayer, or a group of objects. Because you want to mask all of the content in the Screen layer, the clipping object needs to be at the top of the Screen layer, which is what you did in the previous section.

2   Click the <Path> sublayer at the bottom of
    the Screen layer. Drag the selected <Path>
    sublayer up onto the Screen layer name.
    When the layer is highlighted, release the
    mouse button to position the <Path> on the
    top of the layer. The white, rounded
    rectangle will now be on top of the other
    artwork on the Screen layer.

3   Select the Screen layer to highlight it in
    the Layers panel. Click the Make/Release
    Clipping Mask button (⬚) at the bottom of
    the Layers panel.

● **Note:** Deselecting
the artwork on
the artboard is not
necessary to complete
the next steps, but
it can be helpful for
viewing the artwork.

▶ **Tip:** To release the
clipping mask, you can
select the Screen layer
again and click the
same Make/Release
Clipping Mask button.

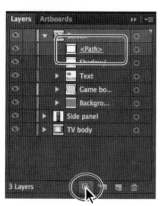

The name of the <Path> sublayer is underlined to indicate that it is the masking
shape. On the artboard, the <Path> sublayer has hidden the parts of the screen
content that extended outside of the shape.

4   Choose File > Save.

Merging layers

To streamline your artwork, you can merge layers, sublayers, or groups. Merging
layers, sublayers, or groups combines the contents into one layer, sublayer, or
group. Note that items will be merged into the layer or group that you selected last.

1   Click the Text sublayer in the Layers panel to
    highlight it, and then Shift-click to highlight
    the Background sublayer.

    Notice that the current layer indicator (◣)
    shows the last highlighted layer as the active
    layer. The last layer you select determines the
    name and color of the merged layer.

● **Note:** Layers can only merge with other layers that are on the same hierarchical level in the Layers panel. Likewise, sublayers can only merge with other sublayers that are in the same layer and at the same hierarchical level. Objects can't be merged with other objects.

2   Choose Merge Selected from the Layers panel menu (▼≡) to merge the content from the three sublayers into the Background sublayer.

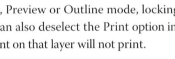

The objects on the merged layers retain their original stacking order and are added above the objects in the destination layer.

3   Double-click the thumbnail to the left of the Background layer name, or double-click directly to the right of the Background layer name. In the Layer Options dialog box, choose Green from the Color menu to match the Screen layer color. Click OK.

Changing the layer color to match the main layer isn't necessary. The Layer Options dialog box has a lot of the options you've already worked with, including naming layers, Preview or Outline mode, locking layers, and showing and hiding layers. You can also deselect the Print option in the Layer Options dialog box and any content on that layer will not print.

4   Alt-click (Windows) or Option-click (Mac OS) the eye icon (👁) to the left of the Screen layer to hide the other layers. Click the blank visibility column to the left of the Shadow/highlight sublayer to show its content on the artboard.

5   Choose Select > All On Active Artboard.

● **Note:** The Align options may not appear in the Control panel but are indicated by the word "Align." The number of options displayed in the Control panel depends on your screen resolution.

6   Make sure that Align To Selection is chosen in the Control panel, and then click the Horizontal Align Center button (⬒) and the Vertical Align Center button (⬌) in the Control panel to align the content to each other.

7   In the Layers panel, choose Show All Layers from the panel menu (▼≡), and then choose Select > Deselect.

8   Choose File > Save.

Locating layers

When working in artwork, there may be times when you select content on the artboard and then want to locate that same content in the Layers panel. This can help you to determine how content is organized.

1   With the Selection tool (▶), in the artwork, click to select one of the small knobs.

    In the Layers panel, you will see the selection indicator to the far right of the Side panel layer and knobs sublayer name.

2   Click the Locate Object button (⊙) at the bottom of the Layers panel to reveal the object within the knobs sublayer.

    Clicking the Locate Object button will open the layer so that the layer content can be seen, and the Layers panel will scroll, if necessary, to reveal the selected content. With an Illustrator file that has a lot of layered content, this can be helpful.

3   Choose Select > Deselect.

4   Click the triangle to the left of the Screen and Side panel layer names to hide the contents of each layer.

Applying appearance attributes to layers

You can apply appearance attributes, such as styles, effects, and transparency, to layers, groups, and objects, using the Layers panel. When an appearance attribute is applied to a layer, any object on that layer takes on that attribute. If an appearance attribute is applied only to a specific object on a layer, it affects only that object, not the entire layer.

● **Note:** To learn more about working with appearance attributes, see Lesson 13, "Applying Appearance Attributes and Graphic Styles."

You will apply an effect to an object on one layer. Then, you'll copy that effect to another layer to change all objects on that layer.

1   Click the triangle to the left of the TV body layer name to show the contents of the layer.

2 Click the target icon () to the right of the bottom <Path> object in the target column.

Clicking the target icon indicates that you want to apply an effect, style, or transparency change to that layer, sublayer, group, or object. In other words, the layer, sublayer, group, or object is targeted. The content is also selected in the Document window. When the target button appears as a double ring icon (either or), the item is targeted; a single ring icon indicates that the item is not targeted.

3 Choose Effect > Stylize > Drop Shadow. In the Drop Shadow dialog box, change the Opacity to **50%**, the X Offset to **0**, the Y Offset to **0.1 in**, and the Blur to **0.1 in**, if necessary. Click OK. A drop shadow appears on the edge of the television shape.

Note: There are two Stylize commands in the Effect menu. Choose the top Stylize menu command, which is in the Illustrator Effects.

Notice that, on the <Path> sublayer, the target icon () is now shaded, indicating that the object has appearance attributes applied to it.

4 Click the Appearance panel icon () on the right side of the workspace to reveal the Appearance panel. If the Appearance panel isn't visible, choose Window > Appearance. Notice that Drop Shadow has been added to the list of appearance attributes for the selected object.

5 Choose Select > Deselect.

You will now use the Layers panel to copy an appearance attribute into a layer and then edit it.

6 Click the Layers panel icon (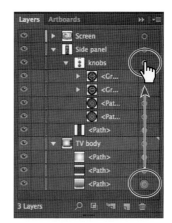) on the right side of the workspace to expand the Layers panel. Click the arrow to the left of the Side panel layer to reveal its contents. If necessary, first scroll down or drag the bottom of the Layers panel down to display the entire list.

7 Press the Alt (Windows) or Option (Mac OS) key, and drag the shaded target icon of the bottom <Path> sublayer in the TV body layer to the target icon of the knobs sublayer, without releasing the mouse button. When the target icon of the knobs sublayer turns light gray, release the mouse button and then the modifier key.

The drop shadow is now applied to the knobs sublayer and all content in that sublayer, as indicated by the shaded target icon.

Note: You can drag and copy the shaded target icon to any layer, sublayer, group, or object to apply the properties found in the Appearance panel.

Now, you'll edit the drop shadow effect for the knobs to make the shadow more prominent.

8 In the Layers panel, click the target icon (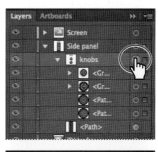) to the right of the knobs sublayer name.

This automatically selects the objects on the sublayer and deselects the object on the TV body layer.

9 Click the Appearance panel icon () on the right side of the workspace to reveal the Appearance panel. In the Appearance panel, click the words "Drop Shadow," scrolling down to find it in the list, if necessary.

10 In the Drop Shadow dialog box, change the Opacity to **80%**, and then click OK.

This will make a subtle gradient change to the knobs.

11 Choose Select > Deselect.

12 Choose File > Save.

Isolating layers

When a layer is in Isolation mode, objects on that layer are isolated so that you can easily edit them without affecting other layers. Next, you will enter Isolation mode for a layer and make a simple edit.

1 Expand the Layers panel by clicking the Layers panel icon, if it's not already showing.

2 Click the triangles to the left of the layers in the Layers panel to close them all.

3 Click to select the Side panel layer.

4 Choose Enter Isolation Mode from the Layers panel menu (▼≡).

   In Isolation mode, the contents of the Side panel layer appear on top of all the objects on the artboard. The rest of the content on the artboard is dimmed and locked, much like when you enter Isolation mode for a group. The Layers panel now shows a layer called Isolation Mode and a sublayer that contains the Side panel content.

5 Select the Selection tool (▶), and Shift-click the two small knobs at the top of the side panel to select them.

6 Press the Down Arrow key twice to move the knobs down.

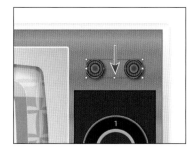

7 Press the Escape key to exit Isolation mode.

   Notice that the content is no longer locked and the Layers panel reveals all the layers and sublayers again.

8 Choose Select > Deselect.

Now that the artwork is complete, you may want to combine all the layers into a single layer and then delete the empty layers. This is called flattening artwork. Delivering finished artwork in a single–layer file can prevent accidents, such as hiding layers and omitting parts of the artwork during printing. To flatten specific layers without deleting hidden layers, you can select the layers you want to flatten and then choose Merge Selected from the Layers panel menu.

Note: If a dialog box appears asking about the clipboard, click Clear Clipboard. This means that content you previously copied in Illustrator (and now is on the clipboard) cannot be pasted into other applications.

For a complete list of shortcuts that you can use with the Layers panel, see "Keyboard shortcuts" in Illustrator Help.

9 Choose File > Save and then File > Close.

Review questions

1 Name two benefits of using layers when creating artwork.

2 How do you hide layers? How do you show individual layers?

3 Describe how to reorder layers in a file.

4 What is the purpose of changing the selection color for a layer?

5 What happens if you paste a layered file into another file? Why is the Paste Remembers Layers option useful?

6 How do you create a layer clipping mask?

7 How do you apply an effect to a layer? How can you edit that effect?

Review answers

1 The benefits of using layers when creating artwork include: protecting artwork that you don't want to change, hiding artwork that you aren't working with so that it's not distracting, and controlling what prints.

2 To hide a layer, click to deselect the eye icon to the left of the layer name in the Layers panel. Select the blank, leftmost column (the Visibility column) to show a layer.

3 You reorder layers by selecting a layer name in the Layers panel and dragging the layer to its new location. The order of layers in the Layers panel controls the document's layer order—topmost in the panel is front-most in the artwork.

4 The selection color controls how selected anchor points and direction lines are displayed on a layer and helps you identify the different layers in your document.

5 The paste commands paste layered files or objects copied from different layers into the active layer, by default. The Paste Remembers Layers option keeps the original layers intact when the objects are pasted.

6 Create a clipping mask on a layer by selecting the layer and clicking the Make/Release Clipping Mask button in the Layers panel. The topmost object in the layer becomes the clipping mask.

7 Click the target icon for the layer to which you want to apply an effect. Then choose an effect from the Effect menu. To edit the effect, make sure that the layer is selected and then click the name of the effect in the Appearance panel. The effect's dialog box opens, and you can change the values.

9 WORKING WITH PERSPECTIVE DRAWING

Lesson overview

In this lesson, you'll learn how to do the following:

- Understand perspective drawing.

- Use and edit grid presets.

- Draw and edit objects in perspective.

- Edit grid planes and content.

- Create and edit text in perspective.

- Attach symbols to perspective.

This lesson takes approximately an hour and a half to complete. If needed, remove the previous lesson folder from your hard disk and copy the Lesson09 folder onto it.

In Adobe Illustrator CS6, you can easily draw or render artwork in perspective, using the Perspective Grid. The Perspective Grid allows you to approximately represent a scene on a flat surface, as it is naturally perceived by the human eye. For example, you can render a road or a pair of railway tracks, which seem to meet or vanish in the line of vision.

Getting started

In this lesson, you'll explore working with the Perspective Grid, adding content to it, and editing on the Perspective Grid.

Before you begin, you'll restore the default preferences for Adobe Illustrator. Then, you'll open the finished art file for this lesson to see what you'll create.

1 To ensure that the tools and panels function exactly as described in this lesson, delete or deactivate (by renaming) the Adobe Illustrator CS6 preferences file. See "Restoring default preferences" on page 3.

2 Start Adobe Illustrator CS6.

● **Note:** If you have not already done so, copy the Lesson09 folder from the Lessons folder on the *Adobe Illustrator CS6 Classroom in a Book* CD onto your hard disk. See "Copying the Classroom in a Book files" on page 2.

3 Choose File > Open, and open the L9end.ai file in the Lesson09 folder, located in the Lessons folder on your hard disk.

4 Choose View > Zoom Out to make the finished artwork smaller, if you want to leave it on your screen as you work. (Use the Hand tool [🖐]) to move the artwork where you want it in the window.) Leave the file open for reference, or choose File > Close.

● **Note:** In Mac OS, when opening lesson files, you may need to click the round, green button in the upper-left corner of the Document window to maximize the window's size.

5 Choose File > Open. Navigate to the Lesson09 folder, located in the Lessons folder on your hard disk. Open the L9start.ai file.

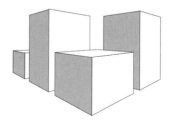

6 Choose File > Save As. In the Save As dialog box, navigate to the Lesson09 folder and name the file **city.ai**. Leave the Save As Type option set to Adobe Illustrator (*.AI) (Windows) or the Format option set to Adobe Illustrator (ai) (Mac OS), and then click Save. In the Illustrator Options dialog box, leave the Illustrator options at their default settings and then click OK.

Understanding perspective

In Illustrator CS6, you can easily draw or render artwork in perspective, using a feature set that works based on established laws of perspective drawing. Perspective in drawing is an approximate representation, on a flat surface, of an image as it is seen by the eye.

Objects drawn in perspective are characterized primarily by the following:

- They are drawn smaller as their distance from the observer increases.

- The perspective objects are foreshortened, which means that an object or distance appears shorter than it actually is, because it is angled toward the viewer.

Understanding the Perspective Grid

The Perspective Grid allows you to approximately represent a scene on a flat surface, as it is naturally perceived by the human eye. For example, you can render a road or a pair of railway tracks, which seem to meet or vanish in the line of vision. The Perspective Grid allows you to create and render artwork in perspective.

1 Choose Reset Essentials from the workspace switcher in the Application bar.

2 Choose View > Fit Artboard In Window.

3 Select the Perspective Grid tool (⬚) in the Tools panel.

The default two-point Perspective Grid appears on the artboard.

● **Note:** If you don't see "Reset Essentials" in the workspace switcher menu, choose "Essentials" before choosing "Reset Essentials."

The figure below shows the Perspective Grid and its parts. As you go through this lesson, you will learn about each part. It may be helpful to refer back to the Perspective Grid options shown in this figure as you progress through the lesson.

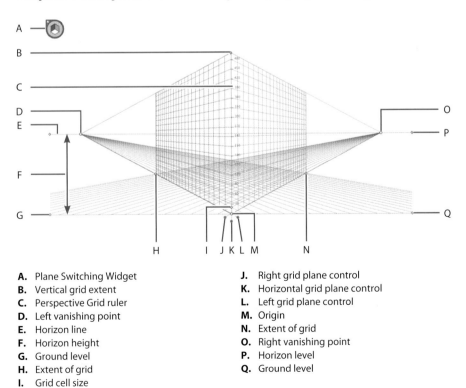

A. Plane Switching Widget
B. Vertical grid extent
C. Perspective Grid ruler
D. Left vanishing point
E. Horizon line
F. Horizon height
G. Ground level
H. Extent of grid
I. Grid cell size

J. Right grid plane control
K. Horizontal grid plane control
L. Left grid plane control
M. Origin
N. Extent of grid
O. Right vanishing point
P. Horizon level
Q. Ground level

Working with the Perspective Grid

In order to begin working with content in perspective, it is helpful to see and set up the Perspective Grid the way you want.

Using a preset grid

To begin the lesson, you'll work with the Perspective Grid, starting with some Illustrator presets.

You use the Perspective Grid to draw and snap content in perspective, although the grid is non-printing. The Perspective Grid, by default, is set up as a two-point perspective, and you can easily change that using presets. A grid in Illustrator can have up to three points of perspective.

Tip: You can show the Perspective Grid without selecting the Perspective Grid tool, by choosing View > Perspective Grid > Show Grid.

1 Choose View > Perspective Grid > One Point Perspective > [1P-Normal View]. Notice that the grid changes to a one-point perspective.

   A one-point perspective can be very useful for drawing roads, railway tracks, or buildings viewed so that the front is directly facing the viewer.

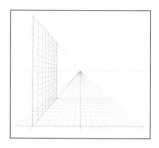

2 Choose View > Perspective Grid > Three Point Perspective > [3P-Normal View]. Notice that the grid changes to a three-point perspective.

   Three-point perspective is usually used for buildings seen from above or below. In addition to showing vanishing points for each wall, there is now a point showing those walls receding into the ground or high in space.

3 To return the grid back to a two-point perspective, choose View > Perspective Grid > Two Point Perspective > [2P-Normal View].

Editing the Perspective Grid

Next, you'll learn how to edit the Perspective Grid. To edit the grid, you can either select the Perspective Grid tool or edit using the Define Grid command. You can make changes to the grid if you have content on the grid, although it may be easier to establish the grid settings before you add content. You can create only one grid per Illustrator document.

1 With the Perspective Grid tool (⌗) selected, drag the horizon line point down below the bottom of the blue sky to move the horizon down, as shown in the figure. The measurement label should show approximately 147 pt.

The location of the horizon line indicates the observer's eye level.

2 With the Perspective Grid tool, drag the left ground level point up, to move the whole Perspective Grid. Drag until the horizon line you adjusted in the previous step is lined up with the bottom of the blue sky.

The ground level point allows you to drag the Perspective Grid to different parts of the artboard or to a different artboard altogether.

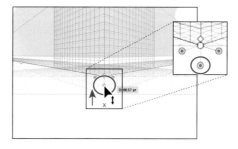

● **Note:** Throughout this section, a red X in the figures shows where to drag from.

● **Note:** The gray lines in some of these figures indicate the initial position of the Perspective Grid, before it was adjusted.

● **Note:** As you drag the Perspective Grid by the ground level point, notice that you can move it in any direction. Make sure that it is still more or less centered horizontally on the artboard.

3 With the Perspective Grid tool, drag the horizontal grid plane control point up about 68 pt so that it's closer to the horizon line.

▶ **Tip:** The location of the ground level in relation to the horizon line will determine how far above or below eye level the object will be viewed.

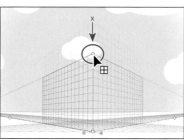

4 With the Perspective Grid tool, click and drag the Vertical Grid Extent point (the top point in the grid) down to shorten the vertical extent.

Making the vertical extent shorter can be a way to minimize the grid if you are drawing objects that are less precise, as you will see later in the lesson.

5 Choose File > Save. Changes you make to the Perspective Grid are saved with this document only.

Setting the grid up for your drawing is an important step. Next, you will access these changes using the Define Grid menu.

6 Choose View > Perspective Grid > Define Grid.

▶ **Tip:** To learn more about the Define Perspective Grid dialog box, search for "Define grid presets" in Illustrator Help.

▶ **Tip:** After setting the Define Perspective Grid settings, you can save them as a preset to access later. In the Define Perspective Grid dialog box, change the settings and then click the Save Preset button.

7 In the Define Perspective Grid dialog box, change the Units to Inches, change the Gridline Every value to **.3** in and change the Viewing Distance to **7** in.

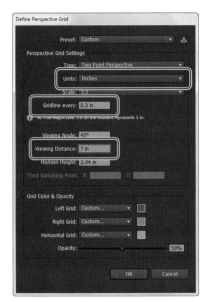

The Viewing Distance is the distance between the observer and the scene. Notice that you can change the Scale of the grid, which you might want to do if real-world measurements are involved. You can edit settings, like Horizon Height and Viewing Angle, which you can also edit on the artboard, using the Perspective Grid tool. Leave the Grid Color & Opacity settings at their defaults. When you have finished making changes, click OK.

8 With the Perspective Grid tool, drag the left vanishing point about −.75 in to the left, until it reaches the left horizon line point. Notice that this changes only the left (blue) grid on the two-point Perspective Grid.

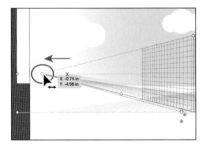

9 Choose Edit > Undo Perspective Grid Edit.

You are able to undo most changes made to the Perspective Grid.

10 Choose View > Perspective Grid > Lock Station Point. This locks the left and right vanishing points so that they move together.

11 With the Perspective Grid tool, drag the left vanishing point about −.75 in to the left again, until it reaches the left horizon line point. Notice that this now changes both grids on the two-point Perspective Grid.

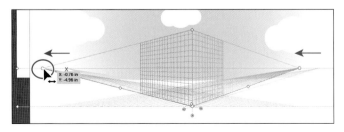

12 Choose File > Save.

13 Choose View > Perspective Grid > Lock Grid.

This command restricts the grid movement and other grid editing features of the Perspective Grid tool. You can only change the visibility and the grid plane position, which you will work with later in this lesson.

● **Note:** When you select a tool other than the Perspective Grid tool, you cannot edit the Perspective Grid. Also, if the Perspective Grid is locked, you can edit it by choosing View > Perspective Grid > Define Grid.

Now that the grid is locked into the correct position, you will begin creating your cityscape by adding content to it.

Drawing objects in perspective

To draw objects in perspective, use the line group tools or rectangle group tools (except for the Flare tool) while the grid is visible. Before you begin drawing using any of these tools, you need to select a grid plane to attach the content to, using the Plane Switching Widget or keyboard shortcuts.

The Plane Switching Widget

When you select the Perspective Grid, a Plane Switching Widget also appears in the upper-left corner of the Document window, by default. You can use this widget to select the active grid plane.

In the Perspective Grid, an active plane is the plane on which you draw an object to project the observer's view of that portion of the scene.

You can change the position of the widget and other options by double-clicking the Perspective Grid tool in the Tools panel.

—From Illustrator Help

A Left Grid(1)
B No Active Grid(4)
C Horizontal Grid(2)
D Right Grid(3)

▶ **Tip:** The numbers in parentheses (Left Grid(1), for instance) refer to the keyboard shortcut assigned to that grid plane.

1 Click the Layers panel icon (◉) to expand the Layers panel. Click the eye icon (◉) to the left of the Background layer to hide its contents on the artboard. Click to select the layer named Left face so that the new content you create is on that layer. Click the Layers panel icon to collapse the panel.

2 Select the Rectangle tool (▪) in the Tools panel.

3 Select the Left Grid in the Plane Switching Widget.

Whichever grid plane is selected in the widget is the grid plane on the Perspective Grid to which you'll add content.

● **Note:** With practice, you'll develop the habit of checking which grid plane is active before drawing or adding content.

● **Note:** You may want
to zoom in for the
next steps.

4 Position the pointer over the top of the Perspective Grid, where the two
planes meet. Notice that the cursor (◄┤) has an arrow pointing to the left,
indicating that you are about to draw on the left grid plane. Drag down and to
the left, to the bottom orthogonal line, as shown in the figure, so that the gray
measurement label shows an approximate width of 3.6 in. Note that it's okay if
your measurements are a little different from those shown.

When drawing on the grid plane, objects snap to the grid lines, by default.

● **Note:** Depending
on the zoom level, your
grid may not match the
figures exactly and
that's okay.

5 With the rectangle selected, change the Fill color in the Control panel to a
medium gray (C=0 M=0 Y=0 K=40 will appear in the swatch tool tip).

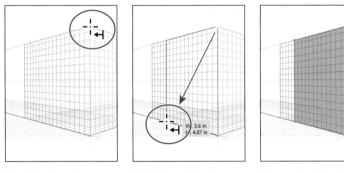

Start drawing.   Create the rectangle.   Change the Fill color.

Next, you will draw another rectangle to create the other side of a building.

▶ **Tip:** You can turn off grid snapping by choosing View > Perspective Grid > Snap To Grid.

6 Press Ctrl++ (Windows) or Command++ (Mac OS) twice to zoom in to the
Perspective Grid. Snapping to the grid doesn't work if you are zoomed out
too far.

7 Click the Layers panel icon (●) to expand the Layers panel. Click to select the
layer named Right face so that the new content you create is on that layer.

8 With the Rectangle tool still
selected, click Right Grid(3) in the
Plane Switching Widget to draw in
perspective on the right grid plane.
Notice that the cursor (├►) now has an
arrow pointing to the right, indicating
that you are about to draw on the right
grid plane. Position the pointer at the
same top point as for the last rectangle
you drew, and drag down and to the
right. When the measurement label

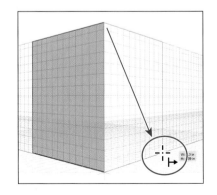

shows a width of approximately 3.3 in and the pointer reaches the bottom of the
right grid plane, release the mouse button.

9 With the rectangle selected, change the Fill color in the Control panel to a light gray (C=0 M=0 Y=0 K=10). Press the Escape key to hide the Swatches panel.

10 Click the X in the upper-left corner of the Plane Switching Widget to hide the Perspective Grid and to see your artwork.

> **Tip:** You can also choose View > Perspective Grid > Hide Grid to hide the grid.

11 Choose View > Fit Artboard In Window.

Next, you will draw a rectangle that will serve as a window for the building. But first, you must show the grid again to continue drawing in perspective.

12 Press Shift+Ctrl+I (Windows) or Shift+Command+I (Mac OS) to show the grid.

> **Tip:** You can also show the Perspective Grid by selecting the Perspective Grid tool or by choosing View > Perspective Grid > Show Grid.

13 Select the Rounded Rectangle tool ( ) by holding down the mouse button on the Rectangle tool ( ) in the Tools panel. Position the pointer over the center of the rectangle you just created. Click once to open the Rounded Rectangle dialog box. Change the Width to **1.5 in** and the Height to **.9 in**. Change the Corner Radius to **.1** in, and then click OK. This will be a window in the building.

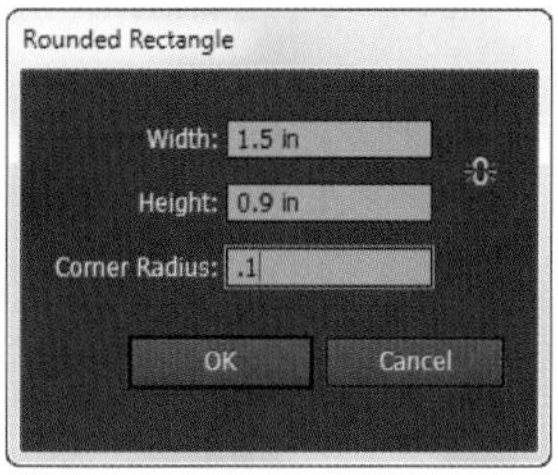

14 Press Ctrl++ (Windows) or Command++ (Mac OS) three times to zoom in.

15 Select the Selection tool ( ), and drag the rectangle down and to the left to position it at the bottom, left of the light gray rectangle.

If you use the Selection tool to drag an object that was drawn in perspective, it maintains its original perspective but it doesn't change to match the Perspective Grid.

16 Choose Edit > Undo Move to return the rectangle to its original position.

Selecting and transforming objects in perspective

You can select objects in perspective using the Perspective Selection tool. The Perspective Selection tool uses the active plane settings to select the objects.

Next, you will move and resize the rectangle you just drew.

1 Select the Perspective Selection tool ( ) by holding down the mouse button on the Perspective Grid tool in the Tools panel. Drag the rounded rectangle down and to the left, to the lower-left corner of the light gray rectangle. See the figure for placement help. Notice that it snaps to the grid as you drag it.

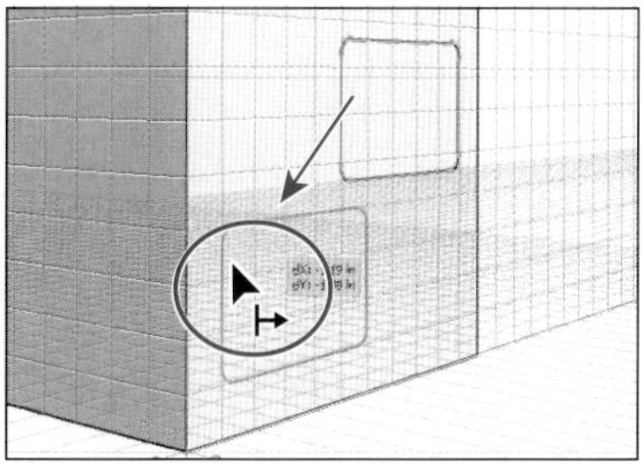

> **Tip:** When drawing in perspective, you can still use the usual keyboard shortcuts for drawing objects, such as Shift-drag.

2 With the rectangle still selected, change the Fill color in the Control panel to the window gradient. Press the Escape key to hide the Swatches panel.

3 With the Perspective Selection tool still selected, click the darker gray rectangle on the left grid plane to select it. Notice that the left grid plane is now selected in the Plane Switching Widget.

4 Select the Zoom tool (🔍) in the Tools panel, and drag a marquee across the lower-left corner of the darker gray rectangle on the left grid plane.

▶ **Tip:** You can open the Transform panel (Window > Transform) and make the height of both rectangles the same.

5 Select the Perspective Selection tool (▶⚏), and then drag the lower-left corner up and to the left, following the bottom grid plane line that leads to the left vanishing point. See the figure below for help. When the measurement label shows a width of about 4.5 in, release the mouse button.

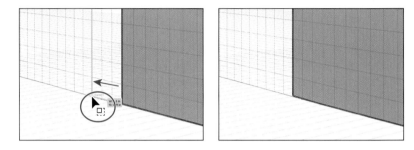

● **Note:** The size does not have to match exactly, as long as the shape is snapped to the Perspective Grid. The width of your rectangles may be different than what you see in the figure, and that's okay.

Scale objects in perspective

You can scale objects in perspective using the Perspective Selection tool. While scaling objects in perspective, the following rules apply:

- Scaling is done in the object's plane. When you scale an object, the height or distance is scaled based on the object's plane and not on the current or active plane.

- For multiple objects, scaling is done for objects that are on the same plane. For example, if you select multiple objects on the right and left planes, all the objects that are on the same plane as the object with the bounding box that is used for scaling are scaled.

- Objects that have been moved perpendicularly are scaled on their respective plane and not on the current or active plane.

—From Illustrator Help

Next, you will duplicate an object in perspective, as well as move an object perpendicular to an existing object.

6 Choose View > Fit Artboard In Window.

7 With the Perspective Selection tool, click to select the light gray rectangle on the right grid plan. Holding down Alt+Shift (Windows) or Option+Shift (Mac OS), drag the selected rectangle to the right on the right grid plane. When the measurement label shows a distance (dX) of approximately 4.75 in, release the mouse button and then the modifier keys.

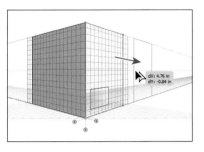

You will use this copy as the face of another building. As with other types of drawings, the Alt or Option key duplicates the object and the Shift key constrains the movement.

With the rectangle copy in place and in perspective, you will now adjust the Perspective Grid so that the grid pattern covers the new shape. You'll do this by editing the grid extent.

8 Select the Perspective Grid tool (⊞) in the Tools panel.

9 Press Ctrl++ (Windows) or Command++ (Mac OS) twice to zoom in.

Notice that the grid pattern in the Perspective Grid starts to expand to the right and left the closer you zoom in.

10 Choose View > Perspective Grid > Unlock Grid, which enables you to edit the grid.

11 With the Perspective Grid tool, position the pointer over the right grid extent widget, indicated by the red X in the figure below, and drag to the left until it reaches the right edge of the copied rectangle.

12 Drag the grid cell widget (circled in the figure) down a bit, until the grid cell size becomes smaller.

Notice that if you drag too far down, the left and right extents of the grid moves away from their accompanying vanishing points. Dragging up would increase the size of the grid cells. Your grid cell size may not match the figure exactly, and that's okay.

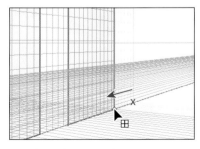

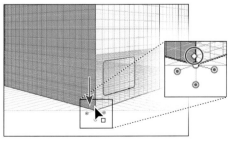

Drag the grid extent widget.   Edit the grid cell size.

Note: Gridlines are set to display on-screen when there is a 1-pixel gap in them. Progressive zooming in will bring into view more gridlines that are closer to the vanishing point. Your grid does not have to match the figures exactly, going forward.

13 Choose View > Perspective Grid > Define Grid, and in the Define Perspective Grid dialog box, change the Gridline Every value to **.25** in. Click OK. This is the same as dragging the grid cell widget on the grid.

14 Select the Selection tool (▸), and click to select the darker gray rectangle on the left grid plane. Change the Fill color in the Control panel to the building face 1 color. Click to select the lighter gray rectangle you created (the other face of the same building), and change the Fill color in the Control panel to building face 2.

15 Choose File > Save.

Now that the copied rectangle is in place and the grid cells display correctly, you will copy the rectangle on the left grid plane so that it becomes the left face of the newly copied rectangle. Next, you will see how to move an object parallel to its current location.

1 Select the Perspective Selection tool (▸◉) in the Tools panel. Click to select the red-colored rectangle on the left grid plane. Holding down the number 5 key, drag the rectangle to the left a bit. Release the mouse and then the 5 key.

This action moves the object in parallel to its current location.

2 Choose Edit > Undo Perspective Move.

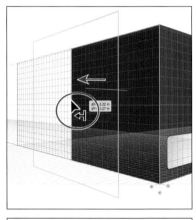

> **Tip:** If you were to select the Draw Behind mode, this step would copy the rectangle and place it behind all other objects.

3 With the Perspective Selection tool selected, hold down the Alt (Windows) or Option (Mac OS) key and the number 5 key and drag the same rectangle to the right. Drag to position it as the left face of the second building. When in position, release the mouse and then the modifier keys.

This duplicates the object and places it at the new location without changing the original object.

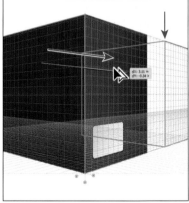

4 With the new copy still selected, choose Object > Arrange > Send To Back. Change the Fill color of the new object in the Control panel to a medium gray (C=0 M=0 Y=0 K=50 will appear in the tool tip).

Next, you will make a copy of the rounded rectangle "window" and then move it to the left grid plane of the red building by pressing a keyboard shortcut to switch planes while dragging.

5 With the Perspective Selection tool selected, select the blue window on the right face of the building. Choose Edit > Copy and then Edit > Paste In Front.

6 With the Perspective Selection tool, drag the copy of the rounded rectangle window to the left. As you drag, press and then release the number 1 key to switch the window to the left grid plane. Drag the window to the lower-left corner of the red rectangle on the left (which is the left side of the red building).

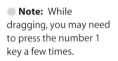
Note: While dragging, you may need to press the number 1 key a few times.

7 Choose Edit > Cut.

8 Click the Layers panel icon () to expand the Layers panel. In the Layers panel, make sure that the Left face layer is selected. Click the Layers panel icon to collapse the panel again.

9 Choose Edit > Paste In Front.

Note: If the rounded rectangle doesn't appear on top of all other objects, choose Object > Arrange > Bring To Front.

10 With the rounded rectangle still selected, press the Right Arrow key and then the Up Arrow key. Notice that pressing the arrow keys snaps a side of the rounded rectangle to the Perspective Grid. Using the arrow keys, position the window in the lower-left corner of the red rectangle, as shown in the figure.

11 Click to select the original rounded rectangle on the right grid plane so that it is the only thing selected. Position it on the same grid lines (relatively) as the copy, using the arrow keys to snap it to the grid, as shown in the figure.

Note: The size of the grid determines the distance an object is moved when pressing the Arrow keys. The larger the grid, the farther the object moves.

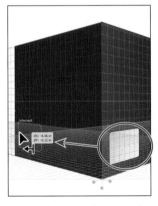

Copy and position the rectangle.

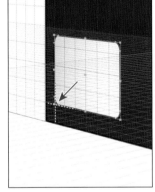

Use the arrow keys to position the left grid rectangle.

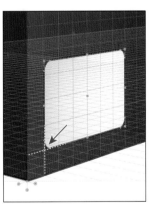

Use the arrow keys to position the right grid rectangle.

12 Press Ctrl+Shift+I (Windows) or Command+Shift+I (Mac OS) to temporarily hide the Perspective Grid.

13 Choose Select > Deselect and then File > Save.

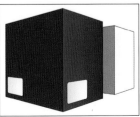

Attaching content to perspective

If you have already created content, Illustrator provides an option to attach the objects to an active plane on the Perspective Grid. You will now add an existing sign for a coffee shop to one of the sides of a building.

1   Choose View > Perspective Grid > Show Grid to show the grid.

2   Choose View > Fit All In Window to see the two artboards.

3   Select the Selection tool (▶), and click to select the Coffee sign on the artboard on the right. Drag the sign close to the right of the gray building you've created in perspective. After you've placed the sign, click once somewhere on a blank area of the main artboard with the grid. This makes the artboard with the Perspective Grid the active artboard and deselects the sign.

4   Choose View > Fit Artboard In Window.

5   Press Ctrl++ (Windows) or Command++ (Mac OS) twice to zoom in to the Perspective Grid and artwork.

Next, you will add the selected sign to the right side of the red building and put it into perspective along with the rest of the artwork on the main artboard.

▶ **Tip:** You can also select the active plane by pressing keyboard shortcuts: 1=Left Grid, 2=Horizontal Grid, 3=Right Grid, and 4=No Active Grid.

6   Select the Perspective Selection tool (▶) in the Tools panel. Select the Left Grid(1) in the Plane Switching Widget to make sure that the sign will be added to the left grid plane.

● **Note:** The above step is an important step that can be easily forgotten!

7   With the Perspective Selection tool, drag the sign so that the top of the sign aligns with the top of the vertical grid extent.

▶ **Tip:** Instead of dragging the object onto the plane using the Perspective Selection tool, you can also select the object with the Perspective Selection tool, choose the plane using the Plane Switching Widget, and then choose Object > Perspective > Attach To Active Plane.

The artwork is added to the grid that is selected in the Plane Switching Widget.

● **Note:** The coffee sign is a group of objects. You can just as easily attach a single object to the Perspective Grid.

8   With the sign still selected, choose Edit > Cut.

9   Click the Layers panel icon (◨) on the right side of the workspace to expand the Layers panel. Click to select the Right face layer. Choose Edit > Paste In Place. This pastes the sign on the Right face layer.

10 Click the Layers panel icon to collapse the panel.

You will now move the coffee sign perpendicular to its current location, along the right side of the building.

11 With the Perspective Selection tool, hold down the number 5 key and drag the coffee sign to the right until it reaches the right side of the red rectangle, as shown in the figure. Release the mouse button and then the modifier key.

12 With the Perspective Selection tool, hold down the Shift key and drag the bottom, middle point of the sign up to make it smaller. When the measurement label shows a Height of about 2.4 or 2.5 in, stop dragging. Release the mouse button and then the Shift key.

Drag the sign into position.   Scale the sign.

● **Note:** If your sign is too close or too far from the red building after resizing, you can drag to position it better, using the Perspective Selection tool.

13 Choose Select > Deselect and then File > Save.

Editing planes and objects together

You can edit the grid planes either before or after there is artwork on them. You can move objects perpendicularly by dragging them, as you've seen, or you can move a grid plane using grid plane controls to move objects perpendicularly.

Next, you will edit the grid planes and the artwork together.

1 With the Perspective Selection tool (▶) still selected, drag the right grid plane control to the right until D: 1 in (approximately) appears in the measurement label, as shown in the figure. This moves the right grid plane but not the objects on it.

● **Note:** Throughout this section, a red X in the figures shows where to drag from.

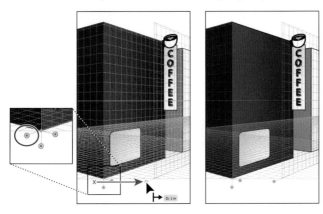

2 Choose Edit > Undo Perspective Grid Edit to return the grid plane to its original position.

▶ **Tip:** If you select an object or objects on the active grid plane and then drag the grid plane control while holding down the Shift key, only the selected objects move with the grid plane.

3 With the Perspective Selection tool still selected, hold down the Shift key and drag the right grid plane control to the right until the measurement label shows about 1 in. Release the mouse button and then the Shift key.

The Shift key moves the grid plane and the artwork on the grid perpendicular to their original positions.

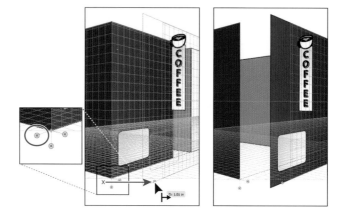

▶ **Tip:** Dragging a grid plane control while pressing Shift+Alt (Windows) or Shift+Option (Mac OS) drags a copy of the objects with the grid plane.

Dragging a grid plane control is not very precise. For more precision, you can move the right grid plane control according to values you enter, which you will do next.

4 Double-click the same right grid plane control you just dragged. In the Right Vanishing Plane dialog box, change the Location to **.5 in** and then select Move All Objects. Click OK.

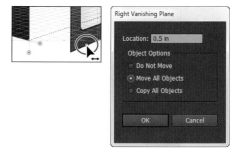

In the Right Vanishing Plane dialog box, the Do Not Move option allows you to move the grid plane and not the objects on it. Copy All Objects allows you to move the grid plane and to bring a copy of the objects on the grid plane with it.

The location in the Right Vanishing Plane dialog box starts at the station point, which is 0. The station point is indicated by the small green diamond on the Perspective Grid, above the horizontal grid control.

Next, you will move the left grid plane using the same method.

5 Double-click the left grid plane control. In the Left Vanishing Plane dialog box, change the Location to **−.4 in** and then select Move All Objects. Click OK.

Grid planes move to the right when you enter a positive value and to the left when you enter a negative value.

Now the grid planes and objects are where they need to be, except for the coffee sign and the left side of the second, gray building, which you will move later. You will now add a rectangle to the red building to fill in the gap left when you moved the planes.

6 Click the Layers panel icon () on the right side of the workspace to expand the Layers panel. Click to select the Center face layer.

7 Click the Layers panel icon to collapse the panel.

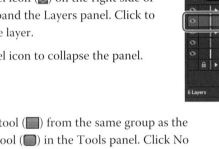

8 Select the Rectangle tool (▣) from the same group as the Rounded Rectangle tool (▣) in the Tools panel. Click No Active Grid(4) in the Plane Switching Widget.

This allows you to draw without perspective.

9 Starting from the upper-right corner of the red rectangle on the left grid plane, drag down and to the right, to the lower-left corner of the red rectangle on the right grid plane, as shown in the figure below.

● **Note:** The corners of the rectangles may not line up perfectly. If you want to ensure that they do, you can select the Perspective Selection tool and position the rectangles to snap to each other.

10 With the rectangle still selected, change the Fill color to the building corner swatch in the Control panel.

11 Choose Select > Deselect and then File > Save.

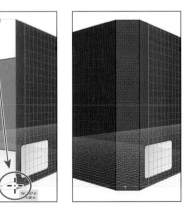

Now that the red building is taking shape, you will reposition the coffee sign and draw some rectangles to attach the sign to the face of the building. This will require that you move a grid plane to match the coffee sign.

Note: If you wanted to simply move the coffee sign in perspective with the Perspective Selection tool, you would not have to move the grid plane to match it.

1 Select the Perspective Selection tool (▶◉) in the Tools panel. Click to select the Coffee sign. Choose Object > Perspective > Move Plane To Match Object.

This moves the left grid plane to match the perspective of the sign. This allows you to draw or add more content in the same plane as the coffee sign.

2 Choose Select > Deselect. Select the Zoom tool (🔍) in the Tools panel, and drag a marquee around the coffee sign to zoom in to it.

3 Making sure that the Left Grid(1) is selected in the Plane Switching Widget, select the Rectangle tool in the Tools panel.

Next, you will draw some rectangles between the sign and the building to attach the sign to the building.

4 Starting on the left edge of the coffee sign, drag down and to the left to create a small rectangle, as shown in the first panel of the figure below. This acts as one attachment point for the sign.

5 With the rectangle still selected, change the Fill color in the Control panel to light blue.

6 Select the Perspective Selection tool (▶◉) in the Tools panel. Holding down Shift+Alt (Windows) or Shift+Option (Mac OS), drag the new rectangle down to create a copy toward the bottom of the sign. Release the mouse button and then the modifier keys. You may need to zoom in further.

7 With the new rectangle copy still selected, Shift-click the first rectangle you just drew and the coffee sign and then choose Object > Group.

8 Choose View > Smart Guides to turn them off.

Tip: Effects can be applied to objects in perspective. For instance, you could apply a 3D extrude effect (Effect > 3D > Extrude & Bevel) to the coffee sign group.

9 Holding down the Shift key, drag the sign group to the right so that it looks like it's attached to the building. The sign position does not have to match the figure below exactly.

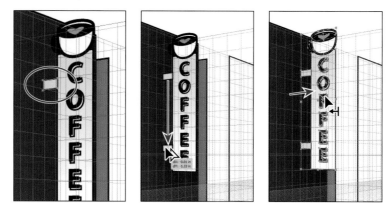

10 Choose View > Fit Artboard In Window.

11 With the Perspective Selection tool, click to select the red rectangle, representing the left side of the building. Choose Object > Perspective > Move Plane To Match Object.

12 Choose Select > Deselect.

▶ **Tip:** To return the left grid plane to the building face, you can also double-click the left grid plane control and change the Location to **–.4** in, select Do Not Move, and then click OK.

Next, you'll move the medium gray rectangle that represents the left part of the second building into the proper position. In order to see a grid plane as you drag the rectangle into position, you can temporarily align the left grid plane to the object.

13 Press Ctrl++ (Windows) or Command++ (Mac OS) twice to zoom in to the Perspective Grid and artwork.

14 Choose View > Smart Guides to turn them on.

15 With the Perspective Selection tool, click to select the medium gray rectangle behind the coffee sign, as shown in the figure below.

● **Note:** If it is difficult selecting the medium gray rectangle behind the coffee sign, you may need to choose View > Outline to select it by the edge and then choose View > Preview.

16 Holding down the Shift key, position the pointer over the lower-right corner point on the medium gray rectangle. Release the Shift key.

The left grid plane is temporarily aligned with the medium gray rectangle, which means that you can draw or add content to the grid on that plane. You can position the pointer over any of the corner points while holding the Shift key to do the same thing.

● **Note:** Smart Guides need to be turned on (View > Smart Guides) in order for you to position the plane automatically, using the Shift key.

17 Drag the middle, right point on the medium gray rectangle to the right so that it aligns with the edge of the light gray rectangle.

● **Note:** When using the Perspective Selection tool to resize or reposition an object in perspective, you do not need to position the grid plane.

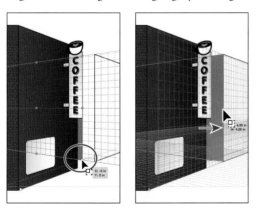

After dragging the rectangle, notice that the left grid plane returns to its original position. This is a way to temporarily reposition a grid plane.

18 Choose Select > Deselect and then File > Save.

Automatic Plane Positioning

Using the automatic plane positioning options, you can select to move the active plane temporarily when you mouse over the anchor point or gridline intersection point by pressing the Shift key.

The automatic plane positioning options are available in the Perspective Grid Options dialog box. To display this dialog box, double-click the Perspective Grid tool (▦) or the Perspective Selection tool (▸◉) in the Tools panel.

—From Illustrator Help

Adding and editing text in perspective

You cannot add text directly to a perspective plane when the grid is visible. However, you can bring text into perspective after creating it off the Perspective Grid. Next, you will add a sign above one of the windows.

● **Note:** You may want to zoom in to the artwork by pressing Ctrl++ (Windows) or Command++ (Mac OS) twice.

1   Click the Layers panel icon (▣) to expand the Layers panel. In the Layers panel, make sure that the Left face layer is selected. Click the Layers panel icon to collapse the panel again.

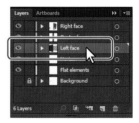

2   Select the Type tool (**T**) in the Tools panel. Click in a blank area on the artboard, and type **Coffee**.

● **Note:** If you don't see the Font Formatting options in the Control panel, click the word "Character" in the Control panel to reveal the Character panel.

3   Select the text with the Type tool, and change the Font to Myriad Pro (if necessary), the Font Size to **48 pt**, and the Font Style to Bold in the Control panel.

4   Select the Perspective Selection tool (▸◉) in the Tools panel. Press the number 1 key on the keyboard to select the left grid, and then drag the text above the rounded rectangle window on the left wall.

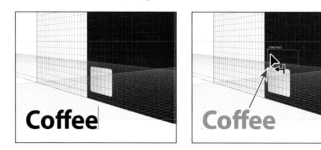

Next, you will edit the text while it is in perspective.

5   With the text object still selected, double-click the text with the Perspective
    Selection tool.

    This enters Isolation mode, allowing you to edit the text instead of the
    perspective object.

▶ **Tip:** You can also enter Isolation mode to edit text by clicking the Edit Text button (■) in the Control panel.

6   In Isolation mode, the Type tool (**T**) is selected automatically. Insert the cursor
    after the Coffee text, press the spacebar, and then type **Shop**. Press the Escape
    key twice to exit Isolation mode and return to the perspective object.

▶ **Tip:** To exit Isolation mode, you can also click twice on the gray arrow that appears below the
document tab at the top of the Document window.

7   Using the Perspective Selection tool, hold down the Shift key and drag the
    upper-right corner of the text object up and to the right to make it a bit larger.
    Release the mouse button and then the modifier key. Make sure that it isn't
    wider than the left side of the building.

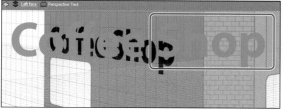

Edit the Coffee text.

Resize the text.

8   Click the Graphic Styles panel icon (■) on the right
    side of the workspace. With the text object selected,
    click the graphic style named Text in the Graphic
    Styles panel. Click the Graphic Styles panel icon to
    collapse the panel.

● **Note:** To learn more about working with graphic styles, see Lesson 13, "Applying Appearance Attributes and Graphic Styles."

    This applies a 3D Extrude effect, as well as strokes,
    fills, and a drop shadow effect to the text object. You can apply many kinds of
    effects, strokes, fills, and more to text in perspective.

9   Choose View > Fit Artboard In Window.

10 Press Ctrl+Shift+I (Windows) or
    Command+Shift+I (Mac OS) to
    temporarily hide the Perspective Grid.

11 Choose Select > Deselect and then
    File > Save.

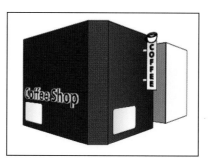

Working with symbols in perspective

● **Note:** To learn more about symbols, see Lesson 14, "Working with Symbols."

Adding symbols to a perspective plane when the grid is visible is a great way to add repeating items, such as windows. Like text, you can bring symbols into perspective after creating them in Normal mode. Next, you will add some windows to the red building from a window symbol that is already created.

Adding symbols to the Perspective Grid

1   Press Ctrl+Shift+I (Windows) or Command+Shift+I (Mac OS) to show the Perspective Grid, and then press Ctrl++ (Windows) or Command++ (Mac OS) twice to zoom in to the Perspective Grid and artwork.

2   With the Perspective Selection tool (▶▣) selected, click the left side of the red building on the left grid plane (the side with the text).

Next, you'll attach a window to the left grid plane and put it on the Left face layer.

3   Click the Symbols panel icon (▣) on the right side of the workspace to expand the Symbols panel. Drag the window1 symbol from the Symbols panel onto the left face of the red building. Notice that it is not in perspective.

4   With the Perspective Selection tool, drag the window to above the Coffee Shop text to attach it to the left grid plane. Then, drag the window toward the upper-left corner of the left side of the red building. Snap it to the grid.

● **Note:** Make sure that the window is close to the top of the building, since you will be adding another row of windows below this one. See the figure for position.

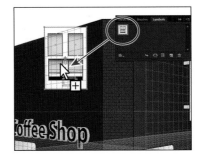
Drag the symbol onto the artboard.

Drag it into perspective.

Transforming symbols in perspective

● **Note:** To edit a symbol that is associated with the Perspective Grid, you can also select the symbol and then click the Edit Symbol button (▣) in the Control panel.

1   With the Perspective Selection tool (▶▣), double-click the window on the left grid plane. A dialog box appears, telling you that you are about to edit the symbol definition. This means that if you edit the content, it will change all of the window symbols on the artboard, which are called instances. Click OK.

2   Select the Selection tool (▶) in the Tools panel. Choose Select > All On Active Artboard. Holding down the Shift key, drag the lower-right corner of the window up and to the left to make it smaller. When the measurement label shows a width of about .6 in, release the mouse button and then the Shift key.

3 Press the Escape key to exit Isolation mode. Notice that the window is now smaller.

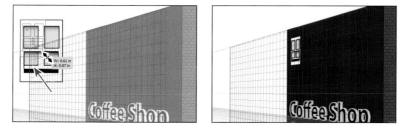

Next, you will align the left edge of the window with the left edge of the rounded rectangle window shape at the bottom of the building face. To do that, you will reposition the grid origin. If you shift the origin, the X and Y coordinates of the horizontal plane and the X coordinate of vertical planes are affected. When you select an object in perspective while the grid is visible, the X and Y coordinates displayed in the Transform and Info panels change with the shift in the origin.

4 Select the Perspective Selection tool (▶▣) in the Tools panel. Click to select the rounded rectangle window on the left side of the red building, below the Coffee Shop text. Choose Window > Transform to open the Transform panel. Notice the X and Y measurements.

5 Select the Perspective Grid tool (▦) in the Tools panel. Position the pointer over the origin point at the bottom of the center, brick face of the red building on the grid. The cursor (▶◦) shows a small circle next to it. Drag the origin point to the lower-left corner of the red rectangle of the left grid plane. It may snap a little to the left of the lower-left point of the rectangle, and that's okay.

▶ **Tip:** You can show rulers on the Perspective Grid by choosing View > Perspective Grid > Show Rulers. This shows you a ruler on each grid plane, in the units set in the Define Grid dialog box.

This sets the 0,0 point (origin) for the X and Y coordinates of the horizontal plane and the X coordinate of vertical planes to the new origin point.

6 Select the Perspective Selection tool in the Tools panel. Click to select the rounded rectangle window, and then click the lower-left reference point in the Transform panel (▦). Change the X value to **.3 in**.

7 Select the window above the rounded rectangle, and change the X value to **.3 in**. This will align the left edge of both objects to each other at the distance you specified from the origin. Don't worry if the Y position you see is different.

● **Note:** To reset the origin point, you can select the Perspective Grid tool in the Tools panel and double-click the origin point.

Drag the origin point.   Reposition the window.   Reposition the other window.

8 Close the Transform panel.

9 Holding down the Shift+Alt (Windows) or Shift+Option (Mac OS) keys, drag the window to the right until the measurement label shows approximately 1 in for dX. Release the mouse button and then the keys. This creates a copy of the window in perspective.

10 Choose Object > Transform > Transform Again to repeat the transformation. Press Ctrl+D (Windows) or Command+D (Mac OS) once to repeat the transformation again. Notice that the copies are in perspective.

● **Note:** When you Shift-click the window(s), you may accidentally move them. If this happens, choose Edit > Undo Perspective Move and try again.

11 With the Perspective Selection tool, Shift-click the other three windows in the row to select them all.

12 Holding down the Shift+Alt (Windows) or Shift+Option (Mac OS) keys, drag the selected windows down, to just above the Coffee Shop text. Release the mouse button, and then release the modifier keys. This creates a copy of the windows in perspective, making a total of eight windows.

Drag a copy of the window.   Repeat the transformation.   Drag a copy of the windows.

13 Choose Select > Deselect.

14 With the Perspective Selection tool, starting above the left side of the red building, drag a marquee across the four windows on the right, above the word "Shop." Shift-click the red rectangle on the left grid plane to deselect it.

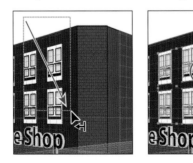

Drag to select the windows.   Shift-click to deselect.

The next step requires several key commands in a precise order, so read carefully.

15 With the four windows selected, drag them to the right. Don't release the mouse button yet. Press the number 3 key to switch to the right grid plane. Hold down the Alt (Windows) or Option (Mac OS) key, and continue dragging the windows close to the upper-left corner of the right side of the red building. Try to align the left edges of the windows with the round rectangle on the right grid plane. When they are in position, release the mouse button and then the modifier key. Leave the windows selected.

The copied windows are on another layer, which is beneath the rectangle on the right side of the building. You need to move the copied windows to the same layer.

Drag and switch planes.   Drag a copy of the windows.

16 Choose Edit > Cut.

17 Click the Layers panel icon (🖼) on the right side of the workspace to expand the Layers panel. Click the Right face layer to select it.

18 Choose Edit > Paste In Place.

You can position the selected windows by pressing the arrow keys.

19 Choose Select > Deselect.

20 Choose View > Fit Artboard In Window, and then choose File > Save.

Releasing content from perspective

There will be times when you want to use objects that are currently in perspective elsewhere, or you want to detach an object from a grid plane. Illustrator allows you to release an object from the associated perspective plane and to make it available as normal artwork. That's what you'll do next.

1 With the Perspective Selection tool (▶◨) selected, click to select the Coffee Shop text on the left side of the red building.

2 Choose Object > Perspective > Release With Perspective.

3 Choose Select > Deselect.

4 With the Perspective Selection tool, Shift-drag the left grid plane control to the left until the measurement label shows a distance of approximately –1 in. Release the mouse button and then the modifier key. This shows that the Coffee Shop text does not move with the grid, since the text has been released from the grid.

5 Choose Edit > Undo Perspective Grid Edit, and then choose Edit > Undo Release With Perspective.

6 In the Layers panel, click the visibility column to the left of the Background layer to show it.

7 Choose Select > Deselect and then File > Save.

● **Note:** The grid is not showing in the figure, but it will still be showing in your document.

Working with the horizontal plane

1 In the Layers panel, click the Horizon layer to select it.

2 Select the Rectangle tool (■), and press the number 2 key to select the Horizontal Grid. Position the pointer about an inch below the bottom edge of the brick building face, drag up to the horizon line, and release the mouse button. This will be a sidewalk.

3 Change the Fill color of the sidewalk rectangle to a gray in the Control panel.

4 Click to select the Left face layer in the Layers panel.

5 Select the Rectangle tool (■), and making sure that the left grid is selected in the Plane Switching Widget, create a door for the red building on the left grid plane.

6 Choose File > Save, and then choose File > Close.

Review questions

1   There are three preset grids. Describe briefly what each could be used for.

2   How can you show or hide the Perspective Grid?

3   Before drawing content on a grid plane, what must be done to ensure that the object is on the correct grid plane?

4   Describe the steps required to move content from one grid plane to another.

5   What does double-clicking a grid plane control allow you to do?

6   How do you move an object perpendicular to the grid?

Review answers

1   A one-point perspective can be very useful for roads, railway tracks, or buildings viewed so that the front is directly facing the viewer. Two-point perspective is useful for drawing a cube, such as a building, or two roads going off into the distance, and it typically has two vanishing points. Three-point perspective is usually used for buildings seen from above or below. In addition to vanishing points for each wall, there is a vanishing point in three-point perspective showing those walls receding into the ground or high in space.

2   You can hide or show the Perspective Grid by selecting the Perspective Grid tool (▣) in the Tools panel, by choosing View > Perspective Grid > Show Grid/Hide Grid, or by pressing Ctrl+Shift+I (Windows) or Command+Shift+I (Mac OS).

3   The correct grid plane must be selected by choosing it in the Plane Switching Widget; by using the following keyboard commands: Left Grid(1), Horizontal Grid(2), Right Grid(3), or No Active Grid(4); or by selecting content on the grid you want to choose with the Perspective Selection tool (▶▣).

4   With the object(s) selected, begin dragging them, without releasing the mouse button yet. Press the number 1, 2, 3, or 4 key (depending on which grid you intend to attach the object[s] to) to switch to the grid plane of your choice.

5   Double-clicking a grid plane control allows you to move the plane. You can specify whether to move the content associated with the plane and whether to copy the content as the plane moves.

6   To move an object perpendicular to the grid, with the Perspective Selection tool, hold down the number 5 key and drag the object perpendicular to the plane.

10 BLENDING COLORS AND SHAPES

Lesson overview

In this lesson, you'll learn how to do the following:

- Create and save a gradient fill.

- Apply and edit a gradient on a stroke.

- Apply and edit a radial gradient.

- Add colors to a gradient.

- Adjust the direction of a gradient blend.

- Adjust the opacity of color in a gradient blend.

- Blend the shapes of objects in intermediate steps.

- Create smooth color blends between objects.

- Modify a blend and its path, shape, and color.

This lesson takes approximately an hour to complete. If needed, remove the previous lesson folder from your hard disk and copy the Lesson10 folder onto it.

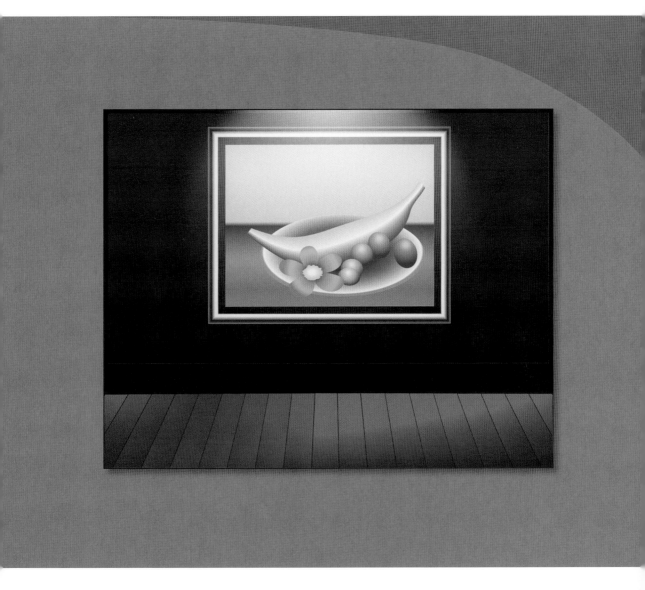

Gradient fills are graduated blends of two or more colors. Using the Gradient tool and Gradient panel, you can create or modify a gradient fill or gradient stroke. With the Blend tool, you can blend the shapes and colors of objects together into a new, blended object or a series of intermediate shapes.

Getting started

You'll explore various ways to create your own color gradients and to blend colors and shapes together using the Gradient tool, Gradient panel, and the Blend tool.

Before you begin, you'll restore the default preferences for Adobe Illustrator CS6. Then, you'll open the finished art file for this lesson to see what you'll create.

1   To ensure that the tools and panels function exactly as described in this lesson, delete or deactivate (by renaming) the Adobe Illustrator CS6 preferences file. See "Restoring default preferences" on page 3.

2   Start Adobe Illustrator CS6.

● **Note:** If you have not already done so, copy the Lesson10 folder from the Lessons folder on the *Adobe Illustrator CS6 Classroom in a Book* CD onto your hard disk. See "Copying the Classroom in a Book files" on page 2.

3   Choose File > Open, and open the L10end.ai file in the Lesson10 folder, located in the Lessons folder on your hard disk.

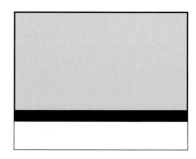

4   Choose View > Zoom Out to make the finished artwork smaller, if you want to leave it on your screen as you work. (Use the Hand tool [✋] to move the artwork where you want it in the window.) If you don't want to leave the document open, choose File > Close.

To begin working, you'll open an existing art file.

● **Note:** In Mac OS, when opening lesson files, you may need to click the round, green button in the upper-left corner of the Document window to maximize the window's size.

5   Choose File > Open, and open the L10start.ai file in the Lesson10 folder, located in the Lessons folder on your hard disk.

6   Choose File > Save As, name the file **gallery.ai**, and select the Lesson10 folder in the Save In menu. Leave the Save As Type option set to Adobe Illustrator (*.AI) (Windows) or the Format option set to Adobe Illustrator (ai) (Mac OS), and then click Save. In the Illustrator Options dialog box, leave the Illustrator options at their default settings and then click OK.

7   Choose Reset Essentials from the workspace switcher in the Application bar.

● **Note:** If you don't see "Reset Essentials" in the workspace switcher, choose Essentials before choosing Reset Essentials.

Working with gradients

A gradient fill is a graduated blend of two or more colors. You can create your own gradients, or you can use the gradients provided with Adobe Illustrator and then edit them and save them as swatches for later use.

You can use the Gradient panel (Window > Gradient) or the Gradient tool (■) to apply, create, and modify gradients. In the Gradient panel, the Gradient Fill or Stroke box displays the current gradient colors and gradient type applied to the fill or stroke of an object.

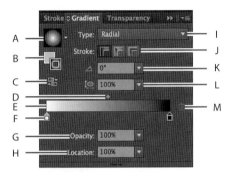

A. Gradient Fill box
B. Fill box/ Stroke box
C. Reverse Gradient
D. Gradient midpoint
E. Gradient slider
F. Color stop
G. Opacity
H. Location
I. Gradient type
J. Stroke options
K. Angle
L. Aspect ratio
M. Delete Stop

In the Gradient panel, the left gradient stop under the gradient slider marks the starting color; the right gradient stop marks the ending color. A gradient color stop is the point at which a gradient changes from one color to the next. You can add more color stops by clicking below the gradient slider. Double-clicking a color stop opens a panel where you can choose a color from swatches, color sliders, or the eyedropper.

Creating and applying a linear gradient to a fill

To begin the lesson, you'll create a gradient fill for the background.

1   Choose View > Fit Artboard In Window.

2   Using the Selection tool (▶), click to select the large yellow rectangle with a black border in the background.

    The background is painted with a yellow fill color and a black stroke, as shown in the Fill and Stroke boxes toward the bottom of the Tools panel. The Gradient box below the Fill and Stroke boxes shows the last created gradient. The default gradient fill is a black-and-white gradient.

3   Click the Fill box to activate it, and then click the Gradient box (□) near the bottom of the Tools panel.

    The default black-and-white gradient appears in the Fill box and is applied to the fill of the selected background shape. The Gradient panel also opens.

4 In the Gradient panel that opens, double-click the white, leftmost gradient stop to select the starting color of the gradient.

A new panel appears when you double-click a color stop. In this panel, you can change the color of the stop, using swatches or the Color panel, which is what you'll do next.

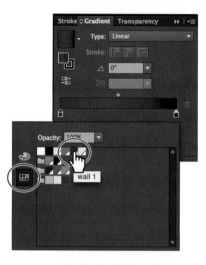

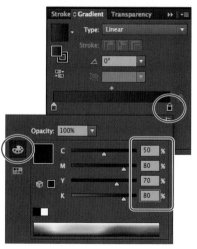

Note: The colors that you will use in gradients in this lesson have been saved in color groups, grouped according to the object you are applying them to, to make them easier to find.

5 After double-clicking the color stop, click the Swatches button (▦) in the new panel that appears. Click to select the swatch named wall 1. Notice the gradient change on the artboard. Press the Escape key, or click in a blank area of the Gradient panel to close the color panel.

6 Double-click the black color stop on the right side of the gradient slider to edit the color.

▶ **Tip:** To move between text fields, press the Tab key. Press Enter or Return to apply the last value typed.

7 In the panel that appears below the Gradient panel, click the Color button (▨) to open the Color panel. Choose CMYK from the Color panel menu (▾▤), if it is not already showing. Change the values to C=**50**, M=**80**, Y=**70**, and K=**80**. After entering the last value, click in a blank area of the Gradient panel to return to the Gradient panel.

Next, you'll save the gradient in the Swatches panel.

8 To save the gradient, click the Gradient Menu button (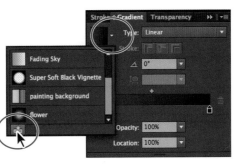) and then click the Add To Swatches button () at the bottom of the panel that appears.

The Gradient menu lists all the default and saved gradients that you can apply.

> **Tip:** You can save a gradient by selecting an object with a gradient fill, clicking the Fill box in the Tools panel, and then clicking the New Swatch button (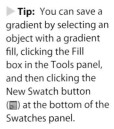) at the bottom of the Swatches panel.

Next, you will rename the gradient swatch in the Swatches panel.

9 Click the Swatches panel icon () on the right side of the workspace to open the Swatches panel. In the Swatches panel, double-click New Gradient Swatch 1 to open the Swatch Options dialog box. Type **wall background** in the Swatch Name field, and then click OK.

10 To display only gradient swatches in the Swatches panel, click the Show Swatch Kinds Menu button (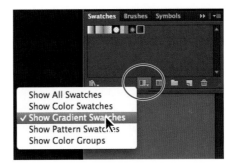) at the bottom of the Swatches panel and choose Show Gradient Swatches from the menu.

11 With the rectangle still selected on the artboard, apply some of the different gradients to the shape fill by clicking them in the Swatches panel. Click the wall background gradient you just saved to make sure it is applied before continuing to the next step.

Notice that some of the gradients have more than two colors. You'll learn how to make a gradient with multiple colors later in this lesson.

12 Click the Show Swatch Kinds Menu button () at the bottom of the Swatches panel, and choose Show All Swatches from the menu. Click the Swatches panel tab to collapse the panel.

13 Choose File > Save, and leave the rectangle selected.

Adjusting the direction and angle of a gradient fill

Once you have painted an object with a gradient, you can adjust the direction, origin, and the beginning and end points of the gradient using the Gradient tool.

Now, you'll adjust the gradient fill in the background shape.

1 Select the Gradient tool (▨) in the Tools panel.

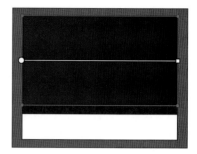

The Gradient tool works only on selected objects that are filled with a gradient. Notice the horizontal gradient annotator (bar) that appears in the middle of the rectangle. The bar indicates the direction of the gradient. The larger circle on the left shows the starting point of the gradient (the first color stop), and the smaller square on the right is the ending point (the last color stop).

▶ **Tip:** You can hide the gradient annotator (bar) by choosing View > Hide Gradient Annotator. To show it again, choose View > Show Gradient Annotator.

● **Note:** If you move the pointer to different areas of the gradient slider, the appearance of the pointer may change. This indicates that different functionality has been activated.

2 Position the pointer over the bar in the gradient annotator.

The bar turns into the gradient slider, much like the one in the Gradient panel. You can use the gradient slider to edit the gradient without opening the Gradient panel.

3 With the Gradient tool, Shift-click the top of the rectangle and drag down to the bottom of the rectangle to change the position and direction of the starting and ending colors of the gradient. Release the mouse button and then the key.

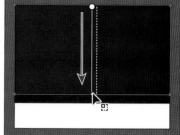

Holding down the Shift key constrains the gradient to 45 degree angles.

4 Practice changing the gradient in the rectangle. For example, drag inside the rectangle to create a short gradient with distinct color blends; drag a longer distance beyond the rectangle edges to create a longer gradient with more subtle color blends. You can also drag up to transpose the colors and reverse the direction of the blend. *Repeat step 3 before continuing to the next step.*

5 With the Gradient tool, position the pointer just off the small white square at the bottom of the gradient annotator. A rotation icon (⟳) appears. Drag to the right to rotate the gradient in the rectangle.

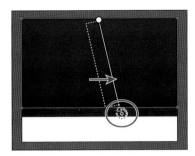

The gradient annotator is rotated to indicate the direction of the gradient when you release the mouse button.

6 Double-click the Gradient tool in the Tools panel to show the Gradient panel. Change the rotation angle in the Angle field to –90 to return the gradient to vertical. Press Enter or Return.

7 With the background rectangle still selected, choose Object > Lock > Selection.

8 Choose File > Save.

● **Note:** Entering the gradient rotation in the Gradient panel, rather than adjusting it directly on the artboard, is useful when you want to achieve consistency and precision.

Applying a gradient to a stroke

Not only can you apply a gradient to the fill of an object, but you can also apply a gradient blend to the stroke of an object. Unlike a gradient applied to the fill of an object, you cannot use the Gradient tool to edit a gradient on the stroke of an object. Next, you will apply a gradient fill and gradient stroke to a rectangle that will become a painting.

1 Click the Layers panel icon (🔲) to expand the panel. Make sure that the triangle to the left of the Gallery layer is toggled open. Click the visibility column to the left of the painting sublayer to reveal its content.

2 With the Selection tool (▶), click to select the white rectangle that appears on the artboard.

3 In the Control panel, change the Fill color to the painting background swatch.

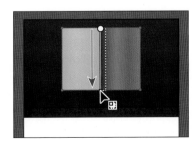

4 Select the Gradient tool in the Tools panel, and make sure that the Fill box is selected toward the bottom of the Tools panel. Position the pointer over the top of the rectangle, and Shift-drag down to the bottom of the rectangle to change the position and direction of the starting and ending colors of the gradient. Release the mouse button and then the key.

5 Change the Stroke weight to **30 pt** in the Control panel.

6 In the Control panel, change the Stroke color to the White, Black gradient. Press the Escape key to hide the Swatches panel.

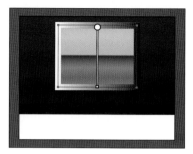

Next, you will use this generic gradient as a starting point for the stroke gradient and then edit it.

Editing a gradient on a stroke

A gradient on a stroke has more options available than a gradient fill. Next, you will add a series of colors to the stroke gradient to create a frame for a painting.

1 Click the Gradient panel icon (▤) on the right side of the workspace to open the panel.

2 Select the Zoom tool (🔍) in the Tools panel, and drag a marquee across the upper-right corner of the selected painting rectangle to zoom in to it.

3 Click the Stroke box in the Gradient panel to edit the gradient applied to the stroke (circled in the figure below).

4 Leave the Type as Linear, and click the Apply Gradient Across Stroke button (▤).

You can apply a gradient to a stroke in three ways: within a stroke (default), along a stroke, and across a stroke.

5 Drag the black color stop to the left until the Location shows approximately **60%**.

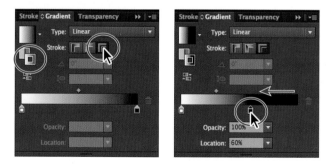

▶ **Tip:** You can delete a color in the color ramp by selecting a color stop and clicking the Delete Stop button or by dragging the color stop downward and out of the Gradient panel.

6 Double-click the white color stop, and click the Swatches button (▦) to show the swatches. Click to select the frame 1 swatch in the top color group. Click outside the panel to accept the selection.

7 Position the pointer below the color ramp, between the two color stops, to add another color stop. When the pointer with a plus (⬚₊) appears, click to add another color stop (see the figure). Double-click that color stop and, with the swatches showing, click the light yellow swatch at the top of the panel.

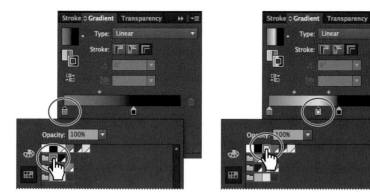

Edit the white color.   Add another color to the gradient.

8 Pressing the Alt (Windows) or Option (Mac OS) key, drag the light yellow color stop to the right, close to the black color stop, and release the mouse button and then the modifier key. This is an easy way to duplicate a color in a gradient.

9 Pressing the Alt (Windows) or Option (Mac OS) key, drag the leftmost (brown) color stop to the right. Release the mouse button and then the modifier key, when it is positioned as you see in the figure below.

10 Click below the color ramp, between the two leftmost color stops, to add a final color stop. Double-click the color stop and, with the swatches showing, click the swatch named frame 2 in the top color group.

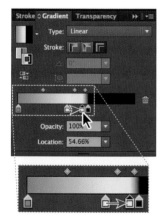
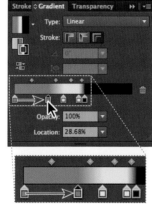
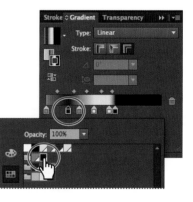

Duplicate the yellow stop.   Duplicate the leftmost color stop.   Add and edit the final color stop.

11 Choose Select > Deselect, and then choose File > Save.

Creating and applying a radial gradient

You can create either linear or radial gradients in Illustrator. Both types of gradients have a starting and ending color. With a radial gradient, the starting color (leftmost color stop) of the gradient defines the center point of the fill, which radiates outward to the ending color (rightmost color stop). Next, you will create and apply a radial gradient fill to a plate.

1 Choose View > Fit Artboard In Window.

2 Expand the Layers panel by clicking the Layers panel icon (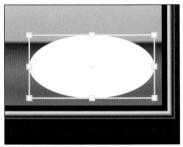) on the right side of the workspace. Make sure that the triangle to the left of the Gallery layer is toggled open. Click to select the visibility column to the left of the plate sublayer (you may need to scroll in the Layers panel).

3 Use the Selection tool (➤) to select the white ellipse in the frame of the painting.

4 Select the Zoom tool (🔍) in the Tools panel, and click the ellipse several times to zoom in.

5 In the Control panel, change the Fill color to the White, Black gradient.

6 Click the Gradient panel icon (▣) to show the Gradient panel. In the Gradient panel, make sure that the Fill box is selected. Choose Radial from the Type menu to convert the linear gradient in the shape to a radial gradient. Keep the ellipse selected and the Gradient panel showing.

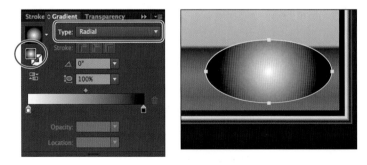

Editing the radial gradient colors

Once you have filled an object with a gradient, you can use the Gradient tool or the Gradient panel to edit the gradient, including changing the direction, color, and origin.

Next, you will use the Gradient tool to adjust the color of each color stop and add two more colors, for a total of four colors in the radial gradient.

1 Select the Gradient tool (▣) in the Tools panel.

2 Position the pointer over the gradient annotator (bar) in the artwork to reveal the gradient slider. Double-click the white color stop on the left end to edit the color. In the panel that appears, click the Swatches button (⊞), if it's not already selected. Select the color called plate 1 in the second color group. Press the Escape key to hide the panel.

● **Note:** When you double-click the color stop, you can see the Location in the panel that appears. As you build this radial gradient, you can copy the values you see in the figures to closely match the positions of the color stops.

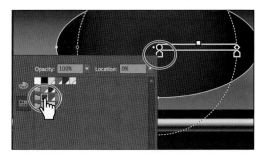

Notice that the gradient annotator starts from the center of the ellipse and points to the right. The dashed circle around it indicates that it is a radial gradient. You can set additional options for radial gradients, as you'll soon see.

3 In the gradient slider, double-click the black color stop on the right. In the panel that appears, select the light yellow swatch at the top of the swatches panel. Press the Escape key to close the panel.

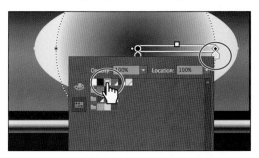

4 Position the pointer beneath the gradient slider. When the pointer with a plus sign appears (k₊), click to add another color to the gradient. See the figure below for placement. Double-click the new color stop beneath the gradient slider. In the panel that appears, select the plate 2 swatch in the second color group. Press the Escape key to close the panel.

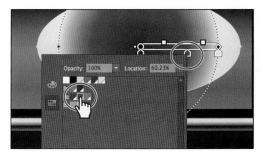

5 Position the pointer beneath the gradient slider, and click to add a fourth (and final) color stop. See the figure for placement. Double-click the new color stop beneath the gradient slider. In the panel that appears, select the plate 3 swatch in the second color group. Make sure that the Location is **97%**. Press the Escape key to close the panel.

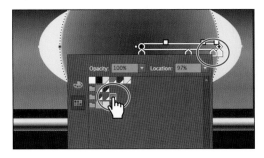

Once the colors are set in the gradient, you can always delete, add more, or even change the order of colors. Next, you will change the order of the last two colors.

6 Double-click the leftmost color stop, and change the Location value to **42%** in the panel that appears. Press Enter or Return to change the value and hide the panel.

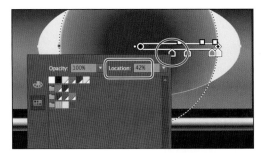

7 Drag the rightmost (yellow) color stop to the left (just to the left of the closest brown color stop). Drag the rightmost brown color stop to the right, all the way to the end of the gradient slider. See the figure for how they should be arranged. Notice that they are still close to each other.

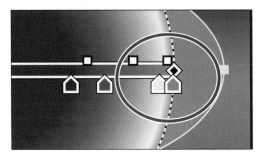

8 Choose File > Save.

Adjusting the radial gradient

Next, you will change the aspect ratio of the gradient, adjust the position, and change the radius and the origin of the radial gradient.

1   With the Gradient tool, position the pointer over the small white box on the right end of the gradient annotator. Click and drag to the right, stopping just past the right edge of the ellipse shape, and release the mouse button. This lengthens the gradient.

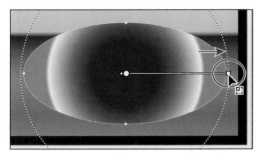

● **Note:** You may not see the dotted circle as you drag the end of the gradient annotator. It appears if you position the pointer over the gradient annotator bar first, before dragging the right end point. That's okay.

2   In the Gradient panel, ensure that the Fill box is selected and then change the Aspect Ratio (▣) to **40%** by selecting it from the menu.

The aspect ratio changes a radial gradient into an elliptical gradient and makes the gradient better match the shape of the plate.

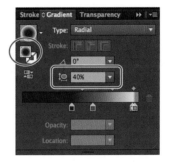

● **Note:** The aspect ratio is a value between 0.5 and 32767%. As the aspect ratio gets smaller, the ellipse flattens and widens.

3   With the Gradient tool, position the pointer over the gradient on the plate. Click the top black circle on the dotted path, and drag up to just past the top of the ellipse shape to change the aspect ratio.

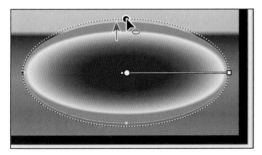

When you release the mouse button, notice that the Aspect Ratio value in the Gradient panel is now larger than the 40% set previously (it's now closer to 50%).

Next, you will drag the gradient slider to reposition the gradient in the ellipse.

4 With the Gradient tool, click and drag the gradient slider up a little bit to move the gradient in the ellipse. Make sure that the bottom edge of the dotted ellipse is above the edge of the ellipse.

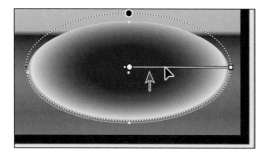 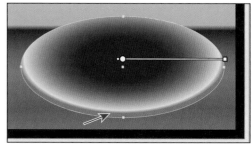

5 With the Gradient tool, click the small white dot to the left of the leftmost color stop and drag to the left.

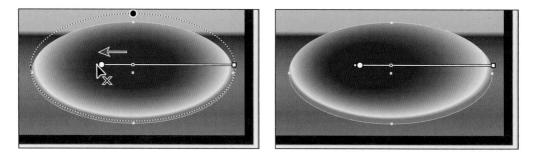

This dot repositions the center of the gradient (the leftmost color stop) without moving the entire gradient bar and changes the radius of the gradient.

6 Choose Edit > Undo Gradient to put the gradient back to the center.

7 Choose Select > Deselect and then File > Save.

Applying gradients to multiple objects

You can apply a gradient to multiple objects by selecting all the objects, applying a gradient color, and then dragging across the objects with the Gradient tool.

Now, you'll paint a flower with a radial gradient fill, and then edit the colors in it.

1 Choose View > Fit Artboard In Window.

2 Click the Layers panel icon ( ) to open the Layers panel. Click to select the visibility column to the left of the flower sublayer.

3 Select the Zoom tool (🔍) in the Tools panel, and drag a marquee across the blue flower shapes to zoom in.

4 Use the Selection tool (►), and click to select one of the blue flower shapes.

5 Choose Select > Same > Fill Color to select all five blue flower shapes.

6 In the Control panel, choose the gradient named flower from the Fill color.

When you apply a gradient to the fill or stroke of multiple selected objects, they are applied independently.

Now, you'll adjust the gradient on the shapes so that the gradient blends across all of them as one object, and then you'll adjust the gradient itself.

7 Make sure that the Fill box is selected at the bottom of the Tools panel.

8 Double-click the Gradient tool (▥) in the Tools panel to select the tool and to show the Gradient panel. Drag from the approximate center of the yellow flower center to the outer edge of one of any one of the petal shapes, as shown in the figure, to apply the gradient uniformly. Leave the flower shapes selected.

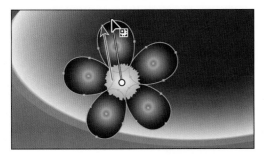 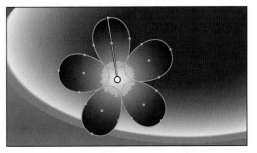

Drag across the flower shapes with the Gradient tool.   The result.

Exploring other methods for editing gradient colors

Up to this point, you've added, edited, and adjusted the position of colors on the color ramp. Next, you will reverse a gradient and adjust the midpoint between colors on the color ramp.

1 In the Gradient panel, with the Fill box selected, click the Reverse Gradient button (▦).

You can also reverse the colors in a gradient by using the Gradient tool to drag across the gradient on the artboard in the opposite direction. This will make it so that the dark color is in the center of the gradient.

2   In the color ramp, in the Gradient panel, drag the leftmost color stop to the right until you see approximately **20%** in the Location at the bottom of the Gradient panel (it doesn't have to be exact).

3   Drag the diamond icon located between the leftmost color stop and the middle color stop to the left, closer to the leftmost color stop. Drag until the Location shows a value of approximately **30%** (it doesn't have to be exact).

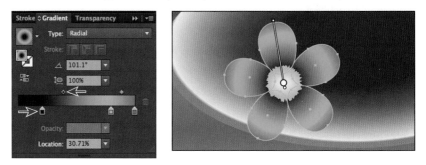

Another way to apply a color to a gradient is to sample the color from the artwork, using the Eyedropper tool, or drag a color swatch onto a color stop.

4   With the flower shapes still selected, click to select the leftmost color stop (the dark color) in the Gradient panel.

5   Choose View > Fit Artboard In Window.

6   Select the Eyedropper tool ( ) in the Tools panel. In the artwork, Shift-click the black rectangle at the bottom of the wall.

Shift-clicking with the Eyedropper tool applies the sampled color to the selected color stop in the gradient, rather than replacing the entire gradient with the color in the selected artwork.

The flower petals are complete. Now, you will group them with the flower center shape and apply a warp to give the whole flower some dimension.

7   Select the Zoom tool ( ) in the Tools panel, and drag a marquee across the blue flower shapes to zoom in.

8   With the Selection tool ( ), Shift-click the yellow center shape in the flower.

9 Choose Object > Group.

10 Choose Effect > Warp > Arc. In the Warp Options dialog box, with Horizontal selected, change the Bend to **−20%** and then click OK.

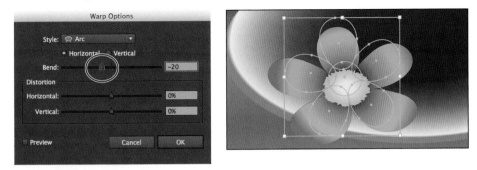

11 Choose Select > Deselect and then File > Save.

Adding transparency to gradients

By specifying different opacity values for the different color stops in your gradient, you can create gradients that fade in or out and that show or hide underlying images. Next, you will create a light for the painting and apply a gradient that fades to transparent.

1 Click the Layers panel icon (■) to open the Layers panel. Click to select the visibility column to the left of the <Path> object.

2 Choose View > Fit Artboard In Window.

3 Using the Selection tool (▶), click to select the white ellipse now showing on the artboard.

4 Open the Gradient panel by clicking the Gradient panel icon. Ensure that the Fill box is selected, click the Gradient menu button (■), and then select White, Black.

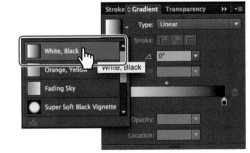

▶ **Tip:** The Fading Sky and Super Soft Black Vignette default gradients are also great starting points for fading to transparency.

5 Choose Radial from the Type menu in the Gradient panel. Double-click the rightmost color stop (the black color). In the panel that appears, click the Swatches button (■) and select the color swatch named White. Press the Escape key once to hide the swatches.

● **Note:** You'll see the purpose of the white-to-white gradient in the next step, when you will change the transparency of the rightmost color stop.

6 With the rightmost color stop selected, change the Opacity to **0**.

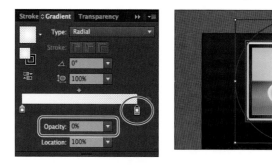

7 Drag the gradient midpoint (the diamond shape) to the left until you see a value of approximately **30%** in the Location field. Click the Gradient panel tab to collapse the Gradient panel group.

8 Press Ctrl+- (Windows) or Command+- (Mac OS) once to zoom out to see the entire selected circle.

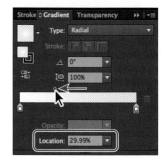

9 Select the Gradient tool (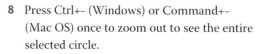) in the Tools panel. Holding down the Shift key, drag from the top to the bottom of the ellipse shape. Be careful not to drag the Aspect Ratio button.

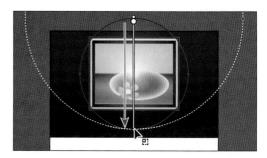

10 In the Control panel, change the Stroke Color to [**None**].

11 Choose Effect > Blur > Gaussian Blur. In the Gaussian Blur dialog box, change the Radius to **60** and then click OK.

12 Choose Select > Deselect and then File > Save.

Working with blended objects

You can blend two distinct objects to create and distribute shapes evenly between two objects. The two shapes you blend can be the same or different. You can also blend between two open paths to create a smooth transition of color between objects, or you can combine blends of colors and objects to create color transitions in the shape of a particular object.

When you create a blend, the blended objects are treated as one object, called a blend object. If you move one of the original objects or edit the anchor points of the original object, the blend changes accordingly. You can also expand the blend to divide it into distinct objects.

Blend between two of the same shape.

Blend between same shape, different colors.

Blend between two different shapes with different fill colors.

Blend along a path.

Smooth color blend between two stroked lines.

Creating a blend with specified steps

Now, you'll use the Blend tool to blend three shapes that will make up the wood floor of the gallery.

1   Choose View > Fit Artboard In Window.

2   Click the Layers panel icon (![icon]) to open the Layers panel. Click to select the visibility column to the left of both the floor and the fruit sublayers. Click the visibility column to hide the <Path>, flower, plate, painting, and wall sublayers. Click the Layers panel tab to collapse the panel group.

Before you blend shapes, you can set the options for how they blend.

3   Double-click the Blend tool (![icon]) in the Tools panel to open the Blend Options dialog box.

4   Choose Specified Steps from the Spacing menu, and change the number of steps to **4**. Click OK.

▶ **Tip:** You can also make a blend by selecting objects and choosing Object > Blend > Make.

5   Scroll down in the Document window so that you can see the three brown floor shapes.

6 Using the Blend tool, position the pointer over the gradient-filled rectangle on the far left. Click when the pointer displays an X (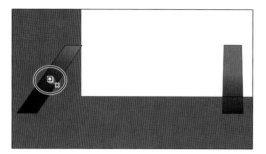). Then, hover over the middle rectangle until the pointer displays a plus sign ( ), indicating that you can add an object to the blend. Click the middle rectangle to add it to the blend. There is now a blend between these two objects.

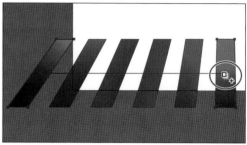

7 Click the rightmost rectangle with the Blend tool pointer (displaying the plus sign) to add it to the blend and complete the blend object.

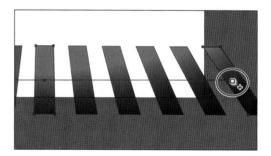

● **Note:** If you wanted to end the current path and blend other objects, you would first click the Blend tool in the Tools panel and then click the other objects, one at a time, to blend them.

Modifying a blend

Now, you'll modify the blend object using the Blend Options dialog box. You'll also create another blend and edit the shape of the path, called the spine, that the objects blend along.

▶ **Tip:** To edit the blend options for an object, you can also select the blend object and then double-click the Blend tool.

1 With the blended rectangles still selected, choose Object > Blend > Blend Options. In the Blend Options dialog box, change the Specified Steps to **9** and then click OK.

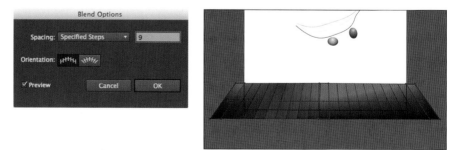

2 Choose Select > Deselect.

3 Select the Zoom tool (🔍) in the Tools panel, and drag a marquee across the green grapes to zoom in. You may need to scroll up in the Document window.

4 With the Blend tool, click the first green grape on the left and then click the green grape on the right to create a blend.

5 Double-click the Blend tool (🖼) in the Tools panel to open the Blend Options dialog box. Change the specified steps to **3**. Click OK.

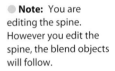

6 Choose View > Outline.

In Outline mode, you can see the outlines of the two original grapes and a straight path between them. These three objects are what a blend object is composed of, by default. It can be easier to edit the path between the original objects in Outline mode.

7 Make sure that the Smart Guides are selected (View > Smart Guides).

8 Select the Direct Selection tool (▷) in the Tools panel. Click the anchor point on the right end of the path to select that anchor point. In the Control panel, click the Convert Selected Anchor Points To Smooth button (🖼) to smooth the curve. With the Direct Selection tool, drag the bottom direction handle up and to the left. See the figure for help.

● **Note:** You are editing the spine. However you edit the spine, the blend objects will follow.

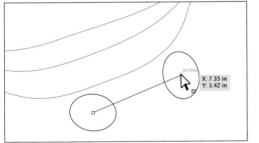
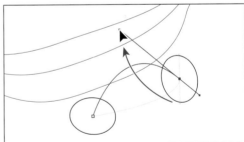

9 Choose View > Preview to see the change.

10 Choose Select > Deselect.

You can modify the blend instantly by changing the shape, color, or position of the original objects. Next, you will edit the position of the grape on the left and see the effect on the blend.

11 With the Selection tool (▶), click the blended grapes to select them.

12 Double-click anywhere on the blend object to enter Isolation mode.

This temporarily ungroups the blended objects and lets you edit each original grape (but not the grapes created by blending), as well as the spine.

▶ **Tip:** A quick way to reshape the spine of a blend is to blend the shapes along another path. You can draw another path, then select the blend as well, and choose Object > Blend > Replace Spine.

> **Tip:** You can reverse a blend by choosing Object > Blend > Reverse Front To Back.

13 Click to select the grape on the left. With the Selection tool, press Shift+Alt (Windows) or Shift+Option (Mac OS) and drag a corner bounding point toward the center to make the grape smaller. Release the mouse button and then the keys.

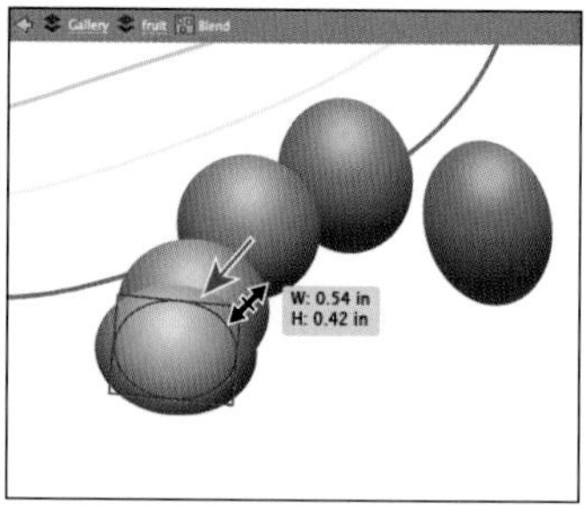

14 Press the Escape key to exit Isolation mode.

The blended objects are considered a single blend object. If you need to edit all the grapes (including the grapes that the blend created), you can expand the blend. Expanding the blend converts the blend to individual objects. You can no longer edit the blend as a single object because it has become a group of individual grape shapes. Next, you will expand the blend.

> **Tip:** To release, or remove, a blend from the original objects, select the blend and choose Object > Blend > Release.

15 Choose Object > Blend > Expand. With the grapes still selected, notice the word "Group" on the left side of the Control panel.

The blend is now a group of individual shapes that you can edit independently.

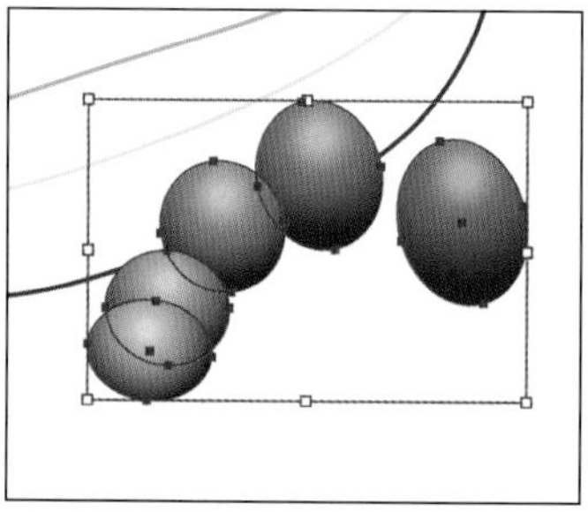

16 Choose Select > Deselect.

17 Choose File > Save.

Creating and editing smooth color blends

You can choose several options for blending the shapes and colors of objects to create a new object. When you choose the Smooth Color blend option, Illustrator combines the shapes and colors of the objects into many intermediate steps, creating a smooth, graduated blend between the original objects.

Now, you'll combine three shapes into a smooth color blend to make a banana.

1 Choose View > Fit Artboard In Window. Press Ctrl++ (Windows) or Command++ (Mac OS) twice to zoom in.

You will now blend the three paths that are behind the blended grapes. All of the paths have a stroke color and no fill. Objects that have strokes blend differently than those that have no stroke.

2 With the Blend tool, position the pointer over the top line until it displays an X ($\boxed{\mathbb{q}}_x$), and then click. Click the middle (yellow) line with the Blend tool pointer that displays a plus sign ($\boxed{\mathbb{q}}_+$) to add it to the blend. Position the pointer over the third line (away from the grapes), and click when a plus sign (+) appears next to the pointer.

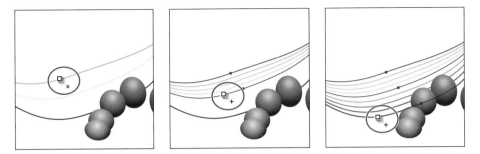

You've created a blend with the same settings as before (a specified step blend). Next, you will change the blend settings for the banana so that it blends as smooth color.

3 Double-click the Blend tool (⬚) in the Tools panel. In the Blend Options dialog box, choose Smooth Color from the Spacing menu to set up the blend options, which will remain set until you change them. Click OK.

4 Choose Select > Deselect.

When you make a smooth color blend between objects, Illustrator automatically calculates the number of intermediate steps necessary to create the transition between the objects. Once you've applied a smooth color blend to objects, you can edit it. Next, you will edit the paths that make up the blend.

5 Using the Selection tool (▶), double-click the color blend (the banana) to enter Isolation mode. Click to select the middle path, and change the Stroke color in the Control panel to any color you want. Notice how the colors are blended. Choose Edit > Undo Apply Swatch to return to the original stroke color.

6 Double-click away from the blend paths to exit Isolation mode.

7 Choose View > Fit Artboard In Window.

8 Open the Layers panel and click to select the visibility column for all of the sublayers, including the Mask sublayer, to make all objects visible on the artboard.

9 In the Layers panel, click to select the Gallery layer.

10 Click the Make/Release Clipping Mask button (▣) at the bottom of the Layers panel.

This uses the first shape (the Mask shape) as a clipping mask to hide artwork that is outside the bounds of the shape.

11 Choose File > Save, and close all open files.

▶ **Tip:** Creating smooth color blends between paths can be difficult in certain situations. For instance, if the lines intersect or the lines are too curved, unexpected results can occur.

Review questions

1 What is a gradient?

2 Name two ways to apply a gradient to a selected object.

3 How do you adjust the blend between colors in a gradient?

4 Name two ways you can add colors to a gradient.

5 How can you adjust the direction of a gradient?

6 What is the difference between a gradient and a blend?

7 Describe two ways to blend the shapes and colors of objects.

8 What is the difference between selecting a smooth color blend and specifying the number of steps in a blend?

9 How do you adjust the shapes or colors in the blend? How do you adjust the path of the blend?

Review answers

1 A gradient is a graduated blend of two or more colors or of tints of the same color. Gradients can be applied to the stroke or fill of an object.

2 To apply a gradient to a selected object, select an object, and do one of the following:

- Select the Stroke or Fill box, and then click the Gradient box in the Tools panel to fill an object with the default white-to-black gradient or with the last selected gradient.

- Change the Fill color or Stroke color in the Control panel to apply a gradient to selected content.

- Select the Stroke or Fill box in the Tools panel, and then click a gradient swatch in the Swatches panel.

- Use the Eyedropper tool to sample a gradient from an object in your artwork, and then apply it to the selected object.

3 To adjust the blend between colors in a gradient, with the Gradient tool selected, and the pointer over the gradient annotator or in the Gradient panel, you can drag the diamond icons or color stops of the gradient slider.

4 To add colors to a gradient, in the Gradient panel, click beneath the gradient slider to add a gradient stop to the gradient. Then double-click the color stop to edit the color, using the panel that appears to mix a new color or to apply an existing color swatch. You can select the Gradient tool in the Tools panel, position the pointer over the gradient-filled object, and then click beneath the gradient slider that appears in the artwork to add a color stop.

5 Drag with the Gradient tool to adjust the direction of a gradient. Dragging a long distance changes colors gradually; dragging a short distance makes the color change more abrupt. You can also rotate the gradient using the Gradient tool and change the radius, aspect ratio, starting point, and more.

6 The difference between a gradient and a blend is the way that colors combine together—colors blend together within a gradient and between objects in a blend.

7 You can blend the shapes and colors of objects by doing one of the following:

- Clicking each object with the Blend tool to create a blend of intermediate steps between the objects, according to preset blend options.

- Selecting the objects and choosing Object > Blend > Blend Options to set the number of intermediate steps, and then choosing Object > Blend > Make to create the blend.

Objects that have painted strokes blend differently than those with no strokes.

8 When you choose Smooth Color blend, Illustrator automatically calculates the number of intermediate steps necessary to create a seamlessly smooth blend between the selected objects. Specifying the number of steps lets you determine how many intermediate steps are visible in the blend. You can also specify the distance between intermediate steps in the blend.

9 You can use the Direct Selection tool to select and adjust the shape of an original object, thus changing the shape of the blend. You can change the colors of the original objects to adjust the intermediate colors in the blend. Use the Convert Anchor Point tool to change the shape of the path, or spine, of the blend by dragging anchor points or direction handles on the spine.

11 WORKING WITH BRUSHES

Lesson overview

In this lesson, you'll learn how to do the following:

- Use four brush types: Art, Calligraphic, Pattern, and Bristle.

- Apply brushes to paths created with drawing tools.

- Paint and edit paths with the Paintbrush tool.

- Change the brush color and adjust brush settings.

- Create new brushes from Adobe Illustrator artwork.

- Work with the Blob Brush tool and the Eraser tool.

 This lesson takes approximately an hour to complete. If needed, remove the previous lesson folder from your hard disk and copy the Lesson11 folder onto it.

The variety of brush types in Adobe Illustrator CS6 lets you create a myriad of effects simply by painting or drawing using the Paintbrush tool or the drawing tools. You can work with the Blob Brush tool, choose from the Art, Calligraphic, Pattern, Bristle, and Scatter brushes, or create new brushes based on your artwork.

Getting started

In this lesson, you will learn how to work with the Blob Brush tool and the Eraser tool. You will also learn how to use four brush types in the Brushes panel and how to change brush options and create your own brushes. Before you begin, you'll restore the default preferences for Adobe Illustrator CS6. Then, you'll open the finished art file for the first part of this lesson to see the finished artwork.

1 To ensure that the tools and panels function exactly as described in this lesson, delete or deactivate (by renaming) the Adobe Illustrator CS6 preferences file. See "Restoring default preferences" on page 3.

2 Start Adobe Illustrator CS6.

● **Note:** If you have not already done so, copy the Lesson11 folder from the Lessons folder on the *Adobe Illustrator CS6 Classroom in a Book* CD onto your hard disk. See "Copying the Classroom in a Book files" on page 2.

3 Choose File > Open, and open the L11end.ai file in the Lesson11 folder, located in the Lessons folder on your hard disk.

4 If you want, choose View > Zoom Out to make the finished artwork smaller and then adjust the window size and leave the artwork on your screen as you work. (Use the Hand tool [✋] to move the artwork to where you want it in the Document window.) If you don't want to leave the artwork open, choose File > Close.

To begin working, you'll open an existing art file.

● **Note:** In Mac OS, when opening lesson files, you may need to click the round, green button in the upper-left corner of the Document window to maximize the window's size.

5 Choose File > Open to open the L11start.ai file in the Lesson11 folder in the Lessons folder on your hard disk.

6 Choose View > Fit Artboard In Window.

7 Choose File > Save As. In the Save As dialog box, name the file **bookcover.ai** and select the Lesson11 folder. Leave the Save As Type option set to Adobe Illustrator (*.AI) (Windows) or the Format option set to Adobe Illustrator (ai) (Mac OS), and then click Save. In the Illustrator Options dialog box, leave the Illustrator options at their default settings and then click OK.

Working with brushes

Using brushes, you can decorate paths with patterns, figures, brush strokes, textures, or angled strokes. You can modify the brushes provided with Illustrator and create your own brushes.

You can apply brush strokes to existing paths, or you can use the Paintbrush tool to draw a path and apply a brush stroke simultaneously. You can change the color, size, and other features of a brush, and you can edit paths after brushes are applied.

Types of brushes

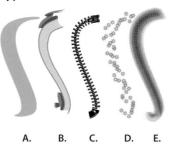

A. Calligraphic brush
B. Art brush
C. Pattern brush
D. Scatter brush
E. Bristle brush

A.   B.   C.   D.   E.

There are five types of brushes that appear in the Brushes panel (Window > Brushes): Calligraphic, Art, Pattern, Scatter, and Bristle. In this lesson, you will discover how to work with all of these except for the Scatter brush.

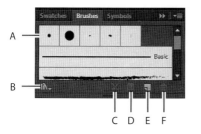

A. Brushes
B. Brush Libraries Menu
C. Remove Brush Stroke
D. Options Of Selected Object
E. New Brush
F. Delete Brush

Using Calligraphic brushes

Calligraphic brushes resemble strokes drawn with the angled point of a calligraphic pen. Calligraphic brushes are defined by an elliptical shape whose center follows the path. You can use these brushes to create the appearance of hand-drawn strokes made with a flat, angled pen tip.

Next, you'll use a Calligraphic pen to create the bunting on the train car.

1 Click the Brushes panel icon (■) on the right side of the workspace to expand the Brushes panel.

2 In the Brushes panel, choose List View from the panel menu (▼≣).

3 Open the Brushes panel menu (▼≣), and deselect Show Art Brushes, Show Bristle Brushes, and Show Pattern Brushes, leaving only the Calligraphic brushes visible in the Brushes panel.

Calligraphic brush examples

Note: A check mark next to the brush type in the Brushes panel menu indicates that the brush type is visible in the panel.

4   In the Control panel, click the Stroke color and choose the light orange swatch. Change the Stroke weight to **2 pt**, and make sure that the Fill color is None.

Calligraphic brushes use the current stroke color when you apply the brushes to artwork.

5   Double-click the Pencil tool () in the Tools panel. In the Pencil Tool Options dialog box, change the Smoothness to **100%** and leave the rest of the settings at their default settings. Click OK.

6   Position the pointer in the upper-left corner of the red train car shape, and draw two "U" shapes on the train car, from left to right, in one continuous motion. This will be the bunting on the car.

7   With the shape you drew selected, select the 5 pt. Oval brush in the Brushes panel to apply it to the line. You may need to scroll down. Notice that the stroke weight changes in the Control panel.

Draw the bunting.

Apply the brush.

The result.

Editing a brush

To change the options for a brush, you can double-click the brush in the Brushes panel. Edits will apply to the current document only, although you can also choose to change artwork to which the brush has been applied. Next, you'll change the appearance of the 5 pt. Oval brush.

● **Note:** The edits you make will change the brush for this document only.

1   In the Brushes panel, double-click the name 5 pt. Oval brush and change the name to **30 pt. Oval**. Press Enter or Return.

2   In the Brushes panel, double-click the 30 pt. Oval brush thumbnail or to the right of the brush name to display the Calligraphic Brush Options dialog box.

▶ **Tip:** The Preview window in the dialog box (below the Name field) shows the changes that you make to the brush.

3   Enter **0** for the Angle and choose Fixed from the menu to the right. Change the Roundness to **10%** and choose Fixed from the menu to the right. Change the Size to **30 pt** and select Preview. Click OK.

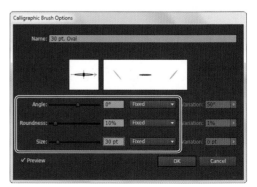

4 In the dialog box that appears, click Apply To Strokes to apply the change to the artwork that has the brush applied.

● **Note:** After clicking Apply To Strokes, the brush may no longer appear on the path. With the bunting path still selected, click the 30 pt. Oval brush again to apply it to the path.

5 Choose Select > Deselect, and then choose File > Save.

Using a fill color with brushes

When you apply a brush to an object's stroke, you can also apply a fill color to paint the interior of the object with a color. When you use a fill color with a brush, the brush objects appear on top of the fill color in places where the fill and the brush objects overlap. Now, you'll fill the bunting shape you created with a fill color.

Path with a fill color and a brush applied to the stroke

1 With the Selection tool (▶), select the bunting shape that you drew.

2 Click the Fill color in the Control panel, and select the CMYK Cyan swatch.

3 Click outside the artwork to deselect it.

● **Note:** Your bunting shape may look different than what you see here, and that's okay.

Removing a brush stroke

You can easily remove a brush stroke applied to artwork where you don't want it. Now, you'll remove the brush stroke on the path above the duck, on the train engine. This path had the original 5 pt. Oval brush you edited applied to it.

1 With the Selection tool (▶), click the dark gray path above the duck.

2 Click the Remove Brush Stroke button (✕) at the bottom of the Brushes panel.

3 Change the Stroke weight to **10 pt** in the Control panel.

4 Choose Select > Deselect, and then choose File > Save.

● **Note:** The path you see may not look the same and that's okay.

Using Art brushes

Art brushes, which include arrow brushes, decorative brushes, artistic brushes, and others, stretch a brush shape (such as Rough Charcoal) or object shape (such as a banner) evenly along the length of the path.

Drawing with the Paintbrush tool

Now, you'll use the Paintbrush tool to apply an art brush to the bear to make it look fuzzy. As mentioned earlier, the Paintbrush tool allows you to apply a brush as you draw.

Art brush examples

Note: If you don't see "Reset Essentials" in the workspace switcher, choose Essentials before choosing Reset Essentials in the workspace switcher.

1 Choose Reset Essentials from the workspace switcher in the Application bar.

2 Select the Zoom tool (🔍) in the Tools panel, and drag a marquee around the teddy bear to zoom in on it.

3 Select the Selection tool (▸) in the Tools panel, and click to select the bear. Choose Select > Deselect. This selects the layer in the Layers panel that the bear is on so that any artwork you paint will be on the same layer.

4 Change the Stroke color to bear brown and the Fill color to None (if necessary) in the Control panel.

Note: A check mark next to the brush type in the Brushes panel menu indicates that the brush type is visible in the panel.

5 Click the Brushes panel icon (🖌) on the right side of the workspace. Open the Brushes panel menu (▾≡), and deselect Show Calligraphic Brushes. Then, select Show Art Brushes to make the brushes visible in the Brushes panel.

6 Click the Brush Libraries Menu button (📚) at the bottom of the Brushes panel, and choose Artistic > Artistic_ChalkCharcoalPencil.

7 In the Artistic_ChalkCharcoalPencil panel, choose List View from the panel menu (▾≡). Click Charcoal - Thick in the list to add the brush to the Brushes panel for this document. Close the Artistic_ChalkCharcoalPencil panel.

You are going to paint around the outside of the bear to give the edges a roughened (fuzzy) look.

8 Select the Paintbrush tool (🖌) in the Tools panel, and then click the Charcoal - Thick brush in the Brushes panel, if it's not already selected. Change the Stroke weight to **.5 pt** in the Control panel.

Notice that the Paintbrush pointer has an X next to it (🖌ₓ). The X indicates that you are about to draw a new path.

9 Draw a long, upward stroke to create the left side of the bear's face, starting at the shoulder and stopping at the ear. Drag across the top of the head from the left ear to the right ear. Finish by dragging a long downward stroke to create the right side of the bear's face, starting at the bottom of the right ear and ending at the right shoulder.

10 Select the Selection tool (▶) in the Tools panel. Double-click the left ear *twice* to enter Isolation mode. Click to select the larger, lighter brown part of the ear.

11 Click the Charcoal - Thick brush in the Brushes panel to apply it. Change the Stroke weight to **.5 pt**, and make sure that the Fill color is bear brown in the Control panel.

12 Press the Escape key to exit Isolation mode. Repeat the steps for the other ear.

13 Choose Select > Deselect, and then choose File > Save.

Editing paths with the Paintbrush tool

Now, you'll use the Paintbrush tool to edit a selected path.

1 With the Selection tool, click to select the last path you drew on the right side of the bear's face.

2 Select the Paintbrush tool (✎) in the Tools panel. Position the pointer near the bottom end of the selected path. An X will *not* appear next to the pointer when it's positioned over a selected path. Drag down and to the left to extend the path a bit under the bear's chin. The selected path is edited from the point where you began drawing.

3 Press and hold the Ctrl (Windows) or Command (Mac OS) key to toggle to the Selection tool, and select the first path you drew with the Paintbrush tool (on the left side of the bear's face).

4 With the Paintbrush tool still selected, move the pointer near the bottom of the selected path and drag down and to the right to extend the path a bit under the bear's chin. See the figure below for placement.

▶ **Tip:** You can also edit paths drawn with the Paintbrush tool using the Smooth tool (✎) and the Path Eraser tool (✎), located under the Pencil tool (✎) in the Tools panel.

5 Choose Select > Deselect, and then choose File > Save.

Next, you will edit the Paintbrush tool options.

▶ **Tip:** Increase the value of the Smoothness option in the Paintbrush Tool Options dialog box to smooth the path by using fewer points as you draw.

6 Double-click the Paintbrush tool (✏) to display the Paintbrush Tool Options dialog box. Select Keep Selected, and then click OK.

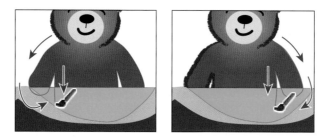

The Paintbrush Tool Options dialog box changes the way the Paintbrush tool functions. Because you selected Keep Selected, the paths now remain selected after you finish drawing them.

7 With the Paintbrush tool selected, position the pointer over the left shoulder and drag down and to the left, to trace around the arm on the left. Paint all the way around the arm and down the side of the bear.

● **Note:** You can release the mouse button at certain points and then continue painting the path. The path remains selected because of the Keep Selected option you set in the Paintbrush Tool Options dialog box.

8 With the Paintbrush tool selected, position the pointer over the right shoulder and drag down and to the right, to trace around the arm on the right. Paint all the way around the arm and down the side of the bear.

● **Note:** When the Keep Selected option is deselected, you can edit a path by selecting it with the Selection tool (▶) or by selecting a segment or point on the path with the Direct Selection tool (▷) and then redrawing over the path with the Paintbrush tool.

9 Double-click the Paintbrush tool in the Tools panel. In the Paintbrush Tool Options dialog box, deselect the Keep Selected option and then click OK.

Now, the paths will not remain selected after you finish drawing them, and you can draw overlapping paths without altering previously drawn paths.

10 Choose Select > Deselect. Choose Select > Object > Brush Strokes. This will select all of the objects with a brush stroke applied, on all artboards.

11 Select the Selection tool in the Tools panel. Shift-click the bunting to deselect it.

12 Click several other brushes in the Brushes panel to see the effects. When you have finished, click the Charcoal - Thick brush again to reapply that brush. Make sure the Stroke weight is .5 pt in the Control panel.

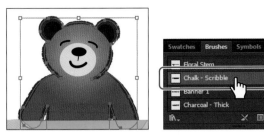

The selected paths.   Try another brush.   The result.

▶ **Tip:** Don't forget the large number of brushes that come with Illustrator. To access them, click the Brush Libraries Menu button (▨) in the lower-left corner of the Brushes panel.

13 Click outside the artwork to deselect it.

14 Choose File > Save.

Creating an Art brush

You can create new Calligraphic, Scatter, Art, Pattern, and Bristle brushes based on your settings. For Scatter, Art, and Pattern brushes, you must first create the artwork you want to use. In this section, you'll use artwork provided with the lesson to create a new Art brush. The Art brush will be used to create a logo for the train engine.

1 Choose View > Fit Artboard In Window.

2 Choose 2 from the Artboard Navigation menu in the lower-left corner of the Document window. This will fit the second artboard in the Document window.

3 Using the Selection tool (▸), click to select the group of stars.

Next, you will make an Art brush from the selected artwork. You can make an Art brush from vector artwork, but that artwork must not contain gradients, blends, other brush strokes, mesh objects, bitmap images, graphs, placed files, masks, or text that has not been converted to outlines.

4 Click the New Brush button (▤) at the bottom of the Brushes panel. This begins the process of creating a new brush from the selected artwork.

5 In the New Brush dialog box, select Art Brush and then click OK.

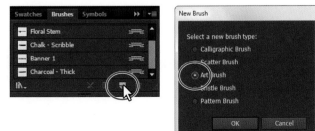

● **Note:** To learn about guidelines for creating brushes, see "Create or modify brushes" in Illustrator Help.

6. In the Art Brush Options dialog box, change the Name to **train logo**. Click OK.

7. Choose 1 from the Artboard Navigation menu in the lower-left corner of the Document window.

8. With the Selection tool selected, click to select the circle around the "RR" on the engine.

9. Select the Zoom tool (🔍) in the Tools panel, and drag a marquee across the circle and the RR in the center of the engine to zoom in to it.

10. Click the train logo brush in the Brushes panel to apply it.

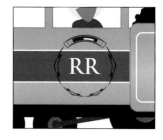

Notice that the original artwork is stretched around the shape. This is the default behavior of an Art brush.

Editing an Art brush

Next, you will edit the train logo Art brush.

▶ **Tip:** To learn more about the Art Brush Options dialog box, see "Art brush options" in Illustrator Help.

1. With the circle still selected, double-click the thumbnail to the left of the train logo name or to the right of the name in the Brushes panel to open the Art Brush Options dialog box. Select Preview to see the changes as you make them. Change the Width to **120%**. This will increase the size of the artwork relative to its original width. Select Stretch Between Guides, and then change the Start to **17 px** and the End to **18 px**. Select Flip Along, and then click OK.

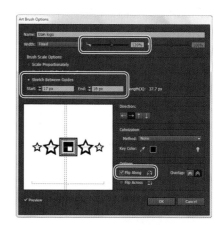

Note: If the stars on your circle are not at the bottom of the circle, you can rotate the circle with the Rotate tool (↻) in the Tools panel to match the position shown in the figure.

2. In the dialog box that appears, click Apply To Strokes to apply the change to the artwork that has the brush applied.

3. Choose View > Fit Artboard In Window.

4. Choose Select > Deselect, and then choose File > Save.

Using Bristle brushes

Bristle brushes allow you to create strokes with the appearance of a natural brush with bristles. You'll start by adjusting options for a brush to change how it appears in the artwork and then paint with the Paintbrush tool and Bristle brush to create a fire effect.

Bristle brush examples

Changing Bristle brush options

As you've seen earlier, you can change the appearance of a brush by adjusting its settings in the Brush Options dialog box, either before or after brushes have been applied to the artwork. When you paint with a Bristle brush, it creates vector paths. It is usually best to adjust Bristle brush settings prior to painting, since it can take some time to update the brush strokes.

1 In the Brushes panel, choose Show Bristle Brushes from the panel menu (▼≣) and then deselect Show Art Brushes.

2 Double-click the thumbnail for the Filbert brush or directly to the right of the brush name to open the Bristle Brush Options dialog box for that brush. Leave the dialog box open for the next step.

3 In the Bristle Brush Options dialog box:

- Leave the Shape set at Flat Curve.

- Make sure that Size is 3 mm. The brush size is the diameter of the brush.

- Change the Bristle Length to **178%**. The bristle length starts from the point where the bristles meet the handle of the bristle tip.

- Change the Bristle Density to **84%**. The bristle density is the number of bristles in a specified area of the brush neck.

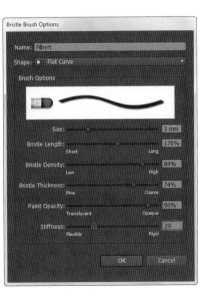

- For Bristle Thickness, set the value to **74%**. The bristle thickness can vary from fine to coarse (between 1% and 100%).

- For Paint Opacity, change the value to **90%**. This option lets you set the opacity of the paint being used.

- For Stiffness, change the value to **29%**. Stiffness implies the rigidness of the bristles.

4 Click OK.

> **Tip:** Illustrator comes with a series of default Bristle brushes. Click the Brush Libraries Menu button (▥) at the bottom of the Brushes panel, and choose Bristle Brush > Bristle Brush Library.

● **Note:** To learn more about the Bristle Brush Options dialog box and its settings, see "Using the Bristle brush" in Illustrator Help.

Painting with a Bristle brush

Now, you'll use the Filbert brush to draw some fire. Painting with a Bristle brush can create a very organic stroke. In order to constrain the painting, you will paint inside a shape. This will mask (hide) part of the painting to be in the shape of a flame.

1   Select the Zoom tool (🔍) in the Tools panel, and drag a marquee around the flame shape to the left of the dinosaur, to zoom in on it.

2   Select the Selection tool (▶) in the Tools panel, and click to select the flame shape. This selects the layer that the shape is on so that any artwork you paint will be on the same layer.

● **Note:** To learn more about the drawing modes, see Lesson 3, "Creating and Editing Shapes."

3   Click the Draw Inside button (⬚) at the bottom of the Tools panel.

● **Note:** If the Tools panel appears as one column, click and hold down the Drawing Modes button at the bottom of the Tools panel, and then choose a Drawing mode from the menu that appears.

4   Choose Select > Deselect to deselect the flame shape. You can still draw inside the shape, as indicated by the dotted lines on the corners of the shape.

5   Select the Paintbrush tool (🖌) in the Tools panel. Choose the Filbert brush from the Brush Definition menu in the Control panel, if it's not already chosen.

6   Change the Fill color to None and Stroke color to flame red in the Control panel. Press the Escape key to hide the Swatches panel. Make sure that the Stroke weight is 1 pt in the Control panel.

▶ **Tip:** If you want to edit paths as you draw, you can select the Keep Selected option in the Paintbrush Tool Options for the Paintbrush tool or select paths with the Selection tool. You don't need to completely fill the shape.

7   Position the pointer at the upper-left tip of the flame shape. Drag down and to the right to loosely follow the top edge of the flame shape. Release the mouse button when you pass the lower-right tip of the flame shape.

When you release the mouse button, notice that the path you just painted is masked by the flame shape.

8   Use the Paintbrush tool (🖌) to provide some texture by drawing more strokes inside the flame shape, using the Filbert brush.

Paint with the Bristle brush.

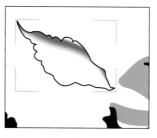
The masked path.

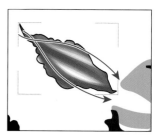
The result.

▶ **Tip:** If you don't like what you just painted, you can choose Edit > Undo Bristle Stroke.

Next, you will edit the brush and paint with another color to build the flame by layering paths.

9 Change the Stroke color to flame orange in the Control panel.

10 Double-click the Filbert brush thumbnail or to the right of the brush name in the Brushes panel. In the Bristle Brush Options dialog box, change the Paint Opacity to **30%** and then click OK.

11 Click Leave Strokes in the dialog box that appears. This changes the brush settings without changing the red flame you already painted.

12 Draw some more paths on top of the red flames, using the Paintbrush tool. Focus the orange paths you draw closer to the dinosaur's mouth.

13 Change the Stroke color to flame yellow in the Control panel.

14 Double-click the Filbert brush thumbnail or to the right of the brush name in the Brushes panel. In the Bristle Brush Options dialog box, change the Bristle Density to **18%** and the Stiffness to **60%**. Click OK.

15 Click Leave Strokes in the dialog box that appears.

16 Draw some more paths on top of the orange flames, using the Paintbrush tool. Focus the yellow paths you draw closer to the dinosaur's mouth.

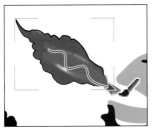
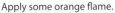

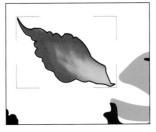

Apply some orange flame. Finish the flame with yellow.

17 Choose View > Outline.

18 Choose Select > Object > Bristle Brush Strokes to select all of the paths created with the Paintbrush tool, using the Filbert Bristle brush.

19 Choose Object > Group, and then View > Preview.

20 Click the Draw Normal button at the bottom of the Tools panel.

21 Select the Selection tool in the Tools panel. Choose Select > Deselect.

22 Double-click the edge of the flame shape to enter Isolation mode. Click the black stroke of the flame shape. Change the Stroke color to None in the Control panel.

23 Press the Escape key to exit Isolation mode.

24 Choose Select > Deselect and then choose File > Save.

● **Note:** When saving, you may see a warning dialog box. Click OK.

The Bristle brush and graphic tablets

When you use a Bristle brush with a graphic tablet, Illustrator interactively tracks the movements of the stylus over the tablet. It interprets all aspects of its orientation and pressure input at any point along a drawing path. Illustrator provides the output that is modeled on the stylus's x-axis position, y-axis position, pressure, tilt, bearing, and rotation.

A cursor annotator that simulates the tip of an actual brush is displayed when using a tablet and stylus that support rotation. This annotator does not appear when other input devices such as a mouse are used. The annotator is also disabled while using the precise cursors.

Note: *Use the Wacom Intuos 3 or higher tablet with Art (6D) pen to explore the full capabilities of the Bristle brush. Illustrator can interpret all 6-degrees of freedom that this device combination provides. However, other devices including the Wacom Grip pen and Art brush pen may not be able to interpret some attributes such as rotation. These uninterpreted attributes are treated as constants in the resulting brush strokes.*

While using a mouse, only x and y-axis movements are recorded. Other inputs, such as tilt, bearing, rotation, and pressure remain fixed resulting in even and consistent strokes.

For Bristle brush strokes, feedback is displayed when you drag the tool. This feedback provides an approximate view of the final stroke.

Note: *Bristle brush strokes are made up of several overlapping, filled transparent paths. These paths, like any other filled path in Illustrator, interact with the paint of other objects, including other bristle brush paths. However, the fill for strokes does not self-interact. Therefore, layered, individual, bristle brush strokes build up and interact with each other, but a single stroke scrubbed back and forth in place does not interact with itself and build up.*

—From Illustrator Help

Using Pattern brushes

Pattern brushes paint a pattern made up of separate sections, or tiles. When you apply a Pattern brush to artwork, different tiles of the pattern are applied to different sections of the path, depending on where the section falls on the path—the end, middle, or corner. There are hundreds of interesting Pattern brushes that you can choose from when creating your own projects, from dog tracks to cityscapes. Next, you'll open an existing Pattern Brush library and choose a train track pattern to create tracks.

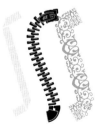

Pattern brush examples

1 Choose View > Fit Artboard In Window.

2 In the Brushes panel, choose Show Pattern Brushes from the panel menu (▼≣) and deselect Show Bristle Brushes.

3 Click the Brush Libraries Menu button (▥), and choose Borders > Borders_Novelty. A brush library panel with various borders appears.

4 Scroll toward the bottom of the Borders_Novelty panel, and click the Train Tracks brush to add it to the panel. Close the Borders_Novelty brush library group.

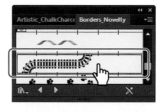

Next, you will apply the brush and then edit its properties.

5 Click the Layers panel icon (◉) on the right side of the workspace to expand the Layers panel. Click the visibility column to the left of the Railroad tracks layer to show the path for the tracks on the artboard. Click the Layers panel icon to collapse the panel.

6 Select the Selection tool (▶) in the Tools panel. Click the path that appears below the train to select it.

7 Choose the Train Tracks Pattern brush from the Brush Definition menu in the Control panel to apply the Pattern brush.

8 Change the Stroke weight to **4 pt** in the Control panel.

Notice that the train tracks follow the curve precisely. A Pattern brush has tiles, as described earlier, that correspond to parts of the path.

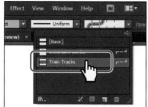 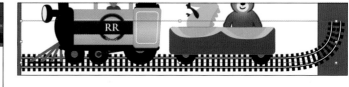

Next, you will edit the brush properties for the selected train tracks.

9 Click the Brushes panel icon (▦) on the right side of the workspace to expand the panel. Click the Options Of Selected Object button (▤) at the bottom of the Brushes panel to edit the brush options for only the selected train tracks on the artboard. This opens the Stroke Options (Pattern Brush) dialog box.

Tip: To change
the size of the railroad
tracks, you can also
change the stroke of
the line on the artboard,
with the brush applied.

10 Change the Scale to **120%** either by
dragging the Scale slider or by typing
in the value. Click OK.

When you edit the brush options
of the selected object, you only see
some of the brush options. The
Stroke Options (Pattern Brush) dialog
box is used to edit the properties of the brushed path without updating the
corresponding brush.

11 Choose Select > Deselect and then File > Save.

Creating a Pattern brush

You can create a Pattern brush in several ways. For a simple pattern applied to
a straight line, for instance, you can select the content that you're using for the
pattern and click the New Brush button (🔲) at the bottom of the Brushes panel.

To create a more complex pattern to apply to objects with curves and corners, you
must first create swatches in the Swatches panel from the artwork that you are
using for the Pattern brush tiles and then create the new brush. For example, to
create a Pattern brush that will be used on a straight line with corners, you might
need to create three swatches, one for the straight line, another for the inside
corner and another for the outside corner. Next, you'll create swatches to be used
in a Pattern brush.

1 Click the Layers panel icon (🔲) on the right side of the workspace to expand the
Layers panel.

2 Click the visibility column to the left of the Frame layer to show its contents.

3 Click the Swatches panel icon (🔲) to expand the Swatches panel, or choose
Window > Swatches.

Now, you'll create a pattern swatch.

4 Choose 2 from the Artboard Navigation menu in the lower-left corner of the
Document window.

5 With the Selection tool (▶), drag the flower into the Swatches panel. The new
pattern swatch appears in the Swatches panel.

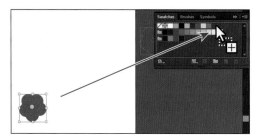

6 Choose Select > Deselect.

7 In the Swatches panel, double-click the pattern swatch that you just created. In the Pattern Options dialog box, name the swatch **Corner** and choose 1 x 1 from the Copies menu.

8 Click Done in the gray bar along the top of the Document window to finish editing the pattern.

9 Repeat steps 5 through 7 to create a pattern swatch of the orange circle located to the left of the flower on the artboard. Name the swatch **Side**.

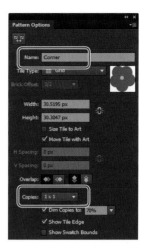

▶ **Tip:** For more information on creating pattern swatches, see "About patterns" in Illustrator Help.

To create a new Pattern brush, you apply swatches from the Swatches panel to tiles in the Brush Options dialog box. Now, you'll apply the pattern swatches that you just made to tiles, to create a new Pattern brush.

10 Click the Brushes panel icon (▦) to expand the panel.

11 Choose Select > Deselect, if there is content selected.

This is an important step! Any content selected will be part of the brush.

12 In the Brushes panel, click the New Brush button (▣).

13 In the New Brush dialog box, select Pattern Brush.

Notice that you can't select the Art Brush or Scatter Brush. That is because artwork needs to be selected in the document first. Click OK.

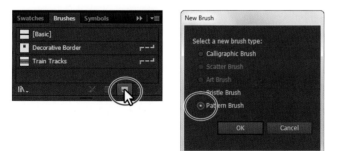

Now, you'll apply the swatches to the tiles for the new Pattern brush.

14 In the Pattern Brush Options dialog box, name the brush **Border**.

Tip: Position the pointer over the tile squares in the Pattern Brush Options dialog box to see a tool tip indicating which tile it is.

15 Under the Spacing option, make sure that the Side Tile box is selected. Below the tile boxes, select Side. The Side swatch appears in the Side tile box.

The Pattern Brush Options dialog box shows the tiles in the new brush you are making. The first tile on the left is the side tile, which is used to paint the middle sections of a path. The second tile is the outer corner tile. The third tile is the inner corner tile. The names of the pattern swatches that are in the Swatches panel are listed under the tiles.

Pattern brushes can have up to five tiles—the side, start, and end tiles, plus an outer corner tile and an inner corner tile to paint sharp corners on a path. Some brushes have no corner tiles because the brush is designed for curved paths.

In the next part of this lesson, you'll create your own Pattern brush that has corner tiles. Next, you'll apply the Corner swatch to the outer corner and inner corner tiles for the new Pattern brush.

16 In the Pattern Brush Options dialog box, select the Outer Corner Tile box (the second tile box from the left). In the pattern swatches list, select Corner. The Corner swatch appears in the Outer Corner Tile box.

17 Select the Inner Corner Tile box (the middle tile box). In the pattern swatches list, select the Corner swatch. The Corner swatch appears in the Inner Corner Tile box. Click OK.

Note: When you create a new brush, the brush appears in the Brushes panel of the current document only.

You won't create a start or end tile for the new brush, because you'll apply the new brush to a path in the artwork next. When you want to create a Pattern brush that includes start and end tiles, you add those tiles the same way as you did the side and corner tiles.

The Border brush appears in the Brushes panel.

Tip: To save a brush and reuse it in another file, you can create a brush library with the brushes you want to use. For more information, see "Work with brush libraries" in Illustrator Help.

Applying a Pattern brush

In this section, you'll apply the Border Pattern brush to a rectangular border around the artwork. When you use drawing tools to apply brushes to artwork, you first draw the path with the drawing tool and then select the brush in the Brushes panel to apply the brush to the path.

1 Click the First artboard button (![icon]) in the lower-left corner of the Document window to return to the first artboard and to fit it in the Document window.

2 With the Selection tool (![icon]) selected, click the white stroke of the rectangle on the border.

3 In the Tools panel, click the Fill box and make sure that None (![icon]) is selected. Then, click the Stroke box and select None (![icon]).

4 Click the Brushes panel icon (![icon]) to expand the panel and choose Thumbnail View from the Brushes panel menu (![icon]).

   Notice that Pattern brushes in Thumbnail view are segmented in the Brushes panel. Each segment corresponds to a pattern tile. The side tile is repeated in the Brushes panel thumbnail preview.

5 With the rectangle selected, click the Border brush in the Brushes panel.

   The rectangle is painted with the Border brush, with the side tile on the sides and the corner tile on the corners.

Now, you'll edit the Border brush.

6 In the Brushes panel, double-click the Border Pattern brush to open the Pattern Brush Options dialog box.

7 In the Pattern Brush Options dialog box, change the Scale to **70%** and the Spacing to **120%** and then select Add Space To Fit. Click OK.

8 In the Brush Change Alert dialog box, click Apply To Strokes to update the border on the artboard.

9 With the Selection tool selected, click to select the arch right above the duck's head. Click the Border brush in the Brushes panel to apply it.

Notice that the flowers are not applied to the path. The path is painted with the side swatch from the Border brush, to which the side tile is applied. Because the path does not include sharp corners, the outer corner and inner corner tiles are not applied to the path.

10 Choose Edit > Undo Apply Pattern Brush to remove the brush from the arch.

● **Note:** Earlier in the lesson, you learned how to remove a brush from an object by clicking the Remove Brush Stroke button (⊠) in the Brushes panel. In this case, you chose Edit > Undo Apply Pattern Brush instead, because clicking the Remove Brush Stroke button would strip the previous formatting from the arch, leaving it with a default fill and stroke.

Editing Pattern brush tiles

You can edit the tiles in a Pattern brush by creating (or updating) swatches and applying the new swatches to the tiles in the Pattern Brush Options dialog box.

You can also change the pattern tiles in a Pattern brush by pressing the Alt (Windows) or Option (Mac OS) key and dragging the new artwork from the artboard onto the tile you wish to change in the Brushes panel.

Changing the color attributes of brushes

The colors that a Scatter, Art, or Pattern brush paints depend on the current stroke color and the colorization method of the brush. If you have not set a colorization method, the default color for that brush is used. For example, the train logo Art brush was applied with its default color (not the current stroke of black) because its colorization method was set to None.

To colorize Art, Pattern, and Scatter brushes, you can use three editing options in the Brush Options dialog box: Tints, Tints and Shades, and Hue Shift.

To learn more about each of these colorization methods, search for "Colorization options" in Illustrator Help.

● **Note:** Brushes colorized with a stroke color of white may appear entirely white. Brushes colorized with a stroke color of black may appear entirely black. Results depend on which brush colors were originally chosen.

Changing a brush color using Tints colorization

Now, you'll change the color of the train logo Art brush using the Tints colorization method.

1   In the Brushes panel, choose Show Art Brushes from the panel menu (▼≡) and deselect Show Pattern Brushes.

2   With the Selection tool (▶), click to select the train logo (the circle with the train logo Art brush applied) below the duck.

3   Pressing the Shift key, click the Stroke color in the Control panel to open the Color panel. Change the values to C=**3**, M=**92**, Y=**100**, K=**16**.

4   In the Brushes panel, double-click the train logo brush to view the Art Brush Options dialog box.

A tool tip appears with the brush name when you position the pointer over it. Select Preview (if necessary) to see the changes you will make, and then move the dialog box off to the side so that you can see your artwork as you work.

5   In the Colorization section of the Art Brush Options dialog box, choose Tints from the Method menu.

The selected path with the train logo brush applied is colorized and displays the brush stroke in tints of the stroke color. Portions of the art that are black become the stroke color, portions that aren't black become tints of the stroke color, and white remains white.

▶ **Tip:** To learn more about how the different colorization methods affect artwork, click the light bulb icon (💡) in the Art Brush Options dialog box.

● **Note:** The Tints And Shades colorization method displays the brush stroke in tints and shades of the stroke color. Tints And Shades maintains black and white, and everything between becomes a blend from black to white through the stroke color.

6 If desired, choose the Tints And Shades colorization method from the menu in the Art Brush Options dialog box to preview the change. Choose the Tints method again, and then click OK. In the warning dialog box, click Apply To Strokes to apply the colorization change to the strokes in the artwork.

You can also choose to change only subsequent brush strokes and leave existing strokes unchanged. When you select a colorization method for a brush, the new stroke color applies to selected brush strokes and to new paths painted with the brush.

7 Pressing the Shift key, click the Stroke color in the Control panel to open the Color panel. Click in the color spectrum bar at the bottom to select a color.

8 When you are satisfied with the color of the train logo, click away from the artwork to deselect it.

9 Choose File > Save.

Changing the brush color using Hue Shift colorization

Now, you'll apply a new color to the Banner 1 brush in the Brushes panel.

1 Click the Layers panel icon (![icon]) on the right side of the workspace to expand the Layers panel. Click the visibility column to the left of the Text layer to show its contents. Click the Layers panel tab to collapse the panel.

2 Select the Zoom tool (![icon]) in the Tools panel, and drag a marquee around the Golden Book Award seal in the upper-left corner to zoom in to it.

3 With the Selection tool (![icon]), click to select the circle in the seal with the brush applied.

4 Click the Brushes panel icon (![icon]) to expand the panel. Double-click the Banner 1 brush in the Brushes panel to reveal the Art Brush Options dialog box. Note that the Banner 1 brush is set to a None Colorization method, by default.

5 In the Art Brush Options dialog box, select Preview, if it's not already selected. In the Colorization section, choose Hue Shift from the Method menu.

You typically choose Hue Shift for brushes that use multiple colors. Everything in the artwork that is the key color changes to the new stroke color when the stroke color is changed.

6 In the Colorization section of the Art Brush Options dialog box, click the Key Color Eyedropper (✐), position the pointer over an orange color in the preview area (to the left of the Colorization settings), and then click, as shown in the figure.

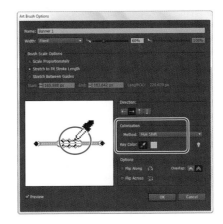

The key color you just sampled (the orange) will now be colorized with the current stroke color. Any orange content in the brush will be yellow. This color appears when you apply the Hue Shift colorization method.

7 Click OK. In the warning dialog box, click Apply To Strokes to apply the colorization change to the strokes in the artwork. You can also choose to change only subsequent brush strokes and leave existing strokes unchanged.

8 Change the Stroke color to flame red in the Control panel. Try other stroke colors for the selected brush strokes before finally choosing flame yellow, as shown in the figure on the right.

9 Choose Select > Deselect.

10 Choose File > Save.

Working with the Blob Brush tool

You can use the Blob Brush tool to paint filled shapes that intersect and merge with other shapes of the same color. With the Blob Brush tool, you can draw with Paintbrush tool artistry. Unlike the Paintbrush tool, which lets you create open paths, the Blob Brush tool lets you create a closed shape with a fill only (no stroke) that you can then easily edit with the Eraser or Blob Brush tool. Shapes that have a stroke cannot be edited with the Blob Brush tool.

Path created with the
Paintbrush tool

Shape created with the
Blob Brush tool

Next, you will use the Blob Brush tool to create a part of the smoke coming from the train engine.

Drawing with the Blob Brush tool

The Blob Brush tool uses the same default brush options as Calligraphic brushes.

● **Note:** If you don't see "Reset Essentials" in the workspace switcher, choose Essentials before choosing Reset Essentials in the workspace switcher.

1 Choose Reset Essentials from the workspace switcher in the Application bar.

2 Choose View > Fit Artboard In Window.

3 Click the Layers panel icon (▧) on the right side of the workspace to expand the Layers panel. Click the eye icon to the left of the Text layer to hide its contents, and then click the visibility column to the left of both the Background layer and the Smoke layer. Click the Smoke layer to select it.

4 Change the fill color to white and the stroke color to None (▨) in the Control panel.

● **Note:** When drawing with the Blob Brush tool, if a fill and stroke are set before drawing, the stroke becomes the fill of the shape made by the Blob Brush tool. If only a fill is set before drawing, it becomes the fill of the shape created.

5 Double-click the Blob Brush tool (✐) in the Tools panel. In the Blob Brush Tool Options dialog box, select the Keep Selected option and change the Size to **30 pt** in the Default Brush Options area. Click OK.

6 Position the pointer just above the black smoke stack to the left of the duck. Drag in a zigzag pattern up and to the right to create some smoke.

Note: When you draw with the Blob Brush tool, you create filled, closed shapes. Those shapes can contain any type of fill, including gradients, solid colors, patterns, and more.

7 Choose Select > Deselect.

Merging paths with the Blob Brush tool

Besides drawing new shapes with the Blob Brush tool, you can use it to intersect and merge shapes of the same color. Next, you will merge the smoke you just created with the white ellipse to the right of it to create one big smoke shape.

1 Click the Appearance panel icon (◉) on the right side of the workspace to expand the panel. In the Appearance panel menu (▾≣), deselect New Art Has Basic Appearance. When this option is deselected, the Blob Brush tool uses the attributes of the selected artwork.

2 With the Selection tool (▶), click the smoke you just drew and Shift-click the white ellipse to the right of the smoke shape.

3 In the Appearance panel, click the word "Path" at the top of the panel so that the drop shadow you apply next isn't applied to the fill or stroke only.

Note: If you see "Mixed Appearances" in the Appearance panel with both shapes selected, then press the letter D to apply the default fill and stroke and then change the stroke to **0** in the Control panel, to remove it.

4 Choose Effect > Stylize > Drop Shadow. In the Drop Shadow dialog box, change Opacity to **35%**, X Offset to **3 px**, Y Offset to **3 px**, and Blur to **2** px. Click OK.

5 Choose Select > Deselect.

6 With the Blob Brush tool selected in the Tools panel, make sure that you see the same attributes as the smoke shapes (a white fill, no stroke, and a drop shadow) in the Appearance panel. Drag from inside the smoke shape you created to the inside of the ellipse to the right, connecting the two shapes.

Note: Notice that the drop shadow is applied to the entire shape as you draw and edit.

Note: Objects merged with the Blob Brush tool need to have the same appearance attributes, have no stroke, be on the same layer or group, and be adjacent to each other in the stacking order.

7 Continue drawing with the Blob Brush tool to make the smoke look more like a cloud. When you release the mouse button, the drop shadow is applied.

If you find that new shapes are being made, instead of the existing cloud shape being edited, undo what you've created; then, with the Selection tool, reselect and then deselect the cloud shape and continue.

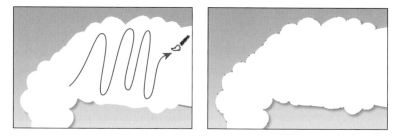

8 With the Blob Brush tool, add more shape to the ellipse part of the smoke on the right side to make it more cloud-like.

9 Choose Select > Deselect and then File > Save.

Editing with the Eraser tool

As you draw and merge shapes with the Blob Brush tool, you may draw too much and want to edit what you've done. You can use the Eraser tool to mold the shape and correct any changes you don't like.

▶ **Tip:** As you draw with the Blob Brush and Eraser tools, it is recommended that you use shorter strokes and release the mouse button often. You can undo the edits that you make, but if you draw in one long stroke without releasing the mouse button, an undo removes the entire stroke.

1 With the Selection tool (▶), click to select the smoke shape.

● **Note:** Selecting the shape before selecting the Eraser tool limits the Eraser tool so that it erases only the selected shape.

2 Select the Eraser tool (⬛) in the Tools panel. Proceed slowly with the next steps, and remember that you can always stop and undo.

3 Position the pointer over the cloud shape, and press the right bracket key (]) several times to increase the size of Eraser brush.

4 With the Eraser tool, drag along the bottom of the smoke shape to remove some of the smoke.

The Blob Brush and Eraser tools have pointers that include a circle, indicating the diameter of the brush.

5   Try switching between the Blob Brush tool and the Eraser tool to edit the smoke.

6   Click the Layers panel icon () on the right side of the workspace to expand the Layers panel. Click the visibility column to the left of the Text layer. Click the Layers panel tab to collapse the panel group.

Note: You may need to select the Selection tool and reposition the text "Ted and Fuego Take a Train" to center the text on the smoke.

7   Choose File > Save, and close all open files.

The Blob Brush tool guidelines

When using the Blob Brush tool, keep the following guidelines in mind:

*   To merge paths, they must be adjacent in stacking order.

*   The Blob Brush tool creates paths with a fill and no stroke. If you want your Blob Brush paths to merge with existing artwork, make sure that the artwork has the same fill color and no stroke.

*   When drawing paths with the Blob Brush tool, new paths merge with the topmost matching path encountered. If the new path touches more than one matching path within the same group or layer, all of the intersecting paths are merged together.

*   To apply paint attributes (such as effect or transparency) to the Blob Brush tool, select the brush and set the attributes in the Appearances panel before you start drawing.

*   You can use the Blob Brush tool to merge paths created by other tools. To do this, make sure that the existing artwork does not have a stroke; then set up the Blob Brush tool to have the same fill color, and draw a new path that intersects all of the paths that you want to merge together.

—From Illustrator Help

Review questions

1 Describe each of the five brush types: Art, Calligraphic, Pattern, Bristle, and Scatter.

2 What is the difference between applying a brush to artwork using the Paintbrush tool and applying a brush to artwork using one of the drawing tools?

3 Describe how to edit paths with the Paintbrush tool as you draw. How does the Keep Selected option affect the Paintbrush tool?

4 How do you change the colorization method for an Art, Pattern, or Scatter brush? (Remember, you don't use colorization methods with Calligraphic or Bristle brushes.)

5 For which brush types must you have artwork selected on the artboard before you can create a brush?

6 What does the Blob Brush tool allow you to create?

Review answers

1 The following are the five brush types:

- Art brushes stretch artwork evenly along a path. Art brushes include strokes that resemble graphic media, such as the Charcoal - Thick brush used in the lesson. Art brushes also include objects, such as the arrow brush.

- Calligraphic brushes are defined by an elliptical shape whose center follows the path. They create strokes that resemble hand-drawn lines made with a flat, angled calligraphic pen tip.

- Pattern brushes paint a pattern made up of separate sections, or tiles, for the sides, ends, and corners of the path. When you apply a Pattern brush to artwork, the brush applies different tiles from the pattern to different sections of the path, depending on where the section falls on the path.

- Bristle brushes allow you to create brush strokes with the appearance of a natural brush with bristles.

- Scatter brushes scatter an object, such as a leaf, along a path. You can adjust the size, spacing, scatter, and rotation options to change the appearance of the brush.

2 To apply brushes using the Paintbrush tool, you select the tool, choose a brush in the Brushes panel, and draw on the artboard. The brush is applied directly to the paths as you draw. To apply brushes using a drawing tool, you select the tool and draw in the

artwork. Then, you select the path in the artwork and choose a brush in the Brushes panel. The brush is applied to the selected path.

3   To edit a path with the Paintbrush tool, drag over a selected path to redraw it. The Keep Selected option keeps the last path selected as you draw with the Paintbrush tool. Leave the Keep Selected option selected (the default setting) when you want to easily edit the previous path as you draw. Deselect the Keep Selected option when you want to draw layered paths with the paintbrush without altering previous paths. When Keep Selected is deselected, you can use the Selection tool to select a path and then edit it.

4   To change the colorization method of a brush, double-click the brush in the Brushes panel to open the Brush Options dialog box. Use the Method menu in the Colorization section to select another method. If you choose Hue Shift, you can use the default color displayed in the dialog box preview or you can change the key color by clicking the Key Color Eyedropper and clicking a color in the preview. Click OK to accept the settings, and close the Brush Options dialog box. Click Apply To Strokes in the alert dialog box if you want to apply the changes to existing strokes in the artwork.

Existing brush strokes are colorized with the stroke color that was selected when the strokes were applied to the artwork. New brush strokes are colorized with the current stroke color. To change the color of existing strokes after applying a different colorization method, select the strokes and select a new stroke color.

5   For Art and Scatter brushes, you need to have artwork selected in order to create a brush using the New Brush button in the Brushes panel.

6   Use the Blob Brush tool to edit filled shapes that you can intersect and merge with other shapes of the same color or to create artwork from scratch.

12 APPLYING EFFECTS

Lesson overview

In this lesson, you'll learn how to do the following:

- Use various effects, such as Pathfinder, Scribble, and Drop Shadow.

- Use Warp effects to distort type.

- Create three-dimensional (3D) objects from two-dimensional (2D) artwork.

- Map artwork to the surfaces of three-dimensional objects.

 This lesson takes approximately an hour to complete. If needed, remove the previous lesson folder from your hard disk and copy the Lesson12 folder onto it.

Effects change the look of an object. Effects are live, which means that you can apply an effect to an object and then modify or remove it at any time, using the Appearance panel. Using effects, it's easy to apply drop shadows, turn two-dimensional artwork into three-dimensional shapes, and much more.

Getting started

In this lesson, you'll create objects using various effects. Before you begin, you'll need to restore the default preferences for Adobe Illustrator. Then, you'll open a file containing the finished artwork to see what you'll create.

1. To ensure that the tools and panels function exactly as described in this lesson, delete or deactivate (by renaming) the Adobe Illustrator CS6 preferences file. See "Restoring default preferences" on page 3.

2. Start Adobe Illustrator CS6.

● **Note:** If you have not already done so, copy the Lesson12 folder from the Lessons folder on the *Adobe Illustrator CS6 Classroom in a Book* CD onto your hard disk. See "Copying the Classroom in a Book files" on page 2.

3. Choose File > Open, and open the L12end.ai file in the Lesson12 folder, located in the Lessons folder on your hard disk.

   This file displays a completed illustration of a soda can.

4. Choose View > Zoom Out to make the finished artwork smaller. Adjust the window size, and leave it on your screen as you work. (Use the Hand tool [🖑] to move the artwork where you want it in the window.) If you don't want to leave the image open, choose File > Close.

To begin working, you'll open an existing art file.

● **Note:** In Mac OS, when opening lesson files, you may need to click the round, green button in the upper-left corner of the Document window to maximize the window's size.

5. Choose File > Open, and open the L12start.ai file in the Lesson12 folder, located in the Lessons folder on your hard disk.

6. Choose File > Save As, name the file **sodacan.ai**, and select the Lesson12 folder. Leave the Save As Type option set to Adobe Illustrator (*.AI) (Windows) or the Format option set to Adobe Illustrator (ai) (Mac OS), and then click Save. In the Illustrator Options dialog box, leave the Illustrator options at their default settings and then click OK.

Using live effects

The Effect menu commands alter the appearance of an object without changing the base object. Applying an effect automatically adds the effect to the object's appearance attribute. You can apply more than one effect to an object. You can edit, move, delete, or duplicate an effect at any time in the Appearance panel. To edit the points that the effect creates, you must first expand the object.

There are two types of effects in Illustrator: vector effects and raster effects. In Illustrator, click the Effect menu item to see the different types of effects available.

Object with a drop shadow effect applied

Note: When you apply a raster effect, the original vector data is rasterized using the document's raster effects settings, which determine the resolution of the resulting image. To learn about document raster effects settings, search for "Document raster effects settings" in Illustrator Help.

- **Illustrator effects**: The top half of the Effect menu contains vector effects. You can apply these effects only to vector objects or to the fill or stroke of a bitmap object in the Appearance panel. The following vector effects can be applied to both vector and bitmap objects: 3D effects, SVG filters, Warp effects, Transform effects, Drop Shadow, Feather, Inner Glow, and Outer Glow.

- **Photoshop effects**: The bottom half of the Effect menu contains raster effects. You can apply them to either vector or bitmap objects.

Applying an effect

Effects are applied using the Effect menu or the Appearance panel and can be applied to objects or groups. In this part of the lesson, you are first going to learn how to apply an effect to a soda can label using the Effect menu and then you will apply an effect using the Appearance panel.

1   Choose Reset Essentials from the workspace switcher in the Application bar to reset the workspace.

2   Choose View > Smart Guides to deselect them.

3   With the Selection tool (⬉), click the text shapes "Sparkling Soda" on the artboard.

4   With the group selected, choose Effect > Stylize > Drop Shadow from the Illustrator Effects section of the menu that appears.

5   In the Drop Shadow dialog box, change the X Offset, Y Offset, and Blur to **.04 in**. Select Preview to see the drop shadow applied to the text shapes. Click OK.

   This applies a subtle drop shadow to the text shapes.

Note: If you don't see "Reset Essentials" in the workspace switcher menu, choose Essentials before choosing Reset Essentials.

Next, you'll apply an effect using a different method, with the same result.

6 With the Selection tool, click the cherries to select the group.

7 With the group selected, click the Appearance panel icon (▦) on the right side of the workspace to expand the Appearance panel.

In the Appearance panel, you will see the word "Group" at the top of the panel, indicating that a group is selected. Effects can be applied to grouped objects.

8 Click the Add New Effect button (fx.) at the bottom of the Appearance panel. You'll see the same listing of effects as in the Effect menu.

9 Choose Stylize > Drop Shadow from the menu that appears.

10 In the Drop Shadow dialog box, change the Opacity to **40%** and leave the X Offset, Y Offset, and Blur set at .04 in. Select Preview to see the drop shadow applied. Click OK.

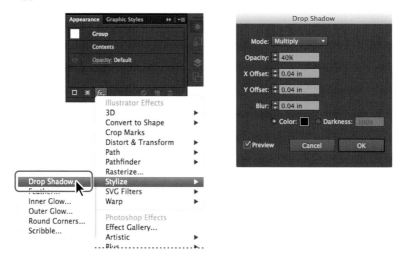

In the Appearance panel, notice that Drop Shadow is now listed in the panel.

11 Choose Select > Deselect.

12 Choose File > Save.

Next, you will edit the two drop shadow effects.

Editing an effect

Effects are live, so they can be edited after they are applied to an object. You can edit the effect in the Appearance panel by selecting the object with the effect applied and then either clicking the name of the effect or double-clicking the attribute row in the Appearance panel. This displays the dialog box for that effect. Changes you make to the effect update in the artwork. In this section, you will edit the drop shadow effect applied to the cherries.

1   With the Selection tool (↖), click the grouped cherry shapes and make sure that the Appearance panel is showing. If it isn't, choose Window > Appearance or click its panel icon (⬤).

Notice the drop shadow effect listed in the Appearance panel. The (🖾) icon to the right of an item listed in the panel indicates that it is an effect.

2   Click Drop Shadow in the Appearance panel. In the Drop Shadow dialog box, change Opacity to **60%** and select Preview to see the change. Try different settings to see their effects (we set the Blur at .03 in), and then click OK.

Next, you will remove an effect from the "Sparkling Soda" text shapes.

Note: Be careful not to click the underlined words "Drop Shadow," which will open the Drop Shadow dialog box.

3 With the Selection tool, click the "Sparkling Soda" text shapes.

4 In the Appearance panel, click to the right or left of Drop Shadow to highlight the attribute row for the Drop Shadow effect, if it's not already highlighted. After highlighting the attribute row, click the Delete Selected Item button (🗑) at the bottom of the panel.

Click the text shapes.

Delete the Drop Shadow.

The result.

5 With the Selection tool, click to select the cherries group again.

6 Choose Object > Ungroup.

Note: When you ungroup the cherries, you will still see the word "Group" at the top of the Appearance panel. That's because each cherry is its own group.

Notice that the drop shadow is gone from the cherries. When an effect is applied to a group, it affects the group as a whole. If the objects are no longer grouped together, the effect no longer applies.

7 Choose Edit > Undo Ungroup, and the drop shadow reappears.

8 Choose Select > Deselect and then File > Save.

Styling text with effects

You can make a warp from objects in your artwork, or you can use a preset warp shape or mesh object as an envelope, like you saw in Lesson 7, "Working With Type." Next, you will use a Warp effect to warp the text at the bottom of the label.

1 With the Selection tool (⬉) selected, select the "NET WT..." type at the bottom of the label.

2 Choose Effect > Warp > Arc Lower.

3 In the Warp Options dialog box, to create an arcing effect, set Bend to **35%**. Select Preview to preview the changes. Try choosing other styles from the Style menu, and then return to Arc Lower. Try adjusting the Horizontal and Vertical Distortion sliders to see the effect. Make sure that the Distortion values are returned to **0**, and then click OK.

Click to select the text.   Apply the Warp effect.   The result.

4 With the warped text still selected, click the visibility icon (⚫) to the left of
   the Warp: Arc Lower row in the Appearance panel to turn off visibility for the
   effect. Notice that the text is no longer warped on the artboard.

5 Select the Type tool (**T**) in the Tools panel, and select and change the "375" text
   on the artboard to **380**.

6 Select the Selection tool, and then click the visibility column to the left of the
   Warp: Arc Lower row in the Appearance panel, to turn on visibility for the
   effect. Notice that the text is once again warped.

⚫ **Note:** You selected the Selection tool again in this step because you originally applied the effect
to the text object with the Selection tool.

7 Choose Select > Deselect.

⚫ **Note:** To learn more about the Appearance panel, see Lesson 13, "Applying Appearance Attributes and Graphic Styles."

Turn off the visibility.   Change the text.   The effect.

▶ **Tip:** It is not necessary to turn the visibility off for the Warp effect before editing the text on the
artboard, but doing so can make it easier.

Next, you will apply multiple effects to the text "CHERRY BLAST" that has been
converted to outlines at the top of the soda label.

1 With the Selection tool (▶), click the "CHERRY BLAST" text shapes to select
   the group.

⚫ **Note:** To learn more about creating outlines from type, see the section, "Creating text outlines" in Lesson 7, "Working With Type."

2 Click the Add New Effect button (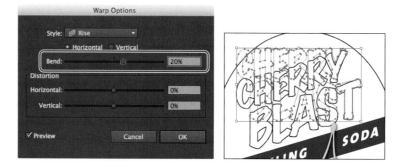) at the bottom of the Appearance panel. Choose Warp > Rise.

3 In the Warp Options dialog box, leave the Horizontal option selected and change the Bend to **20%**. Select Preview to see the change, and then click OK.

Notice how the selected text shapes (in blue) still look like the original shapes but are actually warped. This shows how a live effect allows you to print the text shapes with the Rise effect applied but does not change the underlying object. Also, you can see that the Appearance panel lists the Warp: Rise effect that has been applied to the text shapes.

Next, you will hide the selection anchor points so that you can focus on the outcome.

4 With the "CHERRY BLAST" text shapes still selected, choose View > Hide Edges.

5 In the Control panel, change the Fill color to the swatch named Banner and leave the stroke at black, 1 pt.

6 Choose Edit > Copy, and then choose Object > Hide > Selection.

7 Choose Edit > Paste In Front.

8 With the copy selected, change the Fill color to the swatch named Scribble and the Stroke color to None in the Control panel.

Next, you will apply the Scribble effect to the text shapes.

9 With the text shapes selected, choose Effect > Stylize > Scribble.

● **Note:** The Scribble effect in the figure may not look exactly like yours, and that's okay.

10 In the Scribble Options dialog box, choose Tight from the Settings menu. Select Preview to see the change. Change the Angle to **10**, and the Path Overlap to **-3 pt**, and leave the remainder of the settings as they are. Click OK.

After you make changes in the dialog box, the Settings menu will show Custom, rather than Tight.

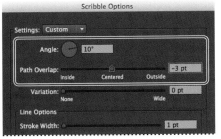

11 Choose Object > Show All.

12 Choose Select > Deselect and then File > Save.

Editing shapes with a Pathfinder effect

Pathfinder effects are similar to working with Pathfinder commands in the Pathfinder panel, except they are applied as effects and do not change the underlying content.

Next, you will apply a Pathfinder effect to several shapes.

1 With the Selection tool (![arrow]), Shift-click to select both the red banner shape behind the "SPARKLING SODA" text shapes and the oval in the background.

2 Choose Object > Group.

You grouped the objects together because Pathfinder effects may only be applied to groups, layers, or type objects.

3 Choose Effect > Pathfinder > Intersect to create a shape that shows where the two shapes intersect.

● **Note:** If you see a warning dialog box when you choose Effect > Pathfinder > Intersect, it's because you didn't group the objects first.

Notice that the Intersect effect appears in the Appearance panel. Clicking Intersect allows you to change the Pathfinder effect and to edit the Intersect effect.

● **Note:** To learn more about the Pathfinder commands, see the "Working with Pathfinder effects" section in Lesson 3, "Creating and Editing Shapes."

● **Note:** To remove the Intersect effect from a group that you just applied it to, click the Intersect effect in the Appearance panel and then click the Delete Selected Item button (![icon]) at the bottom of the panel.

● **Note:** You'll learn more about the Appearance panel in Lesson 13, "Applying Appearance Attributes and Graphic Styles."

4 With the group still selected, choose View > Outline.

The two shapes are still there and completely editable, since the effect being applied is live.

● **Note:** To intersect shapes, you can also use the Pathfinder panel, which will expand the shapes immediately, by default. Using the Effect menu lets you edit shapes independently.

Next, you will copy the oval shape from the group of shapes that has the Pathfinder effect applied.

5 With the Selection tool, double-click directly on the edge of the oval shape to enter Isolation mode.

This allows you to edit just the two shapes that are part of the group.

● **Note:** You are double-clicking the edge because shapes in Isolation mode have no fill, so they can't be selected by clicking in the center.

6 Click the edge of the oval shape to select it. Choose Edit > Copy.

7 Press the Escape key to exit Isolation mode. Choose Select > Deselect.

8 Choose View > Preview, and then choose Edit > Paste In Front to paste a copy on top of the other objects. Leave the oval shape selected.

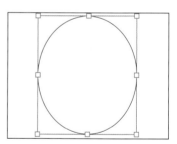

9 Choose File > Save.

Applying the Offset Path effect

Next, you will edit the oval shape by adding multiple strokes to it. You will then edit the multiple strokes by offsetting them against the oval shape. This process allows you to create the appearance of multiple stacked shapes.

1 With the oval shape selected, change the Stroke color to the swatch named Green, the Fill color to the gradient swatch named Center, and the stroke weight to **5 pt** in the Control panel.

2 Click the word "Stroke" in the Control panel, and click the Align Stroke To Outside button (▣) in the Stroke panel. Press the Escape key to hide the panel.

3 Click the Layers panel icon (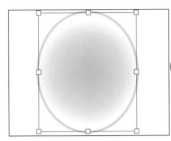) on the right side of the workspace to expand the Layers panel. Click the visibility column to the left of the Background layer to reveal the background shape.

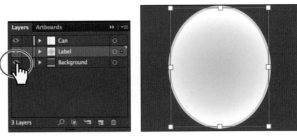

Edit the stroke and fill.   Show the Background layer.   The result.

Next, you will add another stroke to the shape and then edit the gradient fill.

4 Click the Appearance panel icon (■) to expand the panel. Click the arrow to the left of the stroke and fill rows to collapse them, if necessary. With the green shape still selected and the stroke row selected in the Appearance panel, click the Add New Stroke button (■) at the bottom of the Appearance panel. A new stroke appears in the panel, but the shape looks the same.

The shape now has two strokes directly on top of each other that are the same color and same weight.

5 In the Appearance panel, change the Stroke weight for the selected (highlighted) Stroke to **9 pt**.

6 Click the Stroke Color in the Appearance panel, and select the white swatch in the Swatches panel. Press Enter or Return to close the Swatches panel and return to the Appearance panel.

You can add multiple strokes to an object and apply different effects to each one, giving you the opportunity to create unique and interesting artwork.

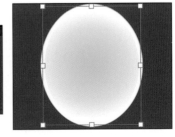

Add a new stroke.   Change the Stroke weight and color.   The result.

7 With the white stroke row selected in the Appearance panel, click the Add New Effect (*fx*) button at the bottom of the Appearance panel. Choose Path > Offset Path.

8 In the Offset Path dialog box, change the Offset to **.2 in**, and click OK.

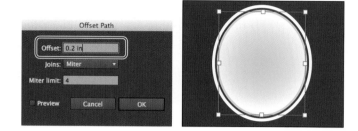

9 In the Appearance panel, click the arrow to the left of the words "Stroke: 9 pt" to toggle it open. Notice that Offset Path is a subset of Stroke. This indicates that the Offset Path effect is applied to only that Stroke.

Now that the artwork is complete, you will scale it and then save it as a symbol in the Symbols panel. Then, you'll apply it to a 3D soda can that you'll create.

10 With the Selection tool selected, hold down the Shift key and click the red rectangle in the background to select both shapes. Choose Object > Arrange > Send To Back.

11 Choose Select > All On Active Artboard. Choose Object > Group.

Applying Photoshop effects

As described earlier in the lesson, the effects in the bottom half of the Effect menu are Photoshop effects. You can apply them to either vector or bitmap objects. Photoshop effects are effects that generate pixels rather than vector data. Photoshop effects include SVG Filters, all of the effects in the bottom portion of the Effect menu, and the Drop Shadow, Inner Glow, Outer Glow, and Feather commands in the Effect > Stylize submenu.

12 With the Group selected, double-click the Scale tool () in the Tools panel.

13 In the Scale dialog box, change the Uniform Scale value to **60%** and select Scale Strokes & Effects. Click OK.

● **Note:** If you scale content and do not select Scale Strokes & Effects, the stroke weights and effects will stay the same when you scale the content.

Document raster effects settings

Whenever you apply a raster effect, Illustrator uses the document's raster effects settings to determine the resolution of the resulting image. It's important to check the document raster effects settings before you start working with effects.

You set rasterization options for a document when creating a new document or by choosing Effect > Document Raster Effects Settings. In the Document Raster Effects Settings dialog box, for all raster effects in a document or when you rasterize a vector object, you can set the Color Model, Resolution, Background, Anti-alias, Create Clipping Mask, and Add Around Object. To learn more about Document Raster Effects Settings, search for "About raster effects" in Help.

—From Illustrator Help

14 Click the Symbols panel icon (), or choose Window > Symbols to expand the Symbols panel. Select the Selection tool and, with the group selected, click the New Symbol button (⬚) at the bottom of the Symbols panel to create a symbol. In the Symbol Options dialog box, name the symbol **soda label** and choose Graphic from the Type menu. Click OK.

Create a new symbol.   Change the symbol options.   The result.

15 Choose Select > Deselect and then File > Save. Keep the file open.

▶ **Tip:** To learn more about symbols, see Lesson 14, "Working with Symbols."

Working with a 3D effect

Using the Illustrator 3D effect, you can control the appearance of 3D objects with lighting, shading, rotation, and other attributes. In this part of the lesson, you'll use two-dimensional shapes as the foundation for creating three-dimensional objects.

You can apply three types of 3D effects:

- **Extrude & Bevel**: Extends a 2D object along the object's Z axis to add depth to the object. For example, if you extrude a 2D ellipse, it becomes a cylinder.

- **Revolve**: Sweeps a path or profile in a circular direction around the global Y axis (revolve axis) to create a 3D object.

- **Rotate**: Uses the Z axis to rotate 2D artwork in 3D space and change the artwork's perspective.

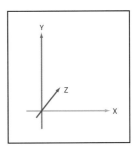

The 3D effect takes advantage of the X, Y, and Z axes.

Below are examples of each type of 3D effect applied to an initial shape on the left.

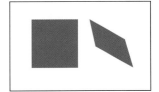

Extrude & Bevel 3D effect   Revolve 3D effect   Rotate 3D effect

Creating a revolved object

In this part of the lesson, you will explore the 3D effect called Revolve. You will create a soda can from an existing path on the second artboard, using the Revolve effect.

1   Choose Window > Workspace > Reset Essentials.

2   Click the Artboards panel icon (▦) to expand the Artboards panel.

3   Double-click Artboard 2 in the panel (not the name) to fit the artboard in the Document window. Click the Artboards panel tab to collapse the panel.

4   Choose Select > All On Active Artboard.

The selected path is half of the shape of a soda can. When you apply the Revolve effect to it, it will be revolved around the right or left edge to create a 360 degree shape, if that's what you want.

● **Note:** The stroke color overrides the fill color of the object, when revolved.

5   Click the Stroke color in the Control panel, and choose None (⬚).

6 Click the Fill color in the Control panel, and select White.

7 Choose Effect > 3D > Revolve. In the 3D Revolve Options dialog box, choose Front from the Position menu. Select Preview to see the changes. You may need to reposition the 3D Revolve Options dialog box to see the artwork.

● **Note:** Depending on the complexity of the shape being revolved and the speed of the computer you are working on, making changes in the 3D Revolve Options dialog box can take some time. It may be helpful to deselect Preview, make some changes, and then select Preview again. That way the shape does not have to "redraw" on the artboard every time a change is made in the dialog box.

▶ **Tip:** The Angle determines the degree of revolution. To create a "cut-away" look, you can change the degree to less than 360.

8 Choose Right Edge from the Offset From menu. Click OK.

This is the edge that your arc revolves around. The result varies dramatically, depending on the side that you choose and whether you have a stroke or fill applied to the original object.

Choose which edge to revolve around.

Left Edge.   Right Edge.

9 Choose File > Save, and keep the file open.

3D Revolve options

In the 3D Options dialog box for the Revolve 3D effect, there are several other options worth mentioning:

- **Angle:** Sets the number of degrees to revolve the path, between 0 and 360.
- **Cap:** Specifies whether the object appears solid (Turn Cap On For Solid Appearance) or hollow (Turn Cap Off For Hollow Appearance).
- **Offset:** Adds distance between the revolve axis and the path, to create a ring-shaped object, for instance. You can enter a value between 0 and 1,000.

—From Illustrator Help

Changing the lighting of a 3D object

The Revolve effect allows you to add one or more lights, vary the light intensity, change the object's shading color, and move lights around the object.

In this section, you will change the strength and direction of the light source.

1   With the soda can shape selected, click the words "3D Revolve" in the Appearance panel.

    If the Appearance panel is not visible, choose Window > Appearance. You may also need to scroll in the Appearance panel or resize it for easier viewing.

2   Select Preview in the 3D Revolve Options dialog box, and click More Options.

You can create custom lighting effects on your 3D object. Use the Preview window in the lower left of the 3D Revolve Options dialog box to reposition the lighting and to change the shade color.

3   Choose Plastic Shading from the Surface menu, if not already selected.

4   In the Preview window (the shaded sphere), drag the white square that represents the light source to the left. This changes the direction of the lighting. Click the New Light button (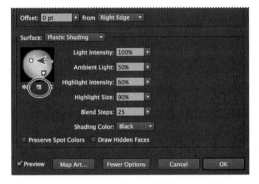) to add another light source to the soda can. Drag the second light source down and to the right.

    Try positioning them in different arrangements, and move the dialog box out of the way to see the artwork.

5   Choose Custom from the Shading Color menu. Click the colored square to the right of the Shading Color menu to open the Color Picker. In the Color Picker, change the color to a medium gray (C=**0**, M=**0**, Y=**0**, K=**50**). Click OK to close the Color Picker, and return to the 3D Revolve Options dialog box.

6   In the 3D Revolve Options dialog box, change Light Intensity to **80%** and the Ambient Light to **10%**. Leave the dialog box open.

    Ambient light controls the brightness uniformly on the surface of the 3D object.

● **Note:** Depending on the speed of the computer you are working on, it may take some time to process changes made in the 3D Revolve Options dialog box.

7   Change the Blend Steps to **40**, and click OK when it is done processing.

8   Choose File > Save.

Surface shading options

In the 3D Options dialog box for Extrude & Bevel and Revolve, Surface lets you choose options for shading surfaces such as:

- **Wireframe:** Outlines the contours of the object's geometry and makes each surface transparent.
- **No Shading:** Adds no new surface properties to the object. The 3D object has the same color as the original 2D object.
- **Diffuse Shading:** Makes the object reflect light in a soft, diffuse pattern.
- **Plastic Shading:** Makes the object reflect light as if it were made of a shiny, high-gloss material.

Note: *Depending on what option you choose, different lighting options are available. If the object only uses the 3D Rotate effect, the only Surface choices available are Diffuse Shading or No Shading.*

—From Illustrator Help

Mapping a symbol to the 3D artwork

You can map artwork to the surface of an object with a 3D effect applied. This artwork can come from Illustrator or from artwork imported from other applications, such as Photoshop. The artwork you map needs to be 2D artwork that's stored in the Symbols panel. Symbols can be any Illustrator art object, including paths, compound paths, text, raster images, mesh objects, and groups of objects. In this part of the lesson, you will map the soda label that you previously saved as a symbol to the soda can.

1   With the soda can still selected, click 3D Revolve in the Appearance panel. Drag the 3D Revolve Options dialog box off to the side, so that you can see the soda can artwork. Make sure that Preview is also selected.

2   Click the Map Art button in the 3D Revolve Options dialog box.

When you map art to a 3D object, you first need to choose which surface to map the art to. Every 3D object is composed of multiple surfaces. For example, an extruded square becomes a cube that is made of six surfaces: the front and back faces and the four side faces. Next, you will choose which surface to map the artwork to.

3 Drag the Map Art dialog box off to the side. Click the Next Surface button () until "4 of 4" appears in the Surface field. In the artwork, notice that Illustrator is highlighting the wireframe and the selected surface in red.

4 Choose soda label from the Symbol menu. Select Preview, if not already selected.

● **Note:** If you select the wrong surface, choose Clear and then map to another surface.

● **Note:** You can work in the Map Art dialog box without selecting Preview, if you find that Preview slows your system down.

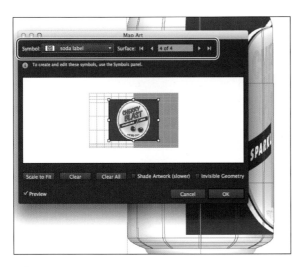

5 Deselect Preview in the Map Art dialog box to speed up the next few steps.

6 Drag the symbol into the light area of the map in the Map Art dialog box.

A light gray color marks surfaces that are currently visible. A dark gray color marks surfaces that are hidden by the object's current position.

7 Select Shade Artwork (Slower). Select Preview to see the artwork with the symbol mapped to it. You may want to reposition or resize the artwork. Then, click OK to close the Map Art dialog box.

▶ **Tip:** If you don't like the position or size of the symbol artwork, you can click the Clear button at the bottom of the dialog box to clear the symbol artwork from the current surface.

▶ **Tip:** You can interact with the symbol in the Map Art dialog box, using the normal bounding box controls to move, scale, or rotate the object.

8 In the 3D Revolve Options dialog box, click the Fewer Options button and then click the left edge of the blue square and drag to the right to spin the 3D object along the Y axis. With Preview selected, release the mouse button when you see a value of -11 in the Y axis field. Make sure that the X and Z values above and below the Y value are 0. Click OK.

The texture now wraps around the soda can. Next, you will edit the soda can color.

To map artwork to a 3D object

When mapping 3D objects, consider the following:

- Because the Map Art feature uses symbols for mapping, you can edit a symbol instance and then automatically update all surfaces that are mapped with it.

- You can interact with the symbol in the Map Art dialog box with normal bounding box controls to move, scale, or rotate the object.

- The 3D effect remembers each mapped surface on an object as a number. If you edit the 3D object or apply the same effect to a new object, there may be fewer or more sides than the original. If there are fewer surfaces than the number of surfaces defined for the original mapping, the extra artwork will be ignored.

- Because a symbol's position is relative to the center of an object surface, if the geometry of the surface changes, the symbol will be remapped relative to the new center of the object.

- You can map artwork to objects that use the Extrude & Bevel or Revolve effect, but you can't map artwork to objects that only use the Rotate effect.

—From Illustrator Help

9 With the Selection tool selected and the 3D object selected, change the Fill color to the swatch named Background in the Control panel.

Notice that the entire shape changes color, except where the symbol artwork is mapped to the surface. At this point, if necessary, you can edit the shape that you started with. If you need to rotate the 3D object, in this situation it's best done in the 3D Revolve Options dialog box.

▶ **Tip:** If you need to edit the shape, it is recommended that you first deselect the visibility column of the 3D Revolve (Mapped) effect in the Appearance panel. Then, when you are finished editing the shape, click the visibility column to show the 3D Revolve (Mapped) effect again.

10 Choose View > Show Edges to show the edges for later lessons.

11 Choose File > Save, and then choose File > Close.

Printing resources

To make optimum decisions about printing, you should understand basic printing principles, including how the resolution of your printer or the calibration and resolution of your monitor can affect the way your artwork appears when printed. Illustrator's Print dialog box is designed to help you through the printing process. For information on working in the print dialog box, see "Print dialog box options" in Illustrator Help.

For information on working with color management in Illustrator, see "Printing with color management" in Illustrator Help.

For information on the optimal ways to print a document, including information on color management, PDF workflows, and more, visit the following site:

* http://www.adobe.com/print/

For information on printing in the Adobe Creative Suite, visit the following site:

* http://www.adobe.com/designcenter/print/CS5-5-printing-guide.html

For a guide to working with transparency in the Creative Suite and how to properly print transparent content, visit the following site:

* http://partners.adobe.com/public/asn/en/print_resource_center/Transparency-DesignGuide.pdf

Note: *While the Transparency-DesignGuide.pdf guide was created for users of Creative Suite 3, it still contains useful information.*

Review questions

1 Name two ways to apply an effect to an object.

2 Where can the effects applied to an object be edited, once they are applied?

3 What three types of 3D effects are available? Give an example of why you would use each one.

4 How can you control lighting on a 3D object? Does the lighting of one 3D object affect other 3D objects?

5 What are the generic steps to map artwork to an object?

Review answers

1 You can apply an effect to an object by selecting the object and then choosing the effect from the Effect menu. You can also apply an effect by selecting the object, clicking the Add New Effect button ([fx]) in the Appearance panel, and then choosing the effect from the menu that appears.

2 You can edit effects in the Appearance panel.

3 The types of 3D effects are Extrude & Bevel, Revolve, and Rotate.

- **Extrude & Bevel:** Uses the Z axis to give a 2D object depth by extruding the object. For example, a circle becomes a cylinder.

- **Revolve:** Uses the Y axis to revolve an object around an axis. For example, an arc becomes a circle.

- **Rotate:** Uses the Z axis to rotate 2D artwork in 3D space and to change the artwork's perspective.

4 By clicking the More Options button in any of the 3D dialog boxes, you can change the light, the direction of the light, and the shade color. Settings for the light of one 3D object do not affect the settings for other 3D objects.

5 Map artwork to an object by following these steps:

a Select the artwork to be used as a symbol, and save it as a symbol in the Symbols panel.

b Select the object, and choose Effect > 3D > Extrude & Bevel or Effect > 3D > Revolve.

c Click Map Art.

d Navigate to the surface by clicking the Next Surface or Previous Surface buttons. Select the symbol from the Symbol menu. Close both dialog boxes.

13 APPLYING APPEARANCE ATTRIBUTES AND GRAPHIC STYLES

Lesson overview

In this lesson, you'll learn how to do the following:

- Create and edit an appearance attribute.

- Add a second stroke to an object.

- Reorder appearance attributes and apply them to layers.

- Copy, turn on and off, and remove appearance attributes.

- Save an appearance as a graphic style.

- Apply a graphic style to an object and a layer.

- Apply multiple graphic styles to an object or layer.

- Align content to the pixel grid.

- Work with the Slice and Slice Selection tools.

- Use the Save For Web command.

 This lesson takes approximately an hour to complete. If needed, remove the previous lesson folder from your hard disk and copy the Lesson13 folder onto it.

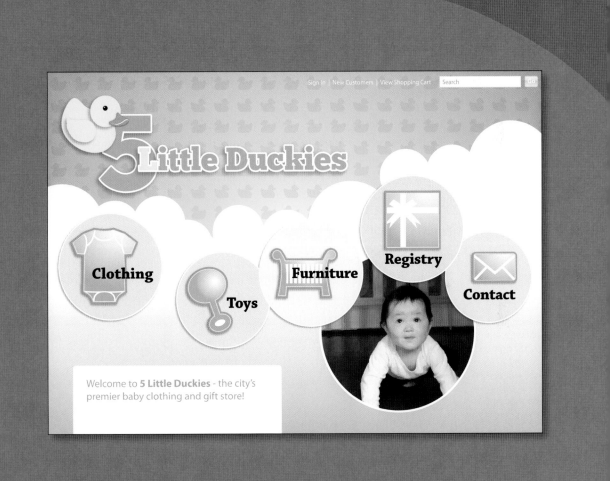

Without changing the structure of an object, you can change its look using appearance attributes, including fills, strokes, effects, transparency, and blending modes. You can save appearance attributes as graphic styles and apply them to another object. You can also edit an object that has a graphic style applied to it and then edit the graphic style—an enormous time-saver!

Getting started

In this lesson, you'll enhance the design for a web page by applying appearance attributes and graphic styles to the type, background, and buttons. Before you begin, you'll restore the default preferences for Adobe Illustrator CS6. Then, you will open the finished art file for this lesson to see what you'll create.

1 To ensure that the tools and panels function exactly as described in this lesson, delete or deactivate (by renaming) the Adobe Illustrator CS6 preferences file. See "Restoring default preferences" on page 3.

2 Start Adobe Illustrator CS6.

    ● **Note:** If you have not already done so, copy the Lesson13 folder from the Lessons folder on the *Adobe Illustrator CS6 Classroom in a Book* CD onto your hard disk. See "Copying the Classroom in a Book files" on page 2.

3 Choose File > Open. Locate the L13end.ai file in the Lesson13 folder in the Lessons folder that you copied onto your hard disk, to view the finished artwork. Leave the file open for reference, or choose File > Close.

    ● **Note:** If a color profile warning dialog box appears, click OK.

The design for the completed web page includes several graphic styles and effects, including gradients, drop shadows, and other graphics. This lesson contains a fictitious business name, made up for the purposes of the project.

● **Note:** In Mac OS, when opening lesson files, you may need to click the round, green button in the upper-left corner of the Document window to maximize the window's size.

4 Open the L13start.ai file in the Lesson13 folder, located in the Lessons folder on your hard disk.

    ● **Note:** If a color profile warning dialog box appears, click OK.

5 Choose File > Save As. In the Save As dialog box, navigate to the Lesson13 folder and open it. Name the file **webstore.ai**. Leave the Save As Type option set to Adobe Illustrator (*.AI) (Windows) or the Format option set to Adobe Illustrator (ai) (Mac OS), and click Save. In the Illustrator Options dialog box, leave the Illustrator options at their default settings and then click OK.

6 Choose View > Fit Artboard In Window.

7 Choose Window > Workspace > Reset Essentials.

    ● **Note:** If you don't see "Reset Essentials" in the Workspace menu, choose Window > Workspace > Essentials before choosing Window > Workspace > Reset Essentials.

Using appearance attributes

You can apply appearance attributes to any object, group, or layer by using effects, the Appearance panel, and the Graphic Styles panel. An appearance attribute is an aesthetic property—such as a fill, stroke, transparency, or effect—that affects the look of an object but does not affect its basic structure. An advantage of using appearance attributes is that they can be changed or removed at any time without changing the underlying object or any other attributes applied to the object in the Appearance panel (Window > Appearance).

1 Click the Appearance panel icon (⬤) on the right side of the workspace to expand the Appearance panel.

2 Select the Selection tool, and click to select the large, yellow number 5 next to the duck.

The different options available in the Appearance panel are described below:

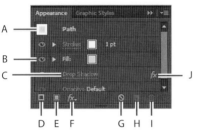

A. Selected object and thumbnail

B. Visibility column

C. Link to options

D. Add New Stroke

E. Add New Fill

F. Add New Effect

G. Clear Appearance

H. Duplicate Selected Item

I. Delete Selected Item

J. Indicates an effect applied

If you apply the Drop Shadow effect to an object, in the Appearance panel you can turn off the Drop Shadow effect, duplicate it, edit it, delete it, and more. You can also copy that effect and apply it to other shapes, groups, or layers. You can even save it as a graphic style and use it for other objects or files.

Editing and adding appearance attributes

You'll start by changing the basic appearance of the selected number 5, using the Appearance panel.

1 With the yellow number 5 still selected and with the Appearance panel showing, select the Fill attribute row by clicking to the right or left of the yellow Fill color box.

Selecting an attribute row lets you change the properties of only that attribute in the selected artwork.

2 In the Appearance panel, click the Fill color box in the Fill attribute row. In the Swatches panel that appears, click the swatch named Blue. Press the Escape key to hide the swatches.

3 Click the triangle to the left of the word "Fill" in the Appearance panel. You will see the Opacity option. Click the word "Opacity" to reveal the Transparency panel. Choose **100%** from the Opacity menu. Press the Escape key to hide the Transparency panel and to return to the Appearance panel.

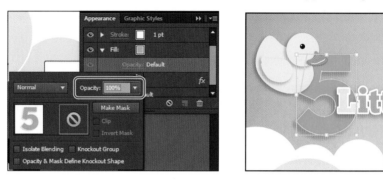

You can change some appearance attributes, like Opacity, in the Appearance panel or elsewhere in the workspace.

4 In the Appearance panel, click the phrase "1 pt" in the Stroke Appearance panel row. Click the underlined word "Stroke" to reveal the Stroke panel. Change the Stroke weight to **3 pt**. Click the Align Stroke To Outside button (■). Press the Escape key to hide the Stroke panel. Leave the Appearance panel open.

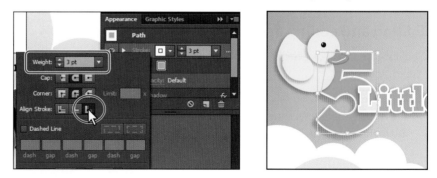

When you select certain attributes in the Appearance panel, like Stroke, new options appear. You can change the Stroke color and the Stroke weight without clicking the word "Stroke" to reveal the Stroke panel.

5 Choose Select > Deselect, and then choose File > Save.

Adding another stroke

Artwork in Illustrator can have more than one stroke and fill applied to them to add interesting design elements. You'll now add another stroke to an object, using the Appearance panel.

1 Select the Zoom tool (🔍), and drag a marquee across the shirt shape underneath the "Clothing" text.

2 With the Selection tool, click to select the shirt shape. In the Appearance panel, change the Stroke weight to **5 pt**. Click the Stroke color box (▣), and select the swatch named Medium gray.

3 Click the underlined word "Stroke," and click the Align Stroke To Outside button (▣). Press the Escape key to hide the Stroke panel, leaving the Appearance panel open.

▶ **Tip:** Other ways to close panels that appear in the Appearance panel, such as the Color panel, include pressing the Escape key or clicking the Stroke attribute row.

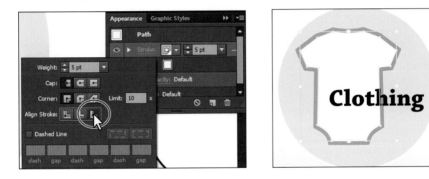

● **Note:** Depending on your operating system, the selection color of objects (the bounding box) may be different and that's okay.

4 In the Appearance panel, click the Add New Stroke button (▣) at the bottom of the panel. A stroke is added above the original stroke row. It has the same color and stroke weight as the first stroke.

5 For the new stroke, leave Stroke weight at 5 pt. Click the Stroke color box in the new appearance row to open the Swatches panel. Select Orange for the color. Press Enter or Return to close the Swatches panel and to return to the Appearance panel.

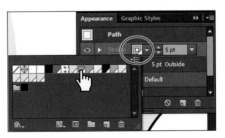

Next, you will add an effect to change the offset of the stroke by bringing it toward the center of the shirt shape.

6 With the Stroke attribute row still selected, click the Add New Effect button (▣) at the bottom of the Appearance panel. Choose Path > Offset Path from the menu that appears.

7   Select Preview in the Offset Path dialog box to see the effect of offsetting as you change the values. Change Offset to **-1 px**, and then click OK.

8   In the Appearance panel, click the arrow to the left of the orange Stroke row to reveal the Offset Path and Opacity attributes. Click the word "Opacity," and choose 70% from the Opacity menu. Press the Escape key to hide the Transparency panel.

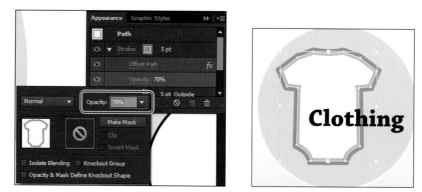

9   Deselect the eye icon () to the left of Offset Path to hide that effect. Notice that the stroke for the shirt shape on the artboard changes. Select the Visibility column to apply the Offset Path effect again.

By clicking the eye icon in the Appearance panel, you disable an attribute without deleting it.

Tip: You can view all hidden attributes by choosing Show All Hidden Attributes from the Appearance panel menu.

10 Choose Select > Deselect, and then choose File > Save.

Adding another fill

You'll now add another fill to an object, using the Appearance panel. This can be a great way to achieve interesting design effects with just one object.

1   Choose View > Fit Artboard In Window.

2   With the Selection tool (▶), click the orange gradient-filled shape behind the "5 Little Duckies" text shapes to select it.

3   In the Appearance panel, click the Fill attribute row to select it.

4   Click the Add New Fill button (▥) at the bottom of the panel.

A new fill is added above the existing fill in the Appearance panel.

5   With the new fill attribute row selected, click the Fill color box and select the Duck pattern. This new fill will cover the existing orange/yellow gradient fill. Press the Escape key to hide the swatches.

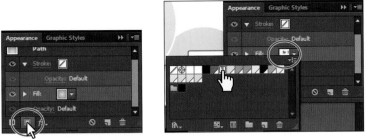

6   Click the triangle to the left of the selected Fill row to reveal the word "Opacity," and scroll down in the panel if necessary. Click the underlined word "Opacity" to reveal the Transparency panel.

7   In the Transparency panel, choose Multiply from the Blending Mode menu. Change the Opacity to **10%**, and press Enter or Return to close the panel.

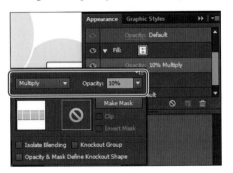

● **Note:** The thumbnail you see in the transparency options may look different, depending on your operating system.

8   Choose File > Save, and leave the shape selected.

Reordering appearance attributes

The ordering of the appearance attribute rows can greatly change how your artwork looks. In the Appearance panel, fills and strokes are listed in stacking order; top to bottom in the panel correlates to front to back in the artwork. You can reorder attribute rows in a way similar to dragging layers in the Layers panel, to rearrange the stacking order. Now, you'll change the appearance of the artwork by reordering attributes in the Appearance panel.

1   Resize the Appearance panel so that you can view all its contents. Click the triangle (▶) to the left of all of the appearance rows to hide their properties.

2   Drag the new Fill attribute row (with the Duck pattern swatch applied) below the original Fill attribute row.

Moving the new Fill attribute below the original Fill attribute changes the look of the artwork. The original yellow/orange gradient fill is now covering the new fill.

3   Choose Edit > Undo Move Appearance Item so that the new Fill row is once
    again between the stroke and original Fill rows in the Appearance panel.

Applying an appearance to a layer

You can also apply simple appearance attributes to layers. For example, to make
everything on a layer 50% opaque, target that layer and change the opacity.

Next, you'll target a layer and add a drop shadow.

1   Click the Layers panel icon (![icon]) to open the panel. In the Layers panel, click the
    triangle to the left of the Buttons layer to view its content, if necessary.

2   Click the target icon (![icon]) to the right of the circles sublayer.

Note: The layer
colors you see may be
different, depending on
your operating system,
and that's okay.

3   Open the Appearance panel, and notice that it says Layer at the top. This
    indicates that any attributes applied will be applied to all content on that layer.
    When you select items that contain other items, such as a layer or group, the
    Appearance panel displays a Contents item, which you can double-click to edit.

4   Click the Add New Effect button (![fx icon]) at the bottom of the Appearance panel,
    and choose Stylize > Drop Shadow.

5   In the Drop Shadow dialog box, change the Opacity to **25%**, the X Offset
    to **-2 px**, the Y Offset to **2 px**, and the Blur to **2 px**. Click OK.

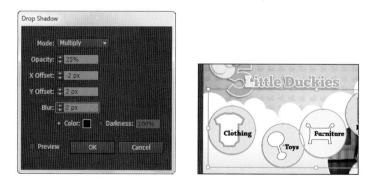

6   Click the Layers panel icon (![icon]), and notice that the target icon now has a shaded
    center (![icon]), indicating that the layer has appearance attributes applied to it.

7   Choose Select > Deselect, and then choose File > Save.

Using graphic styles

A graphic style is a saved set of appearance attributes that you can reuse. By applying graphic styles, you can quickly and globally change the appearance of objects and text.

The Graphic Styles panel (Window > Graphic Styles) lets you create, name, save, apply, and remove effects and attributes for objects, layers, and groups. You can also break the link between an object and an applied graphic style to edit that object's attributes without affecting other objects that use the same graphic style.

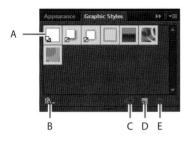

A. Graphic style thumbnail

B. Graphic Styles Libraries Menu

C. Break Link To Graphic Style

D. New Graphic Style

E. Delete Graphic Style

For example, if you have a map that uses a shape to represent a city, you can create a graphic style that paints the shape green and adds a drop shadow. You can then use that graphic style to paint all the city shapes on the map. If you decide to use a different color, you can change the fill color of the graphic style to blue. All the objects that use that graphic style are then updated to blue.

Creating and saving a graphic style

Now, you'll save and name a new graphic style using the appearance attributes you just specified for the shirt shape below the "Clothing" text. You will then apply the same appearance attributes to the other button shapes.

1   Choose Reset Essentials from the workspace switcher in the Application bar.

2   Click the Graphic Styles panel icon (▥) on the right side of the workspace to open the Graphic Styles panel.

3   With the Selection tool (▶), click to select the shirt shape beneath the "Clothing" text.

> **Note:** Depending on your operating system, the bounding box and edges (the yellow outlines in the figure) of some selected objects may be a different color, and that's okay.

> **Tip:** To create a graphic style, you can also click to select the object that you are making the graphic style from. In the Appearance panel, drag the appearance thumbnail at the top of the listing into the Graphic Styles panel.

4 In the Graphic Styles panel, click the New Graphic Style button () at the bottom of the panel.

5 In the Graphic Styles panel, double-click the new Graphic Style thumbnail. In the Graphic Style Options dialog box, name the new style **Icons**. Click OK.

Create a new graphic style.

Double-click the graphic style.

Rename the graphic style.

6 Click the Appearance panel icon and, at the top of the Appearance panel, you will see Path: Icons. This indicates that a graphic style called Icons is applied to the selected artwork (a path).

7 Choose Select > Deselect and then File > Save.

Applying a graphic style to an object

Graphic styles can be easily applied to other objects. Next, you will apply the Icons graphic style you just created to another shape.

1 With the Selection tool (⬥), click to select the baby rattle shape to the left of the text "Toys."

2 Click the Graphic Styles panel tab to reveal the panel, and then click the graphic style named Icons to apply its attributes.

You can also apply a graphic style by dragging its thumbnail directly from the Graphic Styles panel onto an object, even if the object isn't selected.

3 Choose File > Save.

Replacing graphic style attributes

Once you create a graphic style, you can still edit the object that the style is applied to. You can also update a graphic style, and all artwork with that style applied will update their appearance as well.

1   With the Selection tool (⬏), click to select the shirt shape again. In the Graphic Styles panel, you will see that the Icons graphic style thumbnail is highlighted (has a border around it), indicating that it is applied.

2   Click the Appearance panel tab. Change the stroke color of the orange stroke to white. Click the Graphic Styles panel tab to see that the graphic style is no longer highlighted, which means that the graphic style is no longer applied.

3   Press the Alt (Windows) or Option (Mac OS) key, and drag the shirt shape on top of the Icons graphic style thumbnail in the Graphic Styles panel. Release the mouse button and then the modifier key when the thumbnail is highlighted.

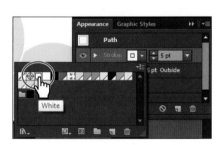
Change the stroke color.

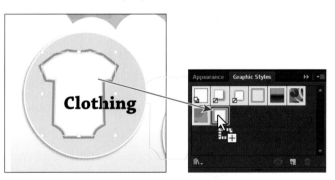
Alt-drag (Windows) or Option-drag (Mac OS) the shape onto the style.

4   Choose Select > Deselect.

5   With the Selection tool, Shift-click the shape behind the text "Furniture," the white shape above the text "Registry," and the white shape above the text "Contact."

6   Click the Icons graphic style in the Graphic Styles panel to apply its attributes.

7   Choose Select > Deselect and then File > Save.

Applying a graphic style to a layer

When a graphic style is applied to a layer, everything added to that layer has that same style applied to it. Now, you'll apply a new graphic style to a layer.

1   Click the Appearance panel tab. You will see No Selection: Icons at the top of the panel (you may need to scroll up). When you apply appearance settings, graphic styles, and more to artwork, the next shape you draw will have the appearance settings listed in the Appearance panel.

2 Click the Clear Appearance button (⊘) at the bottom of the Appearance panel. Select the No Selection appearance name or thumbnail at the top of the panel.

The Clear Appearance button removes all appearance attributes applied to an object, including any stroke or fill. By clicking the Clear Appearance button with nothing selected, you are setting the default appearance for new shapes.

3 Click the Add New Effect button (*fx.*), and choose Stylize > Drop Shadow.

4 In the Drop Shadow dialog box, change the Opacity to **100%**, the X Offset to **-2 px**, the Y Offset to **2 px**, and the Blur to **2 px**. Leave the rest of the settings at default, and click OK. In the Appearance panel, notice that Drop Shadow appears in the list. You may need to scroll in the Appearance panel to see it listed.

Clear the appearance.   Add a drop shadow.   The result.

A new graphic style is created from the current appearance attributes displayed in the Appearance panel, if nothing is selected in the Document window.

5 Click the Graphic Styles panel tab. Alt-click (Windows) or Option-click (Mac OS) the New Graphic Style button (🔲), and name the new style **Icons shadow** in the Graphic Style Options dialog box. Click OK.

Pressing the modifier key opens the dialog box when you click. The graphic style thumbnail shows a box with a slash on the lower-left corner of the thumbnail. This indicates that the graphic style has no stroke and no fill.

Now, you'll target the bases sublayer to apply a drop shadow to all the shapes on that layer. Targeting selects the path(s) on that layer in the artwork.

6 Click the Layers panel icon (🔲) on the right side of the workspace to open the Layers panel.

7 In the Layers panel, click the triangle (▶) to the left of the Buttons layer to expand the layer, if it isn't already. Click the target icon (◎) to the right of the bases sublayer name.

8 Click the Graphic Styles panel icon (), and then click the Icons shadow style thumbnail to apply the style to the layer and all its contents. Keep the shapes selected on the artboard.

Select the layer target icon.

Apply a graphic style.

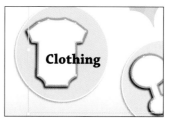

The result.

If you apply multiple graphic styles to an object, the latest graphic style overwrites the previous. If you apply a graphic style to artwork and then apply a graphic style to the layer (or sublayer) that it's on, the graphic style formatting is added together and is cumulative.

Notice that the shape above the text "Registry" does not have the drop shadow applied. That's because that shape is not on the bases sublayer.

9 Click the Layers panel icon (), and drag the <Path> object at the top of the Buttons layer on top of the bases sublayer to add it to that sublayer and to apply the Icons shadow graphic style to the Registry shape.

10 Choose Select > Deselect and then File > Save.

Editing a graphic style applied to a layer

Next, you will edit the drop shadow applied to the layer.

1 Click the Appearance panel icon () on the right side of the workspace to open the Appearance panel.

2 With the Selection tool, click to select the shirt shape beneath the "Clothing" text.

In the Appearance panel, notice the name Layer: Icons shadow at the top of the panel. The Appearance panel shows that the shirt shape is on a layer with a graphic style called Icons shadow applied to it.

3 Click the words Layer: Icons shadow to access the Drop Shadow effect applied to the layer. This also selects all of the shapes on the layer.

> **Tip:** You can also select the bases sublayer target icon in the Layers panel and then edit the effect in the Appearance panel.

4 Click the underlined text Drop Shadow in the Appearance panel and, in the Drop Shadow dialog box, change Opacity to **25%**. Click OK. Leave the Appearance panel showing.

5 Choose Select > Deselect, and then choose File > Save.

Applying an existing graphic style

You can also apply graphic styles to your artwork from graphic style libraries that come with Illustrator CS6. Now, you'll add graphic styles to a button in the design.

1 Choose View > Fit Artboard In Window.

Now, you'll apply an existing graphic style to the Go button that is located off the upper-right corner of the artboard.

▶ **Tip:** Use the arrows at the bottom of the Illuminate Styles library panel to load the previous or next graphic styles library in the panel.

2 Click the Graphic Styles panel tab. Click the Graphic Styles Libraries Menu button (▨), and choose Illuminate Styles. Scroll down in the Illuminate Styles panel, and click the Illuminate Yellow graphic style. Clicking that style adds it to the Graphic Styles panel for the document.

● **Note:** When you click a graphic style from a library, the graphic style is added to the Graphic Styles panel for that document.

3 At the bottom of the Illuminate Styles panel, click the Graphic Styles Libraries Menu button (▨) and choose Additive. In the Additive panel, click the Round Corners 10 pt graphic style thumbnail to add it to the Graphic Styles panel as well. Close the Additive panel.

4 With the Selection tool (▶), click to select the white rectangle off the upper-right corner of the artboard (to the right of the Search field). Be careful not to select the white text "Go" that is on top of it.

5 Right-click (Windows) or Control-click (Mac OS), and hold down the mouse button on the Illuminate Yellow style thumbnail in the Graphic Styles panel to preview the graphic style on the shape. Release the mouse button (and then the Control key on Mac OS) when finished.

Previewing a graphic style is a great way to see how the graphic style will affect the selected object, without actually applying it.

6 Click the Illuminate Yellow graphic style in the Graphic Styles panel to apply it to the shape. Click the Graphic Styles panel tab to collapse the panel group.

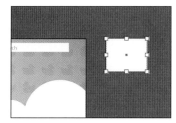

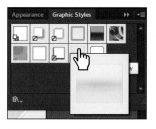

Select the white rectangle.   Preview the graphic style.   The result.

7 Choose File > Save, and leave the shape selected.

Note: You may see a warning icon appear on the end of the Control panel. That's okay. This is a helpful indicator that the topmost fill/stroke is not active.

Applying multiple graphic styles

You can apply a graphic style to an object that already has a graphic style applied. This can be useful if you want to add properties to an object from another graphic style.

1 With the rectangle behind the text "Go" still selected, click the Style menu in the Control panel. In the Graphic Styles panel that appears, click to apply the Round Corners 10 pt graphic style to the Go button shape.

Notice that the fills and the stroke are no longer visible. Graphic styles replace the formatting on selected objects, by default.

2 Choose Edit > Undo Graphic Styles.

3 Click the Style menu in the Control panel again, and Alt-click (Windows) or Option-click (Mac OS) the Round Corners 10 pt graphic style.

Notice that, on the Go button, the fills and stroke are preserved and that the corners are rounded as well (you may need to zoom in). Alt-clicking (Windows) or Option-clicking (Mac OS) adds the graphic style formatting to the existing formatting, rather than replacing it.

Note: If the Style menu doesn't appear in the Control panel, open the Graphic Styles panel by clicking its icon on the right side of the workspace.

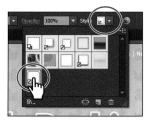

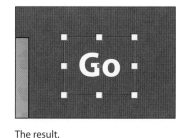

Apply the graphic style.   The result.   The final result.

4 With the Selection tool (▶), Shift-click the text "Go" and choose Object > Group.

5. Click the X, Y, W, or H link in the Control panel to reveal the Transform panel (Window > Transform). Select Scale Strokes & Effects at the bottom of the Transform panel.

6. In the Transform panel, click the Constrain Width And Height Proportions button (![icon]). Change the width (W) to **25**. Press Enter or Return to change the height as well, and hide the Transform panel.

7. Drag the button group to the right of the Search field, using the Smart Guides to align it.

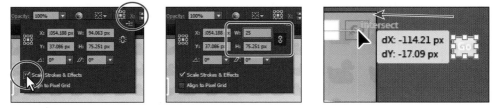

Select Scale Strokes & Effects.   Change the width.   Drag the button into position.

8. Choose Select > Deselect and then File > Save.

Applying a graphic style to text

Next, you'll apply an existing graphic style to some text.

1. With the Selection tool (![icon]), click to select the "Clothing" text. Choose Select > Same > Fill & Stroke to select all five text objects.

2. Click the Graphic Styles panel icon (![icon]) to expand the panel, if necessary. Choose Override Character Color from the Graphic Styles panel menu (![icon]), if it's not already selected.

   When you apply a graphic style to type, the fill color of the text overrides the fill color of the graphic style. To prevent that, choose Override Character Color.

3. Choose Use Text For Preview from the Graphic Styles panel menu (![icon]).

4. In the Graphic Styles panel, right-click (Windows) or Control-click (Mac OS) and hold down the mouse button on the Blue Neon graphic style to preview the graphic style on the text. Release the mouse button (and the Control key on Mac OS), and then click the Blue Neon graphic style to apply it.

   If Override Character Color had been deselected, the fill would still be black.

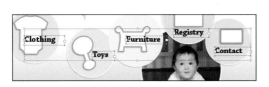

5 Click the Appearance panel tab, and then click the Clear Appearance button () at the bottom of the panel to remove the graphic style formatting.

6 Choose Select > Deselect and then File > Save.

Copying and removing graphic styles

When you create several graphic styles and appearances, you may want to use them on other objects in your artwork. You can use the Graphic Styles panel, the Appearance panel, the Eyedropper tool, or the Live Paint Bucket tool to apply and copy appearance attributes. Now, you'll use the Layers panel to copy an attribute from one layer to another.

1 Expand the Layers panel to see all the layers. With the triangle to the left of the Buttons layer expanded, Alt-drag (Windows) or Option-drag (Mac OS) the target icon () from the bases sublayer onto the target icon of the text sublayer above it.

Using the Alt (Windows) or Option (Mac OS) key as you drag, copies appearance attributes from one layer to another. The shaded target icon () indicates that the layer contains appearance attributes. To move, not copy, an appearance or style from one layer or object to another, drag the target icon. The text now has the same subtle drop shadow applied.

Now, you'll remove the appearance attributes from that layer, using the Layers panel.

2 In the Layers panel, click the target icon to the right of the text sublayer.

3 Drag the target icon to the Trash button () at the bottom of the Layers panel to remove the appearance attribute. Click the Layers panel tab to collapse it.

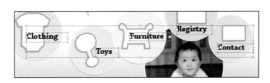

You can also remove attributes of a selected object or layer in the Appearance panel. To do this, select the object and then choose Reduce To Basic Appearance from the panel menu. This removes all appearance attributes except a single fill and stroke.

4 Choose Select > Deselect, and then File > Save.

Creating web graphics

● **Note:** To learn more about what the term raster means, see the section "Vector versus bitmap graphics" in Lesson 15, "Combining Illustrator CS6 Graphics with Other Adobe Applications."

Creating content for the web requires that vector content be converted to raster content. You can do this using the Save For Web command. Images can be saved in a multitude of file formats, such as GIF, JPEG, and PNG. GIF, JPEG, and PNG are optimized for use on the web and are compatible with most browsers, yet they each have different capabilities. The key to the effective use of images on a website is finding the balance of resolution, size, and color to achieve optimal quality.

● **Note:** This section is meant as an introduction to the main tools and processes for saving web content from Illustrator and is not a comprehensive guide. To learn more about working with web graphics, search for "File formats for exporting artwork" in Illustrator Help (Help > Illustrator Help).

Aligning content to the pixel grid

It is critical that raster images look sharp, especially standard web graphics at 72-ppi (pixels per inch) resolution. To enable web designers to create pixel-accurate designs, you can align artwork to the pixel grid. The pixel grid is a grid of 72 squares per inch, vertically and horizontally, that is viewable when you zoom to 600% or higher when Pixel Preview mode is enabled (View > Pixel Preview).

When the pixel-aligned property is enabled for an object, all the horizontal and vertical segments in the object get aligned to the pixel grid, which provides a crisp appearance to strokes. When you create a new document, you can set the Align New Objects To Pixel Grid option at the document level by choosing Web from the Profile menu in the New Document dialog box. This makes all artwork (that is able to be aligned to the pixel grid) align to the pixel grid automatically. You can also align content to the pixel grid later, as you will do in this section.

1 With the webstore.ai file still open, choose File > New. In the New Document dialog box, choose Web from the Profile menu. Click the triangle to the left of the Advanced content, toward the bottom of the dialog box.

In the Advanced settings, you can see that the Color Mode is RGB for all artwork you create, the Raster Effects are 72 ppi, and Align New Objects To Pixel Grid is selected.

2 Click Cancel.

3 In the webstore.ai file, choose File > Document Color Mode and you will see that RGB is selected.

After you create a document, you can change the document color mode. This sets the default color mode for all *new* colors you create.

4 Select the Zoom tool (🔍), and drag a marquee around the text shapes "Little" to the right of the duck in the header, to zoom in closely. This is text that has been converted to outlines (paths).

5 Choose View > Pixel Preview to preview a rasterized version of the design and the pixel grid.

▶ **Tip:** You can turn off the pixel grid by choosing Edit > Preferences > Guides & Grid (Windows) or Illustrator > Preferences > Guides & Grid (Mac OS) and deselecting Show Pixel Grid (Above 600% Zoom).

The artwork in Preview mode

The artwork in Pixel Preview mode

By zooming in to at least 600%, and with Pixel Preview turned on, you can see a pixel grid appear, as in the figure. The pixel grid divides the artboard into 1-point (1/72 inch) increments.

6 With the Selection tool (▶), click to select the group of text shapes that begins with "Little."

7 Click the word "Transform" (or X, Y, W, or H) in the Control panel, and select Align To Pixel Grid at the bottom of the Transform panel. Deselect and select Align To Pixel Grid to see the change on the edge of the text shapes.

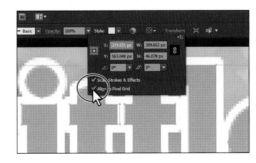

Note: Objects that are pixel-aligned, but do not have any straight vertical or horizontal segments, are not modified to align to the pixel grid. For example, because a rotated rectangle does not have straight vertical or horizontal segments, it is not nudged to produce crisp paths when the pixel-aligned property is set for it.

8 Choose View > Fit Artboard In Window.

9 Choose Select > Object > Not Aligned To Pixel Grid to select all artwork in the document that is able to be, but is not currently, aligned to the pixel grid.

10 Click the word "Transform" in the Control panel, and select Align To Pixel Grid. Leave the Transform panel showing.

11 Choose Align New Objects To Pixel Grid from the Transform panel menu (▼≣).
Press the Escape key to hide the Transform panel.

This sets all *new* artwork to be aligned to the pixel grid automatically. Once again, if you had chosen the Web Profile when creating a document, this would be set already.

12 Choose Select > Deselect, and then choose File > Save.

Text anti-aliasing

The Character panel in Illustrator provides the following text anti-aliasing options: None, Sharp, Crisp, and Strong. You can set anti-aliasing options for each text frame. These text anti-aliasing attributes get saved as part of the document.

While exporting to web formats like JPEG and GIF using the File > Save For Web command, the following options are available in the anti-aliasing drop-down list: None, Art Optimized, and Type Optimized.

- Art Optimized option produces raster for each of these formats in the same way as in earlier versions. However, text anti-aliasing options are not honored while rasterizing the artwork in this case.

- Type Optimized option honors the newly introduced anti-aliasing options for the text frames in the raster produced.

—From Illustrator Help

Slicing content

● **Note:** To learn more about creating slices, search for "Create slices" in Adobe Illustrator Help (Help > Illustrator Help).

If you create artwork on an artboard and choose File > Save For Web, Illustrator creates a single image file the size of the artboard. You can create multiple artboards for artwork that each contain a piece of the web page, like a button, and save each artboard as a separate image file.

You can also design your artwork on an artboard and slice the content. In Illustrator, you can create slices to define the boundaries of different web elements in your artwork. For example, if you design an entire web page on an artboard and there is a vector shape that you want to save as a button for your website, that artwork can be optimized in GIF format, while the rest of the image is optimized as a JPEG file. You can isolate the button image by creating a slice. When you save the artwork as a web page using the Save For Web command, you can choose to save each slice as an independent file with its own format and settings.

Next, you will create a new layer that will contain the slices and then you will create slices for different parts of the artwork.

1   Click the Layers panel icon () to open the Layers panel. Click to select the Top nav layer. Alt-click (Windows) or Option-click (Mac OS) the Create New Layer button ( ) at the bottom of the Layers panel. In the Layer Options dialog box, change the name of the layer to Slices and click OK. Make sure that the new layer named Slices is selected.

Note: To learn more about creating layers, see the section "Creating layers" in Lesson 8, "Working With Layers." The new layer you create may have a different layer color and that's okay.

When you create slices, they are listed in the Layers panel and can be selected, deleted, resized, and more. It helps to keep them on their own layer so that you can more easily manage them, but this isn't necessary.

2   Select the Slice tool ( ) in the Tools panel. Click and drag a slice around the duck, the number 5, and the text "Little Duckies." Don't worry about it fitting perfectly right now; you will edit it later.

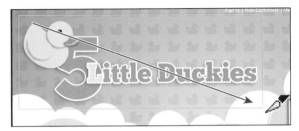

When you create a slice, Illustrator slices the surrounding artwork into automatic slices to maintain the layout of the page. Auto slices account for the areas of your artwork that you did not define as a slice. Illustrator regenerates auto slices every time you add or edit your own slices. Also, notice the number 3 in the corner of the slice you created. Illustrator numbers slices from left to right and top to bottom, beginning in the upper-left corner of the artwork.

Next, you will create a slice based on selected content.

3   Select the Selection tool ( ) and click the Go button group in the upper-right corner of the artboard. You may want to zoom in.

4   Select the Slices layer in the Layers panel to place the new slice on that layer.

5   Choose Object > Slice > Create From Selection.

Illustrator can create slices based on guides you create or on content that you select in the Document window.

Tip: Use the Object > Slice > Make command when you want the slice dimensions to match the boundary of an element in your artwork. If you move or modify the element, the slice area automatically adjusts to encompass the new artwork.

Selecting and editing slices

Note: To learn more about editing slices, search for "Create slices" in Adobe Help (Help > Illustrator Help).

Editing user slices is necessary, for instance, when sliced content changes or when what is included in the slice needs to change.

1 Choose View > Fit Artboard In Window.

2 Select the Slice Selection tool () from the Slice tool group in the Tools panel by clicking and holding down on the Slice tool (✐).

3 Click in the center of the first slice you created over the "5 Little Duckies" text. The selected slice is highlighted, and four corner bounding points appear.

   The Slice Selection tool allows you to edit slices you've created using the different methods. You can also select a user slice with the Selection or Direct Selection tools by clicking the stroke (edge) of the slice or from within the Layers panel.

4 Position the pointer over the left edge of the selected slice. When a double arrow appears, click and drag to the left until it snaps to the left edge of the artboard.

5 Position the pointer over the lower-right bounding point of the selected slice, and click and drag the slice to tighten it around the "5 Little Duckies" text, if necessary.

When slicing content, you should contain all appearance attributes, like drop shadows, in the slice area. This can be difficult if the shadow is blurred quite a bit. Using the Object > Slice > Create From Selection command will create a slice that surrounds all appearance properties, like effects, if those effects are applied directly to the artwork and not to the layer the artwork is on. Using the Slice Selection tool, you can click and drag a slice, copy and paste it, delete it, and much more.

6 Choose Select > Deselect, and then choose View > Lock Slices so that you cannot select them. Choose File > Save.

Using the Save For Web command

After having sliced your artwork, if necessary, you can then optimize that artwork for use on the web. You can use the File > Save For Web command to select optimization options and to preview optimized artwork. This is the last step in the process of creating content for the web.

1 Choose View > Hide Slices.

While working on your artwork, you don't have to have the slices showing. This can make it so that you can concentrate on selecting artwork without selecting slices. You can also hide the layer that the slices are on if you created a layer for them in the Layers panel.

2 Select the Selection tool (![selection tool icon]), and Shift-click the duck, the number 5, the "Little Duckies" text, and the Go button in the upper-right corner.

3 Choose Object > Hide > Other Layers.

When you save the sliced content using the Save For Web command, all content that is showing in a slice will be flattened into a raster image. If you want to have transparency in the selected artwork (part of the image will be see-through), you need to first hide what you don't want to save. The areas where you see the artboard in a slice can be transparent, depending on the type of image you choose.

4 Choose Select > Deselect, and then choose File > Save.

5 Choose View > Show Slices, and ensure that the artwork and drop shadows are contained within the slice. If not, you can resize either slice.

Note: To resize the slices, you would need to make sure that they are unlocked. Choose View > Lock Slices (if a checkmark appears to the left of the menu item, they are locked).

6 Choose File > Save For Web.

7 In the Save For Web dialog box, click the 2-Up tab at the top of the dialog box to select that display option, if it's not already selected.

    This shows a split window with the original artwork on the left and the optimized artwork on the right.

8 With the Slice Selection tool (![slice selection tool icon]) selected, click in the optimized area on the right. Click to select the slice that covers the duck and text artwork, if it isn't selected already. You can tell when a slice is selected because of the light brown border around it.

9 In the Preset area on the right side of the dialog box, choose PNG-24 from the Optimized File Format menu (below Name).

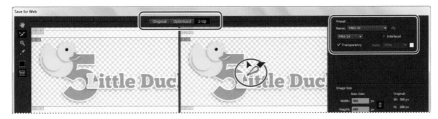

You can choose from four file formats, including GIF, JPEG, PNG-8, and PNG-24, as well as set the options for each in the Preset area. The available options change depending on the file format you select. If your image contains multiple slices that you are going to save, be sure to select each separately and to optimize all the slices.

10 Choose Selected Slices from the Export menu.

Any slices that you select in the Save For Web dialog box will be exported. You can select multiple slices, after you've assigned optimization settings to them, by Shift-clicking the desired slices. By choosing All User Slices from the Export menu, all slices that you created will be exported.

● **Note:** If nothing happens after clicking the Preview button, try clicking again. You may also need to click the Select Browser Menu button to the right of the Preview button and choose Edit List to add a new browser.

11 Click the Preview button in the lower-left corner of the dialog box to launch the default web browser on your computer and to preview the sliced content. After viewing the content, close the browser and return to Illustrator.

12 In the Save For Web dialog box, click Save.

13 In the Save Optimized As dialog box, navigate to the Lesson13 folder in the Lessons folder and open it. Change the name to **logo**, and click Save.

14 Navigate to your Lesson13 folder, and open the images folder that Illustrator generated. In that folder, you will see the single image that is named according to the name entered in the Save Optimized dialog box, with the slice number appended to the end.

▶ **Tip:** When you select slices in the Save For Web dialog box and set optimization settings, they are saved with the slices in the file. That means, if you need to make a change to artwork and save that slice again, you can simply select the slice with the Slice Selection tool and choose File > Save Selected Slices. The saved optimization settings are applied to the artwork, and it is saved where you determine.

● **Note:** If a Save As dialog box appears, save the file in the same location as the original and overwrite the original.

15 Return to Illustrator, and open the Layers panel. Choose Show All Layers from the panel menu (▼≡) to reveal blue icons on the white shapes.

16 Choose File > Save and then File > Close.

Review questions

1   How do you add a second stroke to an object?

2   What's the difference between applying a graphic style to a layer versus applying it to an object?

3   How do you add to an existing graphic style?

4   How do you remove an appearance attribute using the Layers panel?

5   Why do we align content to the pixel grid?

6   Name the three image file types that can be chosen in the Save For Web dialog box.

Review answers

1   Click the Add New Stroke button in the Appearance panel, or choose Add New Stroke from the Appearance panel menu. A stroke is added to the top of the appearance list. It has the same color and stroke weight as the original stroke.

2   After a graphic style is applied to a layer, everything you add to that layer has that style applied to it. For example, if you create a circle on Layer 1 and then move that circle to Layer 2, which has a Drop Shadow effect applied, the circle adopts that effect.

   When a style is applied to a single object, other objects on that layer are not affected. For example, if a triangle object has a Roughen effect applied to its path and you move it to another layer, it retains the Roughen effect.

3   With a graphic style applied to an object, Alt-click (Windows) or Option-click (Mac OS) another graphic style in the Graphic Styles panel.

4   In the Layers panel, click the target icon of a layer. Drag the target icon to the Delete Selection button in the Layers panel to remove the appearance attribute. You can also remove the appearance attribute of a selected object or layer using the Appearance panel. Select the object, and choose Reduce To Basic Appearance from the Appearance panel menu to return the object to its original state.

5   When the pixel-aligned property is enabled for an object, all the horizontal and vertical segments in the object get aligned to the pixel grid, which provides a crisp appearance to strokes.

6   The three image file types that can be chosen in the Save For Web dialog box are: JPEG, GIF, and PNG. PNG has two versions: PNG-8 and PNG-24.

14 WORKING WITH SYMBOLS

Lesson overview

In this lesson, you'll learn how to do the following:

- Work with existing symbols.

- Create a symbol.

- Modify and redefine a symbol.

- Use the Symbolism tools.

- Store and retrieve artwork in the Symbols panel.

- Work with symbols and Adobe Flash®.

 This lesson takes approximately an hour to complete. If needed, remove the previous lesson folder from your hard disk and copy the Lesson14 folder onto it.

The Symbols panel lets you apply multiple objects by painting them on the page. Symbols used in combination with the Symbolism tools offer options that make creating repetitive shapes, such as blades of grass, easy and fun. You can also use the Symbols panel as a database to store artwork and to map symbols to 3D objects.

Getting started

In this lesson, you'll add symbols to a map. Before you begin, restore the default preferences for Adobe Illustrator. Then, open the file containing the finished artwork to see what you are going to create.

1 To ensure that the tools and panels function exactly as described in this lesson, delete or deactivate (by renaming) the Adobe Illustrator CS6 preferences file. See "Restoring default preferences" on page 3.

2 Start Adobe Illustrator CS6.

● **Note:** If you have not already done so, copy the Lesson14 folder from the Lessons folder on the *Adobe Illustrator CS6 Classroom in a Book* CD onto your hard disk. See "Copying the Classroom in a Book files" on page 2.

3 Choose File > Open, and open the L14end.ai file in the Lesson14 folder in the Lessons folder on your hard disk.

If you want to view the finished map as you work, choose View > Zoom Out and adjust the window size. Use the Hand tool (🖐) to move the artwork where you want it in the window. If you don't want to leave the image open, choose File > Close.

To begin working, you'll open an existing art file.

● **Note:** In Mac OS, when opening lesson files, you may need to click the round, green button in the upper-left corner of the Document window to maximize the window's size.

4 Choose File > Open to open the L14start.ai file in the Lesson14 folder, located in the Lessons folder on your hard disk.

5 Choose File > Save As. In the Save As dialog box, name the file **map.ai** and navigate to the Lesson14 folder. Leave the Save As Type option set to Adobe Illustrator (*.AI) (Windows) or the Format option set to Adobe Illustrator (ai) (Mac OS), and click Save. In the Illustrator Options dialog box, leave the Illustrator options at their default settings and then click OK.

6 Choose Window > Workspace > Reset Essentials.

● **Note:** If you don't see "Reset Essentials" in the Workspace menu, choose Window > Workspace > Essentials before choosing Window > Workspace > Reset Essentials.

7 Double-click the Hand tool (🖐) to fit the artboard in the window.

Working with symbols

A symbol is a reusable art object that is stored in the Symbols panel (Window > Symbols). For example, if you create a symbol from a fish you drew, you can then quickly add multiple instances of that fish symbol to your artwork, which saves you from having to draw each fish again. All instances of the fish symbol are linked to the associated symbol in the Symbols panel, so you can easily alter them using Symbolism tools.

When you edit the original symbol, all instances of the fish that are linked to it are updated. You can turn that fish from blue to green instantly! Not only do symbols save time, but they also greatly reduce file size. They can also be used to create SWF files or artwork for Adobe Flash.

• Click the Symbols panel icon (▦) on the right side of the workspace. Take a minute to familiarize yourself with the parts of the Symbols panel.

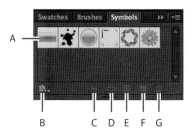

A. Symbols
B. Symbol Libraries Menu
C. Place Symbol Instance
D. Break Link To Symbol

E. Symbol Options
F. New Symbol
G. Delete Symbol

● **Note:** The figure at left shows the Symbols panel with the map.ai file showing in the Document window.

Illustrator comes with a series of symbol libraries, which range from tiki icons to hair and fur. You can access the symbol libraries in the Symbols panel or by choosing Window > Symbol Libraries.

Using existing Illustrator symbol libraries

You will start by adding a symbol from an existing symbol library to the artwork.

1 Choose View > Smart Guides to deselect Smart Guides.

2 Click the Layers panel icon (▦) on the right side of the workspace to expand the Layers panel. Click the Symbols layer to make sure it is selected. Make sure that all of the layers are collapsed by clicking the triangles to the left of the layer names.

When adding symbols to a document, which layer is selected when they are added is the layer they become a part of.

3 Click the Symbols panel icon (▦) on the right side of the workspace to expand the panel.

4 In the Symbols panel, click the Symbol Libraries Menu button (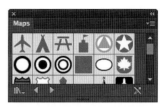) at the bottom of the panel and choose Maps. The Maps library opens as a free-floating panel.

This library is external to the file that you are working on, but you can import any of the symbols into the document and use them in the artwork.

▶ **Tip:** If you want to see the symbol names rather than the symbol pictures, choose Small List View or Large List View from the Symbols panel menu (▼≡).

5 Position the pointer over the symbols in the Maps panel to see their names as tool tips. Click the Rest Area symbol to add it to the Symbols panel for the document. Close the Maps panel.

Every document has a default set of symbols in the Symbols panel. When you add symbols to the panel, as you just did, they are saved with the active document only.

6 Using the Selection tool (▶), drag the Rest Area symbol from the Symbols panel into the UNION PARK area (smaller green area) on the artboard. Drag another into the CENTRAL PARK (larger green area) on the artboard, and leave it selected.

Each time you drag a symbol onto the artboard, an instance of the Rest Area symbol is created. Next, you will resize one of the symbol instances on the page.

● **Note:** Although you can transform symbol instances in many ways, specific properties of instances cannot be edited. For example, the fill color is locked because it is controlled by the original symbol in the Symbols panel.

▶ **Tip:** You can also copy a symbol instance on the artboard and paste as many as you need. This is the same as dragging a symbol instance out of the Symbols panel onto the artboard.

7 Using the Selection tool and holding down the Shift key, drag the upper-right corner of the Rest Area symbol instance in the CENTRAL PARK area, up and to the right, to make it a little larger, while constraining its proportions. Release the mouse button and then the modifier key.

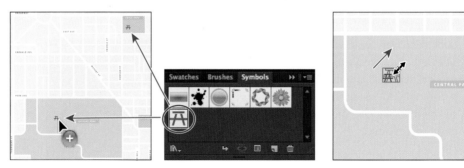

Drag symbol instances onto the artboard.   Resize a symbol instance.

● **Note:** The pointer that you see when dragging a symbol from the Symbols panel into the Document window may look different, and that's okay.

With the symbol instance selected on the artboard, notice that, in the Control panel, you see the word "Symbol" and symbol-related options.

Next, you will edit the Rest Area symbol so that both instances are affected. There are several ways to edit a symbol, and in this section we will focus on one.

8   With the Selection tool (▶), double-click the Rest Area symbol instance in the CENTRAL PARK area on the artboard.

A warning dialog box appears, stating that you are about to edit the original symbol and that all instances will update. Click OK to continue. This takes you into Symbol Editing mode, so you can't edit any other objects on the page.

▶ **Tip:** Another way to edit a symbol is to select the symbol instance on the artboard and then click the Edit Symbol button in the Control panel.

The Rest Area symbol instance you double-clicked appears to change in size. That's because you are looking at the original symbol, not at the resized symbol instance on the page. You can now edit the shapes that make up the symbol.

9   Select the Zoom tool (🔍), and draw a marquee around the symbol instance in the CENTRAL PARK area to zoom in to it.

10 Select the Selection tool and click to select any of the red shapes that make up the picnic bench.

11 In the Control panel, change the Fill color to the swatch named Local Green.

12 With the Selection tool, double-click away from the Rest Area content or click the Exit Symbol Editing Mode button (◀) in the upper-left corner of the artboard until you exit Symbol Editing mode so that you can edit the rest of the content.

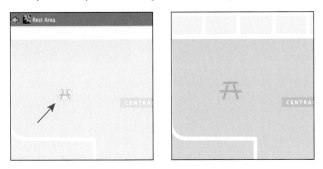

13 Choose View > Fit Artboard In Window, and notice that both Rest Area instances on the artboard now have a green fill.

14 Choose File > Save, and leave the document open.

Creating symbols

● **Note:** You can only use placed art that is embedded (not linked) to create a symbol.

Illustrator also lets you create your own symbols. You can make symbols from objects, including paths, compound paths, text, raster images, mesh objects, and groups of objects. Symbols can even include active objects, such as brush strokes, blends, effects, or other symbol instances. Now, you will create your own symbol from existing artwork.

1 Choose View > symbol content. This takes you to a zoomed in view off the right side of the artboard.

2 With the Selection tool (▶), drag a marquee across the yellow fork content to select it. Drag the selected content into a blank area of the Symbols panel.

▶ **Tip:** By default, the selected artwork becomes an instance of the new symbol. If you don't want the artwork to become an instance of the symbol, press the Shift key as you create the new symbol.

3 In the Symbol Options dialog box, change the name to **Food** and select Graphic as the Type. Click OK to create the symbol.

In the Symbol Options dialog box, you will see a note that explains that there is no difference between a Movie Clip and a Graphic Type in Illustrator, so if you do not plan on exporting this content to Adobe Flash, you don't need to worry about the Type.

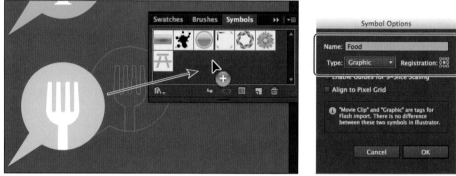

● **Note:** If you are creating artwork for use on the web or for screen display, you can select Align To Pixel Grid in the Symbol Options dialog box to align the instances to the pixel grid. To learn more about the pixel grid, see Lesson 13, "Applying Appearance Attributes and Graphic Styles."

After creating the Food symbol, the original fork group off the right edge of the artboard is converted to an instance of the Food symbol. You can leave it there or delete it, it's up to you.

4 If it isn't already there, drag the Food symbol icon to the right of the Rest Area to change the order of the symbols in the panel.

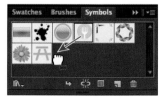

Reordering symbols in the Symbols panel has no effect on the artwork. It can be a way to organize your symbols.

5 Choose File > Save.

Symbol Options

In the Symbol Options dialog box, you will encounter several options that are related to working with Adobe Flash. These options are briefly described below and will be addressed more fully later in this lesson.

- Select Movie Clip for type. Movie Clip is the default symbol type in Flash and in Illustrator.
- Specify a location on the Registration grid where you want to set the symbol's anchor point. The location of the anchor point affects the position of the symbol within the screen coordinates.
- Select Enable Guides For 9-Slice Scaling if you want to utilize 9-Slice scaling in Flash.

—From Illustrator Help

Editing a symbol

In this next section, you will add several instances of the Food symbol to the artwork. Then, you will edit the symbol in the Symbols panel and all instances will be updated.

1 Choose View > Fit Artboard In Window.

2 Using the Selection tool (▶), drag an instance of the Food symbol (the yellow fork) from the Symbols panel to just to the right of the MARKET ST label in the middle of the artboard.

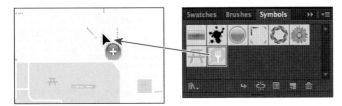

3 Drag another instance of the Food symbol from the Symbols panel just to the right of the EMERALD AVE label. See the figure for placement.

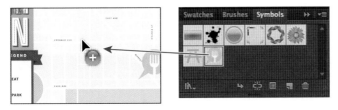

Next, you will learn how to add more instances of a symbol that's already on the artboard, using a modifier key.

4   With the Selection tool (▶), press the Alt (Windows) or Option (Mac OS) key and drag one of the Food symbol instances already on the artboard to create a copy of the instance. Drag it to the right of the WALNUT ST label. When the new instance is in position, release the mouse button and then the modifier key.

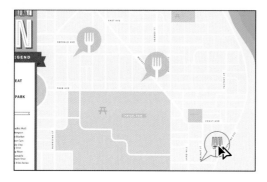

5   Create four more copies by pressing the Alt (Windows) or Option (Mac OS) key and dragging one of the Food symbol instances. Drag them to the right of the EAST AVE, PARK AVE, COAST AVE, and FACTORY ST labels.

You should now have a total of seven Food symbol instances on the artboard.

6   In the Symbols panel, double-click the Food symbol to edit it. A temporary instance of the symbol appears in the center of the Document window.

Editing a symbol by double-clicking the symbol in the Symbols panel hides all artboard content except the symbol. This is just another way to edit a symbol.

7   Press Ctrl++ (Windows) or Command++ (Mac OS) several times to zoom in.

8   With the Direct Selection tool (▷), click to select the yellow shape. Change the Fill color to the swatch named New Local Blue in the Control panel.

Since the fork content is grouped, selecting with the Direct Selection tool lets you select a shape within the group.

9 Choose Select > All, or drag across the shapes with the Selection tool.

10 Choose Object > Transform > Scale. In the Scale dialog box, change the Uniform Scale to **60%** and then click OK.

This allows you to scale all of the symbol instances at once, rather than having to scale each individually. You could make other changes to the symbol artwork in a similar manner.

11 Double-click outside the symbol instance artwork on the artboard, or click the Exit Symbol Editing Mode button () in the upper-left corner of the artboard to see all of the artwork.

12 Press Ctrl+0 (Windows) or Command+0 (Mac OS) to fit the artboard in the window.

13 With the Selection tool, drag the Food instances closer to the street labels.

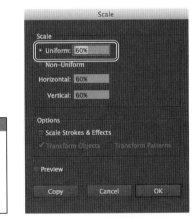

Change the fill color.   Transform the content.   The result.

As you saw earlier, when you double-click an instance of a symbol on the artboard, you edit it in place. By double-clicking a symbol in the Symbols panel, the rest of the artwork is hidden and the symbol appears in the center of the Document window. You can use whichever method suits your workflow.

14 Choose File > Save.

Replacing symbols

Next, you will create a symbol from some other shapes and then replace a few of the Food symbol instances with the new symbol.

1 Choose View > symbol content.

2 With the Selection tool (k), select the green group of shapes with the smiley face (not the two trees).

3   Choose Object > Transform > Scale. In the Scale dialog box, change the Uniform Scale to **60%**, if it's not already 60, and then click OK.

4   At the bottom of the Symbols panel, click the New Symbol button (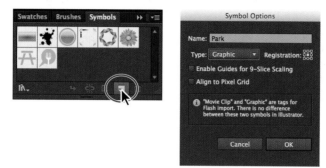). In the Symbol Options dialog box, change the name to **Park** and the Type to Graphic. Click OK.

5   Choose View > Fit Artboard In Window.

6   With the Selection tool, select the Food instance to the right of the PARK AVE label on the artboard. In the Control panel, click the arrow to the right of the Replace Instance With Symbol field to open a panel showing the symbols in the Symbols panel. Click the Park symbol in the panel.

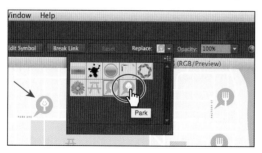

7   Choose Select > Deselect.

8   With the Selection tool, select the Food instance to the right of the COAST AVE label on the artboard. In the Control panel, click the arrow to the right of the Replace Instance With Symbol field to open a panel showing the symbols in the Symbols panel. Click the Park symbol in the panel.

9   With the COAST AVE Park symbol instance still selected, choose Select > Same > Symbol Instance.

This is a great way to select all instances of a symbol in the document. Notice that it also selects the original symbol instance off the right side of the artboard.

10 Choose Object > Group, and then File > Save. Keep the file open.

Symbol layers

When you edit a symbol using any of the methods described, open the Layers panel and you will see that the symbol has its own layering.

Similar to working with groups in Isolation mode, you see the layers associated with that symbol only, not the document's layers. In the Layers panel, you can rename, add, delete, show/hide, and reorder content for a symbol.

Breaking a link to a symbol

At times, you will need to edit specific instances on the artboard but not all of them. Because you can only make changes to a symbol instance like scaling, opacity, flipping, and more, you may need to break the link between a symbol and an instance. This breaks the instance into the original objects or group, if the symbol content was originally grouped, on the artboard.

Next, you will break the link to one of the Food instances.

1 With the Selection tool (▶) selected, click to select the Food symbol instance to the right of the EAST AVE label on the artboard. In the Control panel, click the Break Link button.

   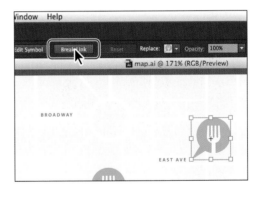

   This object is now a series of paths, as indicated by the word "Path" on the left side of the Control panel. You should be able to see the anchor points of the shapes. This content will no longer update if the Food symbol is edited.

Tip: You can also break the link to a symbol instance by selecting the symbol instance on the artboard and then clicking the Break Link To Symbol button (⊞) at the bottom of the Symbols panel.

2 Select the Zoom tool (🔍), and drag a marquee across the selected content to zoom in.

3 Choose Select > Deselect. Select the Direct Selection tool (▷), and then click the aqua shape.

4 Change the Fill color to the swatch named Mid Gray in the Control panel.

5 Choose Select > Deselect and then File > Save.

Editing symbol options

Using the Symbols panel, you can easily rename or change other options for a symbol, which then updates all the symbol instances in the artwork. Next, you will rename the Rest Area symbol.

1   Choose View > Fit Artboard In Window.

2   In the Symbols panel, make sure that the Rest Area symbol is selected. Click the Symbol Options button (⊞) at the bottom of the Symbols panel.

3   In the Symbol Options dialog box, change the name to **Picnic area** and the Type to Graphic. Click OK.

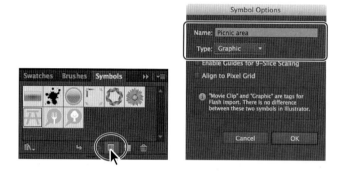

Working with the Symbolism tools

The Symbol Sprayer tool (✺) in the Tools panel allows you to spray symbols on the artboard, creating symbol sets. A symbol set is a group of symbol instances that you create with the Symbol Sprayer tool. This can be really useful if, for instance, you were to create grass from individual blades of grass. Spraying the blades of grass speeds up this process greatly and makes it much easier to edit individual instances or the sprayed grass as a group. You can create mixed sets of symbol instances by using the Symbol Sprayer tool with one symbol and then using it again with another symbol.

Spraying symbol instances

Next, you will save several trees as a symbol and then use the Symbol Sprayer tool to apply those trees to your illustration.

1   Choose View > symbol content.

2   With the Selection tool (➤), drag across the two tree shapes to select them.

3   Drag the trees group into the Symbols panel. In the Symbol Options dialog box, change the name to **Trees** and the Type to Graphic. Click OK.

4   Choose Select > Deselect, and then choose View > Fit Artboard In Window.

5   Select the Symbol Sprayer tool (🖌️) in the Tools panel. Make sure the Trees symbol is selected in the Symbols panel.

6   Double-click the Symbol Sprayer tool (🖌️) in the Tools panel. In the Symbolism Tools Options dialog box, change the Diameter to **1 in** and the Intensity to **5**, if they aren't already, and change the Symbol Set Density to **7**. Click OK.

Note: A higher intensity value increases the rate of change—the Symbol Sprayer tool sprays more and faster. The higher the symbol set density value, the more tightly packed the symbols are as you spray them. If you were to spray grass, for instance, you would want the intensity and density set high.

7   Position the pointer over the CENTRAL PARK label, and click and drag from left to right and from right to left with the Symbol Sprayer, much like using an airbrush or a can of spray paint, to create trees in the park. Release the mouse button when you see some trees on the artboard, like in the figure.

> **Tip:** Make sure to keep moving the pointer. If you don't like the results, you can choose Edit > Undo Spraying and try again.

Notice the bounding box around the Trees symbol instances, identifying it as a symbol set. As you spray, the instances are grouped together as a single object. If a symbol set is selected when you begin to spray with the Symbol Sprayer tool, the symbol instances that you are spraying are added to the selected symbol set. You can easily delete an entire symbol set by selecting it and then pressing the Delete key.

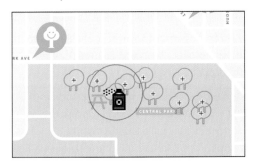

Spray the symbols.

The result.

8 Choose Select > Deselect.

9 Position the Symbol Sprayer pointer over the trees you just created. Click and drag to add more trees.

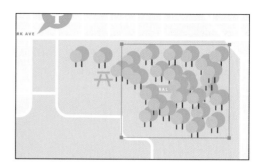

Notice that after releasing the mouse button, you see a bounding box around only the new symbol set. To add symbol instances to an existing symbol set, you must first select the set.

10 With the new symbol set selected, press Delete or Backspace to delete it.

11 With the Selection tool, click to select the first Trees symbol set you created.

Tip: If you don't like the placement of a tree, you can choose Edit > Undo Spraying to remove the instances you sprayed in the previous click.

12 Select the Symbol Sprayer tool, and add more trees to the first symbol set. Try clicking and releasing, instead of clicking and dragging, to add one tree at a time.

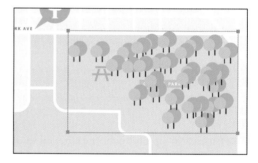

13 Choose File > Save, and leave the symbol set selected.

Editing symbols with the Symbolism tools

Besides the Symbol Sprayer tool, there is a series of Symbolism tools that allow you to edit the size, color, rotation, and more of the instances within a symbol set. In the next steps, you will edit the trees in the Trees symbol set using the Symbolism tools in the Tools panel.

1 With the Trees symbol set and the Symbol Sprayer tool (🔲) still selected, position the pointer over one of the tree instances. Press the Alt (Windows) or Option (Mac OS) key, and click to delete one of the instances in the set.

Tip: If the Symbol Sizer tool is sizing too quickly, double-click the Symbol Sizer tool in the Tools panel and try lowering the Intensity and Density values in the Symbolism Tools Options dialog box.

2 Select the Symbol Sizer tool (🔲) from the Symbol Sprayer tool (🔲) group in the Tools panel. Double-click the Symbol Sizer tool, and change the Intensity to **3** in the Symbolism Tools Options dialog box. Click OK.

3 Position the pointer over some of the trees, and click the mouse button to increase the size of some of the trees. In another area of trees, press the Alt (Windows) or Option (Mac OS) key while you are using the Symbol Sizer tool to reduce the size of the selected symbol set. Make some of the trees smaller than the rest, varying the sizes.

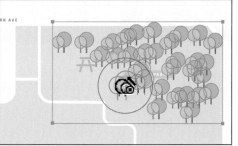

Resize some of the trees.   The result.

Now, you will reposition some of the trees in the symbol set.

4 Select the Symbol Shifter tool () from the Symbol Sizer tool group. Double-click the Symbol Shifter tool. In the Symbolism Tools Options dialog box, change the Intensity to **8**, and then click OK.

The higher the Intensity, the further you can move the symbol instances.

5 Position the pointer over a tree in the selected symbol set, and then drag left or right to move it. Drag the trees away from the CENTRAL PARK label so that you can see the whole thing.

The more you move the pointer, the further you can drag instances. The trees you see in your symbol set may be arranged differently than in the figures and that's okay.

▶ **Tip:** The circle (diameter setting) around the Symbolism tools pointers indicates that any symbol instances within that circle will be affected. Press the left bracket key ([) or right bracket key (]) to change the brush diameter.

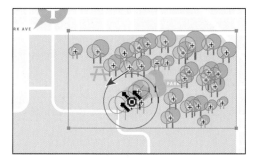

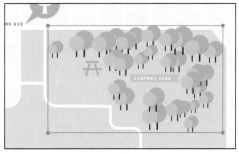

Drag the trees.   The result.

You may notice that, as you drag, some of the trees that should be behind other trees are actually on top of them.

Next, you will fix this with the Symbol Shifter tool.

▶ **Tip:** Shift+Alt-click
(Windows) or Shift+
Option-click (Mac OS) to
send a tree behind.

You may want to zoom in to the symbol set for the next steps.

6 With the Symbol Shifter tool selected, press the left bracket key ([) a few times
to decrease the diameter. Make sure that the circle surrounding the pointer
(that indicates the diameter) isn't much bigger than a tree. Shift-click one of the
trees that should be in front to bring it to the front.

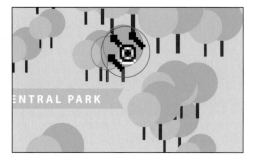

Change the stacking order of instances.

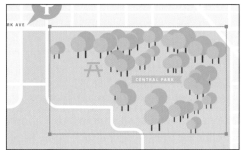

The final result.

7 Select the Symbol Stainer
tool (🖌️) from the Symbol
Shifter tool group in the Tools
panel. With the symbol set
still selected, position the
pointer over the symbol set.
Press the right bracket key (])
several times to increase the
size of the brush.

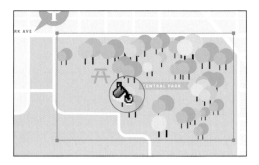

▶ **Tip:** The longer you
press the mouse button,
the more stained
they become. Try
quickly tapping the
mouse button.

8 Change the Fill color in the Control panel to New Local Yellow, and begin
clicking on trees in the symbol set to change their color.

You can always choose Edit > Undo Staining, if you don't like how it's affecting
the trees, or Alt-click (Windows) or Option-click (Mac OS) to decrease the
amount of colorization.

> ▶ **Tip:** There are lots of Symbolism tools for you to experiment with, including the Symbol Styler
> tool (🖿), which allows you to apply graphic styles to symbol instances in the symbol set. To learn
> more about the different types of Symbolism tools available, search for "symbolism tool gallery" in
> Illustrator Help (Help > Illustrator Help).

9 Choose Select > Deselect, and then choose File > Save.

Copying and editing symbol sets

A symbol set is treated as a single object. In order to edit the instances in it, you use
the Symbolism tools in the Tools panel, as you've already seen. You can, however,
duplicate symbol instances and use the Symbolism tools to make the duplicates
look different.

Next, you will duplicate the Trees symbol set.

1 Select the Selection tool (▶), and click to select the Trees symbol set.

2 Press the Alt (Windows) or Option (Mac OS) key, and drag a copy of the instances down and to the left, into the lower-left part of the CENTRAL PARK green area. When it is in position (see the figure), release the mouse button and then the modifier key.

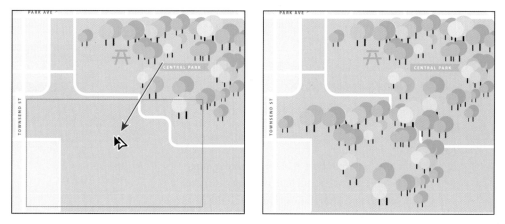

● **Note:** There are many transformations that you can make to a symbol set. You can also drag a point in the bounding box of a symbol set with the Selection tool to resize it.

3 Select the Symbol Shifter tool (🔄) from the Symbol Stainer tool group. Double-click the Symbol Shifter tool, and change the Intensity to **9**. Click OK. Drag the trees in the symbol set so that they fit within the green park area, as you see in the figure.

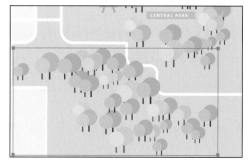

You can change the diameter by pressing the left bracket ([) key or right bracket (]) key. This will help you move more or fewer trees.

4 With the Symbol shifter tool, Shift-click the trees that should be in front, to bring them to the front. Shift+Alt-click (Windows) or Shift+Option-click (Mac OS) to send a tree behind.

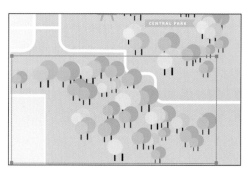

5 Choose Select > Deselect.

6 Choose File > Save.

Storing and retrieving artwork in the Symbols panel

Note: Symbol libraries are saved as Adobe Illustrator (.ai) files.

Saving frequently used logos or other artwork as symbols lets you access them quickly. Unfortunately, symbols you create in one document are not accessible by default in another document. In this next part of the lesson, you will take symbols that you've created and save them as a new symbol library that you can share with other documents or users.

1   In the Symbols panel, click the Symbol Libraries Menu button (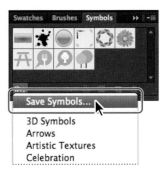) at the bottom and then choose Save Symbols.

> **Note:** When saving symbols as a separate library, the document that contains the symbols that you want to save should be open and active in the Document window.

2   In the Save Symbols As Library dialog box, choose a location, such as your Desktop, to place the symbol library file. Name the library file **map_symbols.ai**. Click Save.

> **Note:** When you first open the Save Symbols As Library dialog box, Illustrator takes you to the default Symbols folder, where you can store the libraries that you create. Illustrator recognizes any libraries stored here and lets you choose them from the Symbol Libraries menu later.

> ▶ **Tip:** If you save the library in the default folder, you can make subfolders and create a folder structure that suits you. You can then easily access them using the Symbol Libraries Menu button or by choosing Window > Symbol Libraries > User Defined > *your symbol library*.

3   Without closing the map.ai file, create a new document by choosing File > New. Leave the default settings, and then click OK.

4   In the Symbols panel, click the Symbol Libraries Menu button (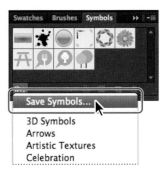) and choose Other Library at the bottom of the menu. Navigate to the folder where you saved the map_symbols.ai library, select it, and then click Open.

The map_symbols library appears as a free-floating panel in the workspace. You can dock it or leave it where it is. It stays open as long as Illustrator is open. When you close Illustrator, and then relaunch it, this panel does not reopen.

5   Drag any of the Symbols from the map_symbols library panel onto the artboard.

6   Choose File > Close, and do not save the new file.

7   Close the map_symbols library.

8   With the map.ai file open, choose File > Save, if necessary, and then File > Close.

Mapping a symbol to 3D artwork

You can apply 2D artwork stored as a symbol in the Symbols panel to selected surfaces on a 3D object. To learn about mapping symbols to 3D artwork, see Lesson 12, "Applying Effects."

Working with symbols and Flash integration

Illustrator also provides excellent support for SWF and SVG file type export. When you export to Flash, you can set the symbol type to Movie Clip. In Adobe Flash, you can choose another type, if necessary. You can also specify 9-slice scaling in Illustrator so that the movie clips scale appropriately when used for user interface components.

You can move Illustrator artwork into the Flash editing environment or directly into the Flash Player. You can copy and paste artwork, save files as SWF, or export artwork directly to Flash. In addition, Illustrator provides support for Flash dynamic text and movie clip symbols.

The following is a generic symbol workflow in Illustrator:

- Step 1: Symbol creation

  When you create a symbol in Illustrator, the Symbol Options dialog box lets you name the symbol and set the following options, specific to Flash: Movie Clip symbol type (which is the default for Flash symbols), Flash registration grid location, and 9-slice scaling guides. In addition, you can use many of the same symbol keyboard shortcuts in Illustrator and Flash, such as pressing F8 to create a symbol.

- Step 2: Isolation mode for symbol editing
- Step 3: Symbol properties and links
- Step 4: Static, dynamic, and input text objects

Next, you will create a button, save it as a symbol, and then edit the symbol options.

1 Choose Window > Workspace > Reset Essentials.

2 Choose File > New.

3 In the New Document dialog box, choose Web from the New Document Profile menu. Keep the rest of the options at their default settings, and then click OK.

4 Choose File > Save As. In the Save As dialog box, name the file **buttons.ai** and navigate to the Lesson14 folder. Leave the Save As Type option set to Adobe Illustrator (*.AI) (Windows) or the Format option set to Adobe Illustrator (ai) (Mac OS), and then click Save. In the Illustrator Options dialog box, leave the Illustrator options at their default settings and then click OK.

5 Choose Window > Symbol Libraries > Web Buttons And Bars.

Note: If you don't see "Reset Essentials" in the Workspace menu, choose Window > Workspace > Essentials before choosing Window > Workspace > Reset Essentials.

6 Choose Small List View from the Symbols panel menu (▼≣).

7 Drag the blue Bullet 4 - Forward symbol from the Web Buttons And Bars panel onto the artboard. Close the Web Buttons And Bars panel menu group.

8 With the Selection tool (▶), Shift-click the upper-right corner of the button and drag to make it roughly twice its original size, releasing the mouse button and then the key.

9 With the button still selected, change the Instance Name in the Control panel to **Home** and press Enter or Return.

The Instance Name is optional when working in Illustrator and is used to identify one symbol instance from another. Entering an instance name for each button is useful if you choose to import the Illustrator content to the stage in Flash (File > Import > Import To Stage).

10 With the button selected, begin dragging it to the right. As you drag, press Shift+Alt (Windows) or Shift+Option (Mac OS) to create a copy. Release the mouse button first and then the modifier keys.

11 In the Control panel, change the Instance Name to **Info** and press Enter or Return.

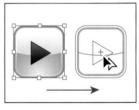

Resize the symbol instance.   Name the instance.   Duplicate the instance.

12 With one of the buttons still selected, click the Symbols panel icon (◳) to open the panel. Click the Symbol Options button (▤) at the bottom of the panel. Make sure that Movie Clip is chosen from the Type menu, select Enable Guides For 9-Slice Scaling, and then click OK.

Next, you'll adjust the 9-slice scaling guides.

13 With the Selection tool, double-click the leftmost button to enter Isolation mode. When the warning dialog box appears, click OK.

14 Select the Zoom tool (🔍) in the Tools panel, and click three times on the leftmost button to zoom in. Choose Select > All.

Choosing Select > All allows you to see the anchor points in the shapes. When you adjust the 9-slice scaling guides, you want to try to position them to indicate the scalable part of the object (usually not the corners).

15 With the Selection tool, drag the rightmost dotted line to the right so that it lines up approximately with the anchor points (circled), as shown in the figure.

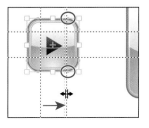

You can use 9-slice scaling (scale-9) to specify component-style scaling for graphic style and movie clip symbols. To maintain the visual integrity of the symbol, corners are not scaled, while the remaining areas of the image are scaled (as opposed to being stretched) larger or smaller, as needed.

16 With the Selection tool, double-click away from the buttons to exit Isolation mode.

17 Choose View > Fit Artboard In Window and then File > Save.

Understanding symbol options for Flash

Movie Clip: Use movie clip symbols to create reusable pieces of animation (in Flash). Movie clips have their own multiframe Timeline that is independent from the main Timeline—think of them as nested inside a main Timeline that can contain interactive controls, sounds, and even other movie clip instances. You can also place movie clip instances inside the Timeline of a button symbol to create animated buttons. In addition, movie clips are scriptable with ActionScript®.

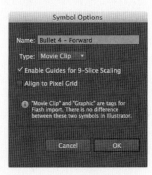

Align to Pixel Grid: To create a pixel-aligned symbol, select the Align to Pixel Grid option from the Symbol Options dialog box. Symbols aligned to the pixel grid remain aligned to the pixel grid at all locations of the artboard, in their actual size.

9-slice scaling: You can use 9-slice scaling (scale-9) to specify component-style scaling for graphic style and movie clip symbols. This type of scaling lets you create movie clip symbols that scale appropriately for use as user interface components, as opposed to the type of scaling typically applied to graphics and design elements.

The symbol is conceptually divided into nine sections with a grid-like overlay, and each of the nine areas is scaled independently. To maintain the visual integrity of the symbol, corners are not scaled, while the remaining areas of the image are scaled (as opposed to being stretched) larger or smaller, as needed.

—From Illustrator Help

Note: If you don't own Adobe Flash CS6, you can install a free trial version from Adobe.com for 30 days, here: http://www.adobe.com/downloads/

For the next section, you need to have Adobe Flash CS6 installed on your machine.

1 Open Adobe Flash CS6.

2 Choose File > New. In the New Document dialog box, make sure that the General tab is selected and that ActionScript 3.0 is also selected as the Type. Click OK.

3 Choose File > Import > Import To Library in Adobe Flash. Navigate to the buttons.ai file you just saved in Illustrator, and then click Open. The Import "buttons.ai" To Library dialog box appears.

   In this dialog box, you can select which artboard to import, which layers to import, how to import the content, and more. The Import Unused Symbols option at the bottom of the dialog box brings all the symbols in the Illustrator Symbols panel into the Flash Library panel. This can be very useful if, for instance, you are developing a series of buttons for a site but they are not on the artboard in Illustrator.

4 Click OK.

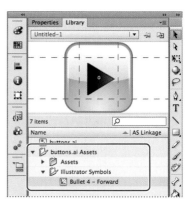

5 Open the Library panel by clicking the Library panel tab on the right side of the workspace. Click the arrow to the left of the folder names to reveal the assets as well as the Bullet 4 - Forward symbol in the Illustrator Symbols folder.

6 Drag the Bullet 4 - Forward symbol onto the stage.

7 Choose File > Close to close the Flash file, and don't save changes. Close Flash, and return to Illustrator. Close all open files in Illustrator.

Review questions

1 What are three benefits of using symbols?

2 How do you update an existing symbol?

3 What is something that cannot be used as a symbol?

4 Name the Symbolism tool that is used for shifting symbol instances in a symbol set.

5 If you are using a Symbolism tool on an area that has two different symbols applied, which one is affected?

6 How do you access symbols from other documents?

7 Name two ways to bring symbols from Illustrator to Flash.

Review answers

1 Three benefits of using symbols are:

   • You can edit one symbol, and all instances are updated.

   • You can map artwork to 3D objects (covered in depth in Lesson 12, "Applying Effects").

   • Using symbols reduces file size.

2 To update an existing symbol, double-click the symbol icon in the Symbols panel, double-click an instance of the symbol on the artboard, or select the instance on the artboard and then click the Edit Symbol button in the Control panel. Then, you can make edits in Isolation mode.

3 Linked images cannot be used as symbols.

4 The Symbol Shifter tool allows you to shift symbol instances in a symbol set.

5 If you are using a Symbolism tool over an area that has two different symbol instances, the symbol active in the Symbols panel is the only instance affected.

6 You can access symbols from saved documents either by clicking the Symbol Libraries Menu button at the bottom of the Symbols panel and by choosing Other Library from the menu that appears; by choosing Open Symbol Library > Other Library from the Symbols panel menu; or by choosing Window > Symbol Libraries > Other Library.

7 To bring symbols from Illustrator to Flash, copy and paste the symbol(s) from Illustrator to Flash, choose File > Import > Import To Stage, or choose File > Import > Import To Library.

15

COMBINING ILLUSTRATOR CS6 GRAPHICS WITH OTHER ADOBE APPLICATIONS

Lesson overview

In this lesson, you'll learn how to do the following:

- Differentiate between vector and bitmap graphics.

- Place linked and embedded Adobe Photoshop graphics in an Adobe Illustrator file.

- Create and edit a simple clipping mask.

- Create a clipping mask from a drawn shape.

- Create a clipping mask from a compound path.

- Make an opacity mask to display part of an image.

- Sample color in a placed image.

- Work with the Links panel.

- Replace a placed image with another and update the document.

- Export a layered file to Adobe Photoshop.

 This lesson takes approximately an hour to complete. If needed, remove the previous lesson folder from your hard disk and copy the Lesson15 folder onto it.

You can easily add an image created in an image-editing program to an Adobe Illustrator file. This is an effective method for incorporating images into your vector artwork or for trying out Illustrator special effects on bitmap images.

Getting started

Before you begin, you'll need to restore the default preferences for Adobe Illustrator CS6. Then, you'll open the finished art file for this lesson to see what you'll create.

1 To ensure that the tools and panels function exactly as described in this lesson, delete or deactivate (by renaming) the Adobe Illustrator CS6 preferences file. See "Restoring default preferences" on page 3.

2 Start Adobe Illustrator CS6.

● **Note:** If you have not already done so, copy the Lesson15 folder from the Lessons folder on the *Adobe Illustrator CS6 Classroom in a Book* CD onto your hard disk. See "Copying the Classroom in a Book files" on page 2.

3 Choose File > Open. Locate the file named L15end.ai in the Lesson15 folder in the Lessons folder that you copied onto your hard disk. This is a poster for a farmers market, and you will add and edit graphics, in this lesson. Leave it open for reference, or choose File > Close.

Now, you'll open the start file from Adobe Bridge CS6.

Working with Adobe Bridge

Bridge is an application that installs when you install either an Adobe Creative Suite 6 component, such as Illustrator, or the entire Adobe Creative Suite 6. It allows you to browse content visually, manage metadata, and more.

● **Note:** The first time Adobe Bridge launches, a dialog box may appear asking if you want Bridge to start at login. Click Yes if you want it to launch at startup. Click No to manually launch Bridge when you need it.

1 Choose File > Browse In Bridge to open Bridge.

2 In the Favorites pane on the left, click Desktop and navigate to the L15start.ai file in the Lesson15 folder. Click the thumbnail in the Content pane.

3 At the bottom of the Content pane, drag the slider to the right to increase the size of the thumbnails in the Content pane.

4 At the top of Bridge, click Filmstrip (or choose Window > Workspace > Filmstrip). This changes the appearance of the workspace to a filmstrip view that provides a larger preview of the selected object. Click Essentials to return to the original workspace.

5 At the bottom of the Content pane, drag the slider to the left until you see all the thumbnails in the Content pane.

6 With the L15start.ai file still selected in the Content pane, click the Metadata panel tab on the right side of the workspace, if it's not already selected, to see the metadata associated with the selected file. This can be camera data, document swatches, and more. Click the Keywords panel tab to reveal the Keywords panel.

Keywords can be associated with objects such as images, which will allow them to be searched for by those keywords.

7 In the Keywords panel, click the plus sign (+) at the bottom to create a keyword. Type **marketposter** into the keyword field, and press Enter or Return. Click to select the box to the left of the keyword, if it's not already selected. This associates the keyword with the selected file.

8 Choose Edit > Find. In the Find dialog box, choose Keywords from the first menu in the Criteria section. Leave the middle field set to contains. Type **marketposter** in the rightmost field of the Criteria options, and then click Find. The Find results appear in the Content pane.

9 Click the X in the upper-right corner of the Content pane, to the right of the New Search button, to close the Find results and return to the folder.

Previewing files and working with metadata and keywords are just a few of the many features available in Bridge. To learn more about working with Bridge, search for "Adobe Bridge" in Illustrator Help (Help > Illustrator Help).

10 Double-click the file L15start.ai in the Content pane to open the file in Illustrator. You may close Bridge at any time.

Note: In Mac OS, when opening lesson files, you may need to click the round, green button in the upper-left corner of the Document window to maximize the window's size.

11 Choose View > Fit Artboard In Window.

12 Choose Window > Workspace > Reset Essentials to reset the Essentials workspace.

13 Choose File > Save As. In the Save As dialog box, navigate to the Lesson15 folder and open it. Name the file **marketposter.ai**. Leave the Save As Type option set to Adobe Illustrator (*.AI) (Windows) or the Format option set to Adobe Illustrator (ai) (Mac OS), and then click Save. In the Illustrator Options dialog box, leave the Illustrator options at their default settings. Click OK.

Combining artwork

You can combine Illustrator artwork with images from other graphics applications in a variety of ways for a wide range of creative results. Sharing artwork between applications lets you combine continuous-tone paintings and photographs with vector art. Even though Illustrator lets you create certain types of raster images, Adobe Photoshop excels at many image-editing tasks. The images can then be inserted into Illustrator.

This lesson steps you through the process of creating a composite image, including combining bitmap images with vector art and working between applications. You will add photographic images created in Photoshop to a poster created in Illustrator. Then, you'll adjust the color of an image, mask an image, and sample color from an image to use in the Illustrator artwork. You'll update a placed image, and then export your poster to Photoshop.

Vector versus bitmap graphics

Illustrator creates vector graphics, also called draw graphics, which contain shapes based on mathematical expressions. Vector graphics consist of clear, smooth lines that retain their crispness when scaled. They are best for illustrations, type, and graphics that need to be scaled to different sizes, such as logos.

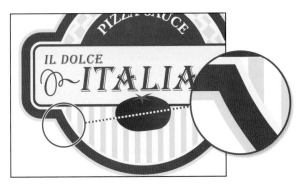

This logo is drawn as vector art, which retains its crispness when scaled to a larger size.

Bitmap graphics, also called raster images, are based on a grid of pixels usually measured in pixels per inch (ppi). They are created by image-editing applications such as Photoshop. When working with bitmap images, you edit groups of pixels rather than objects or shapes. Because bitmap graphics can represent subtle gradations of shade and color, they are appropriate for continuous-tone images, such as photographs, or for artwork created in painting programs. A disadvantage of bitmap graphics is that they lose definition and appear jagged when scaled up.

This logo is rasterized as bitmap art and loses its definition when enlarged.

In deciding whether to use Illustrator or a bitmap image-editing program such as Photoshop for creating and combining graphics, consider the elements of the artwork and how the artwork will be used.

In general, use Illustrator if you need to create art or type with clean lines that looks good at any magnification. In most cases, you'll also want to use Illustrator for laying out a single-page design, because Illustrator offers more flexibility than Photoshop when working with type and when reselecting, moving, and altering images. You can create raster images in Illustrator, but its pixel-editing tools are limited. Use Photoshop for images that need pixel editing, color correcting, and other special effects. Use Adobe InDesign for laying out anything from a postcard to a multiple chapter book, such as this *Classroom in a Book*.

Placing Photoshop files

You can bring artwork from Photoshop into Illustrator using the Open command, the Place command, the Paste command, and drag-and-drop. Illustrator supports most Photoshop data, including layer comps, layers, editable text, and paths. This means that you can transfer files between Photoshop and Illustrator without losing the ability to edit the artwork.

> ● **Note:** Adjustment layers for which visibility is turned off in Photoshop are imported into Illustrator, although they are inaccessible (an adjustment layer applies color and tonal adjustments to your image without permanently changing pixel values). When exported back to Photoshop, the layers are restored.

● **Note:** Illustrator includes support for Device N rasters. For instance, if you create a Duotone image in Photoshop and place it in Illustrator, it separates properly and prints the spot colors.

When placing files using the File > Place command, no matter what type of image file it is (JPG, GIF, PSD, etc.), it can either be embedded or linked. Embedding files stores a copy of the image in the Illustrator file, and the Illustrator file size increases to reflect the addition of the placed file. Linked files remain separate external files, and a link to the external file is placed in the Illustrator file. Linking to files can be a great way to ensure that image updates are reflected in the Illustrator file. The linked file must always accompany the Illustrator file, or the link will break and the placed file will not appear in the Illustrator artwork.

Placing a Photoshop file

1 In Illustrator CS6, choose Window > Layers to open the Layers panel. In the Layers panel, select the Woman layer.

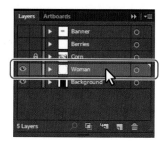

When you place an image, it is added to the selected layer. You'll use the Woman layer for the placed image. The layer already includes the white circle you see on the artboard.

2 Choose File > Place.

3 Navigate to the carrots.psd file in the images folder inside the Lesson15 folder, and select it. Make sure that Link is selected in the Place dialog box.

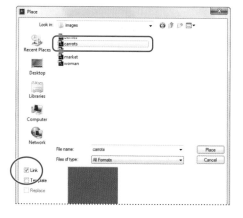

By default, placed Photoshop files are linked to their source file. So, if the source file is edited, the placed image in Illustrator is updated. If you deselect the Link option, you embed the PSD file in the Illustrator file.

4 Click Place.

Notice that the image of carrots is placed in the center of the Document window. It is selected and has bounding points and an X in the center of the image. Also notice in the Control panel that, with the image selected, you see the words "Linked File," indicating that the image is linked to its source file, together with other information about the image. Clicking Linked File in the Control panel opens the Links panel, which you'll do later in this lesson.

Transforming a placed image

You can duplicate and transform placed images just as you do other objects in an Illustrator file. Unlike vector artwork, you need to consider the resolution of the raster image. Next, you will move, resize, and rotate the carrots.psd image.

1 With the Selection tool (➤) selected and the image already selected, drag the image down and to the right so that it is positioned over the top of the white circle in the lower-right corner of the artboard. You may need to scroll down in the Document window.

2 Holding down the Alt+Shift (Windows) or Option+Shift (Mac OS) keys, use the Selection tool to drag the upper-right bounding point toward the center of the image until the width is approximately 4.5 in. Release the mouse button and then the keys.

> **Tip:** To transform a placed image, you can also open the Transform panel (Window > Transform) and change settings there.

After resizing the image, notice that the PPI (Pixels Per Inch) value in the Control panel is approximately 157. The PPI refers to the resolution of the image. Working in Illustrator, if you make an image smaller, the resolution of the image increases. If you make an image larger, the resolution decreases.

3 With the Selection tool, position the pointer just off the upper-right bounding point. The rotate arrows should appear. Drag up and to the left to rotate the image about 13 degrees. With Smart Guides on, you'll see a measurement label. Make sure that the image completely covers the circle.

> **Note:** Transformations performed on a linked image in Illustrator, and any resulting resolution changes, do not change the original image. The changes apply only to the image within Illustrator.

4 Choose Select > Deselect and then File > Save.

Embedding a Photoshop image with layer comps

Designers often create multiple compositions, or comps, of a page layout to show their clients. Using layer comps in Photoshop, you can create, manage, and view multiple versions of a layout in a single Photoshop file.

A layer comp is a snapshot of a state of the Layers panel in Photoshop. Layer comps record the following information about a layer:

- Visibility—whether a layer is showing or hidden

- Position in the document

- Appearance (Layer Style)—whether a layer style is applied to the layer and the layer's blending mode

You create a layer comp in Photoshop by making changes to the layers in your document and clicking the Create New Layer Comp button in the Layer Comps panel. You view comps by applying them in the document. You can export layer comps to separate files, to a single PDF file, to a web photo gallery, or choose one when placing the Photoshop file into Illustrator.

Next, you will place a Photoshop file with layer comps and embed it in the Illustrator file.

1 In the Layers panel, click the visibility column in the Woman layer to hide the contents and then select the Background layer.

2 Choose View > Fit Artboard In Window, in case you zoomed in on the artwork or scrolled in previous steps.

3 Choose File > Place.

Note: Deselecting the Link option embeds the PSD file in the Illustrator file. Embedding the PSD allows for more options when it is placed.

4 Navigate to the market.psd file in the images folder inside of the Lesson15 folder. Deselect the Link option, and then click Place.

5 In the Photoshop Import Options dialog box, set the following options:

- Select Show Preview, if it's not already selected.

- Choose All from the Layer Comp menu.

- Select Convert Layers To Objects.

- Select Import Hidden Layers to import layers hidden in Photoshop.

Click OK.

Note: A color mode warning may appear in the Photoshop Import Options dialog box. This indicates that the image you are placing may not be the same color mode as the Illustrator document. Also, for this image, and going forward, if a color warning dialog box appears after you click OK, click OK in the warning dialog box.

Rather than flatten the file, you want to convert the Photoshop layers to objects, because the market.psd file contains several layers.

6   In the Layers panel, click the triangle (▶) to the left of the Background layer to expand it. Drag the bottom of the panel down, if necessary, so that you can see more of the layers. Click the triangle to the left of the market.psd sublayer to expand it.

Notice the sublayers of market.psd. These sublayers were Photoshop layers in Photoshop and appear in the Layers panel in Illustrator because you chose not to flatten the image when you placed it. Also notice that, with the image still selected on the page, the Control panel shows the word "Group" on the left side and includes a link to Multiple Images. When you place a Photoshop file with layers and you choose to convert the layers to objects in the Photoshop Import Options dialog box, Illustrator treats the layers as separate images in a group.

7   Click the eye icon (👁) to the left of the Color Fill 1 sublayer to hide it.

Note: You may need to drag the left edge of the Layers panel to the left to see the full names.

8   With the Selection tool (▶), drag the market image down so that the bottom edge of the image snaps to the bottom, red bleed guide.

9   Choose Select > Deselect, and then choose File > Save.

Applying color edits to a placed image

▶ **Tip:** For information on color modes and modifying colors with color edits, see "About colors in digital graphics" and "Apply an effect" in Illustrator Help.

You can use color edits in a variety of ways to modify colors in placed images that are embedded. You can convert to a different color mode (such as RGB, CMYK, or grayscale) or adjust individual color values. You can also saturate (darken) or desaturate (lighten) colors or invert colors (create a color negative).

Next, you'll place an image and then adjust its colors. Later in the lesson, you'll apply a mask to this image.

1 In the Layers panel, click the eye icon () to the left of the Background layer to hide it. Click the triangle to the left of the Background layer to collapse it. Click the visibility column in the Corn layer and the Berries layer to show the contents, and then select the Berries layer.

The Corn layer shows an image of corn with the word "LOCAL." You are going to place another image and adjust the color and then mask a copy of it. The corn image and text are an example of what you are about to create.

2 Choose File > Place.

3 Navigate to the berries.psd file in the images folder inside the Lesson15 folder, and then select it. Select Link in the Place dialog box, and then click Place.

● **Note:** As long as the file is open, the Link option is sticky. That means the next time you place an image, the Link option will automatically apply.

4 With the berries image selected, double-click the Rotate tool (↻) in the Tools panel. Change the Rotate Angle to **-90**, and then click OK.

● **Note:** Depending on your screen resolution, the Transform options may not appear in the Control panel. You can click the word "Transform," or you may need to choose Window > Transform to open the panel.

5 Select the top, center point of the Reference Point Indicator (▦) in the Control panel. Change the Y value to **-0.125 in**. Click the Constrain Width And Height Proportions button (▦), change the W value to **70%** (make sure to type in the "%"), and then press Enter or Return.

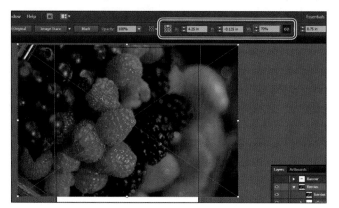

● **Note:** This figure shows the values *before* pressing Enter or Return.

In order to edit colors in the image, the image needs to be embedded in the Illustrator file. If the file is linked, the edits you are about to do can be done in Photoshop and then updated in Illustrator. But sometimes you may want to embed the image so that you don't have to worry about keeping track of a linked image.

6 With the berries.psd still selected on the artboard, choose Edit > Copy and then Edit > Paste In Front. With the new copy selected, choose Object > Hide > Selection.

7 With the Selection tool, click to select the original berries image. Click the Embed button in the Control panel.

If the berries.psd image had layers in Photoshop, the Photoshop Import Options dialog box would open when you embed it, allowing you to set options for embedding the image. On the left end of the Control panel, you will now see the word "Embedded."

8 With the image still selected, choose Edit > Edit Colors > Adjust Color Balance.

9 In the Adjust Colors dialog box, drag the sliders or enter values for the CMYK percentages to change the colors in the image. You can press Tab to move between the text fields. We used the following values to create more of a red cast: C=**-30**, M=**-30**, Y=**-30**, and K=**0**. Feel free to experiment a little. Select Preview so that you can see the color changes. Click OK.

● **Note:** To see the results, you may need to select and deselect Preview as you change options in the Adjust Colors dialog box.

● **Note:** If you later decide to adjust the colors of the same image by choosing Edit > Edit Colors > Adjust Color Balance, the color values will be set to 0 (zero).

10 Choose Select > Deselect and then File > Save.

Masking an image

Clipping paths, or masks, crop an image so that only a portion of the image appears through the shape of the mask. Only vector objects can be clipping paths; however, any artwork can be masked. You can also import masks created in Photoshop files. The clipping path and the masked object are referred to as the clipping set.

Applying a simple clipping mask to an image

● **Note:** You can also apply a clipping mask by choosing Object > Clipping Mask > Make.

In this short section, you'll create a simple clipping mask for the berries.psd image.

1   With the Selection tool (▶), click the berries.psd image to select it. Click the Mask button in the Control panel. This applies a clipping mask to the image in the shape and size of the image.

▶ **Tip:** Another way to create a mask is to use the Draw Inside mode. This mode allows you to draw inside the selected object. The Draw Inside mode can eliminate the need to perform multiple tasks, such as drawing and altering stacking order or drawing, selecting, and creating a clipping mask. To learn more about the drawing modes, see Lesson 3, "Creating and Editing Shapes."

2   In the Layers panel, click the triangle (▶) to the left of the Berries layer to reveal its contents, if you haven't already done so. You may need to drag the bottom of the Layers panel down or scroll in the panel. Click the triangle to the left of the <Clip Group> Sublayer to reveal its contents as well.

● **Note:** You may need to drag the left edge of the Layers panel to the left to see the full names, like we did for the figure.

Notice the <Clipping Path> sublayer. This is the mask you created by clicking the Mask button in the Control panel. The <Clip Group> sublayer is the clipping set that contains the mask and the object that is masked.

Next, you will edit this simple mask.

Editing a mask

In order to edit a clipping path, you need to be able to select it. Illustrator offers several ways to do this.

1   With the berries image still selected on the artboard, click the Edit Contents button (▣) in the Control panel and, in the Layers panel, notice that the berries.psd sublayer (in the <Clip Group>) is showing the selected-art indicator (blue box). Click the Edit Clipping Path button (▣) in the Control panel, and notice that the <Clipping Path> is showing the selected-art indicator (blue box) in the Layers panel.

When an object is masked, you can edit either the mask, the object that is masked, or both. Use these two buttons to select which to edit. When you first click to select an object that is masked, you will edit both the mask and the masked object.

2   With the Edit Clipping Path button (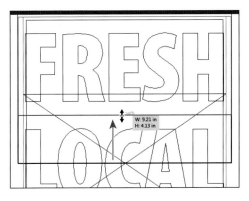) selected in the Control panel, choose View > Outline.

3   Use the Selection tool (▶) to drag the bottom, middle bounding point of the selected mask up to snap the bottom edge of the clipping path to the top edge of the corn image (the line above the word "LOCAL").

▶ **Tip:** You can also edit a clipping path with transformation options like rotate, skew, etc., or by using the Direct Selection tool (▷).

4   Choose View > Preview.

5   With the Selection tool, press and hold the Alt (Windows) or Option (Mac OS) key, and then click and drag the right, middle bounding point to the left. Drag until it snaps to the red bleed guide. Release the mouse button and then the key.

6   In the Control panel, click the Edit Contents button () to edit the berries.psd image, not the mask. With the Selection tool, drag the berries image up a little bit and release the mouse button. Notice that you are moving the image and not the mask.

7   Choose Edit > Undo Move to put the image back where it was.

With the Edit Contents button (■) selected, you can apply many transformations to the image, including scaling, moving, rotating, and more.

8   In the Layers panel, click the triangle (▶) to the left of the <Clip Group> sublayer to hide its contents.

9   Choose Select > Deselect and then File > Save.

Masking an object with a shape

In this section, you'll create a mask for the carrots.psd image in the shape of a circle. In order to create a mask from a shape you draw, the shape needs to be on top of the image, as you'll see.

1 In the Layers panel, click the visibility column to the left of the layer named Woman, to reveal its contents.

2 With the Selection tool (▶), click to select the carrots.psd image on the artboard.

3 Choose Object > Arrange > Send To Back. You should see the white circle as well.

4 Drag a selection marquee across the white circle and carrots.psd image in the lower-right corner of the artboard to select them both.

5 Choose Object > Clipping Mask > Make.

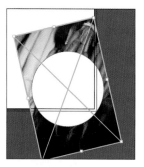 

Both objects selected   The carrots.psd image masked

You can edit the carrots.psd image and the clipping mask separately, just as you did previously with the masked berries image.

▶ **Tip:** You can use text as a clipping mask, if you like. Just create the text, ensure that it's on top of the content to be masked, and then choose Object > Clipping Mask > Make.

6 Choose Select > Deselect, and then choose File > Save.

Masking an object with multiple shapes

In this section, you'll create a mask for the hidden berries.psd image from text that has been converted to outlines. In order to create a clipping mask with multiple shapes, the shapes need to be converted to a compound path.

1 Choose View > Fit Artboard In Window, if necessary.

2 In the Layers panel, click the triangle (▶) to the left of the Background layer to collapse it, if necessary. Scroll up in the Layers panel, if necessary, to see the contents of the Berries layer. Notice that the berries.psd sublayer is hidden.

3 Click the visibility column to the left of the berries.psd sublayer to show the image on the artboard.

4 Click the selection column to the right of the <Group> sublayer at the bottom of the Berries layer. You should see what look like text outlines on the artboard. Choose Object > Arrange > Bring To Front.

With the "FRESH" text shapes selected, you can see the word "Group" on the left end of the Control panel. This was text that was converted to outlines (Type > Create Outlines) so that the letter shapes could each be edited, if necessary.

5 Choose Object > Compound Path > Make.

Notice that the group of letter shapes are placed into one sublayer, called <Compound Path> in the Layers panel. Leave the new compound path selected. The Compound Path command creates a single compound object from two or more objects. Compound paths act as grouped objects. The Compound Path command lets you create complex objects more easily than if you used the drawing tools or the Pathfinder commands.

> **Tip:** To make the letter shapes into a compound path, you can also position the pointer over the letter shapes and right-click or Control-click and choose Make Compound Path.

⬤ **Note:** In order to make a compound path from multiple objects, they don't need to be grouped.

6 With the compound path still selected, Shift-click the berries image on the artboard to select both. Right-click (Windows) or Ctrl-click (Mac OS), and choose Make Clipping Mask.

Notice the Edit Clipping Path button (⬛) and the Edit Contents button (⬛) that now show in the Control panel. This creates a clip group from the FRESH group and the berries.psd image.

> **Tip:** You can also choose Object > Clipping Mask > Make.

7 With the FRESH clip group still selected, click the Graphic Styles panel icon (⬛) to expand the panel. Click the Large text graphic style to apply a drop shadow to the group.

8 Click the Stroke panel icon () to expand the Stroke panel. Change the Stroke weight to **3 pt** and, if necessary, change the stroke color to white by selecting the Stroke box in the Tools panel and choosing the White swatch from the Swatches panel.

9 Choose Select > Deselect, and then choose File > Save.

Creating an opacity mask

An opacity mask is different from a clipping mask, because it allows you to not only mask an object but also to alter the transparency of artwork. An opacity mask is made and edited using the Transparency panel.

In this section, you'll create an opacity mask for the market.psd image so that it fades into the blue color of the background shape.

1 Open the Layers panel and click the triangle (▶) to the left of the Berries layer to collapse it.

2 Click the eye icon (👁) to the left of the Berries, Corn, and Woman layers. Click the visibility column to the left of the Background layer to see its contents. Select the Background layer.

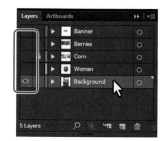

3 Select the Rectangle tool (▭) in the Tools panel, and click in the approximate center of the artboard. In the Rectangle dialog box, change the Width to **8.75 in** and the Height to **4.2 in**. Click OK. This will become the mask.

⬤ **Note:** The object that is to become the opacity mask (the masking object) needs to be the top selected object in the artboard. If it is a single object, like a rectangle, it does not need to be a compound path. If the opacity mask is to be made from multiple objects, they need to be grouped.

4 Press the letter D to set the default stroke and fill.

5 Select the Selection tool (▶), and drag the rectangle so that the bottom of the rectangle snaps to the bottom, red bleed guide and the center of the artboard. Leave the rectangle selected.

6 Press the Shift key, and click the market.psd image to select it as well.

7 Click the Transparency panel icon (◉) on the right side of the workspace to expand the Transparency panel. Click the Make Mask button.

After clicking the Make Mask button, the button now shows as Release. If you were to click the button again, the image would no longer be masked.

The mask in place.   Make the opacity mask.   The result.

Editing an opacity mask

Next, you'll adjust the opacity mask that you just created.

1 In the Transparency panel, Shift-click the mask thumbnail (as indicated by the white rectangle on the black background) to disable the mask.

Notice that a red X appears on the mask in the Transparency panel and that the entire market.psd image reappears in the Document window.

▶ **Tip:** To disable and enable an opacity mask, you can also choose Disable Opacity Mask or Enable Opacity Mask from the Transparency panel menu.

2 In the Transparency panel, Shift-click the mask thumbnail to enable the mask again.

3 Click to select the mask thumbnail on the right side of the Transparency panel.

Clicking the opacity mask in the Transparency panel selects the mask (the rectangle path) on the artboard. If the mask isn't selected, click to select it with the Selection tool (▶). With the mask selected, you can't edit other artwork on the artboard. Also, notice that the document tab shows (<Opacity Mask>/Opacity Mask), indicating that you are now editing the mask.

4 Click the Layers panel icon (▨) on the right side of the workspace to reveal the Layers panel. In the Layers panel, notice that the layer <Opacity Mask> appears, indicating that the mask is selected, rather than the artwork that is being masked.

5 With the mask selected in the Transparency panel and on the artboard, in the Control panel, click the Fill color and select a white-to-black linear gradient, called White, Black.

You will now see that where there is white in the mask, the market.psd image is showing, and where there is black, it is hidden. The gradient between gradually reveals the image from black to white.

6   Choose View > Hide Gradient Annotator.

7   Make sure that the Fill box is selected toward the bottom of the Tools panel.

8   Select the Gradient tool () in the Tools panel. Holding down the Shift key, position the pointer in the center of the mask (horizontally and vertically) and then click and drag up to the top of the mask shape, as shown in the figure. Release the mouse button, and then release the Shift key.

9   Click the Transparency panel icon (■), and notice how the mask has changed appearance in the Transparency panel.

The default gradient applied.

Adjust the gradient.

The result in the panel.

10 Choose View > Show Gradient Annotator.

Next, you'll move the image but not the opacity mask. With the image thumbnail selected in the Transparency panel, both the image and the mask are linked together, by default, so that if you move the image, the mask moves as well.

● **Note:** You only have access to the link icon when the image thumbnail, not the mask thumbnail, is selected in the Transparency panel.

11 In the Transparency panel, click the image thumbnail so that you are no longer editing the mask. Click the link icon (■) between the image thumbnail and the mask thumbnail. This allows you to move just the image or the mask, but not both.

12 With the Selection tool, begin dragging the market.psd image down. As you drag, press and hold the Shift key to constrain the movement vertically. Release the mouse button and then the key to see where it is positioned. Drag until it looks approximately like the figure, always releasing the mouse button and then the key.

● **Note:** The position of the market.psd does not have to match the figure exactly.

13 In the Transparency panel, click the broken link icon () between the image thumbnail and the mask thumbnail.

14 Choose Select > Deselect, and then choose File > Save.

Sampling colors in placed images

You can sample, or copy, the colors in placed images to apply the colors to other objects in the artwork. Sampling colors enables you to easily make colors consistent in a file that combines images and Illustrator artwork.

1 In the Layers panel, make sure that all of the layers are collapsed, and then click the visibility column to the left of the Banner, Berries, Corn, and Woman layers to show their contents on the artboard.

2 With the Selection tool (▶) selected, click the white banner shape behind the "MERIDIEN" text.

3 Make sure that the Fill box is selected toward the bottom of the Tools panel.

4 Select the Eyedropper tool (✓) in the Tools panel, and Shift-click the top green area in the top of the C in "LOCAL," to sample and apply a green color from the corn image.

You can try sampling the color of different images and content if you want. The color you sample is applied to the selected shape.

> ● **Note:** Using the Shift key with the Eyedropper tool allows you to apply only the sampled color to the selected object. If you don't use the Shift key, you apply all appearance attributes to the selected object.

5 Choose Select > Deselect, and then choose File > Save.

Working with image links

When you place images in Illustrator and either link to them or embed them, you can see a listing of these images in the Links panel. You use the Links panel to see and manage all linked or embedded artwork. The panel displays a small thumbnail of the artwork and uses icons to indicate the artwork's status. From the Links panel, you can view the images that are linked to and embedded, replace a placed image, update a linked image that has been edited outside of Illustrator, or edit a linked image in the original application, such as Photoshop.

Finding link information

When you place images, it can be helpful to see where the original image is located, what transformations have been applied to the image (such as rotation and scale), and more information.

1 Choose Window > Links.

Looking in the Links panel, you will see a listing of all of the images you've placed. Images with a name to the right of the image thumbnail are linked, and those images without a name are embedded. You can also tell if an image has been embedded by the embedded icon (▣).

2 Double-click the berries.psd image (which shows the name to the right of the thumbnail) to open the Link Information dialog box.

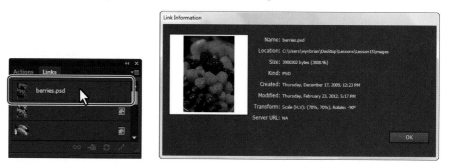

In the Link Information dialog box, you will see information, such as the original location of the image, the kind of file, modification and creation dates, transformation information, and more.

3 Click OK to close the Link Information dialog box.

4 Scroll down in the Links panel, and select the carrots.psd file in the list.

5 Click the Go To Link button (🔁) at the bottom of the Links panel. The carrots.psd image will be selected and centered in the Document window.

6 Click the orange link text "Linked File" in the Control panel to open the Links panel.

This is another way to access the Links panel. If you select a linked image or the image content of a Clip Group, you will see the text "Linked File."

7 In the Control panel, click the filename carrots.psd to reveal a menu of options.

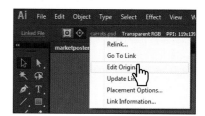

The menu of options that appears mirrors those options found in the Links panel. If you were to select an embedded image, you would instead see the link named Embedded in the Control panel. Clicking that orange link would show the same menu options but with some of them inaccessible.

8   Press the Escape key to hide the menu and leave the image selected.

Replacing a linked image

You can easily replace a linked or embedded image with another image to update the artwork. The replacement image is positioned exactly where the original image was, so no adjustment should be necessary if the new image is of the same dimensions. If you scaled the image that you are replacing, you may need to resize the replacement image to match the original.

Next, you will replace the selected carrots.psd image with another image.

1   In the Links panel, with carrots.psd selected, click the Relink button (⊡) at the bottom of the panel.

2   In the Place dialog box, navigate to the woman.psd image in the images folder in the Lesson15 folder and select it. Make sure that the Link option is selected. Click Place to replace the carrots image with the new one.

The replacement image (woman.psd) appears on the artboard in place of the carrots.psd image. When you replace an image, any color adjustments made to the original image are not applied to the replacement. However, masks applied to the original image are preserved. Any layer modes and transparency adjustments that you've made to other layers also may affect the image's appearance.

3   Close the Links panel group.

4   With the Selection tool (▶) selected, click the Edit Contents button (▣) in the Control panel. Drag the new woman.psd image until it is positioned as you see in the figure.

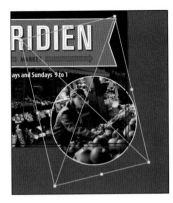

> ▶ **Tip:** You can also press the arrow keys on the keyboard to reposition the image.

5   Click the Edit Clipping Path button (▣) in the Control panel.

6   In the Control panel, change the Stroke color to white and the Stroke weight to **3 pt**.

7   Choose Select > Deselect, and then choose File > Save.

Exporting a layered file to Photoshop

Not only can you open layered Photoshop files in Illustrator, but you can also save layered Illustrator files and then open them in Photoshop. Moving layered files between Illustrator and Photoshop is helpful when creating and editing web or print graphics. You can preserve the hierarchical relationship of the layers by selecting the Write Layers option when saving your file. You can also open and edit type objects.

Tip: In the Export dialog box, the Use Artboards option allows you to export artboards as separate Photoshop PSD files.

1   With the marketposter.ai file still open, choose File > Export.

2   Choose Photoshop (*.PSD) from the Save As Type menu (Windows) or Photoshop (psd) from the Format menu (Mac OS). Navigate to the folder where you'll save the file, and name the file **marketposter.psd**. Click Save (Windows) or Export (Mac OS).

Note: After clicking OK, you may see a warning dialog box. Click OK.

3   In the Photoshop Export Options dialog box, make sure that CMYK is the Color Model, select High (300 ppi) for the resolution, and make sure that Write Layers is selected. Leave the rest of the settings at their defaults. Preserve Text Editability is grayed out because all the text was already converted to outlines. Click OK.

Note: After clicking OK, you may need to give it some time to save the file.

Tip: You can also copy and paste or drag and drop from Illustrator to Photoshop. When you copy and paste, a dialog box appears asking what type of object you'd like to place the content from Illustrator as: Smart Object, Pixels, Path, or Shape Layer. To learn more about bringing Illustrator content into Photoshop, search for "Duplicate selections using drag and drop" in Illustrator Help.

Note: You can open Illustrator files in previous versions of Photoshop, but for this lesson, it's assumed that you are using Photoshop CS6.

4   Start Adobe Photoshop CS6. Open the movieposter.psd file that you exported.

5   Click the Layers tab to view the Layers panel. Notice the layers. Choose File > Close, and don't save the changes.

Note: Artwork that is too complex may be rasterized and flattened to one layer.

6   Close Photoshop CS6, and return to Illustrator.

7   Choose File > Close to close the marketposter.ai file, without saving it.

Illustrator and Adobe InDesign, Adobe Muse, Adobe Fireworks, and Adobe Flash

To learn more about working with Illustrator artwork and Adobe InDesign, Adobe Muse, Adobe Fireworks®, and Adobe Flash, see the PDF file, Adobeapps.pdf, on the *Classroom in a Book* CD.

Review questions

1 Describe the difference between linking and embedding in Illustrator.

2 What kinds of objects can be used as masks?

3 How do you create an opacity mask for a placed image?

4 What color modifications can you apply to a selected object using effects?

5 Describe how to replace an image with another image in a document.

Review answers

1 A linked file is a separate, external file connected to the Illustrator file by an electronic link. A linked file does not add significantly to the size of the Illustrator file. The linked file must accompany the Illustrator file to preserve the link and ensure that the placed file appears when you open the Illustrator file. An embedded file is included in the Illustrator file. The Illustrator file size reflects the addition of the embedded file. Because the embedded file is part of the Illustrator file, no link can be broken. You can update linked and embedded files using the Relink button in the Links panel.

2 A mask can be a simple or compound path. You can use type as a mask. You can import opacity masks with placed Photoshop files. You can also create layer clipping masks with any shape that is the topmost object of a group or layer.

3 You create an opacity mask by placing the object to be used as a mask on top of the object to be masked. Then, you select the mask and the objects to be masked and either click the Make Mask button in the Transparency panel or choose Make Opacity Mask from the Transparency panel menu.

4 You can use effects to change the color mode (RGB, CMYK, or grayscale) or adjust individual colors in a selected object. You can also saturate or desaturate colors or invert colors in a selected object. You can apply color modifications to placed images, as well as to artwork created in Illustrator.

5 To replace a placed image, select the image in the Links panel. Then, click the Relink button and locate and select the replacement image. Click Place.

INDEX

SYMBOLS

* (asterisk), 59
[ ] (bracket keys), 115
caret (caret) symbol, 154
+ (plus sign)
    displayed when dragging tiled content, 49
    indicating overflow text, 218
    next to Selection tool pointer, 79
    in Zoom tool pointer, 49

A

Adjust Colors dialog box, 23, 435
Adobe, *See also* combining Adobe graphics;
    and specific applications
    training and certification programs, 6
    website and Help from, 4–5, 62
Adobe Application Manager dialog box, 7
Adobe Bridge, 426–428
Adobe Fireworks, 446
Adobe Flash
    exporting symbols to, 419–421, 422
    using symbols with, 403
    working with Illustrator artwork in, 446
Adobe Illustrator CS6, *See also* combining
    Adobe graphics; quick tour
    embedding Photoshop image in layer
        comps, 432–433
    exporting layered files to Photoshop, 446
    fonts for, 222
    helpful resources for using, 4–5, 62
    Microsoft documents placed in, 218, 232
    placing Photoshop images in, 20–21, 428,
        430–431
    restoring default preferences, 3
    transforming placed image, 431
    updates for, 7
    vector effects in, 353
    vector graphic advantages of, 35
    version compatibility between Photoshop
        and, 446
Adobe InDesign, 187, 446
Adobe Muse, 446

Adobe Photoshop
    Color Picker in, 187
    compatibility between Illustrator and, 446
    embedding image with layer comps,
        432–433
    importing adjustment layers from, 430
    importing masks from, 436
    placing images in Illustrator, 20–21, 428,
        430–431
    transforming image placed in Illustrator,
        431
    using Illustrator layered files in, 446
    using raster effects in Illustrator, 353, 363
Adobe Updater, 7
AI file type, 419
Align panel, 73, 81
aligning
    anchor points, 73
    applying techniques for, 81
    content, 29
    effect of grouping on, 75
    enabling pixel-aligned content, 392–394
    item to key object, 72–73
    objects equally, 74
    objects on artboard, 74–75
    objects to each other, 72
    paragraphs, 229
    stroke, 98–99
    symbol instances to pixel grid, 406
    undoing alignment, 72
anchor points, *See also* direction handles
    about, 68
    aligning to, 73
    corner and smooth, 151, 153–155, 168–169
    deleting and adding, 166–167
    dragging, 147, 165
    end, 148, 151, 158, 161
    marquee selection of, 70
    nudging with arrow keys, 165, 195
    selecting, 68–69
    snapping to, 131
angle of gradient fills, 300–301
angle of revolution, 366
appearance attributes, *See also* Appearance
    panel

M

Mac OS computers
  adjusting Zoom keyboard
      shortcuts for, 50
  instructions for, 1
  maximizing lesson file's window
      size for, 66, 122
  placement of menu bar for, 59
Magic Wand tool, 70–71
magnification
  adjusting Navigator panel values
      for, 55
  adjusting Zoom tool's, 49
Map Art dialog box, 369
mapping symbol to 3D objects,
      368–371
Maps panel, 404
marquees
  deleting series of shapes within,
      109
  erasing content in, 115
  selecting content with, 69–70
masking images. *See* clipping masks;
      opacity masks
maximum number of artboards, 54
measurement labels
  about, 67
  dX and dY values in, 68, 139
  width and height in, 90
menus
  context, 47
  Harmony Rules, 197
  panel, 47
  View, 48, 51, 99
  Window, 43
merging
  layers, 259–260
  panel groups, 45
  paths with Blob Brush tool,
      345–346, 347
Microsoft Word
  placing documents in Illustrator,
      218, 232
  text file formats supported from,
      217
Microsoft Word Options dialog box,
      218
Missing Profile dialog box, 34
Move dialog box, 173, 251
movie clips
  graphics vs., 406
  using in symbols, 407
moving
  content with artboards, 127
  grouped objects, 75

  layers, 251–253
  objects on layer, 249–250
  shapes with arrow keys, 100, 264
multiple artboards
  creating, 86–88, 123–124
  navigating, 52–53
  saving, 86–87
multiple documents, 57–60
multiple graphic styles, 389–390
multiple strokes, 360–362
multiple sublayer selections, 250
multiple transformations for objects,
      141–142
Muse, 446

N

names
  editing artboard, 53
  viewing layer, 436
naming
  color groups, 192
  selections, 71
  sublayers, 249
navigating
  layers and sublayers, 250
  multiple artboards, 52–53
  between panel fields, 298
  to symbol libraries, 418
  within documents, 55–56
Navigator panel
  customizing, 56
  navigating within documents,
      55–56
negative dX/dY values, 139
nesting groups, 76–77
New Brush dialog box, 329, 337
New Color Group dialog box, 189
New Document dialog box, 87, 179
New Swatch dialog box, 182
9-slice scaling guides, 420–421
nonprintable area, 54

O

object warp, 237–238
objects, *See also* blends; symbols
  adjusting opacity of, 378
  aligning, 72–75, 81
  altering appearance of, 353
  arranging stacks of, 78
  assembling parts of violin,
      172–174
  changing perspective of, 140–141
  choosing border of, 67

  converting Photoshop layers to,
      433
  creating graphic style from,
      383–384
  deselecting, 152, 182, 337
  distorting, 135–136
  dragging copy in grid plane, 282
  drawing behind other shapes, 89,
      96–97
  drawing in perspective, 273–275
  editing 3D lighting, 367–368
  gradient fills for multiple,
      308–309
  graphic styles applied to, 384
  grouping and ungrouping, 75, 77
  hiding, 79–80
  Illustrator controls for coloring,
      179–181
  locating in layer, 261
  locking, 82, 173
  Magic Wand for selecting, 70–71
  making into opacity mask,
      440–441
  masking with shapes, 438
  moving on layer, 249–250
  moving with artboard, 127
  multiple transformations for,
      141–142
  in port and out port of type, 218,
      219
  positioning precisely, 137–139
  reflecting, 132–133, 160
  reshaping text using, 237–238
  revolved, 365–368
  rotating, 134–135
  saving and naming selected, 71
  scaling, 130–132
  selecting, 66–67
  shearing, 136–137
  spacing equally, 74
  threading text between, 219
  unable to merge, 260
  using type object in perspective,
      280–281
  wrapping text around, 238–239
offset option for revolve effects, 366
Offset Path dialog box, 362, 380
Offset Path effect, 360–363
opacity
  adjusting in Appearance panel,
      378
  gradient fill color, 311–312
  modifying drop shadow, 355,
      382, 386
opacity masks
  clipping masks vs., 440

working with overflow text, 218–219

Type On A Path Options dialog box, 242

Type On A Path tool, 241

Type tool, 50, 221

U

undoing
  alignments, 72
  layer reordering, 253
  object grouping, 75, 77
  painting, 332
  Pen tool drawing, 152
  Pencil tool, 172
  perspective, 292
  perspective moves, 278
  symbol spraying, 413, 414
units of measure, 88–89, 129
Up Arrow key, *See also* arrow keys
  adjusting field entries with, 88, 111, 126
  changing corner radius with, 93
  increasing points on star with, 97, 98
  nudging anchor points with, 165, 195
updating Illustrator, 7
user interface, *See also* artboards; panels; workspaces
  adjusting brightness of, 9, 37
  Illustrator views, 51
  improving efficiency with panel groups, 46
  new features of, 8–9

V

vanishing point, 269, 272, 277
vector effects, 353
vector graphics
  advantages of, 35
  applying raster effects to, 353
  bitmap vs., 428–429
  cleaning up traced art, 118
  converting to raster graphics for web, 392
  turning raster into, 116–118
View menu
  adjusting artwork size from, 48
  choosing view modes in, 51
  paint attributes removed in Outline mode, 99
viewing
  swatch name in tool tip, 183

symbol names or images, 404
violin illustration, 156–174
visibility
  making pattern layer visible, 200
  of Pen tool cross hair, 146
  revealing layer, 361
  turning off for Warp effect, 357

W

Wacom tablet, 334
warning dialog box
  convert anchor point tool, 154
  when color modes mismatched, 433
Warp Options dialog box, 235, 357
warping
  flower petals, 311
  hiding visibility of Warp effects, 357
  text, 356–359
Web browser, 398
web graphics
  aligning symbol instances to pixel grid, 406
  creating content for, 392
  previewing on web browser, 398
  saving for web, 396–398
  selecting and editing slices, 396
  slicing, 394–395
weight
  adjusting stroke, 102–105, 161
  customizing Magic Wand to select, 70
  selecting stroke by, 71
white triangle, 184
width
  adjusting shape, 98–99
  saving stroke profiles, 105
Width Point Edit dialog box, 104
Width tool, 18–19, 102–105
Window menu, 43
windows
  conserving space in, 46
  consolidating, 57, 60
  fitting artboard in, 34–35, 48
Windows computers
  hidden files and folders on, 3, 4
  instructions for, 1
workspaces, *See also* artboards
  adjusting brightness of, 9, 37
  areas of, 36
  arranging documents in groups, 60
  components of, 33
  deleting, 47

fitting artboard in window, 34–35, 48
floating and docking panels in, 39–40
hiding/showing rulers, 56–57
moving Control panel within, 41–42
opening and arranging multiple documents, 57–60
resetting defaults, 34, 46–47
saving, 47
scrolling through documents, 50
wrapping
  artwork around objects, 370
  text around objects, 238–239

X

X axis
  measuring distance moved along, 139
  positioning objects to, 137–139
  3D effect, 365

Y

Y axis
  measuring distance moved along, 139
  positioning objects to, 137–139
  3D effect, 365

Z

Z axis for 3D effect, 365
zoom
  adjusting Navigator panel magnification, 55
  magnifying artwork with, 49–50
  using when combining shapes, 107
  using when resizing, 111

Contributors

Brian Wood   Brian Wood is an Adobe Certified Instructor in Dreamweaver CS5, Acrobat 9 Pro, Illustrator CS5, and the author of seven training books (Illustrator, InDesign, and Adobe Muse), all published by Peachpit Press, as well as numerous training videos and DVDs on Dreamweaver & CSS, InDesign, Illustrator, Acrobat, including Acrobat multimedia and forms and others.

In addition to training many clients large and small, Brian speaks regularly at national conferences, such as Adobe MAX, Getting Started with Dreamweaver and CSS tour, The InDesign Conference, The Web Design Conference, The Creative Suite Conference, as well as events hosted by AIGA and other industry organizations. To learn more, visit www.askbrianwood.com

Wyndham Wood   Wyndham Wood is a professional writer with 10+ years of marketing and business experience, including eight years as President of an Adobe Authorized Training Center. In addition to helping write and edit training books, she has authored articles and white papers that have appeared in several industry publications.

Production Notes

The *Adobe Illustrator CS6 Classroom in a Book* was created electronically using Adobe InDesign CS5.5. Art was produced using Adobe InDesign, Adobe Illustrator, and Adobe Photoshop. The Myriad Pro and Warnock Pro OpenType families of typefaces were used throughout this book.

References to company names, websites, or addresses in the lessons are for demonstration purposes only and are not intended to refer to any actual organization or person.

Images

Photographic images and illustrations are intended for use with the tutorials.

Typefaces used

Adobe Myriad Pro and Adobe Warnock Pro are used throughout the lessons. For more information about OpenType and Adobe fonts, visit www.adobe.com/type/opentype/.

Team credits

The following individuals contributed to the development of this edition of the *Adobe Illustrator CS6 Classroom in a Book*:

Project Manager: Brian Wood
Developmental Editor: Wyndham Wood, Brian Wood
Design: Jolynne Roorda
Production Editor: Brian Wood
Technical Editors: Resources Online
Compositor: Brian Wood
Keystroking: Lara Mihata, Mark Stricker, Megan Tytler, Wyndham Wood
Copyeditor: Resources Online
Proofreader: Resources Online
Indexer: Rebecca Plunkett
Cover design: Eddie Yuen
Interior design: Mimi Heft

AdobePress

LEARN BY VIDEO

The **Learn by Video** series from video2brain and Adobe Press is the only Adobe-approved video courseware for the Adobe Certified Associate Level certification, and has quickly established itself as one of the most critically acclaimed training products available on the fundamentals of Adobe software.

Learn by Video offers up to 15 hours of high-quality HD video training presented by experienced trainers, as well as lesson files, assessment quizzes, and review materials. The DVD is bundled with a full-color printed booklet that provides supplemental information as well as a guide to the video topics.

For more information go to
www.adobepress.com/learnbyvideo

Table of Contents never more than a click away

Up to 15 hours of high-quality video training

Lesson files are included on the DVD

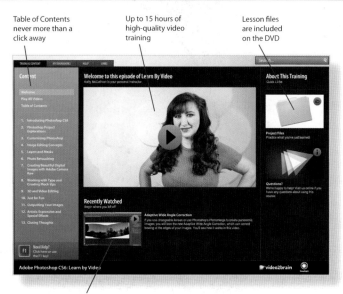

Video player remembers which movie you watched last

Watch-and-Work mode shrinks the video into a small window while you work in the software

Titles

Adobe Photoshop CS6: Learn by Video: Core Training in Visual Communication
ISBN: 9780321840714

Adobe Illustrator CS6: Learn by Video
ISBN: 9780321840684

Adobe InDesign CS6: Learn by Video
ISBN: 9780321840691

Adobe Flash Professional CS6: Learn by Video: Core Training in Rich Media Communication
ISBN: 9780321840707

Adobe Dreamweaver CS6: Learn by Video: Core Training in Web Communication
ISBN: 9780321840370

Adobe Premiere Pro CS6: Learn by Video: Core Training in Video Communication
ISBN: 9780321840721

Adobe After Effects CS6: Learn by Video
ISBN: 9780321840387

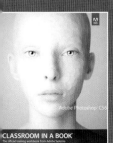

The fastest, easiest, most comprehensive way to learn
Adobe® Creative Suite® 6

Classroom in a Book®, the best-selling series of hands-on software training books, helps you learn the features of Adobe software quickly and easily.

The **Classroom in a Book** series offers what no other book or training program does—an official training series from Adobe Systems, developed with the support of Adobe product experts.

To see a complete list of our Adobe® Creative Suite® 6 titles go to
www.peachpit.com/adobecs6

Adobe Photoshop CS6 Classroom in a Book
ISBN: 9780321827333

Adobe Illustrator CS6 Classroom in a Book
ISBN: 9780321822482

Adobe InDesign CS6 Classroom in a Book
ISBN: 9780321822499

Adobe Flash Professional CS6 Classroom in a Book
ISBN: 9780321822512

Adobe Dreamweaver CS6 Classroom in a Book
ISBN: 9780321822451

Adobe Muse Classroom in a Book
ISBN: 9780321821362

Adobe Fireworks CS6 Classroom in a Book
ISBN: 9780321822444

Adobe Premiere Pro CS6 Classroom in a Book
ISBN: 9780321822475

Adobe After Effects CS6 Classroom in a Book
ISBN: 9780321822437

Adobe Audition CS6 Classroom in a Book
ISBN: 9780321832832

Adobe Creative Suite 6 Design & Web Premium Classroom in a Book
ISBN: 9780321822604

Adobe Creative Suite 6 Production Premium Classroom in a Book
ISBN: 9780321832689

AdobePress

WATCH
READ
CREATE

Unlimited online access to all Peachpit, Adobe Press, Apple Training and New Riders videos and books, as well as content from other leading publishers including: O'Reilly Media, Focal Press, Sams, Que, Total Training, John Wiley & Sons, Course Technology PTR, Class on Demand, VTC and more.

No time commitment or contract required! Sign up for one month or a year.
All for $19.99 a month

SIGN UP TODAY
peachpit.com/creativeedge

creative
edge